Logic and Contemporary Rhetoric

The Use of Reason in Everyday Life

TWELFTH EDITION

Logic and Contemporary Rhetoric

The Use of Reason in Everyday Life

TWELFTH EDITION

Nancy Cavender

Professor Emeritus
College of Marin

Howard Kahane

Late of
University of Maryland
Baltimore County

WADSWORTH
CENGAGE Learning·

Australia • Brazil • Japan • Korea • Mexico • Singapore • Spain • United Kingdom • United States

Logic and Contemporary Rhetoric: The Use of Reason in Everyday Life, Twelfth Edition
Cavender, Kahane

Senior Sponsoring Editor:
Joann Kozyrev

Assistant Editor: Joshua Duncan

Senior Media Editor:
Philip Lanza

Senior Content Project
Manager: Jessica Rasile

Marketing Development
Manager: Joshua I. Adams

Brand Manager: Jennifer
Levanduski

Art Director: Andrei Pasternak

Rights Acquisitions Specialist:
Mandy Groszko

Manufacturing Planner:
Sandee Milewski

Cover Design: Riezebos
Holzbaur/Tim Heraldo

Production Service/
Compositor: S4carlisle
Publishing Services

Cover Image: © hxdbzxy/
shutterstock

For product information and technology assistance,
contact us
at **Cengage Learning Customer & Sales Support,
1-800-354-9706**

For permission to use material from this text or product,
submit all requests online at **www.cengage.com/permissions**
Further permissions questions can be e-mailed to
permissionrequest@cengage.com

Library of Congress Control Number: 2012954320

ISBN-13: 978-1-133-94228-3
ISBN-10: 1-133-94228-8

Wadsworth
20 Channel Center Street
Boston, MA 02210
USA

Cengage Learning is a leading provider of customized learning solutions with office locations around the globe, including Singapore, the United Kingdom, Australia, Mexico, Brazil, and Japan. Locate your local office at **international.cengage .com/region**

Cengage Learning products are represented in Canada by Nelson Education, Ltd.

For your course and learning solutions, visit **www.cengage.com**

Purchase any of our products at your local college store or at our preferred online store **cengagebrain.com**

Printed in the United States of America
2 3 4 5 6 7 17 16 15 14

To Lisa and John

Contents

Preface

I do not pretend to know what many ignorant men are sure of.

—Clarence Darrow

To know that we know what we know, and that we do not know what we do not know. That is true knowledge.

—Henry David Thoreau

We have met the enemy and he is us.

—Walt Kelly's "Pogo"

Education is not simply the work of abstract verbalized knowledge.

—Aldous Huxley

Many people would sooner die than think. In fact, they do.

—Bertrand Russell

You can fool too many of the people too much of the time.

—James Thurber

Now, more than ever, we need to think critically about the world we live in and the decisions we make. We are mired in a recession, bombarded by media hype, blitzed by ads, and overwhelmed by technology. If ever we needed to think clearly about the world at large and the pitfalls we face, this is the time.

To this end, the twelfth edition of *Logic and Contemporary Rhetoric* is designed to help students improve their ability to reason well about problems they encounter in everyday life and about issues debated in the social–political spectrum. (The intent certainly is not to move students to the right or left politically, but rather to help them move up on the scale measuring rational sophistication.)

The text contains examples and exercise items drawn from a broad range of sources—the Internet, television programs, advertisements, literary works, political speeches, newspaper columns, and so on. Students get to sharpen their ability to think critically by reasoning about important topics and issues: Internet ethics, political trends, sexism in the media, economic downturns, steroid abuse, and government doublespeak, to name a few.

It quotes from or refers to writings and comments of Aristotle, Bertrand Russell, Barack Obama, Jerry Seinfeld, Maya Angelou, Winston Churchill, Ann Coulter, Jane Austen, Rush Limbaugh, Alice Walker, Dostoevsky, Pliny the Elder, Sarah Palin, William Shakespeare, Charles Darwin, and a host of others. Examples are drawn from celebrity ads, Obama and Romney political doings, syndicated columnists, works or literature, and hundreds of sources.

Instead of the made-to-order cartoons that appear in some other texts, *Logic and Contemporary Rhetoric* includes drawings from the likes of top-flight cartoonists like David Levine, Edward Sorel, Tom Toles, George Booth, Signe Wilkinson, Bill Watterson and many others, plus comic strips featuring *Calvin & Hobbes*, *Doonesbury*, *Boondocks*, *Peanuts* and others to illustrate points in a lively manner. The trademarks of *Logic and Contemporary Rhetoric* always have been, and still are, ease of comprehension and up-to-date, interesting material. Textbooks need not be dull!

All this is done to sharpen in students the ability to think critically so that they can avoid being manipulated by the media, the advertisers, the political system, and a host of con artists—and ultimately to help them function independently and responsibly in our increasingly complex, challenging society.

This edition is also accompanied by several useful study aids on its CourseMate website. The interactive quizzes, study guides, and flashcards provided there are useful tools to reinforce the material taught in the book. An eBook is also included. The Course-Mate website can be accessed at www.CengageBrain.com.

NEW TO THE TWELFTH EDITION

The principal changes in this edition are these:

1. Hundreds of old examples have been replaced by more up-to-date items culled from (sadly) thousands of new candidates. For example, political items drawn from the Obama and Romney campaigns have replaced outdated ones from previous campaigns. (It is unnerving, though, that examples reflecting the Great Recession are just as relevant this edition as they were in the last.)

2. Dozens of old exercises have been replaced with new ones, including essay questions on current issues like the Supreme Court rulings on Citizens United and the Affordable Health Care Act—court decisions that will affect all students sooner or later.

3. When appropriate, background information has been added to put issues in context and give students perspective. For example, in discussing attack ads that drive political campaigns (Chapter 10), a brief history is given of the deep roots that political attacks have in this country.

4. Although some of the text has been rewritten again to improve organization, style, and flow, the general subject matter covered by this new edition has not changed, but several changes have been made.

   Because presidential campaigns are long on rhetoric and short on substance, the fallacy chapters include a new batch of examples and exercises that reflect the usual fallacious reasoning that muddies the waters of every election. Also, more answers have been added at the back of the book to help students out.

   Chapter 9, on writing argumentative essays, includes a new sample essay on the deliberately provocative subject of whether young people should bother going to college, a topic that must be on the minds of many students nowadays, given the rising costs of higher education and the dismal job outlook.

Chapter 11, on managing the news, has been revised again to reflect the huge transformation that the news media are going through—comparable to what they experienced in the early days of television. The chapter discusses the problems involved as traditional news outlets shrink, but also the benefits that evolve as more and more people access news on the Internet.

As always, new cartoons have been added that liven up the text, but the first one, in particular (of the cat and mouse), perfectly captures the plight of the noncritical thinker.

ORGANIZATION OF THE TEXT

The thought that sparked the original organization of material in *Logic and Contemporary Rhetoric* way back in 1969–1970 was that student reasoning about everyday topics could be improved by acquainting them with a few basic principles of good reasoning and, in particular, by enlightening them concerning common ways in which people are taken in by fallacious arguments and reasoning in everyday life. But a close examination of the ways in which reasoning, in fact, goes wrong in everyday life shows that it does so in a majority of cases first because of a lack of sufficient (or sufficiently accurate) background information; second, because of the psychological impediments (wishful thinking, rationalization, prejudice, superstition, provincialism, and so on) that stand in the way of cogent reasoning; and third, because of a poor understanding of the nature and quality of the various information sources.

Taking account of this insight has resulted in a book that divides into eight parts, as follows:

1. *Good and Bad Reasoning:* Chapter 1 introduces students to some basic ideas about good and bad reasoning, the importance of having good background beliefs, in particular of having well-pruned worldviews, as well as some very rudimentary remarks about deduction and induction and the three overarching fallacy categories employed in Chapters 3, 4, and 5.
2. *Deduction and Induction:* Chapter 2 contains more detailed material on deductive and inductive validity and invalidity.
3. *Fallacious Reasoning:* Chapters 3, 4, and 5 discuss fallacious reasoning, concentrating on how to avoid fallacies by becoming familiar with the types most frequently encountered in everyday life. The point is to help students increase their ability to spot fallacious reasoning by discussing the most common types of fallacious argument and by providing students with everyday life examples on which to practice.
4. *Impediments to Cogent Reasoning:* Chapter 6 discusses wishful thinking, rationalization, provincialism, denial, and so on, and how to overcome them. It explains the attraction and mistaken nature of belief in the paranormal and other pseudosciences. In some ways, this is the most important chapter in the book, because these skewers of rational thought so severely infect the thinking of all of us. (Some instructors pass over this chapter on the grounds that the topic is more appropriately taught in psychology classes, not in classes primarily concerned with critical

reasoning. But the reality here is that many students do not take the relevant psychology classes and that those who do often are provided with a purely theoretical account divorced from the students' own reasoning in everyday life, not with a "how-to" discussion designed to help them overcome these obstacles to rational thought.)

5. *Language:* Chapter 7 discusses the ways in which language itself can be used to manipulate meaning, for instance, via doubletalk and long-winded locutions. (This chapter also contains a section, not common in critical-thinking texts, on the linguistic revolution that has tremendously reduced the use of sexist, racist, and other pejorative locutions in everyday discourse; and it also has a few things to say about the use of politically correct [PC] locutions.)

6. *Evaluating and Writing Cogent Essays:* Chapter 8 deals with the evaluation of extended argumentative passages—essays, editorials, political speeches, and so on. Chapter 9 addresses the writing of these kinds of argumentative passages. (Instructors are urged not to pass over Chapter 9 and urged to have students write *at least* two argumentative papers during the semester. Writing is very likely the best way in which we all can learn to sharpen our ability to reason well. Writing is indeed nature's way of letting us know how sloppy our thinking often is. But it also is the best way to learn how to sharpen our ability to think straight.)

7. *Important Sources of Information:* Chapter 10 discusses advertising as an information source (singling out political ads for special scrutiny); Chapter 11, the media (television, newspapers, radio, the Internet, books, and magazines), in particular, the mass media; and Chapter 12, public school textbooks. (For many people, these are the most important sources of information about how the world works. Instructors are urged not to pass over the chapter on the media too quickly: In this day and age, so much that happens in our lives depends on our being able to assess accurately what the media—in particular, the mass media—tell us.)

8. *More on Cogent Reasoning:* The appendix provides additional material on deduction and induction (including a few words about syllogisms); cause and effect; scientific method; and so on.

Note also that a section at the back of the book provides answers to selected exercise items. It should be remembered, however, that most of the exercise items in this text are drawn from everyday life, where shades of gray outnumber blacks and whites. The answers provided thus constitute author responses rather than definitive pronouncements. Similar remarks apply to the answers to the remaining exercise items provided in the *Instructor's Manual* designed to accompany *Logic and Contemporary Rhetoric.*

THE UNIQUE NATURE OF LOGIC AND CONTEMPORARY RHETORIC

This book is unique among critical reasoning texts in bringing together all of these apparently diverse elements, in particular in stressing the importance of overcoming natural impediments to cogent reasoning; in bringing to bear good background information when dealing with everyday problems; and in so extensively discussing the most important information sources. In this complicated modern world, all of us are laypersons most of the time with respect to most topics; the ability to deal effectively with the "expert" information available to us via the media, textbooks, the Internet, and periodicals—to separate wheat from chaff—thus is crucial to our ability to reason well about everyday problems, whether of a personal or of a social–political nature.

Although the text contains much discussion of theory, this is *not* a treatise on the theory of cogent and fallacious reasoning. Rather, it is designed to help students learn *how* to reason well and *how* to avoid fallacious reasoning. That is why so many examples and exercise items have been included—arranged so as to increase student sophistication as they progress through the book—and why exercises and examples have been drawn primarily from everyday life. Learning how to reason well and how to evaluate the rhetoric of others is a skill that, like most others, requires practice, in this case practice on the genuine article—actual examples drawn from everyday life.

This text provides students with a good deal more than the usual supply of exercise items, but perhaps the most important are those requiring them to do things on their own: find examples from the mass media, write letters to elected officials, do research on specified topics. (The *Instructor's Manual,* available to adopters of the text, suggests several other kinds of student activities—for example, classroom debates on issues of the day—that dovetail nicely with the spirit of the text.)

A true critical reasoning course, or textbook, is unthinkable in a closed or authoritarian society and antithetical to the indoctrination practiced in that kind of culture. The authors of this text take very seriously the admonition that eternal vigilance is the price of liberty. Citizens who think for themselves, rather than uncritically ingesting what their leaders and others with power tell them, are the absolutely necessary ingredient of a society that is to remain free.

ACKNOWLEDGMENTS

Many thanks to the publisher's reviewers for this eleventh edition: Jonathan Gainor, Harrisburg Area Community College; Lori Hoffman, Moravian College; Sughra Hussain, Harrisburg Area Community College; Kate McCorkle, Butte College; Robert Covert, Coastline Community College; and Carlotta Campbell, College of Alameda.

Thanks also to the others who have aided in the preparation of this and previous editions, including Professors Thomas Allen, California Polytechnic University, San Luis Obispo; Don Anderson, Pierce College; Anatole Anton, San Francisco State University; Gary L. Baran, Los Angeles City College; Lawrence Beloof, West Hills Community College; William Bonis, California State University, Long Beach; Gene Booth, University of New Mexico; Donald Burrell, California State University, Los Angeles; Henry C. Byerly, University of Arizona; Joseph Campbell, Washington State University; Alice Cleveland, College of Marin; Monte Cook, University of Oklahoma; Rosemary Cook, Saybrook Institute; Wally Cox, Regent University; Leland Creer, Central Connecticut State University; Robert Cogan, Edinboro University; David Detmer, Purdue University, Calumet Campus; R. V. Dusek, University of New Hampshire; Frank Fair, Sam Houston State University; Dana R. Flint, Lincoln University; Marilyn M. Fry, Coastline Community College; Sidney Gendin, Eastern Michigan University; Norman L. Geisler, Liberty University; James A. Gould, University of South

Florida; J. Anthony Greybasch, Central State University; Paul J. Haanstad, University of Utah; Max O. Hallman, Merced College; Alan Hausman, Hunter College; James Heffernan, University of the Pacific; John Hernandez, Palo Alto College; Mark Herron, National University; J. Thomas Howald, Franklin College; John L. King, University of North Carolina; Charles Landesman, Hunter College and CUNY Graduate Center; Donald Lazere, California Polytechnic State University; Herschel Mack, Humbolt State University; Patrick Maher, University of Pittsburgh; Reed Markham, California Polytechnic University, Pomona; Judith McBride, somewhere in Arizona; Thomas McKay, Syracuse University; Donna Monahan, College of Marin; David Morgan, University of Northern Iowa; Clayton Morgareidge, Lewis and Clark College; Gonzalo T. Palacios, University of the District of Columbia; Ray Perkins, Jr., Plymouth State University; Linda Plackowski, Delta College; Nelson Pole, Cleveland State University; Merrill Proudfoot, Park College; Malcolm Reid, Gordon College; Vincent Riccardi, Orange Coast College; Paul O. Ricci, Cypress College; Paul A. Roth, University of Missouri; Arent H. Schuyler, Jr., University of California, Santa Barbara; Robert Schwartz, University of Wisconsin—Milwaukee; Roger Seanom, University of British Columbia; S. Samuel Shermis, Purdue University; Pamela Spoto, California State University, Chico; Douglas Stalker, University of Delaware; Ben Starr, Modesto Junior College; Joan Straumanis, Kenyon College; John Stroupe, Western Michigan University; Gregory P. Swartzentruber, Villanova University; Roye Templeton, University of Maryland, Baltimore County; John Titchener, University of Maryland, Baltimore County; and Perry Weddle, California State University, Sacramento.

Finally, our very special thanks to the students of Whitman College, the University of Kansas, Bernard Baruch College of CUNY, the University of Maryland Baltimore County, and the College of Marin.

NANCY CAVENDER
Mill Valley, California

What is the use of philosophy, if all it does is enable you to talk . . . about some abstruse questions of logic, etc., and if it does not improve your thinking about the important questions of everyday life?

—Ludwig Wittgenstein

"For God's sake, think! Why is he being so nice to you?"

Cartoon commentary on the state of contemporary rhetoric.

1 Good and Bad Reasoning

It's much easier to do and die than it is to reason why.
— **H. A. Studdert Kennedy**

Read not to contradict and confute, nor to believe and take for granted . . . but to weigh and consider.
— **Francis Bacon**

You can lead a man up to the university, but you can't make him think.
— **Finley Peter Dunne**

You can lead me to college . . . but you can't make me think.
— **Sweatshirt update seen at Duke University**

Ignorance of reality provides no protection from it.
— **Harold Gordon**

Reason is logic, or reason is motive, or reason is a way of life.
— **John Le Carré**

There is much truth to the old saying that life is just one problem after another. That's why problem solving is one of life's major preoccupations. **Reasoning** is the essential ingredient in problem solving. When confronted with a problem, those of us who are rational reason from what we already know, or have good reason to believe, or can find out, to new beliefs useful in solving that problem. The trick, of course, is to reason well. This book is about good reasoning—about how to reason well in everyday life—whether dealing with personal problems or those of a social or political nature.

All of us like to think of ourselves as rational human beings, yet most of what we know is passed on to us by other people. We know, for instance, that the earth is round because we've been told it is, even though our intuition is that it is flat because we walk on flat surfaces every day. In fact, for centuries, the entire world believed it was flat until scientific evidence proved without question that isn't. Much of what we think we know is based on beliefs, sometimes unsupported by accurate information, instilled in us from childhood on. And too often, beliefs collapse into gut reactions to all manner of issues— from gun control to same same-sex marriage to legalizing drugs. A gut reaction is not the same as a rational thought, however, nor is a belief, unless it has been examined for accuracy against conflicting ideas and evidence. Critical thinking, after all, requires information as well as the ability to reason well.

Fortunately, no one is an island. We all have available to us a great deal of knowledge others have gained through experience and good reasoning—accurate information and well-intended advice available to anyone who reaches out for it. Unfortunately, not all information is created equal. Charlatans and fools can speak as loudly as saints or Nobel Prize winners. Self-interest often clouds the thinking of even the brightest individuals. The trick when evaluating the mountain of verbiage we all are exposed to is to separate the nourishing wheat from the expendable chaff. One way to become good at doing this is to think a bit about what makes reasoning good (cogent), as opposed to bad (fallacious).

1. REASONING AND ARGUMENTS

Here is a simple example of reasoning about the nature/nurture issue:

> Identical twins sometimes have different IQ test scores. Yet these twins inherit exactly the same genes. So environment must play some part in determining a person's IQ.

Logicians call this kind of reasoning an **argument**. In this case, the argument consists of three statements:

1. Identical twins often have different IQ test scores.
2. Identical twins inherit the same genes.
3. So environment must play some part in determining IQ.

The first two statements in this argument give reasons for accepting the third. In logic talk, they are said to be **premises** of the argument; and the third statement, which asserts the **claim** made by the argument, is called the argument's **conclusion**.

In everyday life, few of us bother to label premises or conclusions. We usually don't even bother to distinguish one argument from another. But we do sometimes give clues. Words such as *because, since,* and *for* usually indicate that what follows is a premise of an argument. *Therefore, thus, consequently,* and *so* generally signal conclusions. Similarly, expressions such as "It has been observed that . . . ," "In support of this . . . ," and "The relevant data are . . . " are used to introduce premises, while expressions such as "The point of all of this is . . . ," "The implication is . . . ," and "It follows that . . . " are used to signal conclusions. Here is a simple example:

> *Since* it's always wrong to kill a human being [premise], it *follows* that capital punishment is wrong [conclusion], *because* capital punishment takes the life of [kills] a human being [premise].

Put into textbook form, the argument looks like this:

1. It's always wrong to kill a human being.
2. Capital punishment takes the life of (kills) a human being.
∴3. Capital punishment is wrong.[1]

---

[1]The symbol ∴ often is used as shorthand for the word *therefore* and thus indicates that a conclusion follows.

Of course, an argument may have any number of premises and may be surrounded by or embedded in other arguments or extraneous material.

In addition to using transitional words such as *since, because,* and *therefore,* we sometimes employ sentence order—the last sentence in a series stating an argument's conclusion—and occasionally even express a conclusion in the form of a question. When the Los Angeles Galaxy signed David Beckham, international soccer star, an enthusiastic fan gave reasons that hiring him was the right thing to do—not just for the team but for Major League Soccer as well (which isn't nearly as popular in the United States as in other countries). Claiming that Beckham was one of the best players in the world and had star power to popularize the sport, she stated her conclusion in the form of a question: "Doesn't it make sense that he will be a major force in popularizing soccer in this country?"

We should also note that, in daily life, premises and even the conclusions of arguments sometimes are omitted as understood. Life is short, and we don't always bother to spell out matters that are obvious or not at issue or can be taken for granted. In the IQ example given earlier, for instance, the premise that IQ differences must be due either to genetic or to environmental factors was omitted as generally understood. When assessing arguments, we should by all means add omitted premises of this kind when they are relevant.

EXERCISE 1-1

Identify the premises and conclusions in the following arguments. (A few are from student exams—modestly edited.)[2] Remember, sometimes a premise or conclusion may be implied.

Example
Argument
The barometer is falling sharply, so the weather is going to change.
Argument Structure
Premise: The barometer is falling sharply.
Implied premise: Whenever the barometer falls sharply, the weather changes.
Conclusion: The weather is going to change.

1. Since everyone deserves health care, and more than 40 million Americans don't have medical insurance, the United States should institute national insurance.

2. I have my doubts about genetically modified plants. To begin with, we don't have enough information about them to know if they are bad for us in the long run. Then there is the problem of cross contamination if they spread to other areas. The whole thing seems pretty questionable.

3. Barry Bonds will never be the hero that Hank Aaron or Babe Ruth was, even though he set a new home run record. Everyone says he pumped himself up with steroids and tarnished his image forever. Aaron and Ruth got there on their own steam, without any boost from drugs.

---

[2]Starred (*) items are answered in a section at the back of the book.

*4. William Shakespeare: "Forbear to judge, for we are sinners all."

*5. Why not legalize drugs? One thing for sure, we would get rid of the crime syndicates that run the show now. Instead of giving money to the drug lords, the government would rake in billions in taxes. Maybe even enough to pay down the debt.

6. Aristotle: "The Earth has a spherical shape. For the night sky looks different in the northern and the southern parts of the Earth, and that would be the case if the Earth were spherical in shape."

7. Human activities have become the major source of global warming. Over the past 200 years, they have been responsible for the rising carbon dioxide levels from burning fossil fuels and for increased concentrations of other greenhouse gases like methane and nitrous oxide.

*8. Several years ago, National Football League Quarterback Michael Vick was convicted of sponsoring illegal dog-fights and performing acts of cruelty to animals. But he has served his time in federal prison and has worked with the Humane Society to help stamp out dog fighting among young people. So his criminal record shouldn't prevent him from getting into the Football Hall of Fame. He was a great quarterback for the Atlanta Falcons before his prison time, and he's made a great comeback with the Philadelphia Eagles. He deserves the honor.

9. College costs big bucks. When you put out that kind of money, you should be able to decide where your money goes. Students shouldn't have to take introductory courses if they don't want to. Besides, you don't need those basic courses for lots of careers.

10. Giving illegal aliens driver's licenses would undermine our immigration laws. After all, they are here illegally to begin with. Besides, there is the security issue. If anyone can get a license, so can terrorists, and that means they can fly anywhere in the country with just a license for an ID. Who knows how many planes they might blow up?

2. Exposition and Argument

Of course, only those groups of statements that provide reasons for believing something form arguments. Thus, anecdotes are not usually arguments, nor are most other forms of **exposition**. But even in these cases, arguments often are implied. Here is a sales clerk talking about the difference between two digital cameras, an Olympus and a Kodak. "Well, the Olympus has 4.1 megapixels and the Kodak has only 2.2. They both have terrific image quality, but the Olympus is better for cropping and enlarging your prints. The Kodak is $300 less, but it's not as high-powered." Although the clerk's remarks contain no specific argument because no conclusion is drawn, a conclusion is definitely implied. You should choose the Olympus if you want a more high-powered camera; otherwise you should choose the Kodak.

The point is that talk generally is not aimless. A good deal of everyday talk, even gossip, is intended to influence the beliefs and actions of others and thus constitutes a kind of argument. In the camera example, the clerk provided information intended to convince the customer to draw either the conclusion, "I'll buy the Olympus because the range of options is worth the extra $300 to me," or the conclusion, "I'll buy the Kodak because high-powered options aren't worth $300 more to me." In other words, the point of the clerk's chatter was to sell a camera. Similarly, advertisements often just provide product information rather than advance explicit arguments, yet clearly every such ad has an implied conclusion—that you should buy the advertised product.

Nevertheless, it is important to understand the difference between rhetoric that is primarily expository and discourse that is basically argumentative. An argument makes the claim, explicit or implicit, that one of its statements follows from some of its other statements. It at least implies that acceptance of its conclusion is justified if one accepts its premises. A passage that is purely expository gives us no reason to accept any "facts" it may contain (other than the implied authority of the writer or speaker, as, for example, when a friend tells us that she had a good time at the beach).

EXERCISE 1-2

Here are several passages. (Some are from student papers—again, modestly edited.) Indicate which contain arguments and which do not, label the premises and conclusions of those passages that do (as you did in the previous exercise), and explain why you think the other passages do not contain arguments.

Example
Passage from an Agatha Christie's novel Murder on the Orient Express: M. Hercule Poirot, having nothing better to do, amused himself by studying her without appearing to do so. She was, he judged, the kind of young woman who could take care of herself with perfect ease wherever she went. . . . He rather liked the severe regularity of her features and the delicate pallor of her skin. He liked the burnished black head with its neat waves of hair, and her eyes—cool, impersonal and gray.

Evaluation: This is not an argument. The author says Poirot judged (reasoned) that the woman could take care of herself, but does not describe his reasoning. And the rest of the passage simply says that Poirot liked certain features of the young woman.

*1. If we keep burning so much coal and oil, the greenhouse effect will continue to get worse. But it will be a disaster if that happens. So we've got to reduce dependency on these fossil fuels.

2. We are never going to find a cure for diabetes, cancer, Alzheimer's and a lot of other diseases unless we use the most promising research available. Stem cell research is the way to go.

3. Stem cell research sounds like a good idea, but it costs a lot of money, and we don't really know if it will cure people. We don't know what the long term effects will

be either. What if it keeps people alive for 200 years—in a world that is already overpopulated? Besides, it's just wrong to take stem cells from embryos.

*4. My summer vacation was spent working in Las Vegas. I worked as a waitress at the Desert Inn and made tons of money. But I guess I got addicted to the slots and didn't save too much. Next summer my friend Hal and I are going to work in Reno, if we can find jobs there.

5. Legalizing prostitution is bound to increase sexually transmitted diseases. And look what it would do to women. It can't help but lead to their degradation. Besides, most people don't like the idea, anyway.

6. The U.S. Census Bureau estimated that 20.4 million students were enrolled in the nation's 4,495 institutions of higher learning in fall 2008. The average cost of tuition, room, and board for in-state students at four-year public colleges and universities was $14,915, and at private schools, $40,640.

7. Some people in the field of medicine are keen on embedding computer chips inside the body, but I've got a problem with that. True, the chips could provide helpful medical information if I'm unconscious or something, which I guess is the main reason for doing it, but I don't want to make that kind of information available to the government or anyone else, for that matter, who might want to invade my privacy.

8. Too much money is thrown at college football and basketball. It's almost like they are professional sports. In fact, lots of athletes go to college to train for pro teams, not to get an education. All the publicity and hero worship draws attention away from the reason for going to school to begin with. It's no wonder many students pick colleges because of their teams, not their academic standing.

*9. Descartes: "Good sense is of all things in the world the most equally distributed, for everybody thinks himself so abundantly provided with it, that even those most difficult to please in all other matters do not commonly desire more of it than they already possess."

10. Since baseball players who take steroids have an unfair advantage over those who don't, it follows that they should not be inducted into the Hall of Fame, because giving them that honor would corrupt the basic fairness and integrity of the game.

11. Why shouldn't public schools take donations from private business? The government doesn't expend enough money to repair the buildings, let alone pay teachers a decent salary. Besides, big business would demand more for its money—like higher standards and better discipline.

12. Alexis de Tocqueville, *Democracy in America:* Men will never establish any equality with which they will be contented. . . . When equality of condition is the common law of society, the most marked inequalities do not strike the eye: when everything is nearly on the same level, the slightest are marked enough to hurt it.

Hence the desire for equality always becomes more insatiable in proportion as equality is more complete.

3. COGENT REASONING

Reasoning can be either **cogent** (good) or **fallacious** (bad). We reason cogently when we satisfy the following conditions:

1. The premises of our reasoning are believable (**warranted**, justified), given what we already know or believe.
2. We consider all likely relevant information.[3]
3. Our reasoning is **valid**, or **correct**, which means that the premises we employ provide good grounds for accepting the conclusion we draw.[4]

When all three of these conditions of cogent reasoning are not satisfied, reasoning is said to be *fallacious*. Note, by the way, that in daily life, we often speak of arguments as being fallacious or cogent, even though, strictly speaking, it is reasoners—individuals—who reason either fallaciously or cogently. Life is short, and we often speak imprecisely when context makes clear what is intended.

Believable Premises

The first condition of cogent reasoning requires that we bring to bear whatever we already know or believe—our relevant **background beliefs** and information—to determine whether we should or shouldn't accept the premises of an argument being evaluated. Take, for instance, the first premise of the capital punishment argument discussed earlier—the premise making the claim that taking the life of a human being always is wrong. Most of us are not pacifists—we don't believe that it always is wrong to take a human life. Bringing that background belief to bear thus should make us see the first premise of the capital punishment argument as questionable. So we should not accept the conclusion of that argument unless further reasons are presented in its support. (On the other hand, those of us who *are* pacifists obviously should reason differently.)

By way of contrast, consider the stated premise of the following argument:

> Roger Federer must be a terrific tennis player. He won the Wimbledon championship in 2012. (The implied premise is that anyone who took a first at Wimbledon must be an outstanding athlete.)

Tennis fans know that the Wimbledon grand slam championship is one of the most demanding tennis competitions in the world, and acceptance of the stated premise (that Federer won the tournament) was warranted by plenty of background information.

It's interesting to notice that, in effect, evaluating a premise of an argument by bringing background beliefs to bear entails constructing another argument whose conclusion

---

[3]Satisfying this extremely stringent requirement is usually beyond the ability of most of us most of the time. The point is that good reasoners try to come as close as possible to satisfying it, taking into account the importance of drawing the right conclusion and the cost (in time, effort, or money) of obtaining or recalling relevant information. (One of the marks of genius is the ability to recognize that information is relevant when the rest of us fail to notice.)

[4]Provided we know nothing else relevant to the conclusion. Note that reasoning from an unjustified premise may still be cogent if it also employs justified premises that sufficiently support its conclusion. Note also that the term *valid* sometimes is used more broadly than we have used it here.

is either that the premise in question is believable or that it isn't. For example, when evaluating the capital punishment argument discussed before, someone who is not a pacifist might construct the following argument: "I believe that it isn't wrong to kill in self-defense, or in wartime, or to kill those guilty of murder. So I should reject the premise that taking a human life always is wrong."

This brings to mind the fact that in daily life we often are exposed to assertions, or claims, that are not supported by reasons or arguments. Clearly, it is not rational to accept these assertions without evaluating them for believability, and, obviously, their correct evaluation requires us to do exactly what we do when evaluating the believability of the premises of an argument—namely, bring to bear what we already know or believe. Evaluating unsupported assertions thus involves just part of what is done when we evaluate arguments.

No Relevant Information Passed Over

The second criterion of cogent reasoning requires that we not pass over relevant information. In particular, it tells us to resist the temptation to neglect evidence contrary to what we want to believe.

Here, for instance, is the substance of remarks made in fall 2006, by a young woman who just bought a condo with a subprime loan.

> Now is the time to buy a condo. I got a loan without even making a down payment. And interest rates are so cheap. A two-year loan goes for under 5 percent, and I can refinance it later for even less. Besides, I was tired of renting an apartment and wanted a place of my own. It's just money down the drain to rent. The price of condos has really gone up the past few years, so I'm bound to make a profit when I sell. I may be scraping by now, but I can always run up a few credit cards to get along.

Here is the implied argument.

1. This is a good time to buy a condo.
2. Financially it's a good deal since I don't have to make a down payment, and interest rates on short-term loans are low.
3. Real estate will continue to appreciate, and I'll make a profit when I sell.

Alas, this home buyer and thousands like her went into bankruptcy when the housing bubble burst, real estate prices fell, and short-term loans could only be refinanced at higher interest rates than many buyers could afford. Her reasoning neglected to consider her own financial situation and evidence that a little research might have unearthed.

1. The housing market was at an all-time high, and there was bound to be a correction in the market. Past experience shows that housing booms end and prices decline.
2. Short-term loans at very low introductory rates are just teasers that mortgages lenders use to lure consumers into taking out mortgages. Often they are hyped to people with sketchy credit histories and low incomes, in other words, people without the usual qualifications for buying real estate. When the time comes to refinance, usually two years later, the rates shoot up as much as 3 percentage points.
3. Buyers with sufficient incomes who make down payments and qualify for conventional prime rate loans usually can usually ride out a dip in the market, but not

lower income buyers who finance everything on credit. When money is tight, as it began to be in 2007, loan companies refuse to lend to high-risk buyers, who may have to resort to selling at a loss or face foreclosure and possibly bankruptcy.

Hindsight is certainly better than foresight, but with a realistic understanding of one's own financial situation, a little research into the nature of housing markets in general and the shady practices of loan sharks in particular, these points can be figured out by an intelligent person who thinks carefully about the matter. Although it is understandable that the young woman wanted a home of her own, too often common sense gives way to magical thinking.

Valid Reasoning

The third criterion of cogent reasoning requires that the premises of an argument genuinely support its conclusion; or, as logicians like to say, it requires that an argument be valid, or correct. It is vitally important to understand that the validity of an argument has nothing whatever to do with the truth of its premises or conclusion. Validity concerns the nature of the *connection* between the premises and conclusion of an argument, not the truth or believability of its premises. Determining that an argument is valid tells us that *if* we are justified in believing in its premises, *then* we also are justified in believing in the truth of its conclusion. It doesn't tell us *whether* its premises are true. An argument thus can be perfectly valid and have completely false premises, and even have a false conclusion. Here is an example:

1. The Pittsburgh Pirates have won more World Series games than any other major league team. (False premise, alas!)
∴2. They have won more World Series games than the New York Yankees. (False conclusion.)

The argument is valid because if the Pirates *had* won more World Series games than any other major league team, then, obviously (well, it's obvious to baseball fans), they would have won more World Series games than the Yankees. The argument is valid, even though its premise and conclusion both are false. It's valid because anyone who is justified in believing its premise is justified in believing its conclusion.

4. TWO BASIC KINDS OF VALID ARGUMENTS

Premises may correctly support conclusions in two fundamentally different ways. The first way yields *deductively valid* arguments; the second, *inductively valid* (or inductively strong) arguments.[5]

---

[5]Some authorities believe that there is at least one other kind of legitimate argument—namely, the kind in which various alternatives are evaluated. The authors of this text incline to the view that evaluative arguments fall into one or the other of the two basic kinds about to be mentioned. Note also that some authorities restrict the use of the term *valid* so that it refers only to deductively good arguments, even though in everyday life, inductively strong arguments generally are said to be valid. In addition, note that the reasoning process called "mathematical induction" happens to be a kind of deductive reasoning. (Terminology sometimes is misleading.)

Deductive Validity

The fundamental property of a **deductively valid** argument is this: If all of its premises are true, then its conclusion must be true also, because the claim asserted by its conclusion already has been stated in its premises, although usually only implicitly.

Here is an example of a very simple deductively valid argument:

1. If this wire is made of copper, then it will conduct electricity. (Premise.)
2. This wire is made of copper. (Premise.)
∴3. This wire will conduct electricity. (Conclusion.)

Taken alone, neither premise makes the claim that the wire will conduct electricity; but taken together, they do. We cannot imagine what it would be like for both premises of this argument to be true, yet its conclusion turn out to be false. Indeed, it would be contradictory to assert both of its premises and then to deny its conclusion.

It is important to see that it is the **form** of this argument—namely:

1. If some sentence, then a second sentence.
2. The first sentence.
∴3. The second sentence—

that makes it deductively valid, not the truth values of its statements. Letting the capital letter A stand for the first sentence and B for the second sentence, the *form* of the argument can be stated this way:

1. If A then B.
2. A.
∴3. B.

Clearly, every argument having this form is deductively valid, another example being this argument:

1. If Sonia reads *Vogue* magazine, then she's up on the latest fashions.
2. Sonia reads *Vogue* magazine.
3. She's up on the latest fashions.

Logicians, by the way, call the form of this argument, and every argument having this form, *modus ponens*.

It's very important to understand that the deductive validity of an argument guarantees that its conclusion is true *only if* its premises are true. Determining that an argument is deductively valid thus tells us just that *if* its premises are true, *then* its conclusion must be true also; it doesn't tell us *whether* its premises are true and thus doesn't tell us *whether* its conclusion is true.

Here, for instance, is a deductively valid argument having the form *modus ponens* that contains one true and one very likely false premise, and thus does not guarantee the truth of its conclusion:

1. If more people read Agatha Christie's mystery novels than read Shakespeare's plays, then her novels must be better than his plays. (False premise?)
2. Her novels have been read by more people than have Shakespeare's plays. (True premise.)
∴3. Her novels must be better than his plays. (False conclusion?)

Of course, a deductively valid argument that contains a false premise may, luckily, have a true conclusion. But that would be a matter of luck, not of good reasoning.

The fact that a deductively valid argument cannot move from true premises to a false conclusion constitutes its chief characteristic and great virtue. But deductive arguments are limited. They cannot yield conclusions that are not at least implicit in the premises from which they are derived. **Induction** is needed to perform this task.

Inductive Validity

Inductively valid (inductively strong) arguments, unlike deductively valid ones, have conclusions that go beyond what is contained in their premises. The idea behind valid induction is that of *learning from experience.* We often observe patterns, resemblances, and other kinds of regularities in our experiences, some quite simple (sugar sweetening coffee), some very complicated (objects moving according to Newton's laws—well, Newton noticed this, anyway). Valid inductions simply project regularities of this kind observed in our experiences so far onto other possible experiences.[6]

Here is a simple example of an inductively valid argument, of the kind sometimes called *induction by enumeration,* expressed by a rather smart child in Jacksonville, Florida, explaining why he is doubtful about the existence of Santa Claus:

> The tooth fairy turned out not to be real. The Easter Bunny turned out not to be real. So I'm beginning to wonder about Santa.

Admittedly this is a small sample, but perhaps not for a 4-year-old with a limited range of experience.

We use inductive reasoning so frequently in everyday life that its nature generally goes unnoticed. Being informed about induction is a bit like being told that we've been speaking prose all our lives. We start drawing perfectly good inferences of this kind (and some klinkers) at a very early age. By age 5 or 6, the use of induction has taught us a great many of the basic truths that guide everyday behavior—for instance, that some foods taste good and some don't, the sun rises every morning and sets every evening, very hot things burn the skin, some people are trustworthy and some aren't (something most of us seem to need to relearn over and over), and so on.

The great virtue of inductive reasoning is that it provides us with a way of reasoning to genuinely new beliefs, not just to psychologically new ones that are implicit in what we already know, as in the case of valid deductions. However, this benefit is purchased at the cost of an increase in the possibility of error. As remarked before, the truth of the premises of a deductively valid argument guarantees the truth of its conclusion; but the premises of a perfectly good induction may all be true and yet its conclusion be false. Even the best "inductive leap" may lead us astray, because the patterns noticed in our experiences up to a given point may not turn out to be the exact patterns of the whole universe. This happens all too often in daily life—for example, when a restaurant that has served excellent food many times in the past fails us on a special occasion. But it sometimes happens even in the lofty realm of theoretical science. Physicists, for instance, believed for a long time that asbestos does not conduct electricity—a belief supported by

---

[6]This includes those experiences we can't have but might have if we had lived millions of years ago, or if, say, we could go into the interior of the sun without being incinerated.

very good, very strong inductive reasoning—but then discovered that all substances, including asbestos, conduct electricity when cooled down close to absolute zero.

Nevertheless, rational people use induction in formulating their ideas about how things are going to turn out, whether in ordinary, everyday circumstances or in the rather special ones scientists bring about in the laboratory. Induction, thinking of Winston Churchill's famous remark about democracy, is the worst way to expand one's knowledge except for all of the other ways (guessing, wishful thinking, astrology, and so on).

EXERCISE 1-3

Which of the following passages (modestly edited to make them more straightforward than arguments often are in daily life) do you think are deductively valid? Inductively valid? Defend your answers, showing the structure of those you believe to be valid.

1. A friend of mine told me that the herb echinacea would cure my cold or at least reduce the symptoms if I took it four times a day. So I did what he said, but I didn't get better any faster. A few months later I caught another cold and took echinacea again—this time at the first sign I was sick. But no luck. Next time I'll just take some aspirin. Echinacea doesn't work.

2. If I buy these potato chips, I know I'm going to eat the whole bagful at one sitting. But if I do that, I'll upset my stomach. Well, then, if I buy this tempting item, my guts are going to get upset again. Satan, get thee behind me!

3. My father has always voted for Republican candidates, and my mother has also. Hah! Now that I'm old enough to vote, I'm going to vote Democratic. That'll show them.

4. According to statistics compiled by the U.S. Bureau of Census in 2008, full-time workers without high school degrees earned $27,470 a year; high school graduates, $34,197; community college graduates with associate degrees, $44,086; college graduates with bachelor degrees, $57,026; college graduates with professional degrees, $103,411. Is college worth it? Absolutely.

5. SOME WRONG IDEAS ABOUT COGENT REASONING

Having just presented three standards of cogent reasoning and having explained the nature of valid deduction and induction, perhaps we need to mention several recently voiced ideas about logic and good reasoning. According to these modestly trendy ways of looking at the topic, what counts as good reasoning is "culturally relative," or "gender-relative," or even (popular among students) "individually relative." We hear talk of "feminine logic," supposedly different from the "male logic" taught in logic classes (often by female logicians, but let that pass), and of "black intelligence," different from the "Eurocentric" variety foisted on us by white males, as though what makes reasoning good differs from group to group, race to race, or one sex to the other. We all too often hear students say things such as "That may well be true for you, but it isn't true for me," and listen to academics talk disparagingly of "Aristotelian linear reasoning," as opposed to a more "intuitive" type of reasoning, and so on.

A wise person hears one word and understands two.

—**Jewish proverb**

Calvin & Hobbes © Watterson. Reprinted with permission of Universal Press Syndicate. All rights reserved.

Calvin is no match for Miss Wormwood, who easily reads between the lines of Calvin's attempts at ingratiation.

Reading between the Lines

The expression "reading between the lines" has several meanings. One captures the idea of grasping an intended thought that is not expressed, another of getting more information from a statement or argument than it explicitly—or even implicitly—contains, still another of noticing what rhetoric either deliberately or accidentally hides. Reading between the lines often is the essential ingredient in assessing a good deal of the everyday talk we all encounter, in particular political rhetoric and (interestingly) advertisements.

Take the Bufferin ad that states, "No regular aspirin product reduces fever better." Reading between the lines of this ad, we should conclude that Bufferin does *not* reduce fever better than some competing products, because if it did, the ad would make that stronger claim ("Bufferin reduces fever better than any other aspirin product") rather than the weaker one that none reduces fever better. The point is that our own background beliefs should lead us to expect an advertisement to make the strongest claim possible and thus lead us to at least tentatively conclude that a less strong claim is made because stronger claims would be false.

Reading between the lines is the linguistic equivalent of "sizing up" other people—for example, of gleaning information about their beliefs or likely actions from their overt behavior or way of saying something. A good poker player, for instance, looks for signs of bluffing—some players often unwittingly signal a bluff by increasing chatter or by nervous behavior; others do so by feigning lack of concern. Similarly, intelligent voters try to size up political candidates by looking for nonverbal clues and by reading between the lines of campaign rhetoric. (More will be said about campaign rhetoric in Chapters 7 and 10.)

But there is no truth to these ideas about what constitutes good reasoning. It is the height of folly to conclude, say, that an argument having the form *modus ponens* is not valid. Think, for example, what it means to assert seriously that all human beings have a right to life, and then in the next breath to claim, equally seriously, that a particular human being, Smith, has no right to life. What sense is there in first saying that if Jones has been to China, then he's been to Asia, and then asserting that he has indeed been to China but not to Asia? Yet accepting reasonings that violate the standards of deductive logic means precisely accepting some sorts of contradictory assertions or other, because the point of the principles of valid deduction (including the valid principles of mathematics) is to assure that we do not contradict ourselves when we reason from one thing to another. (That's why, to take just one of a thousand examples, double-entry bookkeeping works.)

Similarly, what reason could there be for violating the standards of good inductive reasoning—for denying what experience teaches us? That a large majority of the scientists who laid the groundwork in physics, chemistry, and biology were white males is totally irrelevant to the truth of their basic ideas and theories. *The way the world works does not differ depending on the race or sex of those trying to discover the way the world works!* That is why, to take an everyday example, it is foolish to toss away money on homeopathic medicines: Medical science has shown, over and over again, by means of inductive reasoning, to say nothing of very highly confirmed general biological principles, that homeopathy does not work. The point cannot be stressed too heavily. There simply is no truth whatsoever to the idea that standards of good reasoning differ from group to group, male to female, or person to person.

Doonesbury © G. B. Trudeau. Reprinted with permission of
Universal Press Syndicate. All rights reserved.

There is, however, a good deal of truth to three much different ideas. One is that self-interest, prejudice, and/or narrow-mindedness do in fact often lead people to reason invalidly. Bigotry has a bad name for good reason. Another is that self-interest often motivates us to neglect the values or interests of others, even when we share those values, so that some groups or individuals find their interests frequently neglected. For instance, rich people who believe fairness requires that everyone ought to have an equal chance when starting out in life often forget about equality of opportunity when they argue for the elimination of all inheritance taxes; in families in which both parents work, husbands notoriously tend to paper over their failure to share household and child-rearing duties; in the business world, high executives, while asserting their belief in equal rights for all, frequently overlook the ways in which women, Latinos, and blacks are often passed over for corporate advancement. In all of these cases, the problem is not with the principles of good reasoning. It is with the fallacious nature of the ways in which these principles sometimes are employed.

Those who champion other sorts of "logics" than the standard variety thus may well be mistaken in their target. They attack the principles of good reasoning rather than the failure of their opponents to employ these perfectly good (indeed the *only* good) standards of reasoning correctly, or to reason from acceptable moral or other kinds of values.

A good deal more will be said in later chapters on these matters, in particular about moral and other value claims. For now, the point is just that we must distinguish the principles of good reasoning, which are the same for all, from the ways in which these principles are employed (sometimes fallaciously), and from the differing values that enter into the premises of different reasonings.

6. BACKGROUND BELIEFS

Earlier, we characterized cogent reasoning in terms of three conditions: the validity of connections between premises and conclusions, the believability of premises, and the discovery and use of relevant information. Clearly, satisfaction of the last two of these three conditions requires the employment of background beliefs. That is why bringing one's background beliefs to bear often is the most important task in evaluating an argument for cogency.

Consider, for example, the argument frequently heard in the early 1980s that AIDS was essentially a gay plague inflicted on homosexuals as punishment for their perverse sexual conduct (a claim still occasionally heard). The key premise of this argument was that AIDS can be transmitted sexually only via homosexual conduct, a premise that was supported by the evidence that in the United States a large majority of those reported early on to have the disease were indeed homosexuals. But people with good background information did not accept this argument. For one thing, they knew that in other places around the world—for instance, in Haiti and parts of Africa—large numbers of heterosexuals also had contracted AIDS via sexual contact. And for another, those familiar with some of the basic scientific ideas concerning disease had theoretical (which means higher-level inductive) reasons for believing that AIDS could be transmitted via heterosexual behavior, as are syphilis, hepatitis B, herpes, and so on.

Today, most Americans know that AIDs is transmitted by both heterosexuals and homosexuals, but many people wrongly think that the disease is curable because they have heard about drugs used to treat HIV. In fact, these drugs suppress the viral infection but do not cure it, and no vaccine has been successfully developed to date. Unfortunately, many young people believe they can be cured if they become infected and thus fail to take adequate precautions.

The point is that contrary to the old saying, ignorance is *not* bliss. It just renders us incapable of intelligently evaluating claims, premises, arguments, and other sorts of rhetoric we all are subject to every day. When evaluating arguments and issues, we can't bring relevant beliefs to bear if we don't have them, and we cannot make good judgments if what we believe is off the mark.

7. KINDS OF BACKGROUND BELIEFS

Background beliefs can be divided up in many different ways, an important one being a separation into beliefs about *matters of fact* and beliefs about values. It is a factual question, for example, whether capital punishment is practiced in every society (it isn't); it is a question of values whether capital punishment is morally justified (is it?). In dealing with most social or political issues, we need to separate claims that are about matters of fact from those concerning values, because these two different sorts of claims are defended, or justified, in different ways. The statement, for example, that a given state has a death penalty is proved true, or false, by an examination of relevant government records; the judgment that capital punishment is, or isn't, morally justified as the punishment for heinous crimes is determined by bringing to bear an accepted moral code, or subjective intuitions.[7]

> Knowledge not renewed quickly becomes ignorance.
>
> —Peter Drucker

> Those who cannot remember the past are condemned to repeat it.
>
> —George Santayana

Background beliefs also can be divided into those that are *true* and (unfortunately) those that are *false*. Someone who believes, for example, that capital punishment exists as a practice in every society has a false belief; those who believe that every society punishes murderers in one way or another has a belief that is true. An important reason for regularly testing our background beliefs in terms of our experiences and of what we learn from others is precisely to weed out background beliefs that are false. Education consists of lot more than simply learning a mountain of facts; it also has to do with weeding out beliefs that turn out to be false (or unjustified).

Beliefs also differ as to how firmly they are or should be held. We feel completely sure, completely confident, of some beliefs (for example, that the sun will rise tomorrow); less sure, but still quite confident, of others (for example, that the United States

---

[7]Philosophers and others disagree seriously concerning the question whether there are such things as objective moral principles that all clear-minded, rational individuals are bound to see as correct, or whether moral right and wrong is a matter of subjective opinion—of feelings that can, and perhaps do, differ from person to person.

will still be in existence in the year 2050); and a good deal less sure, but still mildly confident, of others (for example, that we won't get killed some day in an auto accident). The trick is to believe firmly what should be believed, given the evidence, and believe less firmly, or not at all, what is less well supported by evidence.

All of this relates directly to decisions we have to make in everyday life. Wise individuals take into account the probability of one thing or another happening and thus of the confidence they should place in their beliefs about what to do. That's a large part of the truth behind familiar sayings such as "A bird in the hand is worth two in the bush."

8. WORLDVIEWS OR PHILOSOPHIES

As we grow up from childhood into adults, we tend to absorb the beliefs and standards of those in the world around us—our families, friends, and culture. It is no accident that so many of us have the same religious affiliation, or lack of same, as do our parents, that we accept the principles and standards of our own society, and so on.

These beliefs constitute an important part of our **worldviews** or **philosophies**.[8] They tend to be the most deeply ingrained and most resistant to amendment of all of our background beliefs. They become so much a part of us that we often appeal to them without consciously realizing we have done so. They are so intricately woven into the fabric of our belief systems that we often find it hard to isolate and examine individual strands. And when we do examine them, our natural tendency is to reaffirm them without thought and to disparage conflicting claims and evidence, quickly dismissing evidence that might count against them.

Most of these beliefs are general—for example, that killing always is morally wrong, that there is some good in virtually all human beings, or that we all die sooner or later. But not all are. Belief in a monotheistic deity, for instance, or rejection of such a belief, is a particular belief.

But in spite of the example just cited, more general beliefs usually (that is, generally!) are more important than beliefs that are particular, or less general, because they tell us about a wider range of cases and thus tend to be more useful in everyday life. Believing that it rarely rains in July in Los Angeles, for instance, clearly is more useful than believing merely that it won't rain there, say, on July 16, 2014. That is why most of the important beliefs in one's worldview are general and also why most important scientific pronouncements are general—indeed, often extremely general. (Newton's laws, for example, don't just tell us about apples falling from trees or even just about items of all kinds falling toward the Earth. They also tell us about the motion of the Earth around the sun, about the motion of all planets around the sun, about how tides rise and fall, and, in fact, about the motions of all objects whatsoever.) It also is why it is so important, and useful, to expand our worldviews to contain at least a few modestly well-founded beliefs about important scientific theories—for example, about the theory of the evolution of all life on Earth.

---

[8]This includes religious beliefs in the case of those who have religious convictions.

The worldviews of political parties are implied in the words and phrases they use repeatedly in their discourse. University of California linguist George Lakoff came up with a list of words used over and over in the speeches and writings of conservatives and liberals. It's worth examining them to figure out the dominant worldviews reflected in the language.*

Conservatives: character, virtue, discipline, tough it out, get tough, tough love, strong, self-reliance, individual responsibility, backbone, standards, authority, heritage, competition, earn, hard work, enterprise, property rights, reward, freedom, intrusion, interference, meddling, punishment, human nature, traditional, common sense, dependency, self-indulgent, elite, quotas, breakdown, corrupt, decay, rot, degenerate, deviant, lifestyle.

Liberals: social forces, social responsibility, free expression, human rights, equal rights, concern, care, help, health, safety, nutrition, basic human dignity, oppression, diversity, deprivation, alienation, big corporations, corporate welfare, ecology, ecosystem, biodiversity, pollution.

What worldviews did you come up with?

*Taken from Lakoff, G. *Moral Politics: How Liberals and Conservatives Think*. Chicago: University of Chicago Press, 2002.

Compare the worldview reflected in this gem, excerpted from a 1950s women's magazine, to your worldview.

The Good Wife's Guide

- Prepare yourself. Take 15 minutes to rest so you'll be refreshed when he arrives. Touch up your make-up, put a ribbon in your hair and be fresh-looking. He has just been with a lot of work-weary people. . . .
- Listen to him. You may have a dozen important things to tell him, but the moment of his arrival is not the time. Let him talk first—remember, his topics of conversation are more important than yours. . . .
- Make the evening his. Never complain if he comes home late or goes out to dinner, or other places of entertainment without you. Instead, try to understand his world of strains and pressure and his very real need to be at home and relax. . . .
- Don't complain if he's late home for dinner or even if he stays out all night. Count this as minor compared to what he might have gone through that day. . . .

- Don't ask him questions about his actions or question his judgment or integrity. Remember, he is the master of the house and as such will always exercise his will with fairness and truthfulness. You have no right to question him. . . .
- A good wife always knows her place.

—*Housekeeping Monthly,* May 13, 1955

An astute reader noted that he couldn't find a history of this magazine and suspected it was a put-on. He may be right, but anyone raised in the 1950s will recognize the all-too-familiar worldview it reflects.

9. INSUFFICIENTLY GROUNDED BELIEFS

Most of us have strongly held beliefs about a great many controversial issues, and so we tend to respond automatically to arguments about these matters. We feel confident that we know whether marijuana or cocaine should be legalized, whether we should privatize Social Security, whether this candidate or that is more likely to serve all of the people equally if elected to office, and so on. We hold these beliefs, often very strongly, even though a good deal of the time we have insufficient justifying background knowledge and have engaged in too little thought to be able to support our beliefs intelligently or defend them against informed objections. What, for example, do we usually know about candidates running for seats in the U.S. House of Representatives? (In 2012, a significant number of voters did not even know the names of both major party candidates for congressional seats in their districts; fewer still could name both candidates for state legislatures in their districts. Could you?) Too often, we base our vote on our party affiliation (that is, our political beliefs) not on the merit of individual candidates. Clearly, then, weeding out insufficiently grounded background information is vital if we are to improve our reasoning about important, to say nothing of relatively trivial, matters. (It also might be a good idea to find out something about candidates for various offices before stepping into a booth and casting our ballots.)

Having well-supported background beliefs is particularly important with respect to those basic background beliefs that make up our worldviews. Worldviews are like lenses that cause us to see the world in a particular way or filters through which we process all new ideas and information. Reasoning based on a grossly inaccurate or shallow worldview tends to yield grossly inaccurate, inappropriate, or self-defeating conclusions (except when we're just plain lucky), no matter how smart we otherwise may be. Sometimes, the harm is relatively minor (gamblers who waste a few bucks playing "lucky" lottery numbers; astrology column readers who arrange vacation times to fit their sign), but at other times, the harm can be more serious (people with an overly rosy view of human nature who get taken by sharp operators; misanthropes who miss out on the benefits and joys of trusting relationships).

Obviously, then, we need to examine our background beliefs, in particular, those that make up our worldviews, for consistency and believability, and we need to amend them

It is worth noting here that widespread failure to revise worldviews often results in serious political and social unrest and injustice. E. M. Forster captures this poignantly in his novel *A Passage to India,* in which he depicts intense conflicts in colonial India between English masters and their conquered Indian subjects. Believing themselves socially and racially superior, the English relegate the Indians to subordinate positions, never allowing them equality under the British raj. The insensitivity of the British to the plight of their subjects is met with resentment, distrust, anger, and threats of violent retaliation by the Indians. (To make matters worse, the Indians are divided from one another by differing religious and cultural beliefs.) Very few of the British or Indians Forster depicts ever revise their biases and prejudices in the light of new information—for instance, in the light of obvious evidence about the competence of individual Indians or the glaring prejudice of English officials. The novel makes a compelling case for a widespread reexamination of worldviews and other background beliefs if human beings are to arrive at a peaceful, nonexploitative coexistence on planet Earth.

so as to square with newly acquired information. The point is that having a good supply of background beliefs is not just a matter of filling up one's "tank" with gallons of facts. It is at least equally important to improve one's existing stock of beliefs by weeding out those that experience proves to be false, to sharpen vague beliefs, and to replace crude beliefs with those that are more sophisticated—beliefs that penetrate more deeply into the complexities of life and the world.

People who hold different worldviews often clash on a personal level, but when cultures or nations have conflicting worldviews, they can create tension and spark antagonism internationally. One recent example involved a controversy over whether an Afghan should be sentenced to death because he converted from Islam to Christianity. Under Sharia law, a Muslim who rejects Islam may be tried and executed. So when it became known that the man had converted to Christianity, he was put on trial by the Afghan government, whose constitution allows prosecution under Sharia law. When Muslim clerics demanded that he be sentenced to death, prominent leaders in the Western world urged the government to honor human rights principles and free him. The conflicting worldviews caused an uproar on both sides. When the Afghan government looked for ways to drop the case in order to comply with international pressure, the clerics warned that if the man were freed, the people of Afghanistan would kill him. (The government resolved this dilemma by declaring him mentally unfit and citing "investigative gaps" in the case.) When clashes like this multiply and escalate, they may give rise to violence on a large scale. It is probably no exaggeration to say that major conflicts in worldviews are at the heart of most wars.

Socrates is said to have claimed that the unexamined life is not worth living. While clearly an exaggeration, there surely is a great deal of truth in this idea. By the same token, there is a large dose of truth in the idea that an unexamined worldview is not likely to be worth holding, in particular because it will contain little more than an accumulation of the ideas and prejudices of others. Examining worldviews allows us to take control of our lives by actively sorting out our fundamental beliefs, testing them against ideas and information that point to conclusions contrary to what we already believe, and making whatever revisions are indicated in the light of what we have learned. *Doing this helps us to become our own person rather than just a passive follower of others!*

Unfortunately, it is no easy matter for us to examine our worldviews objectively. Psychological studies show that people hold on to their beliefs for dear life, ignoring evidence that undermines them and dredging up weak evidence to support them. This obstacle to rational thought is compounded by our natural tendency to take short-cuts in reasoning that reduce our mental effort, allowing us to slide past unwelcome evidence and leap to hasty conclusions that support our existing beliefs. All this makes rational self-analysis difficult to say the least—but not impossible. To reason cogently, we need to fight this human tendency (discussed further in Chapter 6).

EXERCISE 1-4

1. Using the Internet, go to Google and search for "I have a dream" under the exact phrase option. Figure out which parts of the speech state or imply Martin Luther King's philosophy and explain his worldview.

2. Find at least one item on the Internet or in the mass media (a newspaper or magazine article or a television program) that seems to be based on a worldview contrary to the one you yourself hold. Explain your choice.

3. Find at least one item on the Internet or in the mass media that reflects a typically American point of view you happen to share, and explain what makes it typically American. (This is not as easy to do as it sounds. Recalling the content of the box on E. M. Forster's novel may help prod your memory.)

4. Describe a situation in which you changed your mind on some more or less fundamental belief, and explain what convinced you to do so. (This is a very difficult question for many people to answer, another bit of evidence for the fact that much of what goes on in the accumulation and emendation of important background beliefs happens only on the edge of consciousness.)

EXERCISE 1-5

1. When Barack Obama and Hillary Rodham Clinton ran for the Democratic presidential nomination in 2008, many people thought that the time had come to elect an African American or a woman as president. Never in our history had two candidates from these politically underrepresented groups come so close to leading the nation. What changes in worldviews were reflected in voters' willingness to elect a woman or an African American to the highest position in the country? Compare the worldviews voters might have held before this historic shift to those they held after the election.

EXERCISE 1-6

How do the ideas expressed in the following excerpt from an essay by British philosopher Bertrand Russell compare with those in your own worldview and other background beliefs?

> The aesthetic indictment of industrialism is perhaps the least serious. A much more serious feature is the way in which it forces men, women, and children to live a life against instinct, unnatural, unspontaneous, artificial. Where industry is thoroughly developed, men are deprived of the sight of green fields and the smell of earth after rain; they are cooped together in irksome proximity, surrounded by noise and dirt, compelled to spend many hours a day performing some utterly uninteresting and monotonous mechanical task. Women are, for the most part, obliged to work in factories, and to leave to others the care of their children. The children themselves, if they are preserved from work in the factories, are kept at work in school, with an intensity that is especially damaging to the best brains. The result of this life against instinct is that industrial populations tend to be listless and trivial, in constant search of excitement, delighted by a murder, and still more delighted by a war.

Russell's essay, by the way, appeared in the June 1921 issue of the *Atlantic Monthly*. (The more things change, the more they remain the same?)

EXERCISE 1-7

Here is an excerpt from a speech delivered to the Utah chapter of NOW (National Organization of Women) in May 1997 by Elizabeth Joseph, in which she argues that polygamy is beneficial to women in the modern world:

> I've often said that if polygamy didn't exist the modern American career woman would have invented it. Because, despite its reputation, polygamy is the one lifestyle that offers an independent woman a real chance to "have it all." . . .
>
> As a journalist, I work many unpredictable hours in a fast-paced environment. The news determines my schedule. . . . Because of my plural marriage arrangement, I don't have to worry [about coming home late]. I know that when I have to work late my daughter will be surrounded by loving adults with whom she is comfortable and who know her schedule without my telling them. My eight-year-old has never seen the inside of a day-care center, and my husband has never eaten a TV dinner. And I know that when I get home from work, if I'm dog-tired and stressed-out, I can be alone and guilt free. It's a rare day when all eight of my husband's wives are tired and stressed at the same time.
>
> It's helpful to think of polygamy in terms of a free-market approach to marriage. Why shouldn't you or your daughters have the opportunity to marry the best man available, regardless of his marital status? . . .
>
> Polygamy is an empowering lifestyle for women. It provides me the environment and opportunity to maximize my female potential without all the tradeoffs and compromises that attend monogamy. The women in my family are friends.

You don't share two decades of experience, and a man, without those friendships becoming very special. . . . [P]olygamy [is] the ultimate feminist lifestyle.

Compare Joseph's view to your own on marital arrangements. Do you find her ideas persuasive? Does your worldview jibe with hers? Why or why not? Most of us think of monogamy as "natural," yet polygamy has been common in different parts of the world at different times in history. (Although Utah outlawed the practice in the nineteenth century as a condition of statehood, the anti-bigamy law is rarely enforced in that state. Estimates put the number of polygamists in Utah in the tens of thousands, even though it's impossible to verify the statistics, given the illegal nature of the activity.) Portions of Joseph's speech were reprinted in the February 1998 issue of *Harper's*.

10. Two Vital Kinds of background Beliefs

Background beliefs obviously differ greatly in their importance. Two kinds that are extremely important concern the *nature of human nature* and the *reliability of information sources*.

The Nature of Human Nature

Good beliefs about what we ourselves and other people are like constitute a vital part of everyone's worldview. They are crucial in applying what we know to the problems encountered in everyday life, whether of a personal or a social nature. When can we trust our friends? Is an instructor to be believed who says that students are graded solely on the quality of their exams and not on agreement with the instructor's personal opinions? Will people be sufficiently motivated to work diligently under a socialistic system? Are large numbers of elected officials motivated by selfish interests that frequently override their sense of duty to those who have elected them?

Fortunately, we don't have to start constructing theories about human nature from scratch, since other people, including some of the great writers (Shakespeare, Aristotle, Darwin, Freud) have been at the task for some time now. (Of course, tapping these sources has its risks. Freud, for instance, had some way-off-target ideas on the subject to go along with some extremely penetrating ones.) But even common everyday sayings contain a mother lode of wisdom. Blood *is* thicker than water, and power *does* tend to corrupt, even if it is doubtful that the female of the species is any more vain than the male.

The Reliability of Information Sources

Thoughts about the accuracy, sufficiency, and truthfulness of information sources constitute another vital kind of background belief. As with computers, so also with the human mind: "Garbage in, garbage out." We therefore need constantly to reassess the reliability of important information sources—television, newspapers, magazines, friends, the Internet, teachers, textbooks, and so on. Under what conditions are these sources likely to provide truthful or, at least, sensible information or opinions? When are alleged experts likely even to possess the truth, much less be motivated to tell it to us straight? When are they likely to be prejudiced in ways that may cloud their judgment?

We can't assume automatically that a source is reliable without some *reason* for believing this. As lamented a while back, many people seem to think that if they read it in print or hear it on the TV evening news, then it must be true. Sophisticated reasoners, however, realize that these information sources do not always furnish "the truth, the whole truth, and nothing but the truth"; they don't necessarily provide us with "All the news that's fit to print" (*The New York Times* motto), instead sometimes shaving matters either out of ignorance or from self-serving motives. Intelligent viewers of the scene thus try to determine when these sources are likely to be reliable and when not. That is why a whole chapter in this text, Chapter 10, deals with advertising as an information source; Chapter 11 with the reliability of the media; and Chapter 12, with public school textbooks as information sources.

11. SCIENCE TO THE RESCUE

The mention of Darwin and Freud a while back brings to mind the central place that science plays in modern life and in the construction of accurate stocks of background beliefs—in particular, in the formulation of sensible worldviews. Although no information source is absolutely reliable and no theory exempt from at least a small measure of doubt, the most reliable, the most accurate information comes from the well-established sciences of physics, chemistry, biology, and, to a lesser extent, psychology, the social sciences, and the applied sciences such as engineering. The scientific enterprise is an organized, ongoing, worldwide activity that builds and corrects from generation to generation. The method of science is just the rigorous, systematic, dogged application of cogent inductive reasoning, mixed with all sorts of deductive—including mathematical—reasoning from what has so far been observed over many centuries to theories about how the universe and the many things in it have functioned and are likely to function. Theories falsified by experience are tossed out, no matter whose pet ideas happen to get stepped on. Absolutely no one, starting from scratch, could hope to obtain, in one lifetime, anything remotely resembling the sophisticated and accurate conclusions of any of the sciences, even if that person were a Galileo, Newton, Darwin, and Einstein all rolled into one. *It is foolish indeed to dismiss what science has to say on any topic without very careful thought and without having extremely important reasons for doing so!*[9]

Indeed, one justification for requiring all high school students to take at least one course in a physical or biological science is to allow them to gain an understanding of the great rigor with which scientific principles are tested and proved. But another, easier way to come to understand the power of science as compared to other ways of finding out about the world is to think carefully about the thousands of everyday items available to us today that did not exist 300 years ago, products that owe their existence to the tremendous advances in scientific theory that have been made since the days of Galileo and Newton. Without science, there would be no automobiles, no airplanes (not to mention

---

[9]Note, however, that psychology has just recently come out of its infancy. Note also that there is more chicanery in medical research (because of the profit motive?) than in most other areas of science.

spacecraft), no telephones, electric lightbulbs, air conditioning, or other electric devices of any kind (certainly no computers!), no batteries, no aspirin or other common painkillers, no anesthetics (alcohol used to be the painkiller used during amputations), no antibiotics (or even knowledge of the existence of microbes and thus the extreme importance of cleanliness), no ways to purify drinking water, no indoor plumbing, no eyeglasses, no insulin for diabetics, . . . the list goes on and on. Instead, there were plenty of mosquitoes and flies (and fly paper) everywhere on summer days, and people made do with commodes, outhouses, and well-drawn drinking and washing water. In those days, doctors could cure only a handful of ailments, horse dung and its foul smell were everywhere in every city and town, lighting after dark was furnished by candles or oil lamps, and so on. Before the existence of the scientific, modern, industrial world, the average life span almost everywhere was less than 50 years, much less in most societies.

Of course, to avoid having beliefs contradicted by scientific theory or to apply scientific principles successfully in dealing with everyday problems, one does have to have at least a casual acquaintance with what science has to say on various topics. The problem is that large numbers of people have no idea what science is up to and have only the tiniest stock of scientific facts about the nature of the world. This lack of knowledge about science can have unfortunate consequences. For instance, a growing number of parents have refused to vaccinate their children against whooping cough on the mistaken belief that vaccines are ineffective in preventing the disease and may even be harmful. They believe that a healthy diet and good living is enough and that their refusal to use vaccinations won't affect anyone but their own children. None of these assumptions is accurate, however. The recent increase in whooping cough cases correlates with the increase in vaccine refusals, as studies have shown. For example, a study in Boulder (which has the lowest school-wide vaccination rate in Colorado) found that unvaccinated children were 23 times more likely to get whooping cough than those who had been vaccinated.[10] Not only were they infected, but other children were as well, such as those who were too young to be vaccinated or those who had been vaccinated but did not develop adequate immunity. For immunizations to be effective, a high percentage of children need to be vaccinated to protect the population at large. Ignoring the science has resulted in an outbreak of whooping cough, a disease that had been virtually eradicated for decades.

Unfortunately, it isn't just the average person (or average college graduate?) who is more or less illiterate when it comes to science. Even those who need to know about specific scientific results in order to do their jobs adequately are frequently remiss in this way. During a quite severe drought in California, one government official defended his inaction by stating that "One problem [in deciding whether to enact water rationing measures] is that we have only 110 years of [precipitation] records. Our statistics [on California droughts] aren't very good." Yet, just prior to that time, a U.S. Geological Survey study of giant sequoia tree rings had yielded a record going back more than 2,000 years.

Students sometimes defend their ignorance of science by arguing that they only need to know the science, if any, that is relevant to the job they will perform after graduation

---

[10]This 2009 study, "Parental Refusal of Pertussis Vaccination Is Associated with Increased Risk of Pertussis Infection," was conducted on children enrolled in the Kaiser Permanente of Denver health plan from 1996–2007. (Note that *pertussis is* the medical term for whooping cough.)

from college. But this is a serious mistake. For one thing, it isn't possible to know now what basic scientific ideas will be relevant to a job held several years down the pike. (It isn't really possible, except in unusual cases, to know what sort of job it will *be,* much less what kinds of knowledge are going to be relevant to it.) In this increasingly techno-logical age, more and more jobs require at least a general idea of what science has to say about various topics.

Here is Isaac Asimov, one of the best-known popularizers of science (also famous for his science fiction), explaining why cheating in science is so rare, why getting caught is almost inevitable sooner or later, and thus why scientists on the whole are so much more trustworthy (when they're doing science!) than, say, politicians and other public servants.

Self-Correction

Every once in a while—not often—scientists discover that one of their number has published false data or has plagiarized someone else's work.

This is always deeply embarrassing, especially since these days such news usually receives wide publicity in the nonscientific world.

In some ways, however, these scandals actually reflect credit upon the world of science. Consider:

1. Scientists are, after all, human. There is enormous pressure and competition in the world of science. Promotion and status depend on how much you publish and how soon you publish, for the lion's share of credit comes if you are first with an important theory or observation. Under these circumstances, there is great temptation to rush things; to make up some data you are sure you will eventually find anyway that will support your theory; or to help yourself to someone else's work. The surprise, really, is not that it sometimes happens, but that it doesn't happen much more often. Scientists resist the pressure marvelously well.

2. When it does happen, the mere fact that it is so publicized is a tribute to scientists. If it were a common event, or if people expected scientists to be cor-rupt, it would make smaller headlines and drop out of sight sooner. Single cases of scientific corruption, however, will be talked about for years and inspire arti-cles and books by the score. It's really a compliment.

3. Cases of scientific misbehavior point out how difficult it actually is to carry them out successfully, or even for very long. . . . [A] vital principle in scientific research is that nothing counts until observations can be repeated independently and there, almost inevitably, anything peculiar is uncovered. Science is self-correcting in a way that no other field of intellectual endeavor can match.

4. It is scientists themselves who catch the frauds; no one else is equipped to do so. The point is that scientists do catch them. There is never any cover-up on the grounds that science itself must not be disgraced. However embarrassing the facts may be, the culprit is exposed pitilessly and publicly. Science is self-policing in a way that no other field is.

5. Finally, the punishment is absolute. Anyone who proves to have violated the ethics of scientific endeavor is ruined for life. There is no second chance, no vestige of status. He or she must drop out, forever disgraced.

Add to all this the fact that scientific ethics requires all scientists to labor to find flaws in their own observations and theories—and to publicize these flaws when they find them—and you will understand how stern the requirements are and how astonishing it is that scandal is so infrequent.

—From *SciQuest* (February 1982).
Copyright © by Isaac Asimov.
Reprinted by permission of the Estate of Isaac Asimov.

More to the point, a rudimentary understanding of science also is of immeasurable value when dealing with all sorts of everyday problems that aren't related to earning a living. Consumers spend millions of dollars every year on over-the-counter nostrums that don't work, or may even be harmful, because they don't know simple scientific facts—for instance, that no remedies they can buy will cure the flulike infections common in winter. Every day, people throw their money away on get-rich-quick schemes that defy the most basic principles of economics. Large sums are wasted on fortune tellers, mediums, and other charlatans whom science has proved over and over again cannot deliver the promised goods. (This point is discussed a bit more in Chapter 6.)

Students often are put off science by the sheer complexity of the subject matter. Biology, for example, has to be an extremely complicated science, given that the human body contains trillions of cells, each one of which contains millions of atoms and subatomic particles (did you know this?). So the bad news is that every science quickly goes over the heads of almost all laypeople. But the good news is that with only modest perseverance, people who are reasonably intelligent can learn enough about science to greatly improve their everyday reasoning and thus their chances of success in everyday life. (Clearly, similar remarks apply to mathematics, particularly to arithmetic and simple algebra—note the confusion that occasionally results in supermarkets when the power goes out and clerks need to actually add and subtract to figure out what is owed.)

EXERCISE 1-8

Here are some questions from a science knowledge quiz periodically given by the Pew Research Center as part of a study of the impact of science on society. Give it a try.

1. Which over-the-counter drug do doctors recommend that people take to help prevent heart attacks?

   A. Antacids   B. Cortisone   C. Aspirin

2. According to most astronomers, which of the following is no longer considered a planet?

   A. Neptune   B. Pluto   C. Saturn   D. Mercury

3. What gas do most scientists believe causes temperatures in the atmosphere to rise?

   A. Hydrogen   B. Helium   C. Carbon Dioxide   D. Radon

4. How are stem cells different from other cells?

   A. They can develop into many different types of cells.

   B. They are found only in bone marrow.

   C. They are found only in plants.

5. What have scientists recently discovered on Mars?

   A. Platinum   B. Plants   C. Mold   D. Water

Check your response against the percentage of adult Americans who answered the questions correctly.

1. C 91%   2. B 60%   3. C 65%   4. A 52%   5. D 61%

SUMMARY OF CHAPTER 1

Reasoning is the essential ingredient in solving life's problems. This chapter discusses some of the fundamentals of good reasoning and presents an overview of the material to be covered later on the topic of reasoning well in everyday life.

1. *Reasoning* can be cast into *arguments,* which consist of one or more *premises* (reasons) offered in support of a *conclusion.* In real life (as opposed to in textbooks), arguments usually are not labeled and divided from surrounding rhetoric, nor are their premises and conclusions neatly specified. But clues generally are given. Words such as *because, since,* and *for* usually signal premises; *hence, therefore,* and *so,* conclusions.

2. Not all groups of sentences form arguments. They may be anecdotes or other types of *exposition* or *explanation.*

3. Reasoning is either *cogent* (good) or *fallacious* (bad). Cogent reasoning must satisfy three criteria: It must (1) start with justified (warranted, believable) premises, (2) include all likely relevant information, and (3) be *valid* (correct).

4. There are two basic kinds of valid reasoning: *deductive* and *inductive.* The fundamental property of a *deductively valid* argument is this: If its premises are true, then its conclusion must be true also. This is so because the conclusion of a deductively valid argument already is contained in its premises, although usually implicitly, not explicitly. (Note that a deductively valid argument may have false premises. What makes it valid is that *if* its premises are true, then its conclusion must be also.) Unlike deductively valid arguments, those that are *inductively valid* (inductively correct, strong) have conclusions that go beyond the claims made by their premises, projecting patterns stated in the premises onto additional cases.

5. There is no truth to claims about there being such things as "feminine logic," different from "male logic." Logic is not "gender-relative." Similarly, there is no truth to the idea that something exists called "black logic," different from the "Eurocentric" variety espoused by white male teachers. Good reasoning does not differ from sex to sex or race to race; it is not in any way tied to ethnicity. Furthermore, with respect to facts, at any rate, the idea embodied in the idea that "It may well be true for you, but it isn't true for me" is without merit, as is the academic talk of there being something called "Aristotelian linear reasoning," different from a more "intuitive" type of reasoning. (But more needs to be said, and will be, about beliefs concerning values. The point made in this chapter is that, however we may arrive at value beliefs, reasoning from those beliefs must employ the same principles of logic as does reasoning about purely factual matters.)

6. Background beliefs can be divided in many ways, one being into beliefs about *matters of fact* (snow is white) and beliefs about *values* (Jane Austen's novels are better than those of Stephen King). (Note that when speaking of beliefs here, we have in mind a broad sense covering everything accepted as true, or very likely true, and all value judgments and convictions.)

7. Beliefs also, of course, can be divided into those that happen to be true and those that are false. They also can be differentiated in terms of how firmly they are or should be held, and with respect to whether they concern particular events (Jones went to the show last Wednesday) or those that are general (Copper conducts electricity).

8. Our most important beliefs, taken together, make up our *worldviews* or *philosophies.* They are particularly important because they enter into decisions of all kinds—about what to do or what to believe—that we need to make in everyday life. *Examples:* We all die sooner or later; it's always wrong to betray a friend; the best way to find out about how things work is to use induction and deduction. Note that, although most beliefs in our worldviews are general—even extremely general—a few are not. *Example:* We don't know whether there is or isn't a God (part of the worldviews of agnostics).

9. Unfortunately, we all tend at least sometimes to hold a belief without sufficient reason for doing so—for example, when complicated social or political issues are discussed. This is true even with respect to some of the beliefs that make up our worldviews. But worldviews, just as any beliefs, need to be carefully examined: Does evidence support them? Do we really value this more than that? Having an accurate supply of background beliefs is not just a matter of regularly acquiring more beliefs but also of pruning those we already have.

10. We tend to absorb the beliefs of those around us as we mature from children into adults. Our worldviews, in particular, tend to grow out of family values, religious training, peer group attitudes, cultural heritages, and so on. We often hold these vital beliefs uncritically—indeed, often without realizing that we hold them. Good critical reasoners, on the contrary, try to become aware of and to critically evaluate their background beliefs, especially those making up their worldviews.

11. Beliefs about human nature are of vital importance when reasoning in daily life, because the success or failure of everyday interactions depends on them. Whether we can trust this sort of person or that is an example. That is one reason why reading the writings of great literary and scientific figures is so useful (in addition to being entertaining).

12. Beliefs about the accuracy and truthfulness of information sources also are of great importance, because, as the saying goes, "Garbage in, garbage out." We can't reason well from poor or false information. That is why later chapters in this book deal with several important information sources.

13. Because science plays such an important part in everyone's life these days, it behooves us to become as well acquainted as we can, and as time permits, with the scientific view of the world and with the ways in which scientists come to their conclusions. No one on his or her own could possibly discover even a tiny fraction of what scientists have learned over hundreds of years about the way the world works. (Those who don't see the importance of science in their own lives should reflect on how much we depend, every day, on the fruits of scientific investigations. *Examples:* Electrical devices, painkillers and other modern medicines, toilet paper.) Unfortunately, most people do not have even a reasonably good grasp of what science is up to.

A canine induction by enumeration.

2 More on Deduction and Induction

Truth is more of a stranger than fiction.
—**Mark Twain**

The pure and the simple truth is rarely pure and never simple.
—**Oscar Wilde**

Man has such a predilection for systems and abstract deductions that he is ready to distort the truth intentionally; he is ready to deny the evidence of his senses in order to justify his logic.
—**Fyodor Dostoevsky**

Every man is encompassed by a cloud of comforting convictions, which move with him like flies on a summer day.
—**Bertrand Russell**

1. DEDUCTIVE VALIDITY

In Chapter 1, we distinguished between deductively valid and inductively valid arguments. Here now is a discussion of some of the basic principles of deductive reasoning, which, by the way, the vast majority of people find quite intuitive.

As pointed out in Chapter 1, different arguments may have the same *form,* or *structure.* Here are two arguments that have the same form—namely, *modus ponens:*

(1) 1. If it's spring, then the birds are chirping.
     2. It is spring.
   ∴3. The birds are chirping.
(2) 1. If a world government doesn't evolve soon, then wars will continue to occur.
     2. A world government isn't going to evolve soon.
   ∴3. Wars will continue to occur.

In Chapter 1, we noted that the form of *modus ponens* can be indicated this way:

   1. If *A* then *B.*
   2. *A.*
 ∴3. *B.*

Now, here is another commonly occurring deductively valid form, called ***modus tollens:***

Form: 1. If *A* then *B*.
   2. Not *B*.
 ∴3. Not *A*.

Example: 1. If it's spring, then the birds are chirping.
    2. The birds aren't chirping.
  ∴3. It isn't spring.

Here is still another commonly occurring deductively valid argument form, usually called **hypothetical syllogism:**

Form: 1. If *A* then *B*.
   2. If *B* then *C*.
 ∴3. If *A* then *C*.

Example: 1. If we successfully develop nuclear fusion power, then power will become cheap and plentiful.
    2. If power becomes cheap and plentiful, then the economy will flourish.
  ∴3. If we successfully develop nuclear fusion power, then the economy will flourish.

And here is the deductively valid form called **disjunctive syllogism:**[1]

Form: 1. *A* or *B*.
   2. Not *A*.
 ∴3. *B*.

Example: 1. Either Romney won in 2012 or Obama did.
    2. Obama didn't win.
  ∴3. Romney did.

Note that, while the first premise is true, the second, unfortunately for Romney, is false, as is the conclusion. Nevertheless, the validity of this argument guarantees that *if* both its premises had been true, *then* so would its conclusion have been true.

Finally, here are several argument forms of a different kind (all but the first two are called *syllogisms*):[2]

Form: 1. No *F*s are *G*s.
 ∴2. It's false that some *F*s are *G*s.

Example: 1. No police officers accept bribes.
  ∴2. It's false that some police officers accept bribes. (Uh-huh.)

Form: 1. All *F*s are *G*s.
 ∴2. If this is an *F*, then this is a *G*.

Example: 1. All salamis are tasty.
  ∴2. If this is a salami, then it is tasty. (No dispute on this one.)

---

[1]Strictly speaking, in spite of their names, *disjunctive syllogism* and *hypothetical syllogism* are not syllogisms.
[2]For additional material on deduction and induction see the appendix, and see also: Hausman, Alan, Howard Kahane, and Paul Tidman. *Logic and Philosophy.* 12th ed. Boston: Wadsworth, Cengage Learning, 2013.

Form: 1. All *F*s are *G*s.
             2. All *G*s are *H*s.
            ∴3. All *F*s are *H*s.

Example: 1. All TV evangelists have high moral standards.
             2. All who have high moral standards live up to those standards.
            ∴3. All TV evangelists live up to high moral standards. (Proven by history.)

Form: 1. All *F*s are *G*s.
             2. This is an *F.*
            ∴3. This is a *G.* (Note that this is *not* the form called *modus ponens*!)

Example: 1. All elected officials always tell the truth.
             2. Barak Obama is an elected official.
            ∴3. Barak Obama always tells the truth.

Form: 1. All *F*s are *G*s.
             2. No *G*s are *H*s.
            ∴3. No *F*s are *H*s.

Example: 1. All males are chauvinist pigs.
             2. No chauvinist pigs are likeable.
            ∴3. No males are likeable.

Form: 1. No *F*s are *G*s.
             2. Some *H*s are *F*s.
            ∴3. Some *H*s are not *G*s.

Example: 1. No foreigners can be trusted.
             2. Some newborn babies are foreigners.
            ∴3. Some newborn babies cannot be trusted. (Obviously.)

In daily life, arguments tend to get strung together into larger arguments leading up to a point, a grand conclusion or **thesis**. Here is an example (with logical structure exhibited to the left) in which the conclusion of the first argument is used as a premise in the second, and the conclusion of the second is used as a premise in the third and final argument:

   1. If *A* then *B*.   1. If a world government doesn't evolve soon, then wars will continue to occur.

   2. If *B* then *C*.   2. But if they continue to occur, then nuclear weapons will proliferate

∴3. If *A* then *C*.   3. So if a world government doesn't evolve soon, then nuclear weapons will proliferate.

   4. If *C* then *D*.   4. But if they proliferate, then a nuclear war will be inevitable, sooner or later.

∴5. If *A* then *D*.   5. Which proves that if a world government doesn't evolve soon, we'll end up fighting a nuclear war sooner or later.

   6. Not *D*.   6. But it's ridiculous to think we'll actually have a nuclear war (that is, it's false that we'll have such a war).

∴7. Not *A*.   7. So a world government is going to evolve soon (that is, it's false that a world government won't evolve soon).

EXERCISE 2-1

1. Invent deductively valid arguments having the forms *modus ponens, modus tollens,* disjunctive syllogism, and hypothetical syllogism.

2. Use the conclusion of one of the arguments you have just constructed as a premise in another argument that is deductively valid.

2. DEDUCTIVE INVALIDITY

Any argument that doesn't have a deductively valid form is said to be *deductively invalid.*[3] The number of deductively invalid argument forms is legion, but a few occur so frequently that they've been given names. Here are two examples (to give the flavor):

Fallacy of **denying the antecedent**:

 Form: 1. If *A* then *B*.
     2. Not *A*.
    ∴3. Not *B*.

 Example: 1. If abortion is murder, then it's wrong.
     2. But abortion isn't murder.
    ∴3. Abortion isn't wrong.

The conclusion doesn't follow: Even supposing abortion isn't murder, it may be wrong for other reasons.

Fallacy of **affirming the consequent**:

 Form: 1. If *A* then *B*.
     2. *B*.
    ∴3. *A*.

 Example: 1. If Obama is president, then a liberal is now president.
     2. A liberal is now president.
    ∴3. Obama is president.

The conclusion doesn't follow: Some other liberal may now be president.

EXERCISE 2-2

1. Invent an argument having the form of the fallacy *denying the antecedent,* and then show that it is deductively invalid by explaining how its premises might be true when its conclusion is false.

2. Do the same with an argument having the form *affirming the consequent.*

---

[3]A deductively invalid argument still may be a good argument if it is inductively correct. Arguments that have the forms about to be discussed are bad because they are neither deductively valid nor inductively correct.

3. SYLLOGISMS

A lot more needs to be said about invalid reasoning and will be in later chapters, in particular, Chapters 3, 4, and 5, where various other kinds of fallacious reasoning are discussed. But let's now discuss a few more matters concerning the deductively valid reasonings called **syllogisms.**

We said before that arguments having the form called *hypothetical syllogism,*

    1. If *A* then *B*.
    2. If *B* then *C*.
∴3. If *A* then *C*.

are not true syllogisms (at least not in the sense intended by Aristotle, the inventor of syllogistic logic [4]), while those having the form

    1. All *A*s are *B*s.
    2. All *B*s are *C*s.
∴3. All *A*s are *C*s.

are the genuine article. What makes one the real thing and the other not? The difference between these two kinds of arguments that makes the difference should become clear in the following little exposition as to the nature of syllogisms in traditional syllogistic logic.[5]

In traditional syllogistic logic, a **categorical proposition** is a subject-predicate proposition that asserts or denies a relationship between a **subject class** and a **predicate class**. There are exactly four kinds of categorical propositions (with one variation): **universal affirmative** (*A* propositions), having the form "All *S* are *P*" (*Example:* "All sinners are betrayers."); **universal negative** (*E* propositions), having the form "No *S* are *P*" (*Example:* "No chess players are imbeciles."); **particular affirmative** (*I* propositions), having the form "Some *S* are *P*" (*Example:* "Some men are chauvinists."); and **particular negative** (*O* propositions), having the form "Some *S* are not *P*" (*Example:* "Some logicians are not nitpickers."). The one common variation is that statements such as "Socrates is a man," having as their subject a particular item rather than a class of items, are often honorifically considered to be *A* propositions.

A *syllogism* is an argument containing three categorical propositions, two of them premises, one a conclusion. Here is one of the original examples (dechauvinized):

Syllogism	*Traditional Symbolization*
All humans are mortal.	MAP
All Greeks are human.	SAM
∴All Greeks are mortal.	∴SAP

---

[4]Obviously, something has changed since days of old, and that is why, for example, argument forms such as *hypothetical syllogisms* now sometimes are thought of as the genuine article. The point is that Aristotle and Aristotelians, until recently, would not have considered these other forms to be syllogisms.

[5]For now, let's just note that we replace the *A*s, *B*s, and *C*s in the form of *hypothetical syllogism* by whole sentences, as in "If <u>Art goes to the show</u>, then <u>Betsy will stay home</u>; but the *A*s and *B*s in "All *A* are *B*" are replaced by subjects of sentences, or predicates, as in "All <u>women</u> are <u>fickle</u>."

The term *P,* the predicate of the conclusion, is said to be the syllogism's **major term**; the term *S,* the subject of the conclusion, its **minor term**; and the term *M,* which occurs once in each premise but not in the conclusion, its **middle term**. Every syllogism has exactly three terms (none used equivocally), each one repeated twice but not in the same proposition. There are hundreds of different syllogistic forms (figure out how many), but, of course, only some are valid. The one given above is valid, whereas the syllogism "All Greeks are human; all humans are mortal; therefore, all mortals are Greek" is not.

The valid syllogism about Greeks being mortal is said to be in the **mood** AAA (for obvious reasons). (In this case, the syllogism is said to be in the *first figure,* and its *form* is said to be AAA-I, but let's pass over this complication.) There are, of course, other moods (and figures). Here, for instance, is a syllogism in the mood AII (it happens to be in the third figure):[6]

Syllogism	*Traditional Symbolization*
All things made out of grass are green.	MAG
Some things made out of grass are cigarettes.	MIC
∴ Some cigarettes are green.	∴ CIG

EXERCISE 2-3

1. Invent a deductively valid syllogism that has the same form as the valid syllogism about Greeks being mortal just mentioned.

2. Invent another deductively valid syllogism in some other mood (but not the mood AII).

3. Now invent a deductively invalid syllogism, and explain why you think that it is not valid.

*4. Explain why *disjunctive syllogisms* are not true syllogisms in the sense intended by Aristotle. (Try to do this before looking at the answer in the back of the book.)[7]

4. INDIRECT PROOFS

Another common everyday kind of reasoning is called an **indirect proof** or a **reductio ad absurdum** (reduce to an absurdity) **proof**. We reason in this way when we assume the opposite of what we wish to prove and then deductively derive a conclusion claimed to be false, indeed, often contradictory or otherwise absurd. The point is that if we validly reason to an obviously false conclusion, then our original assumption must be false and hence its negation—the thing we wish to prove—must be true. Here is an example:

---

[6]In the Middle Ages, students determined the validity of syllogistic forms by reciting a chant containing a name for each of the valid cases in each figure. For example, the name "bArbArA" occurs in the chant for the first figure, indicating that the form AAA-1 is valid.
[7]Starred (*) items are answered in a section at the back of the book.

Assume for the moment that when Bill Clinton was president, he offered a night's stay in the Lincoln Room in the White House in return for campaign contributions. Then, since doing so would definitely be at least shady, if not illegal, Clinton would have done something shady if not illegal. But Clinton is an honorable man, so we can be sure that he did not do anything shady or illegal. Therefore, the assumption that Clinton offered a stay in the Lincoln room in return for money must be false. (Notice that the fact that Clinton did, according to most viewers of the scene, rent out the Lincoln bedroom does not detract from the fact that the reasoning in this indirect argument is deductively valid. It just means that one of the premises of this argument must be false.)

An indirect proof can be defeated in either of two ways. One is by showing that there is a mistake in reasoning. (In our example, there is no mistake in reasoning. The argument is deductively valid, which just means that if its premises are true, then its conclusion must be true). The other way is to show that at least one of its premises (other than the assumed premise) is false. (In our example, the likely premise would be...?)

5. TAUTOLOGIES, CONTRADICTIONS, AND CONTINGENT STATEMENTS

A **tautology** is a statement that is *logically,* or *necessarily,* true, or is so devoid of content as to be practically empty (and thus true because completely empty statements, making no claim, cannot be false).[8] *Example:* "Barry Bonds did take steroids, or he didn't." A **contradiction** is a statement that is necessarily false (because it contradicts itself). *Example:* "Barry Bonds did take steroids, and he didn't take them." All other statements are said to be **contingent**. *Example:* "Barry Bonds didn't take them."

We can determine the truth value of a contradiction or of a tautology by logical—deductive—means alone, without the need for any empirical investigation or inductive reasoning. But determining the truth or falsity of a contingent statement requires observation by ourselves or others and, usually, the employment of inductive reasoning. *Example:* Tasting and disliking cooked vegetables several times has led many people to conclude inductively that in general they will dislike cooked vegetables. (Note that there is no contradiction between always disliking cooked vegetables in the past and liking them sometime in the future. Nor does this past dislike guarantee that they always will be disliked in the future.)

EXERCISE 2-4

Which of the following are tautologies, which contradictions, and which contingent statements? Defend your answers. (Be careful; at least one of these is sneaky.)

1. Either Mitt Romney ran for president of the United States in 2012, or a lot of newspapers were mistaken.

---

[8]Note that logicians often use the term *tautology* in a more restricted manner, so as to cover only the logical truths provable by means of what is called *sentential logic*.

2. Either Mitt Romney was on the ballot in Georgia in 2012, or he wasn't.

*3. Romney didn't campaign both for the presidency and for the vice presidency.

4. Snow is always white, except, of course, when it isn't.

5. The news media always report the news accurately.

6. No politicians ever keep any of their campaign promises.

7. Those who laugh last, laugh best.

8. I learned in school that 2 + 2 always equals 4, but I don't believe it.

9. Either you're in favor of an equal rights amendment to the Constitution, or you're against it.

10. Trespassers will be shot and then they'll never trespass again.

11. If you don't play the state lottery, you can't win it.

12. If I didn't get all of the first ten questions here right, then I did get them all right.

6. INDUCTIVE VALIDITY (CORRECTNESS) AND INVALIDITY (INCORRECTNESS)

As indicated before, we can think of induction as a kind of *patterning*. Perhaps the simplest form of induction is the one called **induction by enumeration**, mentioned in Chapter 1. In this kind of inductive reasoning, we reason from the fact that all *A*s observed so far are *B*s to the conclusion that all *A*s whatsoever are *B*s. For example, a study of 100 members of Congress no doubt would show that they all accept campaign contributions from lobbyists intent on influencing legislation, and finding this out would count as good evidence for the inductive conclusion that all 535 members of Congress accept funds of this kind.

Obviously, some inductions of this kind are better than others and make their conclusions more probable. Although there are several modestly different theories about how to determine the probability of the conclusions of enumerative inductions, almost all agree on a few points.

Greater sample size yields greater probability. The more instances in a sample (the instances observed so far), the greater the probability of a conclusion based on that sample. A sample of 100 members of Congress who accept campaign contributions from lobbyists provides a higher degree of probability that all do than a smaller sample, say, of 50 members. The point is that more of the same sort of evidence doesn't change the conclusion of an induction; rather, it changes the degree of probability of that conclusion and thus changes the strength of belief a rational person should have in it.

More representative samples yield higher probabilities than those that are less representative. The quality of a sample is even more important than its size. (Indeed, the higher its quality, the smaller a sample needs to be to yield a given degree of probability.) When sampling apples in a barrel, for instance, it won't do just to sample a few from the top (the classic case); after all, rotten apples are more likely to be at the bottom than at the top of a barrel. Samples that neglect possible rotten apples at the bottom of meta-phorical barrels are said to be *biased* or *unrepresentative*. Obviously, the less biased, more representative a sample, the higher the degree of probability of an inference based on that sample.

One definite counterexample shoots down an enumerative induction. The most im-portant reason that inductive reasoning is superior to many other kinds (for example, of the superstitious or the pseudoscientific variety to be discussed later) is that it does not allow us to pass over evidence that indicates a pet theory is false. For example, if one woman who takes a birth control pill as directed gets pregnant, then no valid enumera-tive induction about the pill's effectiveness can be drawn. (Note that it still may be pos-sible to draw other kinds of valid inductive inferences, including the statistical kind to be discussed shortly.)

However, it often is hard to be sure that what looks like a counterexample really is one. A woman on birth control pills who becomes pregnant, for instance, may have ac-cidentally neglected to take the pills properly, and we may not be aware of that fact. The moral is that it is risky to reject an enumerative induction on the basis of one counterex-ample, or even two, unless we are very sure that at least one is a genuine counterexam-ple. But when we are sure, then an enumerative induction in question must be rejected.

Reasoning by Analogy

Several other kinds of inductive reasoning are very similar to enumerative induction, including **analogical reasoning**. In one version of this kind of inductive reasoning, we reason from the similarity of two things in several relevant respects to their similarity in another. Thus, if we know that two people have similar tastes in books, art, food, music, and TV programs and find out that one likes to watch *Masterpiece Theater* on public television (PBS), then we're justified in concluding by analogy that the other probably does also.

The trouble is that every two things resemble each other in an indefinitely large num-ber of ways. Only *relevant* resemblances count in drawing correct analogies. But what makes a resemblance relevant? The answer is background beliefs about how, in general, things hang together. For example, if the stock market rises and falls in concert with ups and downs in the Olympic elk population over several years, only fools are likely to conclude that the two will fluctuate together in the future, because so much background information contradicts this idea. On the other hand, if stocks were to rise and fall over several years in concert with ups and downs in retail sales, we could reason by analogy that the next change in one will produce a similar change in the other. (Of course, given all of the other factors relevant to stock market prices, an induction of the kind just de-scribed would have to be assigned a very modest degree of probability.)

In another version of analogical induction, we reason from the fact that all examined items of a certain kind have a particular property to the conclusion that a particular as yet unexamined item of that kind will be found to have that property. Finding out that, say, 100 members of Congress accept money from lobbyists, we can conclude by this kind of analogy that a certain other member probably also does so.

As this last example shows, analogical inductions are much safer, and thus have a higher degree of probability, than their enumerative counterparts, because they have much weaker conclusions. Concluding, for example, that a particular member of Congress accepts money from lobbyists is a much weaker, hence safer, prediction than that all members of Congress do so.

Statistical Induction

When drawing a sample from a population, we often find that not all of the examined *A*s are *B*s, so that we cannot draw a valid enumerative induction. But having found that a certain percentage of the *A*s have the property in question, we can conclude by a **statistical induction** that the same percentage of the total population of *A*s have that property. Having found, say, that 480 of the first 1,000 observed tosses of a given coin land face up, we can conclude that 48 percent of all of the tosses with that coin will land face up (thus learning, incidentally, that the coin probably is slightly biased in favor of tails, as many coins are).

Of course, what was said about the quality and, hence, the degree of probability of enumerative inductions also applies to the statistical variety. The larger the sample employed and the more representative it is, the higher the degree of probability of a statistical induction based on that sample.

Higher-Level Inductions

More general, **higher-level inductions** can be used to evaluate those that are less general. For example, we use higher-level induction when we conclude that an automobile engine eventually will wear out or need to be repaired, even though it has run perfectly for 100,000 miles. We overrule a low-level conclusion telling us that, because the car has run perfectly so far, it will do so forever, by appeal to a higher-level, more general induction such as this one: All mechanical devices with moving parts checked up on so far have eventually worn out or needed to be repaired, so very probably this particular mechanical device (the engine in question) also eventually will wear out or need to be repaired.

More general inferences, based on larger samples about more kinds of items, usually have higher degrees of probability than do those that are less general. That is why an enumerative induction about a particular automobile is overruled by a more general one about many mechanical devices. (There are, in fact, even higher-level reasons for tossing out this low-level induction by enumeration—for example, scientific inductions concerning basic principles of physics and chemistry having to do with the effects of friction.)

Reasoning to Causal Connections

When we reason inductively, we often are looking for explanations, or **causes**. For instance, early investigators of the connection between cigarette smoking and lung cancer, emphysema, and heart disease wanted to determine by means of statistical inductions whether smoking *causes* these death-dealing diseases. They found that smokers contract these diseases much more frequently than nonsmokers, and heavy smokers more than light. That is, they discovered a statistical link between smoking cigarettes and contracting these diseases. Finding no higher-level evidence to the contrary, they concluded that cigarette smoking does indeed cause these life-threatening illnesses. (That some people smoke like chimneys and never come down with these illnesses doesn't prove the contrary, but it does suggest that part of the cause of these diseases must be some other, very likely genetic, factor.[9])

The inductive patterns discussed in this chapter are relatively neat and simple. Enumerative induction is an example. But in daily life, and in particular in scientific theorizing, inductive reasoning often is much more complicated and may involve mathematical reasoning (a kind of deductive reasoning) as well. We believe cigarette smoking causes lung cancer, for example, not just because a certain percentage of those who smoke get that deadly disease, but also because the percentage of those who do not smoke and get lung cancer is much lower than for those who do smoke. It is the comparison of the two groups that proves the point. (In fact, the reasoning linking smoking and lung cancer is even more complicated than we have indicated here. For instance, we haven't mentioned how theorists ruled out certain other causal possibilities by carefully selecting the individuals in their samples to rule out the effects of other likely carcinogens.)

Concatenated Inductions

The cigarette–cancer example just discussed brings to mind the fact that in the vast majority of scientific cases, the reasoning employed is of the kind that can be called **concatenated reasoning**—a joining together of inductions and deductions in the discovery of a *pattern* that fits what has been observed or previously reasoned to. In scientific reasoning, inductively confirmed theories of several disciplines typically are brought to bear to reach a conclusion. This is done, for example, in determining the types and significance of the food our ancestors ate before the time of recorded history. Carbon 14 dating is used to determine the approximate date at which, say, animal feces, now fossilized, were deposited at an archeological dig; chemical analysis to reveal what kind of food it was (grain, meat, and so on) and that it was eaten by human beings and not other animals—all of this coupled with anthropological theories about how this sort of food fit into the everyday diet of people in those days. Knowledge of this kind may then be used as part of the evidence in theories about the migrations of ancient peoples and the dispersal of and changes in various kinds of grains, fruits, and domesticated animals.

EXERCISE 2-5

1. What is the difference between an induction by enumeration and analogical reasoning? Provide an example (not mentioned in the text) of each.

2. Explain in your own words what the difference is between an induction by enumeration and a statistical induction. Provide an example (not mentioned in the text) of a valid statistical induction.

3. What is meant by saying that an inference is a higher-level induction? Provide an example (not mentioned in the text).

---

[9]See the section in the appendix concerning necessary and sufficient conditions.

7. A MISCONCEPTION ABOUT DEDUCTION AND INDUCTION

There is a widespread but erroneous idea about the difference between deductive and inductive validity. This is the idea that in deductively valid reasoning, we go from the general to the particular, while in inductively valid reasoning, we move from the particular to the general. But little can be said in support of this idea. For instance, the deductively valid argument

1. All Republican politicians are to the right of Barack Obama.
∴2. All who are not to the right of Barack Obama are not Republican politicians.

moves from the general to the equally general, while the inductively valid argument

1. George Bush (the younger) made promises during the 2000 campaign that he didn't keep.
2. George Bush made promises during the 2004 campaign that he didn't keep.
3. Barack Obama made promises during the 2008 campaign that he didn't keep.
∴4. Barack Obama very likely won't keep all the promises he made during the 2012 campaign.

moves from the particular to the equally particular. And the inductively valid argument

1. So far, all presidential candidates of the Republican Party have been male.
∴2. The next Republican Party presidential candidate will be male.

moves from the general to the particular, not the other way around.

So there isn't much truth to the old idea that deductive reasoning moves from the general to the particular, while inductive reasoning moves from the particular to the general. More accurately, when we reason deductively, we reason to conclusions already contained (implicitly or explicitly) in our premises; when we reason inductively, we move to conclusions by extending patterns or resemblances from one set of events to another set.

Some of those who argue otherwise claim that the idea of deduction moving from the general to the particular is intended to be true only for syllogistic reasoning. Thus, the valid syllogism, "All humans are mortal; Socrates is human; therefore, Socrates is mortal," does indeed move from the general to the particular. The trouble, of course, is that this is not true for the vast majority of other valid syllogisms, including the one mentioned a while back, whose conclusion is that all Greeks are mortal.

8. REASONING COGENTLY VERSUS BEING RIGHT IN FACT

Reasoning correctly and getting a true conclusion are unfortunately not the same thing. We can reason correctly and get a false conclusion, and we can reason fallaciously and get a true conclusion.[10] *Examples:* Scientists in times past reasoned correctly from what was known then to the conclusion that superconductivity occurs only at temperatures

---

[10]In philosophical jargon, we can be *epistemologically right* although *ontologically wrong,* and we can be *epistemologically wrong* but *ontologically right.*

very close to absolute zero, but we now know that this conclusion is false. Astrology buffs reason incorrectly that they will have a good day from the fact that a newspaper column says they will or that the stars are in a certain position in the sky, and then luckily they do have a good day (for completely different reasons having nothing whatever to do with astrology or where the stars happen to be).

On the whole, it's a lot better to reason incorrectly to true—right—conclusions than it is to reason well to false ones.[11] *But the most likely way to be right, in the long run, is to reason correctly!* When people who follow astrology columns thereby do better than they otherwise would have, they're just extremely lucky, not smart. (They're also an extremely rare species of speculator.) In daily life, however, people often equate being smart with being successful, as though success proves reasoning has been cogent. It doesn't, nor does failure prove reasoning fallacious. That's life. Smart people, as they say, "play the odds"—they try to reason well and take their chances in this not-quite-best of all possible worlds, and *in the long run in most cases, they do a lot better than those whose reasoning is excessively fallacious.*

SUMMARY OF CHAPTER 2

1. Different arguments may have the same form, or structure. *Modus ponens, modus tollens, hypothetical syllogism,* and so on, are deductively valid argument forms. Note that in everyday life, arguments frequently get strung together, leading to a grand conclusion, a *thesis.*

2. But lots of other forms are deductively invalid. *Affirming the consequent* and *denying the antecedent* are examples of deductively invalid argument forms.

3. A *categorical proposition* asserts or denies a relationship between a *subject class* and a *predicate class.* There are four kinds of categorical propositions: *universal affirmative* (*A* propositions), having the form "All *S* are *P*"; *universal negative* (*E* propositions), having the form "No *S* are *P*"; *particular affirmative* (*I* propositions), having the form "Some *S* are *P*"; and *particular negative* (*O* propositions), having the form "Some *S* are not *P.*" Statements such as "Socrates is a man," having as their subject a particular item rather than a class of items, are often honorifically considered to be A propositions.

   A *syllogism* is an argument containing three categorical propositions, two of them premises, one a conclusion. *Example:* "No foreigners are trustable. Some newborn babies are foreigners. Therefore, some newborn babies cannot be trusted." The predicate of the conclusion of a syllogism is said to be its *major term;* the subject of the conclusion, its *minor term;* and the term that occurs once in each premise but not in the conclusion, its *middle term.* Every syllogism has exactly three terms (none used equivocally), each one repeated twice but

---

[11]Philosophical slogan: "I'd rather be epistemologically wrong and ontologically right than vice versa, but the best way to be ontologically right is to be epistemologically right." (Philosophical jargon can be just as opaque as that of every other discipline.)

not in the same proposition. There are hundreds of different syllogistic forms (figure out how many), but, of course, only some are valid. *Example:* The syllogism "All Greeks are humans; all humans are mortals; therefore, all mortals are Greek" is not valid.

The *mood* of a syllogism is determined by the kinds of propositions it contains. Thus the syllogism just mentioned is in the mood AAA.

4. In an *indirect* or *reductio ad absurdum proof,* we assume the opposite of what we wish to prove and then deductively derive a conclusion claimed to be false, contradictory, or otherwise absurd. The point is that if we reason validly to a false, or absurd, conclusion, then our original assumption must be false and hence its negation—the thing we wish to prove—must be true.

5. A *tautology* is a statement that is *logically,* or *necessarily,* true or is so devoid of content as to be practically empty. *Example:* "Madonna is world-famous, or she isn't." A *contradiction* is a statement that is necessarily false (because it contradicts itself). *Example:* "Madonna is world-famous and she isn't." All other statements are said to be contingent. *Example:* "Madonna is talented and world-famous."

The truth values of contradictions and tautologies can be determined by logical—deductive—means alone, but the truth or falsity of contingent statements cannot. They are justified by observation or by reasoning, part of which must be inductive, from what we and/or other people have observed.

6. There are several kinds of valid, or correct, inductions. One is *induction by enumeration,* in which we infer from the fact that all *A*s observed so far are *B*s, to the conclusion that all *A*s whatsoever are *B*s.

In general, the larger or the more representative a sample, the greater the probability of an induction based on it. Note that one definite counterexample invalidates an induction. (But we have to be sure that it really is a counterexample.)

Analogical reasoning is very much like induction by enumeration, the chief difference being that analogies yield conclusions about just one case (which is why they have higher degrees of probability than corresponding enumerative inductions), whereas enumerative inductions typically concern a great many.

Statistical inductions also are similar to the enumerative variety, but they move from the fact that a certain percentage of a sample has a given property to the conclusion that the same percentage in the population at large has that property.

We can use more general, *higher-level* inductions to correct, or overrule, lower-level ones. If experience shows that all mechanical devices eventually wear out or need to be repaired, then it isn't reasonable to conclude that a particular auto engine will not, even though it has run perfectly for 100,000 miles.

Inductive reasoning often is used to discover *causes,* as in the case of the statistical induction linking cigarette smoking and various life-threatening diseases.

Reasoning called *concatenated* often brings new evidence together with several already inductively established conclusions, combined with deductive reasoning, to obtain a further conclusion. This is especially true in the sciences. *Example:* Anthropologists or evolutionary theorists reason from principles of physics and chemistry in reaching conclusions from newly discovered evidence.

7. It often is said that deductively valid reasoning moves from general premises to particular conclusions, while inductively valid reasoning moves from particular premises to general conclusions. But this is not correct. *Examples:* The deductively valid argument "If you jump off the Brooklyn Bridge, then you'll be killed. So if you aren't killed, you haven't jumped off the Brooklyn Bridge," moves from the particular to the particular. (By the way, the form of this inference—"If *A* then *B*; therefore, if not-*B* then not-*A*—is sometimes called *contraposition.*) The inductively valid reasoning "If Dan Rather has obtained power, then he has been corrupted by it. He has obtained power. Hence, he has been corrupted by it," moves from the particular to the equally particular (employing *modus ponens,* by the way).

8. Life being what it is, reasoning correctly sometimes results in drawing false conclusions, even from a true premise. *Example:* The person who, having loaned a friend money many times before and having always been repaid, loans the friend money again and gets stiffed. Furthermore, again life being what it is, reasoning fallaciously sometimes results in drawing true conclusions, even sometimes from false premises. *Example:* risking one's life savings at a dice table in Las Vegas employing the "double the bet" method (discussed in the appendix) and winning a small fortune.

But, still again, life being what it is, *in a large majority of cases,* those who reason cogently do better, often a great deal better, than those who reason fallaciously.

"Having concluded, Your Highness, an exhaustive study of this nation's political, social and economic history, and after examining, Sire, the unfortunate events leading to the present deplorable state of the realm, the consensus of the council is that Your Majesty's only course, for the public good, must be to take the next step."

Question-begging advice, following oracular rule number 1: Make pronouncements as empty as possible to minimize the chance of being wrong.

3 Fallacious Reasoning—1

It would be a very good thing if every trick could receive some short and obviously appropriate name, so that when a man used this or that particular trick, he could at once be reproved for it.

—Schopenhauer

Arguments, like men, often are pretenders.

—Plato

Half of being smart is knowing what you're dumb at.

—David Gerrold

We said in Chapter 1 that we reason fallaciously when we fail to satisfy all three of the requirements of cogent reasoning. Accepting premises that we should doubt makes us guilty of the fallacy *questionable premise;* neglecting relevant evidence guilty of the fallacy *suppressed evidence;* and drawing conclusions not suffi-ciently supported by evidence guilty of the fallacy *invalid inference.*

Of course, we must remember that the arguments encountered in daily life tend to be vague, or ambiguous, and premises, and even conclusions, sometimes are omitted as understood. As a result, everyday arguments often can be construed in different ways. Consider the following key line in a TV beer commercial:

More people in America drink Budweiser than any other beer.

Taken literally, this isn't an argument, but it clearly implies that the listener also should drink Bud. So its import might be put this way:

1. More people in America drink Budweiser than any other beer. (Premise.)
∴2. You, too, should drink Budweiser. (Implied conclusion.)

Construed in this way, the ad does contain an argument, but the argument is defective because it contains an invalid inference. That a beer is the most popular does not imply you should drink it. The most popular beer may not be the best beer, and, anyway, perhaps you should drink a cheaper beer and save money or not drink any beer at all. We could, however, just as well restate the argument this way:

1. More people in America drink Budweiser than any other beer. (Premise.)
2. The most popular beer is the best beer. (Implied premise.)
3. You should drink the best beer. (Implied premise.)
∴4. You should drink Budweiser. (Implied conclusion.)

Now the argument is valid but contains at least two questionable premises—that the most popular beer is the best beer and that you should drink the best beer.

Like the Budweiser example, most fallacious arguments can be stated in more ways than one. So there often isn't a single "right" label to apply to fallacious reasoning. This doesn't mean that there aren't plenty of wrong labels to apply, and it surely doesn't mean that merely applying a plausible label is sufficient. The point is to understand *why* an argument is fallacious and why a particular label can be shown to be right. In the case of the Budweiser ad, for instance, it's important to see that being the most popular beer is not by itself sufficient reason for most people to conclude that they should go out and buy it. Labeling just helps us to see that an argument is fallacious (*if it is!*) and helps us to understand why it is fallacious.

Notice, by the way, that in calling the argument itself fallacious, rather than reasoners who may have been taken in by it, we have employed the shortcut way of talking mentioned in Chapter 1. To be precise, we should have said, for example, that anyone who was persuaded by it would be guilty of fallacious reasoning.

Although all fallacious reasoning falls into one or more of the three broad categories just mentioned, over the years, a number of other, narrower fallacy species have been identified that crosscut the three basic types.[1] These labels have come into common use because experience has shown them to be helpful in spotting fallacious reasoning.

Let's now discuss some of the more important of these common fallacy categories and also add some comments concerning the broad fallacy category *questionable premise*.

1. APPEAL TO AUTHORITY

One of the most serious errors in reasoning is to accept the word of someone, in particular an alleged authority, when we should be suspicious. We all have to appeal to experts for information or advice—only fools don't do so with some regularity. In this technological age, we all are nonexperts in most fields. Accepting the word of an authority, alleged or genuine, when we shouldn't makes us guilty of the fallacy called **appeal to authority**.

But which appeals are proper and which fallacious? Clearly, it isn't a good idea to believe that an authority is reliable without having good reason for doing so. Some

---

[1]That is, some instances of a narrower fallacy species may fall into one of the three broad genuses and some into another. Several hundred fallacy categories have been discussed in the literature, but no single source discusses all of them. Only those that occur frequently are discussed in this text, which means that our list is not exhaustive by any means. But the division into the three broad master categories *questionable premise, suppressed evidence,* and *invalid inference* is exhaustive.

alleged authorities don't have the expertise they claim; others can't be relied on to tell it to us straight rather than feed us something more self-serving. Anyway, in some cases we need to do some of our own thinking and research.

So when seeking expert advice, three basic questions need to be addressed if we want to avoid committing the fallacy of appeal to authority:

1. Is the source likely to have the information or good judgment we need?
2. If so, can we trust the authority to tell it to us straight?
3. Do we have the time, desire, and ability to reason the matter out for ourselves (or to understand the expert's reasoning, so that we don't have to rely merely on the authority's word)?

We usually know right away whether we have the needed time and inclination, but the other questions often are rather difficult to answer. However, a few rules of thumb should prove helpful.

Some Authorities Are More Trustworthy than Others

Individuals who are regarded as authorities or experts are not created equal. Some are smart, others stupid; some are well trained in their field, some not; some are more or less honest (a completely honest person being a rarity in any case), others pretty much untrustworthy.

Characters who are less than completely ethical are found in every profession, but some fields attract this type more than others. The fields of law, financial advising, and politics, for instance, notoriously attract sharp operators, but even the clergy is not without its Elmer Gantrys, and doctors who prescribe unneeded surgery are not unknown in the history of medicine.

The news media have its questionable characters as well. Take Rupert Murdoch, for instance, the owner of News Corporation in the United States and News International in Great Britain—and arguably the most powerful media mogul in history. When members of British Parliament questioned him about the extensive, illegal phone tapping and computer hacking carried out by his tabloid reporters, he claimed he knew nothing about it, blaming it on staff members who betrayed him. "I think they have behaved disgracefully," he said, "And I think, frankly, that I'm the best person to see it through." Really? This from the man who ran a media empire in which thousands of phone and computer hackings occurred; officials in the police, armed services and government were bribed for stories, and so were former employees—to keep their mouths shut. Why would anyone give him the authority to clean up the mess?

Even among more scrupulous people, the personal interests of experts are bound now and then to conflict with their duties to clients. Professionals are human, after all, just like the rest of us. Politicians elected to the U.S. Congress are bound to savor the perks, fame, power, and excitement that goes along with their jobs (who wouldn't?), making it rather difficult for them to refuse the fat cat "campaign contributions" (bribes?) needed to gain reelection, and thus making it more difficult still for them to tell voters the straight truth on important issues. (Remember, though, that politics is the art of compromise and, in particular, that candidates do need to get elected to do good work, so they often need at least to shade the truth for that purpose. (See the section in Chapter 10 on political rhetoric for more on this point.)

So when considering expert reasoning or pronouncements, we always need to make a judgment about believability. Does the authority have an axe to grind, a personal interest that might be furthered? Lawyers who speak out against no-fault auto insurance, as they usually do, have to be looked at with a jaundiced eye precisely because the point of no-fault insurance is to reduce legal costs. When members of Congress vote against gun laws, in spite of strong public sentiment favoring gun control in the wake of tragedies like the shootings at the Aurora theatre in Boulder, we aren't being overly skeptical if we wonder whether their judgment has been warped by campaign contributions from interested parties or by narrow constituent interests.

The advice of military experts can be equally suspect if their judgment is skewed by conflicts of interest. During the Iraq War, television newscasts were swamped by interviews with high-ranking retired military officers who assured us for years that the war was justified, the insurgents were under control, the suicide bombings weren't so bad, the surge was working, and so on. It turned out that many of these military experts were recruited by the Pentagon to help sell the war in exchange for access to power and the perks that went along with it—including lucrative business affiliations. So much for expert opinion.

On the other hand, we should be inclined, other things being equal, to accept the word of dentists who urge their patients to brush and floss regularly and of doctors who exhort us to quit smoking cigarettes, precisely because dentists make money when patients get cavities, and doctors profit when people get cancer, have heart attacks, or come down with emphysema. Advice to brush regularly or to quit smoking thus is more likely to be motivated by a professional intent to serve the interests of clients rather than by a desire to further selfish interests.

Authorities in One Field Aren't Necessarily Experts in Another

Famous athletes and movie stars who endorse all sorts of products in television commercials are good examples of professionals speaking outside their fields of expertise. There's no reason to suppose that someone who knows how to act, or to hit home runs, knows any more about washing machines, or shaving cream, than anyone else. The fact that Hugh Jackman was paid to endorse Lipton Iced Tea or Eminem to tout Chryslers proves nothing about the quality of these products, nor is there any reason to suppose that Nikons take better pictures of Ashton Kutcher than Leicas or Panasonics. Yet most of us, irrationally, are suckers when it comes to celebrity TV commercials.

Learn How Best to Appeal to Authorities

It generally is easy to know which sorts of experts to appeal to. Sick people need to consult doctors; someone sued for divorce, a lawyer. It's a lot more difficult to find experts in a particular profession who know their stuff and can be relied on. But even after finding them, we need to become adept at picking their brains. Experts often throw up roadblocks to understanding, especially by overwhelming us with professional lingo. They frequently find it tedious to explain complicated matters to laypeople, and anyway, they may not want to spend the time and effort necessary to do so.

It also is true that laypeople often are unable to follow the complicated reasonings of trained professionals, medical specialists being a case in point. But it usually is possible to get at least a rough idea of what authorities are up to if we are persistent and if we insist that they translate their professional lingo into ordinary discourse. It's hard not to be intimidated by professional jargon or by an authoritarian aura, but it is well worth the effort to resist that sort of intimidation.

Understand What Authorities Can Be Expected to Know

All experts definitely are not created equal. It isn't just that some alleged authorities, as we mentioned before, don't know what they claim to know, or that some aren't completely on the up-and-up. It's also that a good deal more is known about some topics than about others, and that some kinds of information are much more expensive to obtain than others. True experts in some fields thus are more reliable than those in others.

We all are forced by the nature of modern life to seek advice and expert performance from doctors, lawyers, auto mechanics, and other kinds of trained (and often licensed) professionals. But we can't expect the same sorts of definitive answers to our questions or solutions to our problems when consulting these authorities as we can, say, when consulting physicists or chemists. Medicine, for example, while based on biological theory, still is an art: Doctors cannot always be sure of their diagnoses or of how to treat an ailment; the best of them are bound to be mistaken in their judgments now and then. Lawyers cannot be sure how jurors or judges will respond to evidence. Clergymen do not have direct lines to a higher authority.

Become Your Own Expert on Important Controversial Topics

When authorities disagree on a topic of importance, the rest of us need to become our own experts, turning to authorities for evidence, reasons, and arguments, but not conclusions. This is especially true with respect to social and political matters, because experts themselves disagree so much on these issues and because we have to watch out for the intrusion of self-interest into their stated judgments and opinions. Politicians, for example, may be beholden to special interests (as we noted before) or simply be going along with a misguided tide of public opinion. Conservative commentators generally see things differently than do those who are liberal.[2]

But politics is not by any means the only topic where the reasons and reasonings of experts should count for much more than their conclusions. Judges and juries, for example, too often uncritically accept the opinions of psychologists concerning the sanity of those charged with crimes, rather than delving into the reasons behind those opinions. After all, different opinions often can be obtained just by consulting other psychologists.[3]

---

[2]Although labels such as "conservative," "libertarian," "liberal," "right wing," and "left wing" tend to be vague and ambiguous, they still have some content: Those labeled by these terms do tend to differ in their viewpoints, and critical reasoners need to take these differences into account.

[3]This observation conforms to B. Duggan's Law of Expert Testimony: "For every Ph.D. there is an equal and opposite Ph.D."

This holds true even in fields like medicine, where we tend to trust the opinions of experts. For instance, a woman who is advised to have a hysterectomy might be wise to seek a second opinion from another physician. (Women with relevant background information know that many unnecessary hysterectomies are performed for conditions that can be treated by less invasive means.)

One way to gauge the judgment of alleged experts is to check their past records. Professional sports people have a saying that when in doubt, you should go with a winner. Similarly, when expert advice is needed, it makes sense to go with a winner—someone whose track record is good. Those who have been right in the past are more likely than others to be right in the future, other things being equal. Remember, however, that other things are not always equal. Auto mechanics may get out of touch with the latest technology, lawyers who have made their pile may become lazy, and textbook writers (with at least two obvious exceptions!) may eventually go over the hill.

Note, by the way, that most fallacious appeals to authority fall under the broader category *questionable premise,* because underlying the acceptance of the word of an authority is the implicit premise that it is wise to do so. In other words, the fallacy appeal to authority is committed by acceptance of expert advice or information when it isn't wise to do so, perhaps because the authority isn't likely to have the information we desire or may have a serious conflict of interest.

Before going on to a discussion of other fallacies, perhaps notice should be taken of the flip side of the fallacy of appeal to authority—namely, failure to take the word of authorities when we should. After all, salespeople frequently do give us the relevant facts straight; TV news programs do provide us with a good deal of useful information, even if they don't provide us with "the whole truth, nothing but the truth"; politicians sometimes do put aside self-interest and speak out against powerful interests. Being careful when evaluating information sources does not mean becoming completely cynical.

2. INCONSISTENCY

We commit the fallacy of **inconsistency** when we are persuaded to accept the conclusion of an argument that contains self-contradictory statements or statements that contradict each other.[4] Obviously, if two statements are contradictory, then one of them must be false.

Consider, for example, the ways in which inconsistencies intrude into campaign rhetoric. (Campaign rhetoric: The pronouncements of most politicians most of the time.) Candidates for public office do not explicitly say *A* and then immediately assert not-*A*. Instead, the contradictory nature of their pronouncements is concealed in one way or another. For instance, in the same speech, a candidate may assure voters that various government services or payments will significantly be increased (to curry the favor of voters who will profit from them), promise large tax reductions (to gain the support of those burdened by high taxes), and favor a huge reduction in the national debt (to appeal to voter beliefs about the virtues of governmental thrift).[5]

---

[4]Recall the discussion in Chapter 2 about tautologies, contradictions, and contingent statements.
[5]Their argument thus can be put this way: If elected, I won't destroy the government services and payments you want, I will significantly reduce taxes, and I will reduce the national debt. Therefore, you should vote for me.

That is how the vast majority of candidates for high office, including President Bush in 2000 and 2004, President Obama in 2008, and both major presidential candidates in 2012, have played the game. But government services and benefits cost money, and a majority of government expenses are fixed (most notably interest payments on previously contracted debts), so that a package of increased services and benefits, coupled with significant tax and public debt reductions, can be regarded as inconsistent in the absence of a plausible explanation as to how this trick is going to be performed. (In recent times, extremely high military expenditures and huge financial bailouts have made this trick even more difficult than it otherwise would be.) Adding up the figures is one way of determining whether candidates are being consistent, and hence believable, when they promise us the moon.

All presidents are inconsistent at some time or another. Consider, for instance, Barak Obama's shifting positions over the last decade on the Iraq War. In 2002, before he was elected to the Senate, he was adamantly against going to war, but by 2004 he said, "there's not much difference between my position and George Bush's position at this stage"—which was to keep troops in Iraq long enough to stabilize the country. He shifted course again, in 2006 when he came out for full-scale withdrawal once Bush decided to escalate the surge, claiming in 2007 that the war had "made us less safe." However, as commander-in-chief in 2010, he praised the GIs, saying their work had "made America safer."

Does Obama's zigzagging journey from one contradictory position to another mean that he was reassessing the war as he went along or does it reflect shrewd political calculation? It is worth noting that when the American public was for the war in 2004, so was Obama, and when public opinion turned against it in 2006–7, so did Obama—right about the time he was running for president. Once in office, he took care not to offend the military, though, by claiming the troops kept us safe, again reversing his position. Both liberals and conservatives have noted these inconsistencies, by the way, and rightly question Obama's motives.

One reason that politicians get away with inconsistent claims or arguments so often is that voters, being human, tend to see political issues from the point of view of their own self-interest, just as they see personal problems and conflicts with friends and family. Self-interest tends to make us more blind than usual both to fair play and to cogent reasoning. Lots of cigarette smokers, for example, argue against a ban on the sale of cigarettes, on the grounds that we all have a right to ingest harmful substances if we are so inclined. But most of them also, inconsistently, argue against the legalization of heroin because it is harmful to health. Extremist African-Americans who get on their high horses about prejudice against blacks have been known at the same time to inconsistently preach hatred of whites.

But when evaluating the various kinds of rhetoric encountered in everyday life, it is important that we don't misjudge deliberately equivocal, ironic, or humorous rhetoric. It won't do, for example, to brand the literally contradictory bumper sticker that says "Good enough isn't good enough" as contradictory, since it isn't intended to be taken literally. It says, in a humorous way, that we should do better than merely minimally well.

Note that there are ways to be guilty of the fallacy of inconsistency in addition to the obvious one of being inconsistent within a single argument or statement. The earlier example about politicians who, in the same speech, promise lots of government services, lower taxes, and a reduction in the national debt is a case in point. So are the cigarette smokers, also just mentioned, who are against making cigarettes illegal while at the same time are against legalizing the use of heroin.

Another way to be inconsistent is to *argue one way at a given time and another way at some other time, or when talking to one person and then to another.* Of course, there is nothing wrong with changing one's mind—of believing *A* at one time and not-*A* at another. That, after all, is the point of learning from experience. It is when we continue to hang on both to *A* and to not-*A*, trotting out one for use when reasoning about one thing and the other when reasoning about something else, that we are guilty of being inconsistent.

In politics, being inconsistent over time or from audience to audience is called "blowing with the wind." What is popular with constituents in one place or at one time may not be in another. Circumstances thus push politicians into being inconsistent in order to keep up with the latest trends in public opinion or to placate particular audiences. Candidates for office try as much as they can to tell people what they want to hear, and different people want to hear different things. So candidates sometimes switch sides on certain issues to win voter support, as Barack Obama seemed to do when shifting his position on the Iraq War. Mitt Romney's inconsistent positions on multiple issues have been well documented in the press, on news programs and on Internet sites like factcheck.org. He has flip-flopped on global warning, immigration and "Obama's health care act" (despite the fact that it closely resembles his own health care law in Massachusetts). He's shifted positions on the stimulus plan, the no-new-tax plan, and the assault weapons ban. On the abortion issue, he went from pro choice to anti choice or, one might say, multiple choice (echoing Ted Kennedy's quip about him in a 1994 debate for the Senate election). Then there was his infamous comment about the poor. "I'm not concerned about the very poor. We have a safety net there," adding that if the safety net needed repair, "I'll fix it." He was hammered for that first sentence (as will be discussed in Chapter 10), but the claim that he would fix a broken safety net flies in the face of his earlier position on budget cuts, when he endorsed a Republican-backed plan to reduce federal spending drastically—two-thirds of which aimed at cutting programs for the poor. It could be argued that Romney's inconsistencies reflect genuine shifts in attitude, and perhaps they do, but more likely he was blowing with the wind.

We have just gone to some lengths to describe inconsistency as a serious mistake. Yet others have railed against being consistent; witness Ralph Waldo Emerson's famous remark, "A foolish consistency is the hobgoblin of little minds, adored by little statesmen, philosophers and divines."

But there need be no inconsistency in accepting both sides of this coin, provided we notice that consistency is an ambiguous concept. One sense requires us to be consistent in what we believe at any given time. This is roughly the sense meant in this chapter. The other requires us to be consistent now and forever, to stick to our guns no matter what contrary evidence we encounter. This, one must suppose, is the kind of consistency Emerson intended to disparage.

To some extent, we all engage in this sort of inconsistency—politicians are just better at it than most of the rest of us. Occasionally, we do so deliberately, with conscious intent. But often we are trying to fool not just or even the other guy but rather ourselves. Virtually all of us, for instance, are against cheating others, yet at one time or another we can't resist the temptation to do so to our advantage while providing reasons (excuses) to justify what we have done; for example, the excuse that most other people do it, so it's not wrong for us to do so. (This point is discussed at greater length in Chapter 6, where impediments to cogent reasoning are the subject.)

It also must be noted that large organizations have an interesting way to be inconsistent that tends to be rather hard to notice: They have one representative speak out of one side of the mouth while another speaks from the other side. Let's call this sort of chicanery *organizational inconsistency,* thinking of a large organization as a kind of artificial person. (In regarding this as a fallacy, we are, of course, stretching that concept a bit, but for a good purpose, namely, to call attention to this threat to consistent reasoning.)

Another kind of organizational inconsistency occurs when it seems expedient to ignore company policy —which brings us back to Rupert Murdock. Although Murdock's company policy was that the news should be gathered by legal means, many reporters found it expedient to tap phones and hack computers in order to land juicy stories. This practice continued for years before incriminating facts emerged. Indeed, Murdock claimed his lawyers assured him "there was no illegality" except for one incident involving a single rogue reporter. However, whether Murdock was ignorant of these nefarious activities or complicit in them, either way, there was inconsistency between company policy and actual practice.

Another way to be inconsistent is by *saying one thing while doing another.* (Calling this a fallacy again stretches that concept to serve everyday purposes. Strictly speaking, saying one thing and doing another does not make one guilty of a fallacy, because it does not involve an inconsistency between one claim, idea, or argument and another. We include this discussion here to call attention to those who engage in this sort of behavior.

Al Gore was charged with this type of inconsistency when the media revealed that his private consumption of energy was at odds with his praiseworthy public campaign to reduce global warming. The day after he received an Oscar for the best documentary feature, *An Inconvenient Truth,* in which he urged Americans to curb their energy consumption, the Tennessee Center for Policy Research had this to say about Gore's personal energy use: "Gore's mansion...consumes more electricity every month than the average household uses in an entire year, according to the Nashville Electric Service...more than 20 times the national average.... In total Gore paid nearly $30,000 in combined electricity and natural gas bills for his Nashville estate in 2006." Considering how admirable his efforts have been to curb global warming, he might be forgiven a little personal inconsistency. Nonetheless, it would have looked better if he had walked the walk as well as talked the talk.

Of course, mention of the inconsistencies of these politicians should not blind us to the fact that they are not the only ones who are guilty of being inconsistent. The rest of us aren't exactly paragons of virtue where consistency is concerned. Feminists who argue against different "roles" for males and females, yet who don't reciprocate when given expensive engagement rings, or who always leave the driving to their husbands, along with the spanking of errant children, surely are inconsistent.[6]

Inconsistency often is connected in people's minds with hypocrisy—with pretending to believe what one in fact does not, or to be what one is not. The vast majority of candidates for office in the United States during the past 40 years or so have run on platforms opposing legalization of drugs even though some of them smoked dope or sniffed cocaine. Bill Clinton did own up to smoking marijuana, but notoriously claimed that he did not inhale (ho, ho, ho). Should we say that those who were inconsistent in this way were guilty of the sin of *hypocrisy*? At least Barack Obama admitted past drug use in his teens, but attitudes have changed over the years, and Americans seem more willing to accept youthful lapses than they did before.

Readers may note, when they have completed reading the three fallacy chapters in this text, that a good deal more time is spent on the first two fallacies in this chapter than on any of the others. The reason is that these two are very likely the most important. The importance of the fallacy of appeal to authority is obvious: We all are nonexperts about most of the things that matter in everyday life and therefore regularly have to appeal to authorities for information and advice. The importance of the fallacy of inconsistency also should be obvious: It lies in the crucial importance of consistency to cogent reasoning. *At least one of a set of inconsistent statements must be false!*

That is why trying to be consistent is very likely the best way to improve the quality of one's stock of background beliefs (a point to be discussed again later). Having reasoned to a particular conclusion, consistency requires that we ask ourselves whether we would be willing to carry through that line of reasoning when it applies to other cases. If not, then we must give up that line of reasoning or admit to the intellectual crime of being *inconsistent*.

3. STRAW MAN

While the broad fallacy category *suppressed evidence* seldom is mentioned in traditional logic texts, several species of this genus are given great play. One of these is the **straw man** fallacy, which is committed when we misrepresent an opponent's position, or a competitor's product, or go after a weaker opponent or competitor while ignoring a stronger one.[7]

Straw man has always been the stock-in-trade of advertisers and political smear campaigns. A group called Common Sense Issues made a million automated phone calls to voters in the 2008 South Carolina primaries claiming that John McCain "has voted to use unborn babies in medical research." This was a gross distortion of his position to support research on stem cells gathered from embryos.

---

[6]See the article "The Myth of Meritocracy," by Cynthia Tucker, *Atlanta Constitution* editorial page editor and columnist for *Chronicle Features*, that ran in many newspapers on March 30, 1996. See, e.g., Tucker, Cynthia. "The Myth of Meritocracy." *San Francisco Chronicle* 30 March, 1996.

[7]Note, however, that some cases of this fallacy do not fall into the category of *suppressed evidence*. Should we, by the way, replace the name "straw man" by, say, "straw person" or perhaps "false characterization"?

Politicians on both sides of the aisle use straw man arguments to undermine their opponents' position. In the run-up to the Republican primaries, Mitt Romney had this to say about Barack Obama's proposal to raise taxes on high-income Americans to their 1990's level: "President Obama believes that government should create equal outcomes. In an entitlement society, everyone receives the same or similar rewards, regardless of education, effort, and willingness to take risk. That which is earned by some is redistributed to others." This deliberate distortion makes Obama out to be a socialist, when, in fact, he repeatedly championed the free enterprise system and claimed to see nothing wrong with getting rich.

4. FALSE DILEMMA AND THE EITHER-OR FALLACY

In traditional logic, a *dilemma* is an argument that presents two alternatives, both claimed to be bad for someone, or some position. (Dilemmas are discussed further in the appendix.)

The general form of a dilemma can be put this way:

> Either P or Q.
> If P then R.
> If Q then S.
> Therefore, either R or S.

Sometimes the undesired outcomes R and S are identical, sometimes quite different. Here is an example in which they are not quite the same: "Either our fellow citizens are good or they're bad. If they're good, laws to deter crime aren't needed. But if they're bad, laws to deter crime won't succeed. So laws to deter crime either are not needed or won't succeed."

A **false dilemma** is a dilemma that can be shown to be false. One way to do this is to demonstrate that the premise having the form "Either P or Q" is false by showing that there is at least one other viable possibility. This is called "going between the horns" of the dilemma. In the case of the dilemma just mentioned, a viable alternative is that our fellow citizens may be both good (in some ways) and bad (in others).

Another way to defeat a dilemma is to challenge one or both of its other two premises. This is called "grasping the horns" of the dilemma. We might challenge the crime law dilemma, for example, by arguing that even if some citizens are bad, they still can be deterred by laws specifying harsh penalties.

False dilemmas usually are a species of the genus *questionable premise* because any set of statements that sets up a false dilemma needs to be questioned. (Note, by the way, that we can have false trilemmas, false quadrilemmas, and so on.)

The **either-or fallacy** (sometimes called the *black-or-white fallacy*) is very similar to that of *false dilemma*. We're guilty of this fallacy when we mistakenly reason from two alternatives, one claimed to be bad (that is, to be avoided) so that we ought to choose the other alternative. The general form of the fallacy is this:

> Either P or Q.
> Not P.
> Therefore, Q.

where there is at least a third viable alternative, or it is questionable that P is bad. For example, "You have to vote either for the Republican or for the Democratic candidate. But you shouldn't vote for the Republican. So you should vote for the Democrat." A third alternative in this case would be to vote, say, for the Green Party candidate (this is like going between the horns of a dilemma), and some people would challenge the claim that you shouldn't vote for the Republican candidate (this would be like grasping a dilemma by its horns).

One notable example of the either-or fallacy was the second President Bush's battle cry after September 11, "You are either with us or against us in the fight against terror." There were, of course, plenty of options in between. This simplification of a complex situation was a rhetorical device rather than an appeal to reason. A more recent example involved wrangling over ways to reduce the national debt. When the debt-ceiling crisis in 2011 was at its peak and a national catastrophe, default on federal obligations, was just around the corner, politicians on both sides lapsed into either or reasoning. Grover Norquist, president of Americans for Tax Reform, claimed that there were only two solutions to the deficit problem: "spend less or raise taxes." His solution? "There is only one fix for the spending problem: spend less."[8] First, he reduced the options to two alternatives—one good (from his point of view), the other bad. This line of reasoning inevitably led him to the good option—spend less. But even without going very deep into this complex issue, we can see at least one other alternative: spend less *and* raise taxes.

5. BEGGING THE QUESTION

When arguing, either with ourselves or with others, we can't provide reasons for every assertion and then reasons for the reasons, and so on. Some of what we assert must go unjustified, at least for the moment. But when we assume as a premise some form of the very point that is at issue—the very conclusion we intend to prove—we are guilty of the fallacy of **begging the question**.[9] In this sense, *to beg* means "to avoid." When the premise simply states another version of the conclusion, the question of proof is avoided, or *begged*. (The fallacy of begging the question usually falls into the broad category *questionable premise* because a statement that is questionable as a conclusion is equally questionable as a premise.)

In real life, of course, this fallacy rarely, if ever, has the form

    A.
    Therefore, *A.*

---

[8]See Norquist, G. "Read My Lips: No New Taxes." *New York Times* 22 July, 2011.
[9]In a sense, all deductively valid arguments beg the question, because what is said by their conclusions already is said in their premises. In the typical case, part of an argument's conclusion is said in one premise, part in another. That is the point of valid deduction; anyone who accepts the premises of a deductively valid argument and yet rejects its conclusion is guilty of being inconsistent. The difference in the case of the fallacy of begging the question is that the premises state the claim of the conclusion in a way that those who reject the conclusion also will reject the premises for being just as questionable as the conclusion.

Few would be taken in by anything so obvious. Instead, a premise may state a conclusion in different but equivalent words, so that the conclusion is not so obviously begged. This is the way in which the question is begged in one of the classic textbook cases (from the nineteenth century—human gullibility tends to remain constant): "To allow every man unbounded freedom of speech must always be…advantageous to the state; for it is highly conducive to the interests of the community that each individual should enjoy a liberty, perfectly unlimited, of expressing his sentiments."[10]

Although the traditional fallacy of begging the question deals primarily with questions that are at issue, say, as in a debate, over time it has come to have a broader range so as to cover other sorts of questions. Thus, to take a textbook example, we can be said to be guilty of this fallacy when, having asked why chloroform renders people unconscious, we accept the answer that it does so because it is a soporific (a *soporific* being defined as something that induces sleep).

Doctors and other sorts of professionals are frequent perpetrators of this version of begging the question, but they aren't by any means the only ones who set us up for it. Indeed, many times questions are begged quite innocently. Here is an example taken from an article on exclusive men's clubs in San Francisco. In explaining why these clubs have such long waiting lists, Paul B. "Red" Fay, Jr. (on the roster of three of the clubs) said, "The reason there's such a big demand is because everyone wants to get in them."[11] In other words, there is a big demand because there is a big demand. Fay inadvertently (we hope) gave another version of the conclusion in the premise and thus avoided the question of proof.

Note that the fallacy begging the question also has been broadened over time so as to cover cases in which a premise is different from the conclusion of an argument but is controversial or questionable for the same reasons that typically might lead someone to question the conclusion.

Evading the Issue

One effective way to beg the question at issue is simply to avoid it entirely. Doing this makes one guilty of the fallacy **evading the issue**. This approach succeeds when those taken in fail to notice that the issue has been evaded. Perhaps the best way to hoodwink an opponent or dodge a barbed question is to make it appear that the issue or question is indeed being addressed. Politicians frequently evade an issue concerning a complicated problem (the homeless, the national debt, whatever) by speaking instead about the pressing need to solve it. Savvy citizens are not taken in by this sort of chicanery.

Presidential hopeful Mike Huckabee managed a clever evasion in the 2007 YouTube–CNN debate for Republican candidates. When Huckabee, a minister and politician, was asked whether Jesus would support the death penalty, he quipped, "Jesus was too smart to run for public office." And thus he neatly ducked a question suggesting that his Christian scruples were inconsistent with his pro-death penalty stance as governor of Arkansas.

---

[10]Cited by Richard Whately in his excellent book *Elements of Logic* (London, 1826). Whately's fallacy classification is more like the one used in this text than are those of any other text in use today.

[11]Quoted in: Lara, Adair. "The Chosen Few." *San Francisco Chronicle* 18 July 2004.

Politicians are masters at evading the issue. When they are asked hard questions in interviews, they skirt the subject with responses like "That's a complex issue…" and then shift into the message they want to give. Or they claim the question is relevant, then dismiss it to clear the way for topics they do think are more relevant. Or they say things like "That's a good question, but before going into that I want to discuss…" and then go on to spin their own point of view. Evading the issue is so important to politicians that many of them hire media trainers to help them perfect the art.[12]

6. QUESTIONABLE PREMISE—QUESTIONABLE STATEMENT

As we noted earlier, most examples of the fallacies discussed so far fall into the broader category of *questionable premise*. But not all species of questionable premise have received specific names in the literature. So when a premise that is not believable is spotted in an argument and none of these more specific labels apply, we have to fall back on the general term **questionable premise**. That is what we did earlier when we pointed out that a statement in a Budweiser commercial constituted a questionable premise.

Knowing for a fact that a statement is false obviously is a very good reason for questioning it—indeed, for dismissing it. Thus, when a colleague was alleged to be incompetent on grounds that she was an alcoholic, one of the authors of this text rejected the charge on the basis of personal knowledge that the allegation was false. Sometimes a premise that may be believable to one person can strike another as questionable or even false. Take, for instance, the comment of James Reda, Wall Street compensation consultant, about the Obama Administration's plan to limit to $500,000 the salaries of executives of companies that got large amounts of federal bailout money: "$500,000 is not a lot of money, particularly if there is no bonus." Well, maybe to the super rich it isn't a lot of money but to the rest of us it is a fortune and thus his premise is highly questionable.

Remember, though, that hearing something from a trustworthy expert often counts as a reason for believing it to be true. For example, the fact that the overwhelming majority of scientists believe the burning of fossil fuels, such as oil and coal, is polluting the air and causing a rise in worldwide temperatures ought to constitute good reason for believing that there very likely is a greenhouse effect resulting from the use of these fuels.

Finally, it is worth remembering here that in everyday life statements generally do not come labeled as premises or conclusions and also that not all persuasive discourse is put into argumentative form. So there is a good deal of merit in expanding the fallacy of *questionable premise* so that it becomes, say, *questionable statement*.

7. SUPPRESSED (OVERLOOKED) EVIDENCE

The general fallacy category **suppressed evidence**, introduced earlier along with questionable premise and invalid inference, has not received much attention in the fallacy literature, perhaps because theorists tend to see the suppression of evidence as an error

---

[12]For more on this see a fascinating article on media training: Lieberman, Trudy. "Answer the Question." *Columbia Review of Journalism* January/February 2004.

in reasoning but not as a fallacy (as they define that concept). Whether thought of as a fallacy or not, however, it is important that we learn how to bring relevant evidence to bear on an argument and learn how to avoid being taken in by others when they suppress evidence.

Of course, people who suppress evidence often do so inadvertently, one reason that a more all-encompassing label for the fallacy might be *overlooked evidence,* or perhaps *slighted evidence.* It's easy, when strongly committed to a particular side of an issue, to pass over arguments and reasons on the other side. In recent years, advocates on both sides of issues such as capital punishment, abortion, the legalization of marijuana, the depiction of violence on TV, and the legalization of prostitution frequently have been guilty of slighting evidence damning to their side of the issue. Those opposed to "three strikes and you're out" legislation, for instance, tend to neglect the ways in which this kind of law might protect society from repeat offenders; those in favor don't like to talk about the high costs associated with keeping people in jail long past the age at which the vast majority of criminals have ceased to commit violent crimes, or about the fact that a great many of those sentenced under these laws have not committed violent or even serious crimes.

We all, of course, sometimes are motivated by more crass considerations than mere overzealousness. Self-interest is a powerful motivator of deliberately shady reasoning. Take, for instance, the way drug companies manipulated data on drug trials that tested the effectiveness of antidepressants like Prozac and Paxil. The published trials showed that these drugs provided significant relief for 60 percent of people on the drugs, compared to only 40 percent for those on placebos. This evidence was convincing enough to persuade doctors and patients that the drugs were effective. But in January 2008, the *Journal of the American Medical Association* ran a report of a new analysis reviewing data from both the published and unpublished trials of the antidepressants. This analysis revealed that 94 percent of the positive trials were published but only 14 percent of the unconvincing ones were. In effect, the drug companies were suppressing the negative data to win over the government and get FDA approval. Once the unpublished trials were taken into account, the antidepressants had only a slim edge over the placebos. No wonder physicians were puzzled that the drugs didn't seem to work as well on their patients as they did in the published trials.

The point of becoming familiar with the fallacy of suppressed evidence is to sharpen one's ability to spot cases in which relevant evidence is being passed over, whether by others or by ourselves. We need, in particular, to learn how to carry through reasoning so as to see whether all likely relevant information has been considered.

When, for instance, *The New York Times* ran an article (May 10, 2010) about hedge fund managers urging law makers to create "a friendlier environment" for charter schools, it seemed like a gesture of good will on the part of money managers. But the rationale that they are "drawn to the business-like way in which charter schools are run" and that "they applaud the schools' philosophic roots in a free-market model of education" does little to inform us of the hidden agenda. Digging deeper, *The New York Daily News* found that a federal program gives lenders a 39 percent federal tax credit over seven years for construction loans made to charter schools, a tax break that almost doubles the investment. That bit of suppressed evidence would matter little if the charter schools had sufficient income to repay loans with ease, but some of the cash-strapped

> Shall I tell you what it is to know? It is to say you know when you know, and to say that you do not know when you do not know; that is knowledge.
>
> *—Attributed to Confucius (which means that*
> *we do not know for sure that he said it)*

We don't want to be too hasty, or too picky, in leveling a charge of begging the question. Although what Confucius is quoted as saying is literally question begging, it is very likely that what he meant to say (if he actually said it) is that a large part of wisdom is to know what you do and what you don't have good reason to believe and, by implication, not to believe what you do not have good reason to believe. Excellent advice, indeed.

Doonesbury © G. B. Trudeau. Reprinted with permission of Universal Press Syndicate. All rights reserved.

Tokenism: Note that Clint equates his notion of half way with fairness.

schools have had to cut spending on students in order to meet payments. This then, raises questions about the "business like way" in which schools are run for profit.[13]

For lots of us, becoming adept at bringing to bear suppressed or overlooked relevant information is perhaps the most difficult knack required by good reasoning. Sometimes the difficulty is compounded by our limited understanding of the issue at hand. Take, for example, the Environmental Protection Agency's decision in 2002 to omit, for the first time in six years, the chapter on global warming from its annual federal budget. *The New York Times* (September 15, 2002) reported that industrial lobbyists were "praising the decision, contending that carbon dioxide, which is believed to cause global warming, is not a pollutant." In one sense the lobbyists were right—carbon dioxide is not a pollutant; it's a natural gas—but scientists would argue that it has the side effect of trapping heat and thus causing temperatures to rise. Understanding the fallacious reasoning in the lobbyists' argument requires most of us to do a bit of research.

---

[13]See Juan Gonsolez's column in the *New York Daily News* 7 May 2010.

Many people have trouble distinguishing between having no evidence or proof for a claim and having evidence or proof that the claim is false. But having no evidence, say, that vitamin C helps us fight the common cold is quite different from having evidence that it does not do so. Similarly, a lack of clinical proof that marijuana has certain medicinal benefits is much different from having clinical proof that it does not. Lack of *clinical proof,* by the way, also is quite different from having no good evidence whatsoever concerning marijuana's medicinal benefits. In fact, there is a good deal of such "anecdotal" evidence.

In the Italian film *Il Postino* (*The Postman*), the big politician promises, again, that pipes will be built so that the people can have indoor running water, and he actually has construction begin before the election. People again vote him into office, and—surprise—construction immediately stops. Voters have again been suckered by a token gesture and only wake up to that fact when it is too late to make a difference.

8. TOKENISM

Tokenism—mistaking a token gesture for the real thing, or accepting a token gesture in lieu of something more concrete—is another common fallacy.

As might be expected, tokenism is one of the politician's best friends. In 2008, as gas prices soared and voters complained, both Hillary Clinton and John McCain endorsed a plan to suspend the federal excise tax on gasoline (18.4 cents a gallon) for the summer travel season. But this was just a token gesture, a short-term fix that would save consumers little in the long run. In the fiercely competitive election campaign, the proposal was a ploy to win over middle-class voters, hard-hit by the recession and the escalating costs of gas and food.

Another example: A convincing case could be made that early attempts to include a "public option" (involving a government-run health insurance program) in President Obama's health care bill was simply a token gesture to appease the progressive wing of the party. Obama never fought for it, and even supporters of the plan seemed to realize that it was little more than a bargaining chip in health care negotiations.

Actually, his token gesture was a variation on a related ploy—namely, behaving or speaking one way when the heat is on and another when it isn't sufficiently hot to force change. For as long as possible, Bush satisfied those of his Texas constituents and his financial supporters who favored being "tough on criminals," changing when a wider constituency was being wooed during his presidential campaign, much as Texan and former President Lyndon Johnson did in political campaigns way back in the 1960s.

SUMMARY OF CHAPTER 3

All fallacious reasoning falls into one or more of the three broad categories of *questionable premise, suppressed evidence,* and *invalid inference.* But other fallacy categories, crosscutting these broad ones, have come into common use.

1. *Appeal to authority:* Accepting the word of alleged authorities when there is not sufficient reason to believe that they have the information we seek or that they can be trusted to provide it to us (for example, when they have a vested interest), or doing so when we ought to figure the matter out for ourselves. *Example:* Taking the word of energy industry executives that nuclear power plants are safe.

   When appeals must be made to authorities, we should remember that some are more trustworthy than others, and in particular, we should be wary of experts who have an axe to grind. We also should pay attention to the track records of alleged authorities.

2. *Inconsistency:* Accepting the conclusion of an argument that has self-contradictory statements or statements that contradict each other. These contradictory assertions may be made (1) by one person at one time and place, (2) by one person at different times or places (without explaining the contradiction as a change of mind based on reasons), or (3) by different representatives of one institution. While not, strictly speaking, a fallacy, we need to note when there is a contradiction between what someone says and what that person does. *Example:* Al Gore's verbal support of energy conservation compared to his own excessive energy consumption to run his household.

3. *Straw man:* Misrepresenting an opponent's position or a competitor's product to make it easier to attack him or to tout one's own product as superior, or attacking a weaker opponent while ignoring a stronger one. *Example:* Ads accusing John McCain of voting to use unborn babies in medical research.

4. *False dilemma:* A dilemma that can be shown to be false either by "going between the horns" of the dilemma or by "grasping its horns." *Example:* Refuting the dilemma about the futility of laws to deter crime by pointing out that there is a third alternative—namely, that many citizens are both good and bad.

   The *either-or* (*black-or-white*) variation occurs when an argument is based on the assumption that there are just two viable alternatives, one of which is bad (so the other has to be chosen), although there is at least one other viable alternative. *Example:* Refuting the argument that you should vote for either a Republican or a Democrat to a third possibility, say, voting for a Green Party candidate.

5. *Begging the question:* Assuming without proof the question, or a significant part of the question, that is at issue, or answering a question by rephrasing it as a statement. *Example:* In explaining why exclusive men's clubs have such long wait lists, "Red" Fay said, "The reason there is such a demand is because everyone wants to get in them." One way to beg the question is to avoid it entirely and thus evade the issue. *Example:* An elected official who skirts hard questions by shifting into a message he or she wants to give.

6. *Questionable premise—questionable statement:* Accepting a less than believable premise or other statement. *Example:* Accepting the claim that Budweiser is the best beer as a reason for deciding to switch to Bud. (Note that the five fallacies just described are variations of this broader fallacy but that not all species of questionable premise have special names.)

7. *Suppressed (overlooked) evidence:* Failing to bring relevant evidence to bear on an argument. *Example:* Advocates on both sides of the debates about the merits of "three strikes and you're out" laws who slight sensible arguments and objections of their opponents.

8. *Tokenism:* Accepting a token gesture in lieu of the real thing. *Example:* Being satisfied with campaign rhetoric when there is little likelihood of serious intent to carry through.

EXERCISE 3-1

Determine which fallacies (if any) occur in the following passages and state reasons for your answers. Note: Some items may contain more than one fallacy.

Example

> *Passage:* Heard in a debate concerning capital punishment: "Capital punishment is morally wrong. After all, murder is just as wrong when committed by a government as it is when done by an individual person."
>
> *Evaluation:* The speaker *begged the question at issue.* To say that capital punishment is murder is to say that it is a morally wrong killing (note that only wrongful killings are considered to be murder). But the issue was whether capital punishment—governmental killing—*is* murder, so to assume without argument that it is begs the question.

*1. Overheard in a laundry: "What makes me think abortion is murder? When my pediatrician refused to perform an abortion for me, she said she wouldn't be a party to murder. Babies and childbirth are her business, you know."

*2. John Boehner, then House minority leader, had this to say about a minor provision to expand Medicaid family-planning services in President Obama's Stimulus plan. "How can you spend hundreds of millions of dollars on contraceptives? How does that stimulate the economy?"

3. When Barak Obama was a presidential candidate, he included in his policy agenda a plan to "establish a new public insurance program available to Americans who neither qualify for Medicaid or SCHIP nor have access to insurance through their employers." After Obama was elected and healthcare reform was passed without a public option, he said, "I didn't campaign on a public option."

---

* Starred (*) items are answered in a section at the back of the book.

4. Joe Morgan, announcing a Giants–Marlins baseball game and commenting on the Marlins pitcher: "He's been a little erratic, which explains why he hasn't been consistent."

5. When New York Knicks' star forward Amar'e Stoudemire visited Israel in 2011, he said it was a "spiritual and educational" experience that motivated him to practice Judaism for cultural and spiritual reasons, not religious ones. "For me," he said, "it's about learning the total culture. If you research history, I think we're all Jewish. It's the original culture."

6. Excerpt from the second President Bush's 2004 State of the Union address:

> A strong America must also value the institution of marriage....
> Congress has already taken a stand on this issue by passing the Defense of Marriage Act signed in 1996 by President Clinton. That statute protects marriage under federal law as the union of a man and a woman, and declares that one state may not redefine marriage for other states. Activist judges, however, have begun redefining marriage by court order, without regard for the will of the people and their elected representatives. On an issue of such great consequence, the people's voice must be heard. If judges insist on forcing their arbitrary will upon the people, the only alternative left to the people would be the constitutional process. Our nation must defend the sanctity of marriage.

7. Eric Jubler, in an article in which he argued that America should "open up" its wilderness areas: "The purist [conservationist] is, generally speaking, against everything...the purist believes that those who do not agree with him desire to 'rape the land.' "

*8. At a San Francisco fundraiser in May, 2009, Barack Obama explained and defended the attitudes of Midwest workers in small towns that had undergone steady job loss for 25 years: "It's not surprising then that they get bitter, they cling to guns or religion or antipathy to people who aren't like them or anti-immigrant sentiment or anti-trade sentiment as a way to explain their frustrations."

9. Calvin Coolidge is alleged to have been the first to say this: "We must keep people working—with jobs—because when many people are out of work, unemployment results."

10. In an interview with Sarah, Duchess of York, Larry King asked whether she was friends with Prince Charles. She replied, "Well, Larry, the important thing is that I have great respect for the royal family."

11. Argument in a student essay: "Prostitution should not be legalized because it encourages the breakdown of the family. Nevada, where prostitution is legal in ten counties, has the highest divorce rate in the nation, almost twice as high as the national average."

12. Notice from the Hyatt Regency Hotel in New Orleans: "We are pleased to confirm your reservation. It will be held on a space-available basis."

13. It is reported that when Socrates was condemned to death his wife cried out, "Those wretched judges have condemned him to death unjustly!" To which Socrates is said to have replied, "Would you really prefer that I were justly condemned?"

*14. The American Heart Association and the American College of Cardiology select doctors who are experts in their fields to make independent evaluations of cardiovascular science and issue guidelines to doctors in clinical practice. But a study published in 2011 by the Archives of Internal Medicine revealed that more than half the doctors (56 percent of 498) had conflicts of interest. Among those who led the panels, 81 percent had financial interests in companies affected by the guidelines. When the Institute of Medicine (the health branch of the National Academy of Science) recommended that the doctors responsible for setting guidelines cut their ties with conflict-of-interest companies, the president of the American Heart Association said that this could limit the number of doctors available for the work, adding that what makes it difficult is that some well-regarded experts in their field have conducted medical research sponsored by companies.

15. In a segment of the CBS television program *60 Minutes* on April 21, 2007, Leslie Stahl questioned Lou Dobbs about a report aired on his program by one of his correspondents that there had been about 900 cases of leprosy in this country over a 40-year period, but 7,000 cases over the past three years. The report was part of a segment on his April 14, 2005, program in which he claimed that "the invasion of illegal aliens is threatening the health of many Americans." When Leslie Stahl said there didn't seem to be much evidence to support these statistics, he replied, "Well, I can tell you this. If we report it, it's a fact."

16. Question to artist's model: "Why did he paint you so often?" Answer: "Because I'm his model."

*17. From a Dr. Joyce Brothers newspaper column: "Question: You should be more fearful of rape at home because rapes occur more frequently in private homes than in back alleys. Answer: TRUE. Studies indicate that more rapes are committed in the victim's home than in any other place. Almost half took place in either the victim's home or the assailant's; one fourth occurred in open spaces; one fifth in automobiles; one twelfth in other indoor locations."

18. From *Slander,* by Ann Coulter, on the attitudes of liberals: "The liberal catechism includes hatred of Christians, guns, the profit motive, and political speech, and an infatuation with abortion, the environment, and race discrimination (or in the favored parlance of liberals, 'affirmative action')."

19. From a *New Republic* review of the James Michener book *Iberia:* "Michener leads off his chapter on bullfights with an argument between a quintessential

American and Spaniard about brutal sports—which the Spaniard wins by point-ing out that more young men get killed and maimed every year playing American football than in the bullring."

*20. In the aftermath of a 5.8 magnitude earthquake and the terribly destructive Hurricane Irene, Michele Bachmann had this to say at a Florida political rally about God's message to Washington (August 29, 2011): "I don't know how much God has to do to get the attention of politicians. We've had an earth-quake, we've had a hurricane. He [God] said, 'Are you going to start listening to me here? Listen to the American people because the American people are roaring now.' "

21. A *Washington Monthly* article on celebrity chefs (July/August, 2001) quoted Evan Kleinman, chef of Angeli Café in Los Angeles, as saying:

> Basically when it comes to food and food supply, I find it frightening that something so fundamental to life has been left to people whose only con-cern is profit.... I mean as far as I can see, because of that, there are only two kinds of people putting food in their mouths—the ones who have lost the notion that food is something made by human hands and then there are the others...for whom there's still some link with food as a cul-ture of nurturance.

22. Paraphrase of part of a letter to the editor (*Washington Post National Weekly Edi-tion*, March 13–19, 1989):

> "It's true that the Ayatollah Khomeini has gone too far with his death sentence for author Salman Rushdie [because of his "outrageous" book *The Satanic Verses*], but Rushdie also has gone too far by offending all Moslems. I am a strong believer in the freedom of speech. However, books like Rushdie's only create hatred and division and weaken the ties of people to each other. Therefore, his book and others like it should be abolished.

23. When Calvin Klein was asked what the secret of his success was, he answered, "I make clothes women want to wear."

24. *Extra!* (September/October, 2007) quoted a *Washington Post* article (June 10, 2007) arguing that immigrants are "drawn by the great magnet of the American Economy to fill jobs that most Americans won't do."

*25. Sociologist James Q. Wilson: "I am not about to argue [as some sociobiologists do] that there is a 'sympathy gene.' But there must be some heritable disposition that helps us explain why sympathy is so common."

26. *Extra* (July 2010) noted these responses to the arrest of a Pakistani-American suspect arrested in an attempt to bomb Times Square: Michael Bloomberg, mayor of New York, cautioned that the arrest shouldn't lead to scapegoating by religion or ethnicity. Bill O'Reilly's retort on Fox News was "Well, maybe some-body should remind the mayor that Muslim fanatics have been threatening New York City and the entire country for almost twenty years."

27. In attacking a proposed equal rights amendment to the state constitution of Iowa, Pat Robertson argued that the proposal was part of a "feminist agenda...a socialist, anti-family political movement that encourages women to leave their husbands, kill their children, practice witchcraft, destroy capitalism, and become lesbians."

28. An oil and gas industry-backed organization, energyfromshale.org, makes a case for increasing the production of "clean-burning, domestic, reliable supplies" of natural gas by developing more shale sites in this county. The process, known as fracking, involves injecting high-pressure fluid into deep rock formations to release natural gas. The issue is a contentious one, because fracking may cause contamination of ground water and air pollution, among other things, and disposal of waste may be mishandled. With assurances that the oil and gas industry will make sure that fracking is done responsibly, energyfromshale.org notes that "there are only two sides in the debate: those who want our oil and natural resources developed in a safe and responsible way, and those who don't want our oil and natural gas resources developed at all."

29. The day after the Mitchell report was released detailing the widespread use of anabolic steroids in baseball, a fan made this comment on sfgate.com, the *San Francisco Chronicle*'s website (December 18, 2007): "This will send a shock wave through baseball and steroid usage will stop."

30. In the early days of the run-up to the 2012 Republican nomination for the presidency, Newt Gingrich told Greta Van Susteren, on her news program, that the first thing he would do if he were president would be "to exercise a no fly zone [over Libya] this evening." But when President Obama did exactly that, Gingrich told Matt Lauer on the "Today" show "I would not have intervened." (Quoted in Gail Collins's column, March 26, 2011, *The New York Times*.)

31. Jorg Haider, Nazi sympathizer and Austrian Parliament member, in response to an interview with a *Time* magazine reporter (*Time*, February 14, 2000):

    Time: Why did you praise Hitler's employment policies?
    Haider: I think it was only one sentence out of a big debate. My opponents took out one sentence and made a campaign against me, and it was not possible for me to explain myself.

32. Ad for an International Correspondence School journalism course: "Every successful writer started that first story or article with no previous experience. William Shakespeare, Alexander Dumas, Harold Robbins, Danielle Steel, Barbara Cartland—any famous writer you can name started just like you."

*33. In an interview with Vice President Joe Biden (Meet the Press, December 19, 2010), David Gregory asked him whether he agreed with Mitch McConnell that Julian Assange's WikiLeaks was a high-tech terrorist or with others who said it is more like the Pentagon Papers (involving the unauthorized publication of top secret information about the government misleading the public over the US expansion of the Vietnam War). Biden replied, "I would argue that it's closer to being a high-tech terrorist than the Pentagon papers."

34. Walter Burns, in an article in which he argues for capital punishment:

> When abolitionists speak of the barbarity of capital punishment…they ought to be reminded that men whose moral sensitivity they would not question have supported [it]. Lincoln, for example, albeit with a befitting reluctance, authorized the execution of 267 persons during his presidency…and it was Shakespeare's sensitivity to the moral issues that required him to have Macbeth killed.

35. Phyllis Schlafley, an outspoken opponent of the women's liberation movement, in her book *The Power of Positive Women:*

> The second dogma of the women's liberationists is that, of all the injustices perpetrated upon women through the centuries, the most oppressive is the cruel fact that women have babies and men do not. Within the confines of women's liberationist ideology, the abolition of this overriding inequality becomes the primary goal.

"If the coach and horses and the footmen and the beautiful clothes all turned back into the pumpkin and the mice and the rags, then how come the glass slipper didn't turn back, too?"

---

*T*wo important factors in critical or creative thinking are the ability to bring relevant background information to bear on a problem and to carry through the relevant implications of an argument or position to determine whether they hang together. The cartoon illustrates the second of these factors: The child carries through the reasoning in the Cinderella story and finds it wanting. The first factor might be illustrated by a child who realizes there are millions of chimneys for Santa Claus to get down in one night and wonders how he could possibly manage to do so in time.

4 Fallacious Reasoning—2

How happy are the astrologers, who are believed if they tell one truth to a hundred lies, while other people lose all credit if they tell one lie to a hundred truths.

—Francesco Guicciardini

It ain't so much the things we don't know that get us into trouble. It's the things we know that ain't so.

—Artemus Ward

Most instances of the fallacies discussed in the previous chapter fall into the broad fallacy categories *questionable premise* or *suppressed evidence*. Most of the fallacies to be discussed in this and the next chapter belong to the genus *invalid inference*.

1. AD HOMINEM ARGUMENT

There is a famous and perhaps apocryphal story lawyers like to tell that nicely captures the flavor of this fallacy. In Great Britain, the practice of law is divided between solicitors, who prepare cases for trial, and barristers, who argue the cases in court. The story concerns a particular barrister who, depending on the solicitor to prepare his case, arrived in court with no prior knowledge of the case he was to plead, where he found an exceedingly thin brief, which when opened contained just one note: "No case; abuse the plaintiff's attorney." If the barrister did as instructed, he was guilty of arguing **ad hominem**—of attacking his opponent rather than his opponent's evidence and arguments. (An *ad hominem* argument, literally, is an argument "to the person.")

The solicitor's instruction to abuse the plaintiff's attorney bears an uncanny resemblance to the advice Barack Obama's campaign team gave him when he was running against Hillary Clinton in the 2008 Democratic primaries.[1] Recently released memos reveal that his consultants advised him to attack Clinton personally—"to frame the argument along the character fault line." Her policy director for the campaign commented years later that "their campaign was entirely a character attack on Hillary as a liar and untrustworthy. It wasn't an 'issue contrast,' it was entirely personal. And, of course, it worked."

---

[1]Taken from: Izza, Ryan. "The Obama Memos." The *New Yorker* 30 January 2012.

Ad hominems are the staple of mudslingers in both parties. The Obama team not only dished it out, but their candidate got it back in full measure. When Obama was elected to the Senate, Rush Limbaugh repeatedly called him Obama Osama. A sample of the ad hominems hurled at him once he was president include: alien, atheist, crony capitalist, loser, Muslim, Nazi, socialist, and tar baby. To round things off, one pundit summed him up as sanctimonious, demagogic, self-righteous and arrogant. On the Republican side, Mitt Romney was derided as a flip-flopper, liar, Mormon cultist, predatory capitalist, and vulture capitalist—by members of his own party! For good measure, the Democrats labeled him a fraud, parrot, war monger, budget buster, and economic traitor. The unions topped that with Romney Gekko, after the notorious Gordon Gekko, in the film *Wall Street*, whose mantra was "Greed is Good." Whew! And to think that some people actually *want* to run for president.

It is important not to confuse ad hominem arguments with those in which the fallacy is *straw man*. The difference is that straw man attacks misrepresent an opponent's position, whereas those that are ad hominem abuse an opponent directly.

Attacks on Character or Credentials Sometimes Are Relevant

Although attacks on a person usually are irrelevant to that individual's arguments or claims, sometimes they are very relevant indeed. Lawyers who attack the testimony of courtroom witnesses by questioning their expertise or character are not necessarily guilty of arguing ad hominem. They may be trying to gauge the integrity of the witness to determine whether his or her testimony is credible.

The judgment of expert witnesses may be particularly difficult to assess because they often express opinions or arguments against which the typical layperson is unable to argue directly. When doctors, lawyers, or other experts testify, often the best we can do is try to evaluate their honesty or judgment. Evidence that a psychologist testifying in court has been convicted of perjury, or spends a great deal of time testifying in court, would be a good reason to prefer the conflicting testimony of experts on the other side of the case.

Of course, negative evidence concerning an expert rarely proves that the authority's pronouncements are false. At best, character attacks just provide grounds for disregarding their testimony, not for deciding that it is false. If a doctor who advises operating on a patient turns out to be held in low esteem in the profession, it is rash to conclude that *therefore* no operation is necessary.

What has just been said about attacking the credentials of experts applies to organizations and their pronouncements as well. For example, that a research organization receives most of its funds from the pharmaceutical industry and also regularly issues reports favorable to drug company interests constitutes a very good reason to be suspicious of its output.

Guilt by Association

One of the important variations on the ad hominem argument is that of **guilt by association.** According to an old saying, people can be judged by the company they keep. But is this true? Is it rational to judge people in this way?

The answer is that it is—up to a point and under certain circumstances. In the absence of contrary evidence, a man frequently seen in the company of several different women known to be prostitutes is rightly *suspected* of being connected with their occupation. Similarly, a person who frequently associates with several known agents of a foreign government is rightly suspected of being an agent of that government.

But suspicion is very different from certitude. Judgments based on a person's associations rarely have a high degree of probability. Suspecting that someone uses the services of prostitutes is much different from knowing that he does. (It is, however, good reason to look further, assuming we care enough about the matter.) Someone frequently in the company of prostitutes may turn out to be a sociologist conducting an investigation. A person often seen in the company of foreign spies may turn out to be a friendly counterspy or even just an associate.

Establishing guilt by association between politicians is particularly tricky. When Jack Abramoff, the Republican lobbyist, was indicted for bribery and corruption, a photograph of him shaking hands with the second President Bush hit the media. The obvious implication was that Bush was involved in Abramoff's nefarious activities, though there was no evidence to suggest that he had ever been with the lobbyist except at a few White House receptions, where it is customary for the president to shake hands with guests. Bush himself denied knowing Abramoff at a news conference in January 2006. However, Abramoff claimed that he had seen Bush in almost a dozen settings, and Secret Service records revealed that he had made at least seven visits to the White House—six in 2001 and one in 2004. But so far there is no evidence that Bush was in cahoots with Abramoff and probably there never will be. Unless ongoing investigations prove otherwise, the president cannot be charged with guilt by association.

2. Two Wrongs Make a Right

Those who try to justify a wrong by pointing to a similar wrong perpetrated by others often are guilty of the fallacy sometimes called **two wrongs make a right** (traditional name: *tu quoque*—Latin, "you're another"). For example, in the 2000 presidential election, over 1,900 Palm Beach County, Florida, citizens voted for two candidates for the same office, thus invalidating their ballots. Democratic Party representatives claimed that the vast majority of these double votes resulted from confusion brought on by an illegally designed ballot, thwarting voter intent. A Republican Party spokesperson dismissed their complaint by pointing out that in the 1996 presidential election over 15,000 ballots in Palm Beach County were invalidated for that reason, without creating a huge uproar. But surely, the fact that the 1996 election had a problem does not justify having the same problem in the year 2000.

Justifying a vengeful retaliation in sports may fall into this category as well. In recent years, the baseball commissioner has clamped down on aggressive acts of retaliation between players by fining and suspending them for violence on the field. But in the rough-and-tumble "good old days," retaliation was the way they settled scores. If a pitcher hit the batter, one of the players on the other team would take him down by sliding into first base, cleats high, when the pitcher was covering the base. The umpires would turn a blind eye, and the players would get revenge and the satisfaction of taking care of the problem themselves.[2] Nonetheless, slamming into a player like a fullback because a pitcher on the other team knocked down a batter is using one wrong to justify another.

---

[2]For more discussion of retaliatory behavior in baseball see: Chass, Murray. "End of an Age That Was Ruled by Retaliation." *New York Times* 18 March 2008.

Fighting Fire with Fire

Like most other fallacies, the two wrongs fallacy seems plausible because of its resemblance to a more legitimate way of reasoning—in this case to the plausible idea that we sometimes are justified in "fighting fire with fire." Killing in self-defense illustrates this nicely. We feel justified in fighting one evil (the unjustified attack on our own life) by doing what otherwise would constitute another evil (taking the life of the attacker). So the two wrongs fallacy is not automatically committed every time one wrong is counteracted by another. The crucial question is whether the second wrong is genuinely needed to fight, or counteract, the first.[3]

The Handbook of Political Fallacies, by British political philosopher and reformer Jeremy Bentham (1748–1832), is one of the classic works on political rhetoric and fallacies. Here are excerpts from his account of the first of four "causes of the utterance of [political] fallacies" (another excerpt appears in Chapter 6).

First Cause...: Self-Conscious Sinister Interest

[I]t is apparent that the mind of every public man is subject at all times to the operation of two distinct interests: a public and a private one....

In the greater number of instances, these two interests...are not only distinct, but opposite, and that to such a degree that if either is exclusively pursued, the other must be sacrificed to it. Take for example pecuniary interest: it is to the personal interest of every public man who has at his disposal public money extracted from the whole community by taxes, that as large a share as possible...should remain available for his own use. At the same time it is to the interest of the public...that as small a share as possible...should remain in his hands for his personal or any other private use....Hence it is that any class of men who have an interest in the rise or continuance of any system of abuse no matter how flagrant will, with few or no exceptions, support such a system of abuse with any means they deem necessary, even at the cost of probity and sincerity....

But it is one of the characteristics of abuse, that it can only be defended by fallacy. It is, therefore, to the interest of all the confederates of abuse to give the most extensive currency to fallacies....It is of the utmost importance to such persons to keep the human mind in such a state of imbecility that shall render it incapable of distinguishing truth from error....

Students inclined to complain that too many of the fallacy examples in this text come from politicians should seriously reflect on Bentham's remarks, especially because government today deals with so many matters that determine the quality of all of our lives.

---

[3]This passes over questions concerning retributive justice. If retributivists are right, we sometimes are justified in punishing those guilty of unfairly harming others even though in doing so we fail to fight the original harm (or fail to rehabilitate the criminal or deter others from similar offenses).

Two Wrongs and Hypocrisy

The two wrongs fallacy also sometimes seems plausible—not fallacious—for another reason: Those who argue this way may intend to imply that their opponents are being hypocritical, and often this charge is accurate and may even have some merit. The town drunk isn't the one to tell us we've had one too many and are making fools of ourselves, even if we are. (That's the import of the reply, "You're a fine one to talk.") Similarly, the philanderer who finds out about his wife's infidelity is hardly the one to complain that she has deceived him. But when we become outraged at the chutzpah of our accusers, we shouldn't lose sight of the fact that their hypocrisy doesn't justify our own failures.

Common Practice and Traditional Wisdom

As the traditional Latin name *tu quoque* suggests, the fallacy two wrongs make a right originally was intended to cover only those cases in which an individual or group responds to a charge by charging the accuser or accusers with a similar crime. But over time, it has come to include related, indeed overlapping, sorts of fallacious arguments. One of these is **common practice**, committed when a wrong is justified on the grounds not that one other person or group, but rather lots of, or most, or even all others do the same sort of thing.

For example, when former Senator George Mitchell released an explosive report naming baseball players who took anabolic steroids, many hard-core fans defended superstars like Roger Clemens, Barry Bonds, and Mark McGwire. They argued that these players were taking steroids because lots of other players took them. Since the performance level of everyone on drugs was much better than before, the competition was keener. "How can you blame these guys?" one fan asked. "They did what they had to do to stay competitive." Well, you can blame them, of course, for rationalizing that it was okay to take performance-enhancing drugs because it was common practice to do so.

Another example is the all-too-common rationalization students use for cheating on tests or plagiarizing papers: "Everyone is doing it." In fact, almost everyone may well be plagiarizing from online sources nowadays. Surveys done from 2006-10 at the Center for Integrity have shown that only 29% of students think that copying from the Internet is "serious cheating."[4] Many students blithely copy and paste their essays together without giving a thought to citing sources. Nonetheless, common practice is hardly justification for academic dishonesty —particularly from a teacher's point of view.

A related fallacy, sometimes called **traditional wisdom**, is committed when a wrong or an unsuitable practice is justified on grounds that it follows a traditional or accepted way of doing things. We do, of course, want to learn from past experiences, so we shouldn't assume that *just because* things have been done certain ways in the past, that way must be the right or best way now. All innovations go against past practices—from the introduction of plows that dig deeper furrows (resisted by North African farmers on the grounds that their fathers and grandfathers had farmed the traditional way), to the elimination of practices based on racial, religious, or gender bias in the United States, or

---

[4] See: Gabriel, Trip. "For Students in the Internet Age, No Shame in Copy and Paste." *New York Times* 2 August 2010.

to do away with practices based on the caste system in India, which force "untouchables" to do dirty work, such as collecting "night soil" (human excrement).

In some cases, practices that once made perfect sense no longer do because of changing circumstances or increased knowledge. In others, the fallacy in arguing for the retention of common practices is due to the wrongheadedness or unfairness of those old ways of doing things. Those who benefit from these practices find it hard to entertain the idea that there could possibly be anything wrong with them. In England, for instance, women for centuries had no legal rights under the common law. It wasn't just that women were disenfranchised. Fathers could marry a daughter to whomever they pleased, and after marriage, a woman's husband became the owner of her property. It took a very long time for these and similar legal injustices to be rectified; they were defended, for one thing, on the grounds that women had no legal rights because they never had had any. (In nineteenth-century England and America, the idea that women should have the vote was met with great hilarity in all-male circles of power, and political cartoons in newspapers and magazines poked fun at "lady suffragettes.")

It's often easier to see the questionable nature of customs in distant times or other cultures than in one's own. Consider the centuries-old tradition in some Middle Eastern countries of "honor" killing, the practice of killing girls or women who have sexual relations out of wedlock or are suspected of other sexual improprieties. In the Arab world, an unchaste woman brings shame on the family and sometimes the relatives themselves kill her to "cleanse the honor" that has been soiled. Hundreds of women are killed for reasons of honor each year. Yet activists trying to tighten the laws against honor killings are faced with massive opposition that portrays their campaign as an assault on Arab ways. The traditional wisdom is that an unchaste woman deserves to die.

Similar remarks apply to other societies, a very important example being India, where there also is the inhuman practice of murdering a wife whose family fails to come up with a sufficiently large dowry. Note also that in many Middle Eastern and African countries, traditional wisdom requires that young girls, just before puberty, be given a clitorectomy so as to reduce the temptation to engage in sex out of wedlock.

Of course, those who conform to these customs see them as good; it is other people, both inside and outside these cultures, who find fault with them. The point is that traditional beliefs need to be reevaluated and changed when found wanting.

But, again, we don't want to go overboard. Every change brings with it risks that may not have been calculated correctly. The "three strikes and you're out" laws, for example, were generally enacted without careful consideration of the likely consequences of such a serious departure from past practice. The point of such a bill is to assure that those who repeatedly commit serious violent crimes are not released from jail to again commit heinous offenses. But most of these measures enacted so far fail to distinguish correctly between seriously violent repeat felons and others, or to consider the cost of incarcerating criminals long past the time when they are likely to commit violent crimes (most of which are committed by young men). They also fail to take account of the motivation these bills provide for two-time losers to shoot to kill rather than allow themselves to be captured and tried a third time.

W. Somerset Maugham summed things up nicely when he said, "Tradition is a guide, not a jailer."

3. IRRELEVANT REASON (NON SEQUITUR)

Traditional logic textbooks often discuss a fallacy called *non sequitur* (literally, "it does not follow"), usually described as being committed when a conclusion does not follow logically from given premises. In this sense, any fallacy in the broad category *invalid inference* can be thought of as a non sequitur. But other writers describe this fallacy more narrowly.

Let's replace the ambiguous term *non sequitur* with the expression **irrelevant reason**, used to refer to reasons or premises that are irrelevant to a conclusion when the error doesn't fit a narrower fallacy category such as ad hominem argument or two wrongs make a right.

At a 2011 Congressional hearing on climate change, a lawyer claimed that the EPA cannot declare that greenhouse gas emissions are a health threat. His reason? Public health has improved over the same period of time that greenhouse gas emissions have been rising.[5] However, public health is better now because medical and scientific advances have decreased infant mortality, increased life expectancy, and improved our health in general, but these factors are irrelevant to the long-term effects of greenhouse gas emissions that require decades of study and have yet to be determined.

Sometimes irrelevant arguments defy logic. Shortly after the attack on the World Trade Center, Michael Kelly had this to say in "Pacifist Claptrap."

> Organized terrorist groups have attacked America. These groups wish the Americans to not fight. The American pacifists wish the Americans to not fight. If the Americans do not, the terrorists will attack America again. And now we know such attacks can kill many thousands of Americans. The American pacifists, therefore, are on the side of future mass murders of Americans. They are objectively pro-terrorist.[6]

Ah, those crafty pacifists. Little did we realize their murderous intent.

How about this excerpt from a United Airlines commercial?

> We humans are a social animal. That's why United flies to more places than any other airline.

This commercial says that the reason United flies to more places is that "we humans are a social animal," a fact that is totally irrelevant to (United's) flying to more places than competing airlines. Their use of the phrase "that's why," implying that a reason supports a conclusion, is completely off base. The appeal of United's spiel is to emotion, not to brain power, not to reason. Note, by the way, that a reason is not automatically irrelevant just because it is false. For example, the old superstition that walking under a ladder brings bad luck is false, but it isn't irrelevant to the question whether a person should or shouldn't engage in this practice; were it true, it would be a very good reason indeed for not walking under ladders.

Note also that a reason may be irrelevant when looking at a matter from one point of view but not from another. Take, for example, the remark by a psychological clinician,

---

[5]Krugman, Paul. "The Truth, Still Inconvenient." *New York Times* 4 April 2011.
[6]Kelly, Michael. *Washington Post* 26 September 2001, quoted in *Extra!,* November/December, 2001.

© Dan Wasserman, *The Boston Globe,* Tribune Media Services

A humorous (we hope) equivocation.

quoted in *Science News* magazine, that abandoning the old and standard ways of classifying mental disorder in favor of new ones "will result in denial of insurance coverage for treatment of serious psychological disturbances." Looked at from the point of view of psychiatric *theory,* this remark is irrelevant, but from the point of view of psychiatric *practice,* it is very relevant indeed.

4. EQUIVOCATION

A term or expression is used *equivocally* in an argument when used to mean one thing in one place and another thing in another.[7] Accepting an argument that is invalid because we are fooled by an equivocal use of language makes us guilty of the fallacy that you will not be surprised to learn is generally called **equivocation.**

---

[7]As used in everyday life, the term *equivocation* often connotes the use of equivocation to deceive. As used here, it does not necessarily carry this connotation. We do, of course, have to remember that equivocation is frequently employed in daily life to make invalid arguments appear to be valid.

When a TV evangelist said that we all should stop sinning and "be like Jesus," someone in the audience expressed doubt that he was up to that, pointing out that, after all, "Jesus is the son of God." In reply, the evangelist told the doubter that he could indeed stop sinning because, "You're the son of God, too." But the evangelist was guilty of equivocation, because the doubter meant that Jesus is the son of God in the special way that (according to Christian doctrine) only Jesus is held to be, while the evangelist had to mean that the doubter was the son of God in the metaphorical sense in which (again according to Christian theology) we all are children of God.

Equivocation is a common fallacy because it often is quite hard to notice that a shift in meaning has taken place. As might be expected, given human nature, less than completely ethical manipulators frequently take advantage of the ease with which people can be fooled in this way. The sugar industry, for instance, once advertised its product with the claim that "Sugar is an essential component of the body . . . a key material in all sorts of metabolic processes," neglecting the fact that it is *glucose* (blood sugar), not ordinary table sugar (sucrose), that is the vital nourishment. It's true, of course, that table sugar does turn into blood sugar in the body, but it provides that necessary ingredient without also providing the other sorts of vital nutrients found in fruits, grains, and other more complete food sources that contain plenty of sucrose.

Advertisements of this kind for food and other health products are successful because a large majority of consumers know very little about how the body functions—what sorts of food are required for good health and what sorts are unhealthy. They tend to get their information about these vital matters from television commercials, other advertisements, and TV talk shows. So they are ready-made suckers for every fad that comes down the pike. For example, many food products have been advertised as especially healthy because they are low in cholesterol, or even cholesterol-free, while containing the usual (high) levels of fats, which the body then uses to make cholesterol. The ambiguity taken advantage of here is, again, the difference between what is in a food and what is in the bloodstream. Low blood cholesterol levels are good; low food cholesterol levels combined with high fat content definitely are not good. (Note that some foods advertised to be cholesterol free or even fat free contain partially hydrogenated oils, much less heart healthy than the fats listed on packages by law.)

Sometimes legal action is taken against companies for misleading advertising. When Phillip Morris was sued for deceiving smokers into thinking "light" cigarettes were less harmful than regular ones, a company spokesman said that the word *light* referred to taste, not content, but surely he was equivocating. Most smokers would tend to think that "light" meant that the cigarettes had less tar and nicotine—if only to rationalize their bad habit.

Interestingly, terms that can be used either relatively or absolutely, like *rich* and *poor,* sometimes cause trouble. Poverty, for instance, is exceedingly unpleasant anywhere, at any time. But the poor in the United States today are richer in absolute terms with respect to material wealth than the vast majority of people who lived in days of old or who live today in the so-called Third World countries of Africa, Central and South America, and Asia. This important truth is masked by the fact that the term *poor,* in its relative sense, does apply to those Americans who are poor compared to other Americans, though they may be rich compared to most people who lived in the past or who live in Third World countries today. (Do we make ourselves perfectly clear?)

It is he that sitteth upon the circle of the earth.

—Isaiah 40:22

Ambiguity

Almost any statement can be interpreted in various ways if we have a mind to do so. The Bible is a happy hunting ground for those intent on taking advantage of the ambiguity of natural languages, because so many people take what it says to be the word of the Ultimate Authority. This passage from Isaiah was once used to prove that the Earth is flat, but when the discoveries of Copernicus, Kepler, and Newton made the idea of a flat Earth untenable, the Isaiah quote was reinterpreted to prove that those who wrote the Bible knew the Earth is a sphere.

But Ambiguity Often Serves Useful Purposes

Students sometimes get the idea that *ambiguity,* certainly equivocation, always is bad. But it isn't. Ambiguous uses of language, especially metaphorical ones, and even equivocations, can be employed for all kinds of good purposes. The well-known psychologist Carl Rogers, for example, used equivocation very effectively in the following passage to emphasize a point:

> As a boy I was rather sickly, and my parents have told me that it was predicted I would die young. This prediction has been proven completely wrong in one sense, but has come profoundly true in another sense. I think it is correct that I will never live to be old. So I now agree with the prediction that I will die young.[8]

Ambiguous uses of language also serve to grease the wheels of social intercourse. Benjamin Disraeli, the nineteenth-century British prime minister, often used ambiguity to soften his replies to letters, while still coming close to being truthful, as in his reply to an unsolicited amateur manuscript: "Many thanks; I shall lose no time in reading it." (In most other contexts, of course, equivocation of this kind is rightly considered to be rather sneaky.)

Ambiguity also serves very useful purposes in literature, particularly in metaphoric passages. It enables writers to introduce multiple meanings quickly into a text in a way that adds significance to what is being said by drawing attention to often rather subtle connections without hitting us over the head with them. For example, the title of Joseph Conrad's great novel *Heart of Darkness* doesn't refer just to the central part of the African jungle, but also captures some of the moral horror of the principal character, Kurtz, succumbing to the dark temptations of colonial African life, and by extension, it draws attention to the corruption and depravity "civilized" people are capable of when they give in to their base instincts. It also suggests the appalling abuses of power

---

[8]Rogers, Carl. *The Carl Rogers Reader.* New York: Houghton Mifflin, 1989. Reprint of article in *Journal of Humanistic Psychology* (Fall 1980).

resulting from the exploitation of Africans and their lands by European colonials at the turn of the century. The ambiguity lurking in the title of Conrad's novel thus prepares us for the complex moral issues addressed in his classic work.

5. APPEAL TO IGNORANCE

When good reasons are lacking, the rational conclusion to draw is that we just don't know. But when we greatly desire to believe something, it's tempting to take the absence of evidence, and thus absence of refutation, as justification for believing that it is true. Doing this makes us guilty of the fallacy **appeal to ignorance** (traditionally known as *argumentum ad ignorantiam*). Some people have argued, for example, that we should believe there is no intelligent life on other planets anywhere in our galaxy, since no one has been able to prove that there is; indeed, until recently, when the existence of other planets was confirmed, it was sometimes argued that there were no planets anywhere other than our own tight little island.

The fallacy in this sort of reasoning can be seen by turning it on its head. If appeals to ignorance could prove that no life exists on other planets, then it equally well could prove just the opposite. After all, no one has proved that life does *not* exist on any of these planets. In the absence of good evidence for a claim, the right thing to do is to be *agnostic* on the issue, to neither believe nor disbelieve. Ignorance proves nothing, except, of course, that we are ignorant. During the Iraq War, the Bush administration could have said that the opposition was guilty of appeal to ignorance when it claimed that because no weapons of mass destruction were found, there must not be any hidden weapons. As of this writing, they still haven't been found, but you never know—they may turn up.

There are, however, cases in which the failure of a search does count against a claim. That happens when whatever is searched for would very likely have been found if it existed. Given all the sky watching that has gone on in the past 10,000 years, the claim that there exists a planet-sized object between Earth and Mars is disproved by the failure

In 1950, when Senator Joseph R. McCarthy (Republican, Wisconsin), was asked about the fortieth name on a list of 81 names of people he claimed were communists working for the United States Department of State, he responded that "I do not have much information on this except the general statement of the agency that there is nothing in the files to disprove his communist connections."

Many of McCarthy's followers took this absence of evidence as proof that the person in question was indeed a communist, a good example of the fallacy of appeal to ignorance. This example also illustrates the importance of not being taken in by this fallacy. McCarthy never backed up his charges with a single bit of relevant evidence, yet for several years he enjoyed great popularity and power, and his witch hunt ruined many innocent lives before, finally, McCarthy and "McCarthyism" were brought down in congressional hearings that revealed the true character of this miserable person.

of anyone to observe it. Similarly, the failure to find evidence of a virus in a blood test justifies a doctor's conclusion that the patient isn't infected with that virus. These are cases not of reasoning from ignorance but rather of reasoning from the *knowledge* that we would have found the item looked for if it had been there to find.

Note, however, the importance of *appropriately* searching. That telescopes have searched the sky for several hundred years, and naked eyes for thousands, without spotting a god up there proves absolutely nothing about the existence of a god in the sky, since deities are not conceived of as the kind of entities that can be seen in this way.

6. COMPOSITION AND DIVISION

The fallacy of **composition**, also sometimes called the *salesman's fallacy,* but more accurately the *consumer's fallacy,* is committed when someone assumes that a particular item must have a certain property because all of its parts have that property. Auto dealers, for example, frequently try to get prospective customers to fall for this fallacy by touting low monthly payments while neglecting total costs, hoping their marks will assume that if the monthly payments are low, then the total cost must be low also. Washers and dryers used to be sold by telling customers that it takes "only 50 cents a day" to buy one. Of course, 50 cents a day adds up to $365 in two years (a lot of money until rather recently), something buyers seldom thought to figure out even though the arithmetic involved was on the grade school level.

The fallacy of **division** is committed when we assume that all (or some) of the parts of an item have a particular property because the item as a whole has it. The fallacy of division thus is the mirror image of the fallacy of composition. While infrequently fallen for in everyday life, cases do happen. An example is concluding that all the rooms in a large, fancy, hotel must be large, as guests often do when making reservations at places such as the posh Plaza Hotel in New York (where in fact lots of rooms are rather tiny).

7. SLIPPERY SLOPE

In a typical **slippery slope argument**, an action is objected to on the grounds that once it is taken, another action, and then perhaps still another, is bound to be taken, down a "slippery slope," until some undesirable consequence results. According to a slightly different version, whatever would justify taking the first step would also justify all the others, but since the last step isn't justified, the first isn't, either.

Arguing that a slope is slippery without providing good reason for thinking that it is, or when the slope clearly is not, makes us guilty of the **slippery slope fallacy.** For example, a Canadian-style "single-payer" health care system has often been objected to on grounds that it is a kind of socialized medicine and that its adoption would lead to socialized insurance of all kinds, socialized railroads, airlines, and so on, without sufficient reason being presented for believing this would be the case. (Are there any?) It also sometimes is argued that whatever would justify a single-payer system of health care also would justify all sorts of other socialistic measures, again without justifying this conclusion.

Earlier editions of this text at this point had a section on a variation of the fallacy slippery slope called the *domino theory*. Back in the nasty old Cold War days, dominoes were alleged to be in danger of falling all over the globe. Perhaps the chief reason advanced by the Johnson and Nixon administrations for our involvement in the war in Vietnam was that if Vietnam fell to the communists, the rest of Southeast Asia would also, and then countries in Central America (Nicaragua, El Salvador, and so on) and even parts of South America (in particular, Chile). Although we were defeated in Vietnam, it is primarily communist dominoes that have fallen—perhaps the reason that the domino theory has gone out of fashion.

Too often slippery slopes are used to incite fear or demonize minority groups or movements. In 2010, when Muslims in Murfreesboro, Tennessee, attempted to build an Islamic Center, people opposed to the plan rallied against it. In response, TV evangelist Pat Robertson had this to say on his show *The 700 Club* (Christian Broadcasting Network. 19 August 2010):

> You mark my word, if they start bringing thousands and thousands of Muslims into that relatively rural area, the next thing you know they're going to take over the city council. Then they're going to be having a public ordinance that calls for public prayers five times a day. Then they're going to be having ordinances... [for] foot washing in all the public restrooms. . . etcetera, etcetera. And before long, they're going to demand, demand, demand. . .and little by little, the citizens of Murfreesboro. . . are going to be cowed.

A malicious slippery slope if there ever was one—aimed at group of people who represented only 1% of the town's population.

Note, however, that some slopes may well be slippery. The slippery slope fallacy is committed only when we accept without further justification or argument that once the first step is taken, the others are going to follow, or that whatever claims (however inaccurate) would justify the first step would in fact justify the rest. Consider this explanation of an economic slide that could have occurred after the housing market crashed in 2007.[9]

> As homeowners see the value of their homes decline, they become more likely to delay purchases of the big items—like automobiles, electronics and home appliances—that are ballasts of the American economy. When those purchases decline, large manufacturing firms, suddenly short on funds, could begin laying off employees. Those workers, uncertain about the future, might in turn stop buying Starbucks lattes and movie tickets, and in a worst-case scenario, that could spur coffee shops and theaters to begin layoffs of their own.

---

[9]Duhigg, Charles. "Depression, You Say? Check Those Safety Nets." *New York Times* 23 March 2008.

This may seem like a slippery slope fallacy at first glance, but a similar chain reaction did occur during the Great Depression in 1929, resulting in persistent, widespread unemployment. It was, indeed, a slippery slope, and one that threatened to repeat itself when the credit markets froze up and the stock market plunged in 2008.

SUMMARY OF CHAPTER 4

1. *Ad hominem argument:* An irrelevant attack on an opponent rather than on the opponent's evidence or arguments. *Example:* Rush Limbaugh calling Barack Obama "Obama Osama." Note, however, that not all character attacks are fallacious, as they may not be when challenging the integrity of a supposedly expert witness.

    We're guilty of the variation on this fallacy called *guilt by association* when we judge someone guilty solely on the basis of the company that person keeps.

2. *Two wrongs make a right:* Justifying a wrong by pointing to a similar wrong perpetrated by others. *Example:* Baseball players justifying aggressive retaliation against a pitcher on the other team because he hit a batter and knocked him down. Note, however, that when fighting fire with fire, what would otherwise be a wrong often isn't, as when someone kills in self-defense.

    Although there is an air of hypocrisy to a charge coming from an equally guilty party, this doesn't make an accurate charge any less on target.

    Variations: Common practice, in which a wrong is justified because it is commonly engaged in. *Traditional wisdom,* in which a wrong is justified because that's the way things always have been done.

3. *Irrelevant reason:* Trying to prove something with evidence that is or comes close to being irrelevant. (Some other term, such as *ad hominem argument,* may also apply.) *Example:* The commercial that says the reason United flies more places is that "we humans are a social animal," a fact irrelevant to United's flying more places than other airlines.

4. *Equivocation:* Using a term or expression in an argument in one sense in one place and another sense in another. *Example:* The TV evangelist's use of the expression "son of God" to refer to Jesus Christ and to a parishioner, in order to persuade the parishioner that he could "be like Jesus" and stop sinning. Note, however, that intentional ambiguity, even equivocation, is not always fallacious. It isn't, for example, when used for metaphoric effect.

5. *Appeal to ignorance:* Arguing that the failure to find evidence refuting a claim justifies believing that it is true. *Example:* Arguing that there is no intelligent life on other planets since no one has been able to prove there is. Note, however, that the failure of *appropriate* searches sometimes does support rejection of a claim.

6. *Composition:* Assuming that an item has a certain property because all or most of its parts have that property. *Example:* Assuming a commodity is inexpensive because of low installment payments.

    Division: Assuming that all or most parts of an item have a property because the whole item has it. *Example:* Assuming the rooms in a large hotel are large.

7. *Slippery slope:* Accepting a claim that a particular action must be avoided because, if taken, it would lead to another action, and another—down a slippery slope to undesirable consequences, when no or insufficient reason has been presented to justify that claim. *Example:* Arguing that adoption of a single-payer health plan will lead to adoption of all sorts of other socialistic measures.

EXERCISE 4–1

Determine which fallacies (if any) occur in the following short passages and justify your answers (as you did when working on Exercise 3-1). (Some of these passages may contain fallacies discussed in the previous chapter.)

1. During the mass protests in Egypt in 2011, Jim Lehrer, *News Hour* anchor, asked Vice President Joe Biden whether Egypt's President Hosni Mubarak should be seen as a dictator. Biden replied: "Look, Mubarak has been an ally of ours in a number of things and he's been very responsible. . . relative to geopolitical interests in the region. . . I would not refer to him as a dictator." (PBS *News Hour* 27 January 2011, quoted in *Extra!,* March 2011.)

2. In a column about Al Gore's book *The Assault on Reason*, David Brooks roundly criticized the book, but wrote that it was "well worth reading. It reminds us that whatever the effects of our homogenizing mass culture, it is still possible for exceedingly strange individuals [meaning Al Gore] to rise to the top." (*New York Times* 29 May 2007)

3. Charlton Heston (then president of the National Rifle Association), in an interview after the 1999 shootings at Columbine High School, told ABC's *This Week* that he opposed President Clinton's attempt to limit handgun purchases to one a month. "Before you know it, it becomes no guns."

*4. Football player Roger Craig, on George Seifert's promotion to head coach of the National Football League's San Francisco 49ers: "I think George will do an excellent job, because he's been searching for a head coaching job for some time, and what better place to start his head coaching job." (In fact, Seifert did have an excellent record with the 49ers before being canned.)

5. From a 1972 article in the *Hartford Courant* still relevant today on the possibility of women priests in the Catholic Church: "Citing the historic exclusion of women from the priesthood,...the study [of a committee of Roman Catholic bishops] said '. . . the constant tradition and practice, interpreted as divine law, is of such a nature as to constitute a clear teaching of the Ordinary Magisterium [teaching authority of the church].' "

*6. Bumper sticker seen in California when a handgun bill was before voters of that state:

Gun Registration Equals Mass Extermination
First Register Guns, Then Register the Jews

---

*Starred (*) items are answered in a section at the back of the book.

7. In an article for the *Atlanta Constitution* (March, 1996) Cynthia Tucker pointed out how the rich and powerful often are given special privileges. "These revelations make the case for affirmative action. People of color, who rarely have power or connections, are just seeking the same favors available to those who [already] have them."

8. At a donor dinner for the 2012 presidential campaign, Mitt Romney said that the 47 percent of Americans who "pay no income taxes" are people who are "dependent upon government, who believe that they are victims, who believe the government has a responsibility to care for them, who believe that they are entitled to health care, to food, to housing, to you-name-it. That that's an entitlement. And the government should give it to them."

9. Jan Berger in the *Baltimore Evening Sun:* "Weeks of patient investigation have revealed that the gas leaked at Bhopal [India—with thousands of casualties] because something went wrong."

*10. Rush Limbaugh, on his February 29, 2012 show, caused a furor when he lashed out at a college coed who testified before Congress in favor of religiously affiliated schools providing insurance coverage for contraception. Limbaugh's response was "What does that say about the college coed...who goes before a congressional committee and essentially says that she must be paid to have sex? What does it make her? It makes her a slut, right? It makes her a prostitute. She wants to be paid for having sex. She's having so much sex she can't afford the contraception."

11. Claim made by opponents of an initiative to legalize marijuana for medicinal purposes: "It would be foolish to permit the sale of marijuana to seriously ill people on the recommendation of their physicians. That just opens the floodgates to the complete legalization of that dangerous drug."

12. A letter to the editor of *Connoisseur* magazine defended a previous article favoring bullfighting from "the protesting letters you are sure to receive," by reminding readers that bulls selected for the arena live twice as long as those destined for McDonald's and die in a far more noble fashion.

13. When President Bush attempted to justify sending 20,000 more troops to secure Iraq in 2007, congressional leaders asked him why he thought this strategy would succeed when previous efforts had failed. Bush responded, "Because it has to." (quoted in the *New York Times* 11 January 2007)

*14. Indian mystic Vivekananda: "There is no past or future even in thought, because to think it you have to make it present."

15. From a conversation with a friend (not verbatim): "Sure, I've told you before that I believe everyone's opinion counts on moral matters like abortion. But not *everyone's* opinion counts—I wouldn't want Hitler's to count. Well, [name deleted] isn't a Hitler, but she sleeps around like sex was going out of style next week or something. She's just a slut, and she's broken up at least one marriage I know about. Why should her opinion count on anything? Why should we listen to her opinion on the abortion business?"

16. In a Virginia court ruling against President Obama's health care law, Judge Henry E. Hudson argued that a law requiring most Americans to buy health insurance was unconstitutional and that it "exceeds the constitutional boundaries of congressional power." Judge Hudson cautioned that the law would "invite unbridled exercise of federal police powers" and would give Congress "boundless" authority to force Americans "to buy an automobile, to join a gym, to eat asparagus."

17. Jules Crittenden, an embedded journalist for the *Boston Herald* in the Iraq War, defended himself from criticism for bringing home some illegal "souvenirs" from Iraq (*Boston Herald* 23 April 2003): "I understand and share the world's concern about the disappearance of legitimate Iraqi national treasures that are in fact treasures of human civilization," Crittenden wrote in an open letter to journalists in this country. "However, those are matters separate from the time-honored tradition among soldiers of bringing home reminders of some of the most intense experiences of their lives. There was no exception to that historical practice in this war...[until reporters and soldiers were subject to search by federal agents on returning to the United States]."

18. Argument heard all too frequently in introductory philosophy classes: "We're perfectly entitled to believe there is a God. After all, every effort by atheists to prove otherwise has failed."

19. Lewis Carroll, in *Through the Looking Glass:* " 'You couldn't have it if you did want it,' the Queen said. 'The rule is jam tomorrow and jam yesterday—but never jam *today*.' 'It must sometimes come to jam today,' Alice objected. 'No it can't,' said the Queen. 'It's jam every *other* day: today isn't any *other* day, you know.' "

20. As the country slid into the Great Recession in 2008, Phil Gramm, former senator from Texas, told Americans to stop complaining about the economy, calling them "a nation of whiners." He said, "You've heard of mental depression; this is mental recession."

21. Robert Ringer in *The Tortoise Report* touting gold as an investment: "Two thousand years after the human flesh had disappeared, the gold that adorned it [an ancient Egyptian corpse] remained virtually unchanged. That's a real hard act for paper money to follow."

22. Margaret Morissey, an anti-garbage activist, was interviewed on *As It Happens,* a Canadian news program (February 2002) about her arrest for blocking trucks from dumping garbage on a hill overlooking St. Brides, Newfoundland. The arrest occurred despite the fact that it was illegal to use the hill as a dumpsite. When she asked the mayor why the dumping was still allowed, he said, "We've been doing it for 30 years."

23. Overheard on the bus to Atlantic City: "I just play the quarter slots when I go to Atlantic City. That way, I don't lose too much money."

*24. Sigmund Freud: "Our own death is...unimaginable, and whenever we make the attempt to imagine it we can perceive that we really survive as spectators."

25. Excerpt from an article in *Extra!* (June 2003) critical of embedding journalists with military units during the Iraq War: "Embedding was the brainchild of Assistant Defense Secretary Victoria Clarke, formerly with Hill and Knowlton, the PR firm infamous for promoting the false baby-incubator story during the first Gulf War."

26. When John Bolton was nominated for the position of ambassador to the United Nations in 2005, repeated testimony was given in Senate hearings about his bad temper and his abrasive manner with subordinates. (One person went so far as to call him a "serial abuser.") But he was defended by Danielle Pletka, a vice president at the American Enterprise Institute, who said, "This is a disgrace, the idea that temperament is suddenly important. There are legions who have gone before John, as well as members of Congress, who have behaved appallingly."

27. St. Augustine, in *De Libero Arbitrio:* "See how absurd and foolish it is to say: I should prefer nonexistence to miserable existence. He who says, I prefer this to that, chooses something. Nonexistence is not something; it is nothing. There can be no real choice when what you choose is nothing."

28. When Ralph Nader announced on *Meet the Press* that he was running for president in the 2004 election, he said, "George Bush is a giant corporation masking as a human being."

29. Item from the *Philadelphia Inquirer* (August 28, 2003) about an atheist, Sherrie Wilkins, suing a school board in Camden, New Jersey over school uniforms: "Citing the equal protection clause of the U.S. Constitution, Wilkins' lawsuit argues that atheists should have the same rights as religious parents [since the school district allows parents to opt out of the requirement on religious grounds]....[Furthermore] as an atheist, Wilkins said in court documents, she objects to the uniforms because they 'hinder her children's creativity...and freedom of expression.' Uniforms also symbolize militarism, which she opposes, she said."

30. In the run-up to the Senate confirmation of appointments to the Supreme Court, Senate Republicans threatened to strip Democrats (the minority party) of their right to use the filibuster as a way to prevent the confirmation of judges. The Democrats argued that the filibuster had been around for 200 years and scrapping it would be "changing rules in the middle of the game." Further, it would undermine the constitutional principle of "checks and balances" that protected Americans from one-party rule. (Discussed in: Bai, Matt. "The Framing Wars." *New York Times Magazine* 17 July 2005.)

31. A lobbyist, whose job is to get people to call or write to members of Congress, responding to the charge that this sort of activity makes the "political playing field" uneven (because big money can afford these endeavors much better than small): "Everyone knows that the playing field isn't level in this country in the business arena, or in others for that matter. Nobody complains about that. Why fuss about the funding for what I do?"

32. Excerpt from a letter to the editor of the *Pacific Sun* (September 2000): "Nowhere on the official Ralph Nader website is there any mention of concern about how women are treated in the media. I can't help but infer that this kind of human dignity is not high on his agenda."

*33. Another one from ex-senator Phil Gramm, defending his argument that food stamps should be cut: "We're the only nation in the world where all our poor people are fat."

It's dangerous to conclude that A *is the cause of* B *just because* B *follows* A.

5 Fallacious Reasoning—3

Figures don't lie, but liars figure.
—Old saying

There are lies, damn lies, and statistics.
—Benjamin Disraeli

It's very difficult to make predictions, especially about the future.
—Casey Stengel

Let's now continue our discussion of fallacious reasoning with several fallacies that generally fall into the broad category *invalid inference.*

1. HASTY CONCLUSION

The fallacy of **hasty conclusion** is committed when we draw a conclusion from relevant but insufficient evidence. This fallacy is committed in many different ways and circumstances, ranging from judging political candidates primarily on the basis of 30-second TV commercials to concluding that a neighbor is having an affair on the basis of one or two suspicious clues.

Of course, if we mere human beings were as lucky as Hercule Poirot or Miss Marple, or the other famous fictional detectives, our overly hasty conclusions would frequently turn out to be correct. Here, for example, is the archetype of the great fictional detective Sherlock Holmes making one of his amazing "deductions" when first introduced to Dr. Watson in Sir Arthur Conan Doyle's *A Study in Scarlet:*

> Here is a gentleman of the medical type, but with the air of a military man. Clearly an army doctor, then. He has just come from the tropics, for his face is dark, and that is not the natural tint of his skin, for his wrists are fair. He has undergone hardship and sickness, as his haggard face says clearly. His left arm has been injured. He holds it in a still and unnatural manner. Where in the tropics could an English army doctor have seen much hardship and gotten his arm wounded? Clearly in Afghanistan.

What Holmes observed about Watson was consistent with all sorts of other possibilities that in real life might have been actualities. Doctors don't look that much different from other professionals. Some men with a military air (whatever that might be) never have been in the military. Among Englishmen in those days, when Britain ruled the waves, naval military men were just as common as army types. Tanned faces can result from exposure to nontropical sunlight. A still and unnatural arm carriage may be the legacy of a childhood accident, a haggard expression due to anguish at the loss of a close relative. And even supposing the person in question were a military man who had been wounded in battle in Afghanistan, he still might just have come from a funeral in Italy, South Africa, Brighton, or Timbuktu. The conclusion drawn by Holmes may have been a good guess, but stated with the typical Holmes air of infallibility, it surely was hasty.

Fallacies are endemic to political rhetoric and hasty conclusions are no exception. In recent years, politicians have been eager to reform school performance under President Bush's No Child Left Behind and President Obama's Race to the Top, using the simplistic method of linking teacher evaluations to student performance on standardized tests. The theory is that good teachers will produce students who score well on these tests. But this fails to take into account many of the complex factors involved in student performance, such as problems with tests that may not reflect the actual curriculum or problems with students who have poor language or math skills to begin with and need more time and instruction than is available. It is therefore hasty to conclude that because a class scores below average, the teacher is ineffective.

2. SMALL SAMPLE

Statistics frequently are used to project from a sample to the "population" from which it was drawn. This is the basic technique that underlies several kinds of inductive reasoning and is the method employed by most polls, including those conducted by Gallup, Harris, and the Nielsen television ratings. But when we accept a conclusion based on a sample that is too small to be a reliable measure of the population from which it was drawn, we are guilty of the fallacy of the **small sample**, a variety of the fallacy *hasty conclusion.* No sample of 100 to 500 voters, for instance, can possibly reflect accurately the entire voting population of the United States.

Scientists, of all people, aren't supposed to commit statistical fallacies (or any fallacies, for that matter), but they're human. In an interesting, one might say comical, example, researchers drew a conclusion about the mating vocal responses of primate species based on a sample of three human couples (each observed engaged in sex exactly once), a pair of gibbons, and one troop of chacma baboons.

The general question as to when a sample is sufficiently large is extremely difficult to answer and is a matter of great interest to statisticians and other scientists. Obviously, though, all other things being equal, the larger the percentage of a population from which a sample is drawn, the more confident we can be that it reflects that population as a whole.

3. UNREPRESENTATIVE SAMPLE

In addition to being large enough, a good sample should be *representative* of the population from which it is drawn. Indeed, the more representative a sample is, the smaller it needs to be to be significant. When we reason from a sample that isn't sufficiently

> Sample size does not overcome sample bias.
>
> **—Saying popular among statisticians**

representative, we commit the fallacy of the **unrepresentative sample** (sometimes called the fallacy of **biased statistics**, although that name also applies to cases where known statistics that are unfavorable to a theory are deliberately suppressed).

The example just mentioned, about primate mating responses, illustrates the fallacy of the unrepresentative sample as well as that of the small sample. For one thing, only three of the dozens of primate species were checked—chimps, gorillas, lemurs, tarsiers, and so forth, may be quite different. (In fact, orangutans turn out to be much different from all other primates in their sex practices.) For another, there is plenty of reason to believe that no sample of three human couples could possibly be representative of all *Homo sapiens,* given the tremendous variety of sex practices engaged in by members of our species.

As usual, relevant background information is crucial when we try to determine whether a sample is likely to be representative of the population from which it was drawn (or is likely to be sufficiently large, for that matter). Good reasoning *always* requires good background information.

4. QUESTIONABLE CAUSE

We commit the fallacy of **questionable cause** when we label something as the cause of something else on the basis of insufficient or unrepresentative evidence, or when doing so contradicts well-established, high-level theories.[1] (Questionable cause is a broader version of the traditional fallacy *post hoc, ergo propter hoc* (literally, "after this, therefore because of this"). Note that the fallacy questionable cause often overlaps that of hasty conclusion or of small sample.)

As just mentioned, it isn't easy to determine whether a sample is sufficiently large or representative. This is true in particular because judgments on these matters often depend on seeing the relevance of background information and *bringing it to bear.* All too often, people make judgments about causal connections on the basis of observed correlations, often quite small, that contradict very general, very well-confirmed, and quite easily understood higher-level theories about what sorts of causes can result in what kinds of effects. People often do so because they lack the relevant and *accurate* background information; sometimes they are motivated by wishful thinking to ignore contrary evidence or theories (a topic to be discussed at some length in the next chapter).

Many people have little or no understanding of the general way in which things work in this world. As they experience life, they don't try to figure out how things work in general or attempt to gain some of the knowledge that has been gleaned over time by

---

[1]This doesn't mean that these higher-level theories are exempt from refutation. Evidence that persistently runs contrary even to the highest-level, most general scientific theories eventually, and sometimes rather swiftly, overturns them, as, for example, old ideas about the motions of continents, and related matters, were overturned by evidence favoring the currently held theory concerning plate tectonics.

The Small Society. Reprinted by permission of the Washington Star Syndicate, Inc.

It isn't always easy to determine what is the cause of what.

others. Instead, they attend almost exclusively to immediate events and problems. They may see science as some kind of magical box from which gadgets like television sets, computers, and jet planes are extracted by bearded drudges with German accents, or by youthful nerds. Having relatively little background information to bring to bear on experience, they are unable to assess either the adequacy of evidence or the possibility that a general idea might be true. Think, for instance, of those who believe in ESP (extrasensory perception) despite the failure of every scientific test to confirm it.

Or consider the apparent rise in autism cases that certain groups have blamed on child immunizations, particularly the measles, mumps, and rubella vaccination (MMR).[2] They reason that since the rise in autism cases has coincided with an increase in recommended childhood vaccinations, certain vaccines must be the cause of autism in some children. The MMR immunization, given to toddlers between 15 and 17 months, comes at about the same time that parents begin to observe signs of autism. But this low-level reasoning fails to take into account the fact that autism typically begins to emerge at the end of the second year, whether the child is immunized or not, as rigorous scientific studies have shown. Yet the coincidental appearance of symptoms of autism at the time the vaccine is given, plus the media coverage of the plight of autistic children, have persuaded many people that vaccinations are the cause.

They continue to do so even after the original study, done in Great Britain, was roundly discredited and retracted by *Lancet*, the British medical journal that first published it. A 2010 analysis found "clear evidence of falsification of data," and the *British Medical Journal* called it an "elaborate fraud." The main author of the study, Dr. Andrew Wakefield, and his colleagues were charged with altering facts to suit their hypothesis, and Dr. Wakefield was stripped of the right to practice medicine in Great Britain. Yet many parents cling to their belief that childhood vaccines cause autism.

---

[2]For more on this see: Jacoby, Susan. *The Age of American Unreason.* New York: Pantheon Press, 2008. 219–220; and more specifically: Madsen, Kreesten, et al. "A Population-Based Study of Measles, Mumps, and Rubella Vaccination and Autism." *New England Journal of Medicine* 347 (November 7, 2002).

For many people, economics is just as baffling as the hard sciences. Critics were inclined to blame the second President Bush for the downturn in the economy during his last year in office. But the fact that the country slid into a recession during his last year doesn't prove that his policies caused the economy to slow down. True, his administration sank billions of dollars into the Iraq and Afghanistan Wars, but wars tend to stimulate the economy in the short run. (The long run is another matter, as future generations will discover when the tax burden to pay for these wars falls on them.) The reasons are more complex, and economists are still sorting them out, but one cause was certainly the crash of the bloated housing market. When the housing bubble burst in 2007, inflated real estate values sank like a stone, home foreclosures skyrocketed, the stock market skittered around, and the nation's largest financial institutions teetered on the brink of bankruptcy as they looked for bailouts from the government. But President Bush did not cause the chain reaction. Although his administration certainly contributed to it by reducing government oversight of the financial industry, the groundwork was laid by previous administrations that deregulated financial markets over a period of thirty years, allowing an unregulated shadow banking system of hedge funds and investment banks to evolve, bypassing the safety regulations imposed on traditional banks, and thus paving the way for the credit crisis in 2008.

For a brief period when Barack Obama took office, President Bush continued to take the heat for the weak economy, but as the recession deepened and unemployment rose, the blame shifted to Obama. Republicans hammered him for driving up the deficit; Democrats fought back with the charge that the deficit was a toxic legacy from Bush. In fact,

The
General Surgeon
has determined that breathing
is dangerous to your health.
This conclusion
was drawn from a survey
of 100 Canadian rats
that have died
within the past 5 years.
All were
habitual breathers.

Reprinted by permission of American Greetings Corporation, Cleveland, Ohio.

Greeting card humor illustrating some fallacy or other, no doubt.

both presidents increased federal spending extensively, but other factors they had little control over had greater influence—not the least of which was the massive hit to the federal budget from the loss of tax revenues as the recession bottomed out. Nonetheless, when it's time for elections, the sitting president in a bad economy usually is held responsible no matter what other forces are at work. The economic well-being of the United States depends on many complex factors, here and around the world, that a president does not and cannot control. This doesn't mean that, by promoting unsound economic policies, a president cannot be a part of the cause of an economic downturn. The point is that it is simplistic to give him or her the lion's share of the blame without further argument.

The fallacy questionable cause also sometimes is committed because items are incorrectly classified—poorly sorted into different kinds. Any items, no matter how different from one another, have some things in common, so that there always is some reason for grouping them together in our thoughts. When we classify items to discover cause/effect relationships, we need to make sure we have bunched together just the right sorts of cases. In some areas of the United States, for instance, a larger percentage of nonwhite children do poorly in school compared to students who are white, a fact that has led some people to conclude that being nonwhite is the *cause* of their doing less well in school (that there is a genetic difference involved here), an interesting and very serious example of the fallacy questionable cause.[3]

Research on gun control is a common source of questionable causation. One recent example is an analysis of the correlation between gun ownership and homicides in the 62 most urbanized counties in the United States.[4] The analysis was conducted for the *New York Times*, by Daniel Webster, codirector of the Johns Hopkins Center for Gun Policy and Research. Counties with higher rates of gun ownership had higher rates of homicide per capita (adjusting for age of residents). This finding suggests that effective gun control results in fewer homicides, but the man who conducted the analysis, Daniel Webster, pointed out that the correlation doesn't necessarily prove that gun control measures deserve the credit. Other factors may be involved, like increased police protection or citizen watch groups. To confuse matters further, gun law studies may contradict each other. For instance, several years ago the Center for Disease Control and Prevention reported that there wasn't enough evidence to conclude that gun control measures were effective at all. And the National Research Council could find no "causal relationship between the ownership of firearms and the causes or prevention of criminal violence or suicide" in an extensive 2004 study of the available research on this issue.

As might be expected, the statistical variety of questionable cause, in which a mere statistical correlation is taken to provide proof of a causal connection, is quite common.

---

[3]Notice that in the United States, nonwhite is an ethnic, not a racial, category. Most Americans who think of themselves as African-American are racially both of white (European) and African-American (African) descent; a few are of African and Asian stock; and a very few are descended from European, African, *and* Asian forebears (Tiger Woods being a well-known example). Similar remarks apply to members of many other groups. Mexican Americans, for example, tend to be descended from European (chiefly Spanish) and Asian forebears. Interestingly, the exact or even approximate place of origin of the Asian peoples who originally populated Mexico is hotly disputed by anthropologists and other scientists.

[4]Luo, Michael. "In Firearms Research, Cause is Often he Missing Element." *New York Times* 26 January 2011.

It's true that every statistical correlation has some significance and, in the absence of reasons to the contrary, increases the likelihood (probability), however slightly, that there also is a causal connection between the things correlated. But when there are reasons to the contrary, or when the statistical sample in question is too small or unrepresentative, we make a mistake in jumping to the conclusion that we've found a causal connection.

Sometimes alleged causal connections based on statistical surveys are too silly to take seriously, because they are so obviously contrary to well-supported background beliefs. An example is the theory that smoking marijuana causes college students to get better grades, based on one dubious statistical study in which marijuana smokers averaged slightly higher grades than nonsmokers. This theory actually gained modest acceptance in some, ah, "high"-minded circles during the 1970s. (And what are the background beliefs that should make you doubt smoking dope causes an increase in grades?)

5. QUESTIONABLE ANALOGY

We reason by *analogy* when we conclude from the observed similarity of two or more items in some respects to their similarity in another.[5] Sports fans, for example, may have reasoned by analogy when they concluded that the 2012 Olympic Games would be fun to watch, given that they were fun to watch in previous years. Caffeine lovers do so when they reason from the fact that coffee has kept them awake several nights in a row to the conclusion that drinking it again tonight will keep them awake.[6] The general form of such reasoning is that the items mentioned are alike in certain respects, so they will be alike in some other way.

But we aren't always justified in reasoning by analogy. When we do so anyway, we are guilty of the fallacy of **questionable analogy**, sometimes referred to as **faulty comparison**.

Analogical reasoning can be fallacious for several different reasons. The sample on which it is based may be too small or not sufficiently representative, it may conflict with conclusions drawn by higher-level reasoning, or there may be a lack of relevant similarity between the items implied to be alike. Here is an example based on a much too small sample:

> I've won at blackjack twice in a row by drawing a card when holding cards totaling 18, so I conclude by analogy that I'll win next time I draw on 18.

This analogy also is defective because it ignores the higher-level theory of probability, which says that your chances of success when drawing on 18 are quite low.

Some analogies seem to be apt on the surface but collapse under closer scrutiny. For instance, in an op-ed article for the *New York Times* (January 1, 2007), the historian Arthur Schlesinger, Jr., used this analogy to illustrate the folly of ignoring the lessons of

---

[5]Analogical reasoning thus is very similar to induction by enumeration. Indeed, the latter can be thought of as a kind of analogical reasoning.

[6]Recall, though, the earlier discussion of the fallacy questionable cause. It isn't easy to be positive that it's the coffee keeping us awake.

the past: "As persons deprived of memory become disoriented and lost, not knowing where they have been and where they are going, so a nation denied a conception of the past will be disabled in dealing with its present and its future." Although both examples deal with a loss of past experience, the first involves forgetting all experience, as Alzheimer's patients do, but the second involves ignoring past experience—quite a different phenomenon.

In some cases, the analogy is so wide of the mark that its questionable nature should be obvious. For example, after the prisoner abuse scandal at the Abu Ghraib prison, Saudi Arabian writer Daud al-Shiryan was quoted in the media saying, "This will increase the hatred of America, not just in Iraq but abroad. . . .Abu Ghraib was used for torture in Saddam's time. People will ask now what's the difference between Saddam and Bush. Nothing!" President Bush didn't authorize the prison abuse, to begin with, and the abuse that did occur, though bad enough in its own right, was in no way comparable to the torture and killing that went on under Hussein.

Not uncommonly, questionable analogies surface in a court of law. In 2003, many American tourists were annoyed to discover that credit card companies were charging a currency conversion fee for items purchased abroad. One irate customer filed suit against Visa and MasterCard for intentionally hiding the fee from cardholders. The attorney for MasterCard argued, "That's not hiding, that's not concealing—that's how business is done in this country." The defense went on to explain that "while consumers naturally understand that commercial suppliers of goods and services impose a mark-up over their costs, the proposed decision would condemn as 'embedding' the standard practice that a seller tells its customer its price to them, not which part of the price reflects its cost and which part its mark-up." However, to compare hidden credit card fees to the undisclosed markup of commercial goods is certainly questionable. The consumer knows the cost of an item in a retail store because it is clearly marked on the price tag, but when using a credit card abroad, the consumer has no idea of the total amount because of the hidden conversion fee.

In 2009, Congress passed the Credit Card Accountability Responsibility and Disclosure Act, requiring companies to disclose hidden fees on foreign transactions, among other things. But those crafty bankers figured out how to transform and bury that fee by redefining the term *foreign*. Now it includes any transaction that touches a foreign bank, even if the entire exchange takes place in U.S. dollars—like booking foreign flights on domestic planes through online travel sites. And now *that's* how business is done.

Some analogies are easily seen to be fallacious, others as clearly apt. But the evaluations of still others often require a good deal of thought. Consider this analogy in a letter to the editor arguing against stricter handgun control laws: When a drunk driver runs over a child, we go after the driver, not the car. When someone kills a child with a gun, we go after the gun. But shouldn't we go after the person who murders with a gun, not the gun itself? In this case, there clearly is a relevant resemblance between the two cases—killing with a car or with a gun—so there is something to the analogy. But there also are important differences, as there often are, and the question is whether they are both relevant and sufficient to make the analogy questionable. For example, private autos are an extremely important kind of transportation in our society; banning their use would dramatically change all sorts of things in everyday life. Handguns serve few legitimate purposes in private hands; AK-47s and the like, none at all. Restricting their use would make relatively little difference in most of our lives. Furthermore, most auto deaths result from accidents or negligence, rarely from deliberate intent to murder. Guns frequently are used deliberately to murder other people. Note that the letter writer omits the fact that, when people use guns for nefarious purposes, we go after the gun user as well as the gun itself, and also the fact that we outlaw autos believed to be unsafe to drive. The point of all of this is that we don't want to label analogies questionable, or apt, too quickly; in some cases, we need to consider all sorts of factors. Good critical reasoners need to become adept at bringing background information to bear when evaluating analogies, just as most other sorts of reasoning.

This example also illustrates the difficulty in bringing one's relevant background beliefs to bear when evaluating an argument. All of the relevant differences just mentioned are common knowledge, yet we often fail to bring information of this kind to bear when evaluating an argument. (Did you in this case?)

Before turning to a discussion of other fallacies, perhaps it should be noted that we need to distinguish between *explanatory* analogies used to explain and *argumentative* analogies used to prove a point. When we argue or reason analogically, we present evidence for a conclusion; when we use an analogy to explain, we merely liken the thing explained to something already familiar. In Plato's famous analogy of the cave, for example, the people in the cave who merely see the shadows of things are likened to those who restrict themselves to the ever-changing world of everyday experience, while the people who come out into the sunlight and see the objects themselves are likened to the philosophers who reason to the unchanging reality that lies behind everyday experiences. The analogy explains Plato's ideas about a world beyond that of mere everyday experiences, but it doesn't prove that there is such a world or in any way argue that there is. (Plato himself very likely intended his cave myth to be explanatory, not argumentative, but it often is construed otherwise.)

The point here is that we shouldn't accuse those whose analogies are intended to explain of being guilty of the fallacy questionable analogy. (They may, of course, serve very poorly to explain, but that is another matter.) Anyway, as just remarked, explanatory analogies sometimes are mistakenly taken to prove what they merely explain, and in this case, we are indeed justified in accusing those who do this of the fallacy questionable analogy.

Finally, we need to notice that, in everyday life, it often is difficult to determine whether an analogy is intended to explain or to prove; no doubt some are intended to serve both purposes. In any case, as with explanations in general, it is hard to separate the mere explanatory nature of an analogy from its power to persuade. (Recall, for example, the salesperson's explanation about cameras in Chapter 1, where the intent was to persuade a customer to buy a camera, not merely to explain the differences between one camera and another.)

6. QUESTIONABLE STATISTICS

Statistics always seem so precise and *authoritative*. It sounds so much more believable, for instance, to claim that the typical child watches an average of 4,286 acts of violence on TV by age 18 rather than just that kids typically watch an awful lot of TV violence. But how could anyone know such an exact fact? There would have to be a lot of guesswork and extrapolation from very small samples to arrive even at an informed rough estimate as to these sorts of matters. This doesn't mean that we ought simply to dismiss these statistics; it just means that we have to understand their limitations.

Statistics on the state of the economy are a case in point. Take the ones published by the federal government on business conditions in the United States. One of the major problems with these statistics is that their *margin of error* (not always provided) often is greater than the "significant" differences they report. This becomes evident when we consider that the government's later revisions of its own figures often reflect a change larger than the alleged margin of error.

In addition, problems arise from the need to use a base year in determining long-run trends. Those who want to show that a given year has had a high rate of growth can choose a low base year; those intent on proving a low rate of growth, a high base year. Meanwhile, the precisely true rate of growth may remain in doubt.

In the case of figures concerning the gross national product, we have several other reasons for being suspicious. One is that a good deal of commerce in the United States today is illegal. Think only of racketeering, gambling, drug traffic, prostitution, and the hiring of illegal aliens to do migrant farm labor or household cleaning and other low-paying, tedious, and often backbreaking jobs. Reliable statistics concerning illegal activities are by their nature hard to come by. Calculating, say, the commerce in illegal drugs has to be done indirectly, by reference to the sale of legal drug equipment, drug busts, and so on. Another reason for suspicion is that a good deal of otherwise legal commerce is done "off the books," so that no taxes need to be paid or so that restrictive laws can be avoided. How are we to assess the value of goods when one kind is bartered for another?

Statistics on corrupt activities are just as hard to come by, particularly in a country like Russia, where corruption is endemic and bribery is the norm rather than the exception (Russians shell out bribes for all manner of things, from paying off traffic cops to getting better medical treatment.) So when Transparency International, a group monitoring corruption, estimated that corruption in Russia had grown sevenfold from 2001 to 2006, or that the value of bribes paid to bureaucrats was almost equal to the country's revenue in a given year, we have to assume that these are little more than guess-timates. The same goes for estimates made by INDEM, an independent Russian think tank, that businesses in Russia spend 7 percent of their budget on bribes.[7] How is it possible to come up with these statistics when bribery, by its very nature, usually occurs under the table?

Sometimes statistics are based on soft information and are thus questionable. For years, doctors have urged us to reduce our intake of fatty foods, but a 2006 study funded by the Women's Health Initiative (WHI) seemed to contradict this advice. The study—following 48,835 women aged 50–79 for an average of 8.1 years—revealed no significant statistical difference in the rates of colorectal cancer, heart disease, or stroke between the group on the low-fat diet and the comparison group on the normal diet. But the study was problematic because the data were drawn from the participants' memories of what they ate—sometimes up to a year earlier! (Do you remember what you ate last week, let alone a year ago?) Evidence that their memories were unreliable becomes

---

[7]See: Mainville, Michael. "Bribery Thrives as Big Business in Putin's Russia." *San Francisco Chronicle* 2 January 2007.

clearer when we consider this finding: Women who weighed 170 pounds on average claimed they consumed 1,700 calories a day at the beginning of the study and 1,500 calories at the end. Yet these women lost only 1 pound over many years in the WHI study.[8] How could that be? Either their memories were faulty or they were shaving off calories. More likely, they consumed 500–700 more calories a day than they reported. Given the apparent unreliability of these reports, it is questionable that low-fat diets fail to protect women from certain illnesses. No matter, this dubious science made headlines and probably allowed many women to rationalize eating the fatty foods they craved.

The government's figures on unemployment also need to be viewed with a good deal of suspicion. These figures are calculated partly on the basis of information gathered via polls of "representative" individuals. How these people respond depends on the precise wording of the questions they are asked (a point soon to be discussed further), and this in part depends on what the government considers to be full-time, compared to part-time, employment, and who is said to be seeking employment, compared to those who have given up the search. (It also depends on how truly representative the government's samples happen to be.) Early in 2012, for instance, the Obama administration was upbeat about the drop in unemployment from a dismal 8.9% in October 2011, to a slightly less dismal 8.3% in January 2012. But that report was based on people out of work for less than a year, and didn't reflect the rate of those out of work for over a year. The total percent of the unemployed, plus workers who wanted full-time jobs but had to settle for part-time, is 15.1%, nearly double the amount cited. Of course, it is to the advantage of every administration to quote the official rate of the Bureau of Labor Statistics (BLS), which is the lowest, but all you have to do is check out the unemployment figures released monthly by the BLS to get a more accurate picture of the various categories and percentages of people out of work in this country.

All of this certainly does not mean that government statistics on commerce and employment should be tossed into the nearest wastebasket. But it does mean that precise official figures should be taken for what they are: the best *approximations* we have of business activity—valuable primarily in showing very-long-term trends, but often calculated so as to serve short-term political interests.

By way of contrast, consider a correctly cautious claim typical of those frequently made by scientists (*Science News,* January 19, 1991): Scientists using sophisticated techniques to determine the age of ancient cliff drawings in west Texas estimated that the drawings were painted "3,865 years ago, *give or take a century*" (italics added).

Finally, it's important to have some idea as to which sorts of statistics can be known, even in theory. Some statistics simply are unknowable. Here is a letter one of the authors of this text received several years ago that contains examples of unknowable statistics it would be hard to top:

> Dear Friend: In the past 5,000 years men have fought in 14,523 wars. One out of four persons living during this time have been war casualties. A nuclear war would add 1,245,000,000 men, women, and children to this tragic list.

---

[8]For more on this see: Ness, Carol. "Down to a Science." *San Francisco Chronicle,* 16 March 2006.

It's ludicrous to present such precise figures as facts. No one knows (or could know) the exact number of wars fought so far, to say nothing of the number of war casualties. (Does anyone even know the true casualty rates just for all of the wars that have occurred in the past ten years?) As for the numbers in a nuclear conflict, the casualty rate would depend on who fought such a war, and, in any event, it is a matter on which even so-called experts can engage in only the wildest sorts of speculations.

7. QUESTIONABLE USES OF GOOD STATISTICS

As we've just seen, statistics that are obviously questionable are a problem. But perfectly good statistics also can cause trouble—for two reasons. The first is the inability of so many people to understand the significance of this statistic or that, made worse by the natural tendency in all of us to pay attention to statistics that support conclusions we already have drawn. The second is the ability of charlatans to bamboozle the rest of us via cleverly employed statistics. (That's the import of the old saying that figures don't lie, but liars figure.)

Since the No Child Left Behind Act was adopted by Congress, statistical shenanigans have abounded. In order to satisfy the mandate that students be proficient in reading and math by 2014, some educators have made creative use of statistics to show how well their schools are doing. Because the law allowed each state to develop its own standards and tests, the temptation to lower standards and inflate grades proved irresistible. In 2005, nearly 85% of New York fourth graders tested proficient in math on state tests, but only 36% on national exams. In Georgia, 87% of fourth graders met state proficiency standards in reading, but only 26% on national tests.[9] These examples reflect a national trend in redefining proficiency. A 2009 federal study found that from 2005–7, fifteen states lowered their proficiency standards in reading or math tests for fourth and eighth graders.[10]

In 2011, President Obama made a special point in his State of the Union address of praising Bruce Randolf School of Denver for graduating 97% of its first senior class, a triumph for a school once considered one of the worst in Colorado. (The high school had been added to the low ranking middle school.)[11] But it turned out that when a researcher at Louisiana State University examined the data, he found that yes, indeed, 97% of the senior class had graduated, but ACT test scores were far below average and thus most students were not prepared for college. So the high rate of graduation really meant that standards were lowered to allow more students to graduate. When the stakes are high, it's tempting to make statistics lie.

Then there are the politicians who made much of the fact that in 2011, 47% of Americans did not pay federal income tax. While this statistic is accurate according to the Tax Policy Center, it is misleading because some politicians misinterpret it to mean that almost half the people in this country pay no taxes at all. In fact, the great majority do pay other taxes. Nearly 90% of nontaxpaying households earn low incomes that exempt

---

[9]Ravitch, Diane. "Every State Left Behind." *New York Times* 7 November 2005.

[10]Dillon, Sam. "Federal Researchers Find Lower Standards in Schools." *New York Times* 29 October 2009.

[11]Diane Ravitch, "Waiting for a School Miracle," the *New York Times*, June 1, 2011.

them from federal taxes, but not from payroll and excise taxes, nor state and local income taxes, nor sales and property taxes.[12] So when politicians complain that half the population is getting a free ride, they are wrong. It is simply a ploy to con the public into thinking that nontaxpayers are scamming the system

The misuse of statistics is just as common in economics as it is in education and politics. For instance, a libertarian defending the current economy on a radio talk show claimed that less than 10 percent of Americans used to own stocks, but now up to 45 to 50 percent do. Thus, an ordinary wage earner who saves can take part in the increase in wealth the stock market provides. Although his figures are about right, he neglects two important points. First, the 45 to 50 percent includes retirement funds invested by companies, not individuals—the ordinary earner simply draws a pension from the invested fund. Second, a tiny portion of stockholders own most of the stock and get rich, and the gap between the rich and the rest of us has been getting a good deal larger.

Another example, the Death Penalty Information Center indicated that from 1990 to 2006, the murder rate was higher in states with the death penalty than in those without it. Those opposed to the death penalty on grounds that it does not deter homicides take this to be evidence supporting that conclusion.

But sophisticated critical reasoners wondered whether doing so made them guilty of the fallacy questionable cause (or perhaps hasty conclusion?). For it very well may be that states with death penalties had a higher rate of murder to start with and that perhaps they opted for this harsh penalty to try to reduce the amount of serious crime. To prove their point, those opposed to the death penalty on these grounds would have to present statistics showing that serious crime remained the same, or increased, after a death penalty was imposed in particular states. Otherwise, the comparison is of apples and oranges. (Remember that the number of serious crimes tends to increase in hard economic times and decreases in good.)

8. Polls: An Important Special Case

A well-conceived and well-executed poll can be a fruitful way to find out all sorts of things, from the voter strength of a political candidate to Fido's preferences in dog food. Unfortunately, not all polls are created equal.

One problem is that the way in which a question is asked seriously influences the answers one can expect. It is extremely difficult, if not impossible, to word a question in a way that is completely neutral. At the height of the Watergate scandal, for instance, a Gallup poll asked the question:

> Do you think President Nixon should be impeached and compelled to leave the presidency, or not?

Thirty percent said yes. But a Pat Caddell private poll asked the question this way:

> Do you think the President should be tried, and removed from office if found guilty?

---

[12]Williams, Roberton. "Why Do People Pay No Federal Income Tax?" Tax Policy Center of the Urban Institute and Brookings Institution. Web. 27 July 2011.

Fifty-seven percent answered yes to that one. So 30 percent answered yes to the question worded one way, 57 percent when the same question was put another way.

Information left out of questions can skew poll results enormously. Here, for example, are two different questions on late-term abortion that had radically different responses.[13] An ABC poll asked "Do you think the late-term abortion procedure known as dilation and extraction, or partial birth abortion, should be legal or illegal?" Sixty-two percent said "illegal." But a follow-up question was asked, adding additional information. "What if it would prevent a serious threat to the woman's health?" Only 33 percent responded "illegal" to this question.

Statistics seem to baffle almost everyone. Several years ago, when 200 educators were asked what percentage of children read at grade level or below, 78 percent failed to provide the correct answer—50 percent. Even teachers have a hard time keeping straight on the difference between comparative and absolute scales.

Another comparative rating that causes confusion is the IQ rating: Half of those who take the test must be rated at 100 or below, given that 100 merely marks the halfway point in results.

Cartoon by Tom Meyer © *San Francisco Chronicle.* Reprinted by permission.

---

[13]Quoted in "Framing the Abortion Issue." *Extra!,* July/August 2007.

The importance of framing the issue has not escaped those intent on skewing poll results one way or the other. Here, for example, are a couple of loaded question in the "2000 Official NRA Gun Owners Survey":

> Do you think gun owner names should be subject to surprise inspection by the Bureau of Alcohol, Tobacco, and Firearms?

> Do you think gun owners like you should be required to pay expensive liability insurance for every gun you own?

What gun owners in their right minds would answer "yes" to these questions?

Of course, when it comes to slanted poll questions, the Democratic and Republican Parties take a back seat to no one. Here is an example from the 2010 mailings conducted by the Republican National Committee:

> Do you believe that the best way to increase the quality and effectiveness of public education in the U.S. is to rapidly expand federal funding while eliminating performance standards and accountability?

What voters would answer "yes" to this question?

The biggest problem with polls, though, is the difficulty of tapping a truly representative sample. The 1936 *Literary Digest* poll, based on names lifted from telephone directories and auto registration lists, is perhaps the most famous example of an extremely biased poll. It predicted that Alf Landon would defeat Franklin Roosevelt, while the actual result was a tremendous landslide for Roosevelt. The magazine (which went out of business shortly afterward—questionable cause?) failed to take into account the fact that few people in the bottom half of the American population had telephones or autos in those days, so that their sample was completely unrepresentative of American voters.

Of course, the art of polling has come a long way since 1936, or even 1948, when polls predicted an easy victory for Thomas E. Dewey over Harry Truman. The *Chicago Tribune*—whose motto, incidentally, was and still is "The World's Greatest Newspaper"— was so sure Dewey would win that it grossly misinterpreted early returns and printed one of the most infamous headlines in newspaper history—"Dewey Defeats Truman"—which an exultant Truman held up to the crowd at his victory celebration.

But it still is difficult to get a representative sample of the voting population by polling only 1,500 or so potential voters—the standard practice today. In theory, a very carefully selected sample of roughly this size should be almost as reliable as one of 15,000 (a poll of this size would be much too expensive and is never conducted). But in practice, for all sorts of reasons, things frequently don't work as planned. This doesn't mean that we should not pay attention to polls. They often are the best or even the only way we have of testing the water. It just means we have to pay heed to them in an intelligent manner. A presidential election poll taken in September is of much less value, other things being equal, than one conducted in October; polls paid for by one side or the other are worth less than those conducted by truly independent organizations. But most important, we have to remember that even the best polls have a batting average well below 100 percent.

Presidential polls were particularly tricky in 2012. Starting with the run-up to the Republican primaries early in 2011, the public ranked candidates from lukewarm to poor. So things got off to a pretty dismal start. But once the Super Pacs began pouring in money (thanks to Citizens United), each new candidate soared to the top. One month it was Mitt Romney, then Michelle Bachmann, Herman Cain, Rick Perry, Newt Gingrich, and Rick Santorum—with Ron Paul bopping in and out. The media dubbed each one the flavor of the month. And so it continued—forever, it seemed. In almost none of the polls did the public show any enthusiasm for the odds-on favorite, Mitt Romney, but ever so slowly he built his delegate base. Polls were taken daily, yet none of them could predict the Republican candidate for months. (One can only imagine how gleeful the Obama administration was over this chaotic state of affairs.) This state of affairs continued right up to the election—with Barack Obama and Mitt Romney roughly tied in the final days. In an election that close, even the most sophisticated polls couldn't predict Obama's victory.

Note, by the way, that there is no such thing as a "poll fallacy," even though, as just illustrated, polls do give rise to fallacies such as questionable statistics and hasty conclusions.

9. FALSE CHARGE OF FALLACY

It often is all too easy to charge others with fallacious reasoning. This is particularly true when people change their minds and embrace positions they previously denied. The temptation is to charge them with the fallacy of inconsistency. But making a given statement at one time and one that contradicts it at a later time does not necessarily indicate inconsistency; we may have good grounds for changing our minds.

Take the person who says, "I used to believe that women are not as creative as men, because most of the intellectually productive people I knew about were men; but I've changed my mind, because I believe now (as I didn't then) that environment (culture, surroundings), not native ability, has been responsible for the preponderance of intellectual men." Surely, that person cannot be accused of the fallacy of inconsistency, since he (or she!) has explained the change of mind.

Anyway, in good textbook style, let's say that those who falsely accuse others of fallacy are themselves guilty of making a **false charge of fallacy**.

Of course, falsely accusing someone of inconsistency is not the only way in which someone might be guilty of false charge of fallacy. Recall, for example, the earlier discussion of the distinction between analogical reasoning and explanatory analogies; clearly, we are guilty of making a false charge of fallacy if we accuse someone of perpetrating a questionable analogy when his or her intent is not to prove something but merely, via an analogy, to explain it.

We are also guilty of falsely charging someone with a fallacy when we take literally an ironic jab at the opposition. In the following letter to the editor, for example, the writer clearly intends to be ironic:

> Billions of dollars and two decades later, the War on Drugs has successfully eliminated illegal drugs from the face of America. The country is finally free of pot, coke, and heroin. With this as a model, the War on Junk Guns is bound to be successful.

Claiming that the writer is guilty of questionable premise or suppressed evidence because the War on Drugs hasn't eradicated illegal drugs clearly constitutes a false charge of fallacy. The letter writer just employs sarcasm to remind us ironically that the War on Drugs has been a failure.

Exercise item from the second edition of a certain textbook on logic and contemporary rhetoric:

Newspaper story: Thor Heyerdahl has done it again, crossing the Atlantic in a papyrus raft designed according to ancient Egyptian tomb carvings. Landing in the Western Hemisphere on the island of Barbados, he was greeted by the Barbados prime minister, Errol Barrow, who declared, "This has established Barbados was the first landing place for man in the Western World."

This was a very un-PC remark by Barrow, but that is not the point here. The point is that the correct answer to this exercise item was supposed to be hasty conclusion, *but a student from Barbados pointed out that the prime minister was known for his sense of humor. Another false charge of fallacy, this time by the (here nameless) author of the critical reasoning textbook in question.*

Note, by the way, that some of the alleged fallacies that have been discussed in logic textbooks since time immemorial are not generally fallacious, at least according to the criteria set up in this text. Take the fallacy called ***appeal to force*** (traditional name: *argumentum ad baculum*—"argument to the cudgel," or "appeal to the stick"), committed, it is said, when a conclusion is accepted after a threat of force of one kind or another. Lawmakers, for instance, sometimes are charged with commission of this fallacy when they are convinced to vote a certain way by the implied threats of lobbyists to stop the flow of campaign contributions.

But legislators whose arms are twisted in this way generally are not guilty of a fallacy—the arm twisting doesn't convince them of the merits or demerits of particular legislation but rather of the personal (career) benefits to be gained by voting as lobbyists "suggest" they should. We need to know here, though, that self-interest frequently motivates people, lawmakers included, to believe what they otherwise would see to be false. More is said in Chapter 6 about the power of self-interest to influence beliefs.

Quibbling

When deciding whether someone has or has not committed a fallacy, we don't want to **quibble**. We don't want to take advantage, for instance, of the fact that life is short, and, in everyday life, we don't usually bother to spell out every detail. Some things can, and should, be taken for granted.

Consider the American Medical Association (AMA) ad that stated:

100,000 doctors have quit smoking.
Maybe they know something you don't.

Students have called this ad fallacious because, among other reasons, it suppresses evidence as to what kind of doctors have quit. ("Maybe it was horse doctors." "They don't say if they were doctors of medicine.") But this sort of response amounts to nothing better than quibbling. It resembles the remark of a student who objected to Shakespeare's wonderful line, "He jests at scars, that never felt a wound" (*Romeo and Juliet*), on grounds that *he* (the student) had felt a wound—a mere scratch—and still jested at scars. (Other students have objected to the line on the grounds that Shakespeare incorrectly used *that* instead of *who,* but they [the students!] were guilty of another, grammatical sort of quibbling—to say nothing of hubris, in having the temerity to "correct" the grammar of someone who may well be the greatest writer to ever work in the English language.)

This (finally!) concludes our discussion of fallacies, unfortunately restricted to just a few of the more common varieties that have been discussed in one place or another in the literature. While it is useful to become adept at aptly applying specific names to cases of fallacious reasoning, the point of acquiring this skill, after all, is to learn how to improve one's own reasoning and to be better able to spot the fallacious reasoning of others. Remember, though, that what counts is not the ability to apply a label to poor reasoning. Labels certainly are useful in getting adept at spotting bad arguments, but seeing that they are bad and understanding why they are bad is the name of the game.

In any case, we will soon see that spotting fallacies is only part of the larger enterprise of evaluating more complicated passages containing related arguments that are intended to form a coherent whole. *Extended arguments* of this kind—argumentative essays—are discussed in Chapters 8 and 9.

SUMMARY OF CHAPTER 5

1. *Hasty conclusion:* Accepting an argument on the basis of relevant but insufficient information or evidence. *Example:* Sherlock Holmes's conclusion that Dr. Watson was an army man just back from Afghanistan.

2. *Small sample:* Drawing conclusions about a population on the basis of a sample that is too small to be a reliable measure of that population. *Example:* Conclusions drawn about primate mating habits based on a sample of three human couplings, a gibbon mating, and those of one troop of baboons.

3. *Unrepresentative sample:* Reasoning from a sample that is not representative (typical) of the population from which it was drawn. *Example:* The sample of primates just mentioned.

4. *Questionable cause:* Labeling A as the cause of B on evidence that is insufficient, negative, unrepresentative, or in serious conflict with well-established high-level theories. *Example:* Blaming President Bush or President Obama for the downturn in the economy when other, more complex factors are at work.

5. *Questionable analogy:* Drawing an analogical conclusion when the cases compared are not relevantly alike. *Example:* Comparing Bush to Hussein in the prisoner abuse scandal at Abu Ghraib.

6. *Questionable statistics:* Employing statistics that are questionable without further support. *Example:* Accepting government statistics on short-term business trends as completely accurate rather than just educated approximations.

Extreme example: Employing unknowable statistics about how many wars have been fought in the past 5,000 years and how many casualties there have been.

Note, by the way, that the quality of statistics sometimes differs a great deal from time to time and place to place.

7. *Questionable uses of statistics:* Perfectly good statistics also sometimes are a problem—for two reasons. The first is the inability of so many people to under-stand the significance of this statistic or that, made worse by the natural ten-dency in all of us to see statistics as favoring conclusions we already have drawn. The second is the ability of charlatans to bamboozle the rest of us via cleverly employed statistics. *Example:* Accepting evidence that the murder rate in states that have adopted a death penalty for serious crimes is higher than in states that have not done so as proof that the death penalty does not deter crime, without further evidence that this statistical evidence has a causal foundation; it could well be, for example, that states adopting death penalties had even higher murder rates than other states and have adopted a death penalty in an attempt to do something about that unfortunate fact.

8. *Polls:* Although polls are an important source of information, they need to be dealt with cautiously. Polls can be misleading (1) because of the way in which questions are worded—often deliberately to obtain the desired statistics; (2) because they ask the wrong questions; (3) because respondents don't want to appear ignorant, immoral, odd, or prejudiced; or (4) because they are based on a sample that is too small or unrepresentative. *Example:* The NRA survey asking loaded questions skewed to get negative responses to government control of gun owners.

9. *False charge of fallacy:* Erroneously accusing others of fallacious reasoning. *Example:* Accusing someone of fallacy who has changed his mind about the lack of creativity of women in the light of contrary evidence.

Note that ironic rhetoric that, if taken literally, would be fallacious, may well not be. Note also that we don't want to be overly critical of the reasoning of others to the point that we are guilty of *quibbling*.

Some of the alleged fallacies that have been handed down to us in logic textbooks often are not fallacious. For example, legislators who vote so as to satisfy lobbyists are not usually guilty of the fallacy of appeal to force: They become convinced by the implied threats of the lobbyists to vote as "suggested" because of self-interest, not because they change their minds about the merits of the legislation. Sad.

EXERCISE 5-1

1. In the wake of terrorist attacks across Europe, the French National Assembly passed a law banning the Islamic burqa and niqab—full body veils that mask the identity of the wearer. This legislation provoked a wave of protests in groups ranging from civil rights activists to Muslim extremists. In defense of the law, Jean-Francois Cope, the majority leader in the French Assembly, argued that covering the face poses a serious threat to public safety, particularly now that

security cameras are commonly used to identify criminals.[14] As evidence, he cited a recent case in which criminals dressed in burqas committed armed robbery in a Paris suburb. He said that the French are "passionately attached" to individual liberty, but that sometimes they must compromise for the greater public good. To make his point, he argued that a U.S. law prohibiting people "from strolling down Fifth Avenue in the nude does not constitute an attack on the fundamental rights of nudists. Likewise, wearing headgear that fully covers the face does not constitute a fundamental liberty." Rather, it undermines the common good of the community.

Identify the fallacies in this passage and explain them.

2. The National Science Foundation reported that two different polls conducted by telephone two weeks apart came up with much different results on the question of whether Americans support embryonic stem cell research—even through the pollsters used similar methodologies.[15] The Coalition for the Advancement of Medical Research (CAMR) found that nearly 75 percent of Americans supported this type of research, but a poll conducted two weeks later by the United States Conference of Catholic Bishops (USCCB) reported that "48 percent of Americans oppose federal funding of stem cell research that requires destroying human embryos." Only 39 percent approved. Why were the results so different? The answer is in the way the questions were framed.

CAMR question: I'm going to read you a brief description of embryonic stem cell research, and then get your reaction. Embryonic stem cells are special cells that can develop into every type of cell in the human body. The stem cells are extracted from embryonic cells produced in fertility clinics and then frozen days after fertilization. If a couple decides that the fertilized eggs are no longer needed, they can choose to donate the embryos for research or the clinic will throw the embryos away. Scientists have had success in initial research with embryonic stem cells and believe that they can be developed into cures for diseases such as cancer, Parkinson's, heart disease, juvenile diabetes, and spinal cord injuries. Having heard this description, do you strongly favor, somewhat favor, somewhat oppose, or strongly oppose medical research that uses stem cells from human embryos?

USCCB question: Stem cells are the basic cells from which all of a person's tissues and organs develop. Congress is considering the question of federal funding for experiments using stem cells from human embryos. The live embryos would be destroyed in their first week of development to obtain these cells. Do you support or oppose using your federal tax dollars for such experiments?

Evaluate the way the issue is framed in each question and explain how the questions influenced the survey results.

---

[14] Cope, Jean-Francois. "Tearing Away the Veil." *New York Times* 5 May 2010.
[15] For further discussion see "Public Attitudes about S & T [Science and Technology] in General," http://nsf.gov/statistics/, (2006).

3. Here is a paraphrase of a letter to the editor of the *Nutrition Action Health Letter:*

I am a diabetic who has found the artificial sweetener NutraSweet to be "a total nightmare." I thought it would be a good substitute for sugar [diabetics have to severely limit their intake of sugar]. But when I started using it, I began to have serious headaches that my doctor could not account for. So under my doctor's supervision, I stopped using NutraSweet and my headaches stopped. Going back onto NutraSweet was followed by a renewal of my headaches. I did this back and forth three times and the scenario was the same each time: "no NutraSweet, no headache; NutraSweet, headache."

Do you agree with the unstated implication of this letter—that taking the NutraSweet was the cause of the headaches? Defend your answer against likely objections.

4. Comment on this quote (attributed to Rush Limbaugh) from an ad urging people to join the National Organization for Women. "What if a man claimed the right to rape using the same principle found in the theory that it is his body and he has the right to choose?"

5. Earlier in this chapter, we questioned the use of Death Penalty Information Center (DPIC) statistics concerning the death penalty to show that that extreme form of punishment does not deter crime more than lesser penalties. What about a *Harper's Index* item indicating that the chances of a white teenager arrested on a drug charge being tried in adult court, rather than a juvenile court, are about 1 in 70, while for blacks the chances are 1 in 18? Is the implied conclusion that black teenage offenders are discriminated against compared to whites justified on the basis of this evidence?

*6. Comment on the following statistic listed in the November 2000 *Harper's Index:* Points by which the average SAT score of a home-schooled student exceeds that of other United States students—81.

EXERCISE 5-2

Determine which fallacies (if any) occur in the following short passages and justify your answers (as you did when working on Exercises 3-1 and 4-1). (Note again that some of these passages may also contain fallacies discussed in previous chapters and some *may not* contain fallacious reasoning.)

*1. In the run-up debate to the 2012 Republican primaries, Michelle Bachmann denounced Texas governor Rick Perry for issuing an order requiring Texas school girls to be vaccinated against a sexually transmitted virus. In a follow-up interview, she linked the vaccine to mental illness when she told the story of a distraught woman who approached her after the debate claiming that the shot had

---

* Starred (*) items are answered in a section at the back of the book.

left her daughter mentally retarded. Bachmann concluded with a warning that Perry was forcing young girls to receive "an injection of what could be potentially a very dangerous drug."

2. The *New York Times* (January 20, 2005) reported that Germaine Greer, a well-known Australian feminist and literary scholar, quit the cast of *Celebrity Big Brothers,* a British reality show, after only five days. On this program celebrities are confined in a house where they interact with one another while viewers vote on who should go or stay. Greer complained that contestants were encouraged to bully, living conditions were poor, food was stale, and towels were filthy. Even worse, she claimed that they were subjected to "lockdowns" in their bedrooms, where they were prohibited from eating, using the bathroom, or sleeping. When other contestants refused to join her revolt against *Big Brothers* thought police, she quit in disgust and denounced the show as a "fascist prison camp."

3. From a Bob Schwabach "On Computers" newspaper column: "There aren't just a couple of brands [of IBM-compatible computers] for those [very low] prices; there are dozens. Do they work? Someone I know has been running one continuously for five months, and it's never missed a beat."

4. During the wars in Afghanistan and Iraq, the U.S. government placed a value on human lives that suffered wrongful deaths caused by the U.S. military and made "condolence payments" to family members. They did the same for Americans killed in al Qaeda attacks on September 11, 2001. Here are some statistics on the worth of human life taken from "A Scale for the Price of Life," by Tom Engelhardt (*San Francisco Chronicle* 20 May 2007).

   A civilian killed in Haditha, Iraq, by U.S. Marines: $2,500.

   A civilian killed near Jalalabad, Afghanistan, by U.S. Marines: $2,000.

   A civilian killed by al Qaeda terrorists on September 11: $1.8 million.

5. Smoking pot definitely leads to heroin use. A report by the U.S. Commissioner of Narcotics on a study of 2,213 hard-core narcotics addicts in the Lexington (Kentucky) Federal Hospital shows that 70.4 percent smoked marijuana before taking heroin.

6. In the Supreme Court's hearing on the constitutionality of the Affordable Health Care Act, the question of whether people can legally be required to buy health care insurance or pay a penalty was argued at length. One reason in favor of the law was that the mandate simply regulates how people pay for healthcare services they are virtually certain to use at some time in their lives. To which Justice Scalia replied, "Everybody has to buy food sooner or later, so you define the market as food. Therefore everybody is in the market. Therefore, you can make people buy broccoli."

7. From a student essay: "It is wrong to criticize advertisers for manipulating people through psychological ploys because that's what makes ads effective."

8. Overheard in a local bar: "You women are wrong to be for censoring pornography, even if it's true, and I'm pretty sure it isn't, that porno stuff makes a few men more likely to rape. Would you want to ban miniskirts, bikini outfits, low-cut dresses, and such—require women to wear Muslim-style outfits—if it's true that scanty clothes make some men more likely to rape?"

9. Donna Brazile, Democratic strategist, had this to say about women in politics (quoted in the *San Francisco Chronicle* 4 August 2010)":

   "If we had more women in politics this country would be farther ahead—because women are not afraid to ask for directions when they're lost."

10. A disgusted baseball fan on hearing about Barry Bonds's alleged use of performance-enhancing drugs: "They ought to let him play ball. The next thing you know, they'll be taking away records from people because they had an extra bowl of Cheerios." (*San Francisco Chronicle* 2 September 2006)

11. The president of a college who shall go unnamed here justifying the reduction of salaries for adjunct (part-time) teachers who are paid only 75 percent of the rate paid to full-time staff per course: "I don't see the problem here. No other college in the state pays more than we do."

12. Comment in *Time* article (14 May 2001) by Tom Green, a self-proclaimed fundamentalist Mormon, who was indicted in Utah on four counts of bigamy: "Mormons say polygamy is immoral and wrong, but the church was founded by polygamists. That is hypocrisy."

*13. Simon Cowell, of American Idol fame, commenting on Piers Morgan's qualifications to replace Larry King as CNN talk host:

   "Piers is interested in people and that means a great interviewer." (Quoted in *Vanity Fair*, October 2010, p. 276.)

14. In a speech at the Naval Postgraduate School in Monterey, California, Albert Gonzales, the president's White House counsel, justified the second President Bush invading Iraq without a congressional declaration of war. When one officer asked how Bush could legally do this, Gonzales said that we had conducted 100 military actions in the past without a congressional declaration of war; furthermore, past presidents often declared war without a congressional declaration.

15. Hendrik Hertzberg, *New Yorker* columnist, had this to say about Fox News in his "Talk of the Town" article, The Debate Debate, February 13 and 20, 2012:

   TV journalism's most pathological mutation, Fox News, propagandizes for the Republican right as faithfully, slickly, and humorlessly as Russian state TV does for Vladimir Putin.

16. Bill Gates, commenting on the government's antitrust suit against Microsoft: "Forcing Microsoft to include Netscape's competing software in our operating system is like requiring Coca-Cola to include three cans of Pepsi in every six-pack it sells." In response, the chief of the Justice Department antitrust division, Joel Klein, said Microsoft's actions are similar to one company owning all the

supermarkets and refusing to carry any soda brand other than its own. In your opinion, who won this little to-and-fro, and why?

17. From a student essay: "The U.S. Department of Health states that only 3–5 percent of sexually transmitted diseases in this country are related to prostitution."

18. Paraphrase of part of a letter in a December 1990 "Ann Landers" advice column:

    My parents didn't give me much guidance about social behavior, morals, or sex. But I read your column—you were one person I learned from. You said not to go for looks and popularity, but to pay attention to "the quiet one in the corner." So about nine years ago, I married an average-looking guy who is a "great father and a good provider," and have been very happy. Thanks very much for your excellent advice.

19. President Obama, at a townhall meeting in Cannon Falls, Minnesota (August 15, 2011), had this to say about the House Republicans refusal to compromise on closing the deficit by eliminating some tax loopholes for the wealthy as well as cutting trillions from the budget:

    "It's not that complicated, but it does require everybody being willing to make compromises . . . in my house if I said, you know, Michelle, honey, we got to cut back, so we're going to have you stop shopping completely, you can't buy shoes, you can't buy dresses, but I'm keeping my golf clubs. You know, that wouldn't go over so well."

*20. A letter to the editor of the *New York Times* (August 6, 2010) argued that since same-sex marriage is "contrary to divine and natural law," it should be forbidden "by human law as well."

21. In September 2005, a Danish Newspaper, *Jyllands-Pasten,* published cartoons of the prophet Muhammad that were reprinted in several other countries over the next few months, causing a storm of protest throughout the Islamic world. Current Islamic interpretation decrees that the Koran prohibits depicting the image of Muhammad (though it has not always been interpreted this way in the past), but one cartoon went so far as to caricature the prophet as a terrorist. The outcry was even greater when a report later emerged that two years earlier the paper had refused to print cartoons of Christ because they might be offensive and were not funny. The editor claimed that the case was "ridiculous to bring forward now. It has nothing to do with the Muhammad cartoons. In the Muhammad drawings case, we asked the illustrators to do it. I did not ask for these cartoons [of Christ]. That's the difference."

22. Comment by Dr. James M. Orient, Executive Director of the Association of American Physicians and Surgeons, on President Clinton's February 2000 proposed $3,000 fine on tobacco manufacturers for each underage smoker:

    What's next? Fining auto makers for each speeding driver, nailing Hershey for every diabetic who eats a candy bar, or gouging MacDonald's for all obese people who order a Big Mac?

EXERCISE 5-3

Here are a few more short passages to be evaluated.

*1. A response to the criticism of the danger of the *Cassini* space mission because it contained 72.3 pounds of plutonium: "Would you decide not to drive a car because you might have an accident and harm others?"

*2. Although traditional Jewish practices forbid eating the meat of the pig, a large minority of Jews in Israel have developed a taste for bacon, pork, and the rest. This offended Orthodox Jews, who wanted to pass a law prohibiting the sale of these products. Explained Rabbi Avraham Shapira, a leader of Orthodox Jews, in the fall of 1985 (a law concerning meat from the pig was passed in 1990): "Our law is not to forbid people to eat pork. We are very democratic here. What we want is people not to be able to sell pork. It hurts every religious man when he passes through a city in Israel and he sees a shop with pork in the window."

3. Parts of a speech given by Paul Ryan to the Rand Society in 2005 were quoted extensively in the media when he became the Republican Party's vice-presidential candidate in 2012. This statement, in particular, was cited in several articles: "[T]he reason I got involved in public service, by and large, if I had to credit one thinker, one person, it would be Ayn Rand. And the fight we are in here, make no mistake about it, is a fight of individualism versus collectivism."

4. When New York mayor Michael Bloomberg announced that New York public schools would use student test scores to evaluate teachers and to help decide which ones would get tenure, the teacher's union fought back, claiming that he put too much emphasis on standardized testing. Bloomberg defended his decision, claiming that banning the use of test scores would be like "saying to hospitals, 'You can evaluate heart surgeons on any criteria you want—just not patient survival rates!' "

5. Taken from a student's paper (paraphrased):

    The prohibition amendment, which made drinking alcohol illegal early in this century, reduced consumption by 50 percent. When the amendment was repealed, the consumption of alcohol almost tripled. This shows that Americans take the law seriously; when something is illegal, they tend to stay away from it.

    Instructor's comment on the student's paper: "This must be why we have no drug problems today."

6. Missouri Representative Todd Akin defended his position on abortion in a television interview when he was asked if he would support abortions on women who were raped. "It seems to me first of all, from what I understand from doctors, that's really rare," he said. "If it's legitimate rape, the female body has ways to try to shut the whole thing down." (KTVI, St. Louis TV station. 18 August 2012.)

7. Newspaper Association of America's spokesperson Paul Luthringer (quoted in *Extra!,* September/October 1995), responding to a survey that found only 19 percent of sources quoted or referred to on newspaper front pages were

women: "The fact that women are quoted less than men has nothing to do with the state of journalism, but has more to do with who—male or female—is the first to return a reporter's call."

*8. From a *Science News* article:

[Scientists] produced their map of the vegetation existing 18,000 years ago by sifting through published reports on ancient pollen and other plant remains in sediments from around the world. They then estimated how much carbon dioxide was locked within the plants, soil and peat in specific regions. Continental vegetation and soils contained far less carbon dioxide during the Ice Age than they do today, researchers report. . . . Carbon storage on the continents totaled 968.1 billion tons 18,000 years ago, compared with 2,319.4 billion tons now, an increase of 140 percent.

9. The *New York Times*, 17 June 1988, reported that, when several women's groups protested the Pakistani law that accords the legal testimony of women half the weight of the testimony of men, Qazi Hussain Ahmed, leader of the Islamic party, said, "These laws do not affect women adversely. Our system wants to protect women from unnecessary worry and save them the trouble of appearing in court."

10. Craig Stoll, a San Francisco restaurant owner, defended his decision to prohibit diners from bringing their own wine into his pizzeria. "I don't know why people feel so entitled to bring their own [bottle]. What if you collected fine tablecloths from all over the world and you don't ever cook at home so you want to bring one in to eat off of? It's ridiculous." ("The Taming of the Screw," *San Francisco Chronicle* 6 April 2006.)

*11. Item in *Science 80* (November/December 1979):

The chief trouble with the word "superstition" is that it always applies to the beliefs of someone else, not your own. The entire history of science shows that, in varying degrees, much that even the greatest scientists believed to be fact is today either false or else somewhat less than factual, perhaps even superstitious. It follows that what the best scientists today believe to be fact will suffer the same fate.

12. On a segment of "Your World" (Fox News, January 4, 2008), host Neil Cavuto asked author Marc Rudov why he said that Hillary Clinton's nagging voice was the reason men overwhelmingly picked Barack Obama rather than Clinton in Iowa (at the Democratic caucuses). Rudov replied, "When Barack Obama speaks, men hear, 'Take off for the future.' And when Hillary Clinton speaks, men hear, 'Take out the garbage.' "

13. Rick Santorum had this to say in an interview on the Christian web site Caffeinated Thoughts (October 2012): "Many in the Christian faith have said, 'Well, that's O.K. Contraception's O.K.' It's not O.K. because it's a license to do things in the sexual realm that is counter to how things are supposed to be."

14. A letter to the *San Francisco Examiner* from a physician argued that if juries award sums like $10.5 million to plaintiffs who have contracted toxic shock syndrome—even though that disease wasn't known to medical science when the damage took place—perhaps we can now expect lawsuits against pharmaceutical companies and physicians by the relatives of people who died of pneumonia before 1943, on the grounds that as-yet-undiscovered penicillin hadn't been prescribed.

*15. When it was pointed out to Stephen Schneider, a climatologist at Stanford's Institute for International Studies, that he was recommending action now even though he was only 90 percent sure that global warming was occurring because of atmospheric emissions, he replied, "Why do we need 99 percent certainty when nothing else is that certain? If there were only a 5 percent chance the chef slipped some poison in your dessert, would you eat it?"

16. Peter Singer in his book *Animal Liberation:* "The racist violates the principle of equality by giving greater weight to the interests of members of his own race when there is a clash between their interests and the interests of those of another race. The sexist violates the principle of equality by favoring the interests of his own sex. Similarly, the speciesist allows the interests of his own species to override the greater interests of members of another species. The pattern is identical in each case."

17. When Charles Gibson, ABC anchor, asked 2008 vice-presidential candidate Sarah Palin about her foreign policy experience, Palin made an off-the-cuff remark that she could see Russia from her house. Katie Couric, CBS anchor, followed this up in another interview, asking her to explain how proximity to Russia "enhances your foreign policy credentials."

    Palin: Well it certainly does because our, our next-door neighbors are foreign countries, there in the state that I'm executive of. And there . . .

    Couric [interrupting]: Have you ever been involved in any negotiations, for example, with the Russians?

    Palin: We have trade missions back and forth. It's very important when you consider even national security issues with Russia. As Putin rears his head and comes into the airspace of the United States of America, where do they go? It's Alaska. It's right over the border. It is from Alaska that we send those out to make sure that an eye is being kept on this very powerful nation because they are right there. They are right next to our state.

18. Hitler's version of Darwin's theory of evolution by natural selection (from *Mein Kampf*): "No more than Nature desires the mating of weaker and stronger individuals, even less does she desire the blending of a higher with a lower race, since if she did her whole work of higher breeding over perhaps hundreds of thousands of years, might be ruined with one blow."

19. When Sharif el-Gamal, a real estate developer, proposed building an Islamic Center near ground zero, the site of the 9-11 attack, Newt Gingrich opposed it

(on "Fox and Friends," August 16, 2010): "We would never accept the Japanese putting up a site next to Pearl Harbor. There is no reason for us to accept a mosque next to the World Trade Center." (Quoted in Hulse, Carl. "G.O.P. Seizes On Islamic Center Near Ground Zero as Election Issue." *New York Times* 17 August 2010.)

20. Part of a political column by George Weigel (November 29, 1992), in which he argued against the *Roe v. Wade* Supreme Court decision:

> The hard sociological fact is that abortion on demand (the regime established by *Roe*) has been the greatest deal for irresponsible or predatory men in American history. Why? Because whatever else is said, *Roe* frees men from responsibility for the sexual conduct they consensually enter. *Roe* is alleged to have empowered women; in fact, *Roe* legally disempowered women from holding men accountable for their sexual behavior where that behavior had unplanned results.

*21. From an article in the January/February 1994 issue of *Quill* magazine about the claim by Dr. John Pierce (University of California, San Diego) that the Joe Camel cigarette ads were responsible for "a sharp increase in teen smoking":

> His study shows that first-time smokers among Californians from the ages of 16 to 18 had steadily declined from 12.5 percent in 1975 to 6.2 percent in 1988, but then began sharply increasing again. Joe Camel, a cool-looking, cartoonish character, was introduced as the Camel symbol in 1988. Teenage smoking immediately began increasing by 0.7 percent a year, through 1990. In 1992, Pierce conducted another study that showed Joe Camel was as familiar a character as Mickey Mouse to children as young as six.

> The *Quill* article also indicated that because of his research, Dr. Pierce stated that he believes we should ban all tobacco advertising. When asked whether this wasn't censorship contrary to the Constitution's First Amendment, he replied, "There is no free speech [issue] here. The issue is to protect our children from being influenced into an addiction that will cause cancer."

*22. Since the 55-mile-per-hour speed limit was introduced by President Carter, traffic fatalities in the United States have dropped almost in half. So now that the Republican Congress (in 1995) has repealed the 55-mph limit, we can expect traffic fatalities to go back to where they were—almost double what they are now. (Note: We now have the advantage of hindsight, since we can find out whether the repeal did or did not go back to where they were or significantly increased. But do this exercise item without resort to later information of this kind. By the way, did traffic fatalities significantly increase?)

23. In an interview with Bloomberg News (August 9, 2009), President Obama was asked whether he favored capping the pay of Wall Street executives. He responded, "Why is it that we're going to cap executive compensation for Wall Street bankers but not Silicon Valley entrepreneurs or NFL football players?"

*24. Taken from an item in *Extra!* (December 2003):

> Fox News anchor Brit Hume . . .argued (August 26, 2003) that U.S. soldiers were better off than Californians. "Two hundred seventy-seven U.S. soldiers have now died in Iraq, which means that statistically speaking U.S. soldiers have less of a chance of dying from all causes in Iraq than citizens have of being murdered in California, which is roughly the same geographical size. The most recent statistics indicate California has more than 2,300 homicides each year, which means about 6.6 murders each day. Meanwhile, U.S. troops have been in Iraq for 160 days, which means they're incurring about 1.7 deaths including illness and accidents each day."

25. The *Los Angeles Times* ran an article in November 2005 about the covert U.S. military practice of paying Iraqi newspapers and television stations to run articles with reassuring news about the war in Iraq. Although propagandistic in nature, the articles were presented as unbiased news accounts. In defending the policy on National Public Radio, Charles Krohn, a former Army spokesman, said, "I don't think there's any need for secrecy, but I think it's pretty well understood that it's the custom in that country to pay journalists and to pay newspapers. And certainly I think the record that Saddam [Hussein] has done this and others do it is pretty well established."

EXERCISE 5-4

*A letter to the editor of *Free Inquiry* (Winter 1999/2000) argues against hanging copies of the Ten Commandments in public schools on the grounds that it may promote church attendance, which may well be harmful. As evidence, the writer cites statistics from two different issues of *Scientific American*. The first (July 1999) notes the percentage of adults in the United States and in European countries who attended church at least once a month in the 1990s. The second (August 1999) lists the criminal population per hundred thousand behind bars during that period. Evaluate these statistics and explain why you think they do or don't support the claim that churchgoing may be harmful.

	40 Percent or More Attending Church	
Country	Percentage Attending Church	Number in Jail per 100,000
Ireland	88	55
Poland	74	170
U.S.	55	668
Italy	47	85
Canada	40	115
Mean	61	219

Under 20 Percent Attending Church		
France	17	95
Norway	13	55
Sweden	11	65
Finland	11	60
Iceland	9	40
Mean	12	63

EXERCISE 5-5

Find several fallacy examples of your own, perhaps gleaned from newspapers, magazines, television programs, textbooks (hopefully not this one, but anything is fair game), or what have you, provide a name in each case if you can, and carefully explain why the passage is fallacious.

Calvin & Hobbes © Watterson. Reprinted with permission of Universal Press Syndicate. All rights reserved.

6 Psychological Impediments to Cogent Reasoning: Shooting Ourselves in the Foot

Memory says, "I did that." Pride replies, "I could not have done that." Eventually, memory yields.

—**Nietzsche**

Every dogma has its day.

—**Abraham Rotstein**

Think with your head, not your guts.

—**Old saying**

Populus vult decipi. (The people want to be deceived.)

—**Ancient Roman saying**

Nothing is so firmly believed as what we least know.

—**Montaigne**

How strange it is to see with how much passion
People see things only in their own fashion.

—**Molière**

I wouldn't have seen it if I hadn't believed it.

—**Insightful takeoff on an old saying**

Good reasoning is a matter of character as well as brain power. If human beings were completely rational animals, learning how to reason well would be a relatively easy task. We would simply learn which patterns of reasoning are good and which bad, and then make all of our reasoning conform to good patterns while avoiding the bad. Even if we started out with poor background beliefs, repeated use of valid deductive and inductive inferences, based on all of what we have experienced so far, would soon set things straight.

Unfortunately, human beings are not completely rational, although rationality is an important part of our makeup. This chapter is concerned with that other part of human nature—the nonrational, emotional component that prevents us from being perfect reasoners. While no one can completely eliminate these nonrational impediments to cogent reasoning, any more than a leopard can change its spots, understanding how they work can help us to reduce the harm they do to our attempts at completely rational thought.

1. LOYALTY, PROVINCIALISM, AND THE (HERD INSTINCT)

Throughout history, individual chances for success at most things—getting enough food, attracting and holding a mate, successfully raising children—have depended on two fundamental factors. The first is the success of the groups we belong to in their competitions with other groups. Members of primary in-groups (nations, tribes, cultures) defeated by competing out-groups generally suffer serious harm to their chances of having a good life or any life at all. That is why we all feel a tug of **loyalty** to our own in-group; a society that has too many disloyal people has little chance against other, more cohesive groups. (Note, however, that the strength of this tug differs greatly from person to person.)

But being a member of a successful in-group is of little value if others in the group do not allow us reasonable chances for success in whatever it is we want to do. That is an important reason why we all are so anxious to get along with the other members of the groups to which we owe loyalty. The person who is completely out of step with everyone else is not likely to be successful, even if the group as a whole thrives and multiplies.[1] Enter the **herd instinct** that tends to keep our beliefs, and thus our actions, within the bounds of what society as a whole will accept. Finding ourselves in a culture in which everyone covers certain parts of the body, we feel uncomfortable leaving those parts naked. Those belonging to Muslim or Orthodox Jewish groups find eating any part of the pig abhorrent. In Western societies, virtually everyone avoids eating the meat of horses and dogs; in China, dog meat is a delicacy.

Of course, there is no harm in feeling embarrassed if caught in public with the wrong attire or in finding shellfish repugnant. But the herd instinct sometimes leads people to do horrendous things, as they do when mobs carry out vigilante justice or when whole nations acquiesce to unfair practices. Refraining from eating the flesh of the cow, as Hindus do, is one thing; branding some of one's compatriots as "untouchables" is another.

The point is that it is part of human nature to find it easy and natural to believe what everyone else in our society believes, and foolish to believe what others find foolish. This is no doubt one reason for what sociologists call **culture lag,** the tendency of practices and beliefs to persist long after whatever conditions made them useful or sensible have disappeared.

We all desire to have at least a minimal status in the groups that we belong to, for the reasons just mentioned. But the higher our status, the better our chances. That's why most of us have such a strong desire to make a better than minimally good appearance when in public. We want to look intelligent, informed, and decisive—to shine compared

---

[1]For more on this way of looking at the human repertoire, see: Kahane, Howard. *Contract Ethics: Evolutionary Biology and the Moral Sentiments.* Lanham, Md.: Rowman & Littlefield, 1995; and Wilson, James Q. *The Moral Sense.* New York: Free Press, 1993.

> Man is a social animal; only in the herd is he happy. It is all one to him whether it is the profoundest nonsense or the greatest villainy—he feels completely at ease with it—so long as it is the view of the herd, and he is able to join the herd.
> —**Søren Kierkegaard**

to others. And that is why, for instance, millions of Americans who had never heard of Osama bin Laden before the devastating terrorist attack on the World Trade Center, who had no idea what the Taliban was until it gave refuge to bin Laden, and who knew next to nothing about Islam and the Muslim religion, let alone the meaning of *jihad,* formed almost instant opinions on the invasion of Afghanistan and later Iraq. After the two-pronged war began, newspapers across the country were filled with letters to editors expressing demands for this action or that. The need to be in the swim, to talk "intelligently" about topics of the day, leads us to form and broadcast these quick opinions based on superficial evidence. And once we have pronounced them, the need to avoid appearing to have been wrong in public leads us to hang onto those beliefs, often in the face of conflicting evidence. The underlying psychological mechanism is the desire to gain, and retain, the status in the eyes of others in our group that is vital to success in everyday life.[2]

It also should be noted that hardly any of the large societies common in today's world are completely cohesive. Nations such as the United States, Canada, India, China, and Russia are composed of all sorts of diverse subgroups, the United States being one of the two most diverse cultures in history. (The other was the Soviet Union before its disintegration.) Most people are completely loyal to their own nation but also have a special interest in the fates of subgroups. They therefore tend to see things not just from the point of view of the mainstream culture but also from that of smaller groups within the primary culture. We see the results of this in current political rhetoric designed to appeal to "special interest" groups such as religious fundamentalists, African Americans, Latinos, Jews, and so on. (Note, by the way, that we all have a very special interest in the welfare of members of our own families.)

Provincialism stems in large part from this natural tendency to identify with the ideas, interests, and kinds of behavior favored by those in groups with which we identify. That is why blacks tend to sympathize with blacks, Jews with Jews, women with women. (Think of the polls in the 2008 presidential primaries that showed blacks and men in general favoring Barack Obama and women favoring Hillary Clinton—until well into the primaries.)

Of particular importance is the fact that we tend to see things from the point of view and interests of our primary culture—our primary in-group—especially when there is conflict with other groups. The result is a kind of belief provincialism operating at various levels—leading Americans, for example, to pay relatively little attention to what happens to the peoples of the rest of the world and to misconstrue what is happening there. That is why, although the United States was founded on the principles of democracy and fair play, a great many Americans have failed to notice that since World War II

---

[2]Erving Goffman's fascinating book *The Presentation of Self in Everyday Life* (New York: Doubleday, 1959; Penguin, 1969) still is an excellent source of information on these matters.

the United States government has helped to overturn several democratically elected governments around the world (for instance, in Chile) and attempted to murder Cuba's Fidel Castro. It is difficult to swallow unpleasant truths when loyalty and the herd instinct reinforce what others in our group vehemently assert, and when provincialism narrows our range of interests and tends to make us see everything in terms of the interests of our own primary group.

2. PREJUDICE, STEREOTYPES, SCAPEGOATS, AND PARTISAN MIND-SETS

Loyalty and provincialism often lead to **prejudice**, including prejudice against all or almost all members of other groups, and to thinking in terms of unverified **stereotypes** that support prejudicial beliefs. But being prejudiced against others is quite different from simply having a bad opinion of them. We are prejudiced only when our nasty beliefs about others are not justified by sufficient evidence. So prejudice can be defined as thinking ill of others without sufficient warrant.

African-Americans in particular have been the butt of prejudice in this country, flagrantly before the civil rights movement, but after that in more devious ways. Racial slurs were masked in code phrases like "welfare mothers" or "crime in the streets" or "state's rights." Over time, these covert references were driven underground by politically correct attitudes that put the lid on anyone who "played the race card," but political correctness also tended to dampen healthy discussions about race. It wasn't until Barack Obama ran in the 2008 presidential primaries that robust discussions of prejudice and race returned to the public forum—and, sadly, so did racial slurs. Obama himself was dubbed the "food stamp president" by Newt Gingrich in the 2012 Republican primaries. Not content with this racially charged ad hominem, Gingrich doubled down with an attack ad claiming that "more people have been put on food stamps by Barack Obama than any president in history."

Prejudicial attitudes often lead to stereotypical thinking that involves attributing certain oversimplified characteristics, often negative, to a specific group of people. Of course, no group of any size is composed of people who resemble one another as do peas in a pod, so it is foolish to be prejudiced against every member of such a group. It's just silly to think that the French all are great lovers, that all Jews and Scots are unusually frugal, or that all women are more emotional than men. It *is* true, though, that people in a given large social group generally are different in many ways from those in other groups. The French as a group are modestly different from Germans, as are Iranians from Pakistanis, something anyone can notice simply by going from one of these countries to the other. The trouble with stereotypical thinking is rather that, even when accurate with respect to groups as a whole (and they often are not), it fails to take account of the differences among individual members.

> "Ignorance—that is to say, fear of the unknown—is the source of the most invidious prejudice."
>
> **—Justice John Paul Stevens**

During the 2008 presidential primaries, Hillary Clinton was a lightning rod for stereotypical and sexist comments about women. Her positions on the issues were often drowned out by media hype on her appearance and her emotional control (or lack thereof). At various times, she was criticized for having thick ankles, wearing pants suits, styling her hair like a helmet, and—showing cleavage. If tears came to her eyes (which happened once), she was a weak sister; if she remained controlled, she was an ice princess. Contrast that brief, tearful show of emotion to John Boehner's frequent bouts of weeping in public over everything from funding Iraq troops to celebrating the Republican party's victory in 2008. When that election won him the position of speaker of the House, much was made of his crying, but never once was this seen as a sign of weakness. This curious reversal of the stereotype that tough men don't cry reflects a welcome change in attitude that allows men to express emotion, but no such latitude is given to women in public office. Imagine the reaction if Nancy Pelosi had burst into public tears just once when she was speaker of the House.

Women in high position regularly face sexist scrutiny. When Elena Kagan was up for confirmation to the Supreme Court, the media commented on her dress and mannerisms in ways never directed at male justices. Like most professional women, Kagan had to appear highly qualified but not too masculine; well dressed, but not too feminine. A fashion columnist in the *Washington Post* had this to say about her appearance:[3] her "dowdy" style was "unabashedly conservative," with a "generous sprinkling of frumpiness"—all of which "made her so much older." As far as body language goes, she sat "hunched over," with "her legs ajar," and in fact never seemed to cross her legs at all. The column noted that although Kagan knew the cameras were on her, she didn't seem to care. She was just "intent on being comfortable"—which is damning with faint praise. No male Supreme Court nominee was ever subjected to this kind of sexist scrutiny. An ironic footnote: an article in the same edition was titled "Does the *Post* Treat Women Badly."

The list could go on, but one more example will do. Widespread coverage of Senator Michelle Bachmann's appearance dogged her throughout her short-lived campaign for the 2012 Republican presidential nomination. A *Newsweek* cover featured a photograph of her pretty face looking vacant and startled, like a deer caught in the headlights. The *Huffington Post* compared her long eyelashes to the fake lashes of evangelist Tammy Faye Bakker, who slathered on make-up with a trowel. The *New York Times* called attention to the fact that she spent $4,700 on a hair and make-up artist over a two-week period. The *New Yorker* noted that her campaign staff knows that "her image depends on carefully groomed glamour." And that is just a small sampling of the media obsession with her appearance. It's no wonder that her staff controlled her image with an iron grip. They had only to look back to the last campaign to see how the press lasered in on the looks of Hillary Clinton and Sarah Palin. (Remember Palin's $150,000 wardrobe?) No one paid much attention to John Kerry's pricey, tailored suits in the previous campaign.

One of the most widely stereotyped groups, particularly in this country, is teenagers. Consider this quote: "Our youth now love luxury. They have bad manners, contempt for authority; they show disrespect for their elders, and love to chatter in places of exercise. They no longer rise when elders enter the room. They contradict their parents, chatter

---

[3]See: Givhan, Robin. "Elena Kagan's Artful Plumage: D.C. Frump," *Washington Post* 23 May 2010.

before company, gobble food, and tyrannize their teacher." And who is responsible for that rant against teens? None other than Socrates, that wise old philosopher, though whether he actually said it is debatable. Nonetheless, it reminds us that teenagers have had a bad rep throughout the ages and are stereotyped today much as they were in the fifth century BCE. Yet most people, even parents of teens, know that the great majority of young people are reasonably well-behaved, polite, and respectful of their elders.

The flip side of prejudice and intolerance directed against members of other groups is overtolerance of—even blindness to—the defects and foibles of our own group and its members. Loyalty tends to make us see our own leaders as a good deal more intelligent, informed, and honest than in fact they are (or than it would be reasonable to expect the leaders of any society to be) and to regard the general run of our compatriots as better on average than the people in other societies. People are particularly prone to loyalty to the government in times of war, as was evident during the early months of the war in Iraq, when the media were so uniformly patriotic that it was considered taboo for journalists to break ranks and criticize the government—this, despite the fact that unprecedented protests were occurring throughout the world. (More discussion on this is in Chapter 11.) Clear thinkers need to overcome this reverse prejudice in favor of people in their own in-groups, especially of in-group leaders (an important reason for the inclusion in this text of so many examples illustrating the clay feet of quite a few elected officials).

Prejudice against members of other groups, particularly of minorities within a larger culture, often is reinforced by the need to find **scapegoats**—others we can blame for the ills of the world—when in fact we ourselves may bear a large measure of responsibility. That a group being trashed cannot possibly have produced the troubles it is charged with rarely makes a difference.

The classic scapegoat in the Christian world has always been the Jews. In days of old, when Christian theology was interpreted to say that lending money at interest constituted the sin of usury, Jews therefore became important moneylenders. Blaming them for calamities then sometimes had the practical motive of serving as an excuse for the repudiation of outstanding loans. But at most times, the primary point of anti-Semitism has been simply to place the blame for ills elsewhere.

Everyone nowadays is familiar with the way in which the Nazis used the Jews as scapegoats, and with their attempt to exterminate all European Jews. So it might be supposed that picking on the Jews would have little appeal these days. Yet anti-Semitism is still very common in many places. In Russia, to take one example, Jews are commonly held responsible for the ills produced by 70 years of Soviet communism. (The thin thread of truth behind this ridiculous idea—note that Stalin was not Jewish—is that a very few of the high officials in the Communist Party and in the Soviet government were Jews.) In other Eastern European countries, Jews were similarly often held responsible for the problems generated by Soviet domination. This was true even in Poland, where only about 10,000 out of more than 3 million Jews survived the German attempt at genocide and still resided in Poland.

One might suppose that the murder of millions of Jews in Europe during World War II, and the still existing anti-Semitism just described, would make Jews, of all people, the least likely to relegate others to second-class citizenship. And yet in Israel, the first primarily Jewish state in about 2,000 years, Israeli Arabs do not have the same status as Israeli Jews, and Arab lands in the West Bank have been taken from them and given to

Jewish "settlers." Not that the Arabs have been paragons of virtue—think only of the stated objective of several Arab and other Islamic countries to destroy Israel.

And then there are the genocidal tribal battles going on in Africa, the mass destruction and murder in the former Yugoslavia, hostilities between Hindus and Muslims in India, the savage revenge killings between Shiites and Sunnis in Muslim countries, and so on. In every case, those on both sides in these ethnic battles feel justified in their vindictive hatred and prejudice against the "enemy."

Prejudice and scapegoating, of course, also occur in the United States. As usual, small or less powerful groups tend to be the ones picked on, including people of African or Asian descent, Latinos, Native Americans (American Indians), and, naturally, Jews. Since the attack on the World Trade Center, an irrational prejudice against Middle Easterners has sprung up in this country. Yet almost all Middle Easterners in the United States are peaceful, productive members of society who are just as horrified at the terrorist attacks as everyone else. Only a handful are involved in terrorist activities.

Increasingly, we have been scapegoating immigrants, particularly Latinos. They are blamed for taking jobs from Americans, draining our education and medical resources, and posing the threat of terrorism. Anti-immigration sentiment is highest in areas where unemployment is at its worst, and people look for someone else to blame when faced with job losses and higher costs of living. Some politicians have been so riled up over the issue that they have introduced legislation to end the Fourteenth Amendment's guarantee of citizenship to children of unauthorized immigrants. Senator Lindsay Graham had this to say about it. "People come here to have babies. They come here to drop a child, it's called 'drop and leave.' " (*Fox News*, July 28, 2010.) The fear is that these "anchor babies" go back to their country only temporarily. Once grown, they will legally return to the United States for their education and bring the rest of their family with them. Yet Politifact (August 6, 2010) finds nothing in immigration research that supports the notion of "drop and leave." Rather, all the data suggest that people come here to work.[4] The loaded language used to describe these immigrants is designed to inflame and mislead the public.

Scapegoating immigrants has a long history in this country, as it has in most countries for that matter. When a wave of Irish immigrated to the United States during the potato famine in the 1840s, they were stereotyped as dirty, ignorant, alcoholic, and violent, and were blamed for society's ills. The same thing happened to the Poles when a million and half swamped Ellis Island in the early twentieth century. That's when Polish jokes started making them out to be stupid, lazy, and inferior. It is a sad tendency of human nature that people tend to move blame and responsibility away from themselves and project it onto others by vilifying and blaming them for things they didn't do.

Thinking in terms of unverified stereotypes and scapegoats often results from a **partisan mind-set** that leads people to perceive evidence and to judge arguments via an "us against them" or a "my right view against your wrong view" attitude. We all are tempted to arrange facts to fit our side of an issue and tend to be blind to the import of evidence supporting any other side. Good reasoners fight this tendency in all of us to favor ideas already held and see our side automatically as right and the other guy's as wrong. Those with a partisan mind-set give in to this all-too-human tendency, generally without being aware that they have done so. This is true, for example, of some individuals who

---

[4]See: Hollar, Julie. "Time to 'Drop and Leave' Loaded Language." *Extra!* March 2011.

are vigorously engaged in the social or political arenas. That is why it can be so maddening to discuss touchy issues with some very committed people—they tend to be deaf to counterevidence and counterarguments. (Another reason, of course, is that we ourselves may be "hearing impaired" when it comes to the reasons and arguments of others.)

A really good critical reasoner has a mind-set that is completely different from those who see everything from a partisan point of view. This does not mean that good reasoners lack a sense of loyalty! It means simply that they have an open mind rather than a mind that sees everything from the point of view that "our side always is right and the other side always wrong"—a mind open to the truth, wherever it may lie.

3. SUPERSTITIOUS BELIEFS

Prejudice against members of other groups at least has group loyalty going for it. That can't be said about **superstitions**. It is true, though, that superstitions often are based on some small scrap of evidence or other. Bad things obviously do occasionally happen after a mirror is broken. Coincidences do happen. And even newspaper astrology columns are moderately accurate once every blue moon.

The difference between superstitious and sensible beliefs is that sensible beliefs are based on sufficient evidence that justifies those beliefs, not on carefully chosen scraps of support. Superstitious beliefs are generally based on biased evidence or on small or unrepresentative samples (discussed in Chapter 5)—evidence from which all negative cases have been removed. Bad things do happen on Friday the 13th, but so do lots of good things. And bad things happen on other days also, so that there is nothing remarkable about the fact that they happen on Friday the 13th. Superstitious people ignore facts of this sort and pay attention just to the evidence supporting their superstitious convictions.

The odd thing about superstitious beliefs is that their complete irrationality doesn't seem to stop even the most brilliant people from having them. Chess grand masters, for example, display amazing intelligence and insight when playing that great intellectual game, not to mention incredible memories. In the 2010 world chess championship match, for instance, grandmaster Veselin Topalov was so spooked out about playing a tiebreaker on May 13th with world champion "Vishy" Anand that he wound up losing the match the day before instead of going into overtime. Apparently he had lost a championship match on the 13th to Vladimir Kamik in 2006, and to avoid a tiebreaker on the 13th in 2010, he wound up playing an erratic final game on the 12th, losing what would have been the tie game. "I just didn't want to play on the 13th," he said, thus neatly combining a superstition with a rationalization. But the number 13 is not bad luck for every one. It was a lucky number for former world chess champ Garry Kasparov, who was born on April 13 (well, he was an Aries, so that explains his great ability) and he was the 13th world chess champion. Where is the logic in this logic-driven game?

4. WISHFUL THINKING AND SELF-DECEPTION

As we have just seen, loyalty, prejudice, stereotypical thinking, the herd instinct, and superstition tend to give us beliefs that do not square with reality. Beliefs acquired in these nonrational ways often result from **wishful thinking**—believing what we would like to be true, no matter what the evidence—or from **self-deception**—consciously believing what at a deeper level we know to be dubious. It is a very human trait indeed to believe that which we would like to be true and to deny those things we find unpalatable (or, as in the case of our own eventual death, extremely hard to accept).

An extreme example in literature is Jay Gatsby's idealization of Daisy Buchanan in *The Great Gatsby,* by F. Scott Fitzgerald. Gatsby persists in deceiving himself about her character despite mounting evidence that she not only is self-centered, irresponsible, and fickle, but also has let him take the blame for a crime she has committed. His self-deception is so great it could be called a **delusion**—one that leads tragically to his own death. Gatsby's adoration of Daisy is an exaggerated example of what many people feel in the early stages of love. We commonly indulge in wishful thinking about our lovers and deceive ourselves about their imperfections despite evidence to the contrary (hopefully imperfections of much less magnitude than Daisy's).

When the stakes are high, we have a natural tendency to deceive ourselves rather than face reality. This tendency is just as prevalent in world leaders as it is in the average person. A classic case is British Prime Minister Neville Chamberlain's decision to sign an agreement with Hitler in 1938 to achieve, in his words, "peace in our time." Chamberlain was so conscious of the horror another world war would bring, and so desperately anxious to spare his nation and the civilized world from such a disaster, that his judgment was destroyed, and he failed to see Hitler's intent in spite of all sorts of evidence that many others, including Winston Churchill, perceived for what it was.[5]

In more recent times, a few weeks after the Iraq War began in 2003, President Bush announced the end of major conflict in Iraq under the now infamous banner "Mission Accomplished." Well, eight years later when the war finally wound down, it wasn't hard to peg that one as wishful thinking. A lesser-known pronouncement made at the same time by Donald Rumsfield, then Secretary of Defense, was that major conflict was at an end in Afghanistan as well. (Ho Ho Ho)

Sometimes the stakes are so high that a world leader goes off the deep end, as was the case with the delusional Muammar Qaddafi, deposed Libyan dictator. In the midst of the Libyan insurgency, when rebels were pulling down posters of Qaddafi and putting up their own flag, reporters tried to get him to concede that the people had gone to the streets to protest.[6]

His reply? "They are not against us. No one is against us. . . They love me. All my people are with me, they love me all. They will die to protect me, my people." When a reporter asked him why, then, the rebels who captured Benghazi said they were against him, he said, "It's al-Qaeda. It's not my people," and then went on to blame the uprising on the hallucinogenic drugs that Osama bin Laden had given his people! And so Qaddafi, once a master of doublespeak, rambled into la-la-land, defending his delusions to the end. Fortunately, our self-deceptions tend to result in less global evils, although they still may have catastrophic consequences for ourselves or friends. Think of the large number of people who drink and then drive. Or consider the significant percentage of adults in every industrial country who still smoke cigarettes or chew tobacco in the face of overwhelming

---

[5]In fairness to Chamberlain, note that a very few historians claim, on rather sparse evidence, that Chamberlain knew chances for peace were not great and wanted to gain time for Britain to rearm.
[6]From an interview given by Qaddafi to BBC Middle East editor, Jeremy Bowen and ABC's Christiane Amanpour, 1 March 2011.

evidence linking tobacco to all sorts of fatal illnesses, including heart disease, various kinds of cancer, and emphysema. Millions of people everywhere continue to puff or chew away, undeterred even by warning labels on tobacco products like this one:

SURGEON GENERAL'S WARNING: Smoking Causes Lung Cancer, Heart Disease, Emphysema, And May Complicate Pregnancy.

In Chapter 4, we presented the first of four "causes of the utterance of fallacies" that Jeremy Bentham described in his famous book The Handbook of Political Fallacies. *Here is an excerpt from the second of the four, which happens to be relevant to the topics discussed in this chapter:*

Second Cause: Interest-Begotten Prejudice

If every act of the will and hence every act of the hand is produced by interest, that is, by a motive of one sort or another, the same must be true, directly or indirectly, of every act of the intellectual faculty, although the influence of interest upon the latter is neither as direct or as perceptible as that upon the will.

But how, it may be asked, is it possible that the motive by which a man is actuated can be secret to himself? Nothing, actually, is easier; nothing is more frequent. Indeed, the rare case is not that of a man's not knowing, but that of his knowing. . . .

When two persons have lived together in a state of intimacy, it happens not infrequently that either or each of them may possess a more correct and complete view of the motives by which the mind of the other is governed, than of those which control his own behavior. Many a woman has had in this way a more correct and complete acquaintance with the internal causes by which the conduct of her husband have been determined, than he has had himself. The reason for this is easily pointed out. By interest, a man is continually prompted to make himself as correctly and completely acquainted as possible with the springs of action which determine the conduct of those upon whom he is more or less dependent for the comfort of his life. But by interest he is at the same time diverted from any close examination into the springs by which his own conduct is determined. From such knowledge he would be more likely to find mortification than satisfaction.

When he looks at other men, he finds mentioned as a matter of praise the prevalence of . . . social motives. . . . It is by the supposed prevalence of these amiable motives that he finds reputation raised, and that respect and goodwill enhanced to which every man is obliged to look for so large a proportion of the comforts of his life. . . .

But the more closely he looks into the mechanism of his own mind, the less able he is to refer any of the mass of effects produced there to any of these amiable and delightful causes. He finds nothing, therefore, to attract him towards this self-study; he finds much to repel him from it. . . .

Perhaps he is a man in whom a large proportion of the self-regarding motives may be mixed with a slight tincture of the social motives operating upon the private scale. In that case, what will he do? In investigating the source of a given action, he will in the first instance set down the whole of it to the account of the amiable and conciliatory motives, in a word, the social ones. This, in any study of his own mental physiology, will always be his first step; and it will commonly be his last also. Why should he look any further? Why take in hand the painful probe? Why undeceive himself, and substitute the whole truth, which would mortify him, for a half-truth which flatters him?

5. RATIONALIZATION AND PROCRASTINATION

Perhaps the most common form of self-deception is **rationalization**. We engage in this kind of psychological ploy when we ignore or deny unpleasant evidence so as to feel justified in doing what we want to do or in believing what we find comfortable to believe. Rationalization is nicely illustrated by the old joke about the psychiatrist and a delusional patient who believes he is dead. To prove to the patient that he is alive, the psychiatrist first gets him to agree that dead men don't bleed and then makes a cut in the man's arm, which, of course, bleeds. Smiling, the psychiatrist tilts his chair back and waits. "Well," says the dismayed patient, "I guess I was wrong. Dead men do bleed." He thus manages to sustain his delusion by rationalizing away undeniable proof to the contrary.

Another example, from the play *Cabaret:* A credulous German is reading the latest Nazi propaganda. Scowling he says, "The Jews own all the banks. And they're behind an international communist conspiracy too." Whereupon his clearer-thinking companion observes, "But bankers are capitalists and communists are opposed to capitalism. How can Jews be both?" The first man pauses, then nods knowingly and rationalizes: "They're very crafty."

Rationalization is often used to justify an act that violates one's personal code. In a revealing study of prison staff who worked on execution teams, a group of Stanford psychologists found that team members were more likely to disengage themselves morally from executing criminals than prison guards not on the team.[7] The "executioners" were more inclined to dehumanize inmates on death row, to claim that they were a threat to society ("they can escape and kill again"), and to cite the financial burden on society of life imprisonments. Such rationalizations (buttressed by suppression and denial) let them slide out of taking moral responsibility.

And then there are media rationalizations, like the ones Nancy Grace and a CNN spokeswoman came up with after they aired a grueling interview with a mother who committed suicide not long after appearing on Grace's talk show. In it, Grace badgered

---

[7]See more on this study in: Carey, Benedict. "When Death Is on the Docket, the Moral Compass Waivers." *New York Times* 7 February 2006.

the woman about the disappearance of her 2-year-old son, demanding that she disclose her whereabouts at the time her son went missing. The woman, a suspect in the case, stumbled over her words, groping for answers, as Grace pressed her for a confession. At the bottom of the screen, a text box appeared noting "Since show taping, body [of the mother was] found at grandparent's home." When a viewer called to ask if Grace thought she had pushed the woman over the edge, she replied that her show wasn't to blame for what happened. "The truth is not always nice or polite or easy to go down. Sometimes it's harsh and it hurts." Well, that's one way of rationalizing the effect of a brutal attack. A CNN spokeswoman justified the broadcast, saying that they decided to air the interview just hours after the suicide with the idea that it would continue to draw attention to the case in the hope of helping to find the missing 2-year-old. Right. So CNN was actually helping the police investigation—not rationalizing a sleazy attempt to sensationalize a tragic event.[8]

Rationalization often leads to **procrastination**—to putting off for tomorrow what common sense tells us needs to be done today. Young smokers often tell themselves that they'll quit a few years down the pike before any serious harm is done; students are famous for delaying work on term papers until the day before they're due. (Recall the old song about how "*Mañana* is good enough for me" and the Spanish saying *Mañana será otro día,* "Tomorrow will be another day.") It is an all-too-human tendency to favor immediate gratification at the risk of possible long-term harm. In general, the more likely or more serious the long-term harm, the less likely that an intelligent person will choose immediate gratification. The trouble is that most of us tend to weigh long-term harms or losses too lightly when compared with short-term gains.

Sometimes these types of self-deception affect an entire nation. When Thomas Jefferson wrote the line "all men are created equal" in the Declaration of Independence, apparently he didn't mean all men: He meant all property-owning men, and that certainly didn't include African-Americans (let along women). Nonetheless, he did not think slaves should be considered property and believed that slavery was morally at odds with the principles of the American Revolution. Yet he rationalized owning slaves himself (200, more or less, at any given time), selling them off when he needed the money, and freeing only a handful at his death. Jefferson was a complicated man, who seemed able to hold two opposing ideas in his mind yet remain enough in denial of the moral contradictions not to worry too much. And so he procrastinated raising the issue of freeing the slaves, partly out of ambivalence and partly out of the very real opposition from the South, where slavery was endemic and fiercely defended. Eventually he said it was up to the next generation to free the slaves.[9]

The unwillingness of human beings to face unpleasant reality often is revealed strikingly in important works of fiction. In his novel *Heart of Darkness,* for example, Joseph Conrad describes the way in which Europeans who invaded Africa in the nineteenth century rationalized their exploitation and degradation of native populations. He thus chronicled a case of self-deception and rationalization engaged in by a whole group of

---

[8]From: Nevius, C. W. "CNN Talk Show Reaches a New Depth of Sleaze." *San Francisco Chronicle* 15 September 2006.

[9]For more on Jefferson's attitudes on slavery, see *American Sphinx,* an excellent, engaging biography of this complex man, by Joseph Ellis.

people over an extended period of time. In his novel, set in the Belgian Congo at the turn of the century, European invaders claim that their aim is to enlighten and civilize the African natives—to "wean those ignorant millions from their horrid ways." But it becomes evident as the story develops that the colonial traders have only one mission—to plunder the land for ivory.

Here is a short excerpt from Jane Austen's celebrated novel Sense and Sensibility *that nicely reveals a kind of rationalization all too common in real life. The excerpt (from Chapter 2) starts with John Dashwood explaining to his wife Fanny why he intends to give his stepmother and half-sisters £3,000 (about $300,000 in present U.S. currency) from his very comfortable inheritance:*

"It was my father's last request to me, . . . that I should assist his widow and daughters."

"He did not know what he was talking of, I dare say; ten to one but he was light-headed at the time. Had he been in his right senses, he could not have thought of such a thing as begging you to give away half your fortune from your child." [In fact, it was very much less.]

"He did not stipulate any particular sum, my dear Fanny; he only requested me, in general terms, to assist them, and make their situation more comfortable than it was in his power to do. . . ."

"Well, then, *let* something be done for them; but *that* something need not be three thousand pounds. . . . [W]hen the money is once parted with, it never can return. Your sisters will marry, and it will be gone forever. If, indeed, it could ever be restored to our poor little boy—"

"Perhaps then, it would be better for all parties if the sum were diminished by one half—five hundred pounds [each] would be a prodigious increase in their fortunes!"

"Oh! beyond anything great! What brother on earth would do half so much for his sisters, even if *really* his sisters! And as it is—only half blood! . . ."

". . . As it is, without any addition of mine, they will each have above three thousand pounds on their mother's death—a very comfortable fortune for any young woman."

"To be sure it is: and, indeed, strikes me that they can want no addition at all. . . ."

"That is very true, and, therefore, I do not know whether, upon the whole, it would not be more advisable to do something for their mother while she lives rather than for them. . . . A hundred a year would make them all perfectly comfortable." . . .

"[I]t is better than parting with fifteen hundred pounds at once. But then if Mrs. Dashwood should live fifteen years, we shall be completely taken in. . . . [P]eople always live forever when there is an annuity to be paid them. . . ."

"I believe you are right, my love; it will be better that there should be no annuity in the case. . . . A present of fifty pounds now and then will prevent their ever being distressed for money, and will, I think, be amply discharging my promise to my father."

"To be sure it will. . . . . I am convinced within myself that your father had no idea of your giving them any money at all. . . . Altogether they will have five hundred a-year amongst them, and what on earth can four women want for more than that?—They will live so cheap! Their housekeeping will be nothing at all. They will have no carriage, no horses, and hardly any servants; they will keep no company and can have no expenses of any kind! Only conceive how comfortable they will be! . . . They will be much more able to give *you* something!"

And so, the wealthy Dashwoods not only manage to rationalize their way out of helping John's stepmother and half-sisters but convince themselves that their much poorer relatives are better able to give something to them!

Although a work of fiction, *Heart of Darkness* was based on the true conditions that existed in the Belgian Congo at the turn of the century. In 1876, when the Belgians began their colonization of the Congo, their monarch, King Leopold, who literally took personal ownership of the Congo, described his intent as "to open to civilization the only part of our globe where Christianity has not yet penetrated and to pierce the darkness which envelops the entire population." But in fact the king was a tyrant; the colonials, profiteers; and the Congolese, virtual slaves. When news of the atrocities committed against African natives reached Europe, a vague uneasiness rippled across the continent, but Europeans managed to deal with these reports by rationalization. If the natives rebelled, the sentries had to defend themselves, didn't they? Weren't some natives bound to die in the civilizing process in any case? Et cetera.

Reprinted by permission of Paul Miller.

In *Heart of Darkness,* Conrad punctured European rationalizations about what they were doing in Africa in a graphic way by concentrating on a few characters whose development revealed the underlying truth that the European claim to be bringing civilization to the Africans was a smokescreen whose consequence (and unconscious intent?) was not to deceive the natives but rather to deceive the Europeans themselves.

Anyone who dismisses the *Heart of Darkness* portrayal of mass self-deception as just fiction—a story—or thinks that this sort of thing only happened a long time ago might reflect on the present-day confiscation of native lands in Brazil, Indonesia, and elsewhere, where the destruction of indigenous ways of life and peoples is justified in the name of "the integration of native populations into modern life" or "maximal use of resources."

6. OTHER DEFENSE MECHANISMS

When we rationalize or procrastinate, we usually are consciously aware of our actions. But there are a number of psychological strategies (defense mechanisms) that we generally are not consciously aware of using to avoid negative emotional feelings. Because they involve distortion of reality, these defense mechanisms can seriously undermine our ability to think critically.

In **suppression**, we avoid thoughts that are stressful by either not thinking about them or, more commonly, by thinking nonstressful thoughts. In this way, we manage to avoid the anxiety associated with the stress-provoking situation. Although suppression may reduce stress in the short run, it often has negative consequences later on. For instance, a student failing a statistics course may block his anxiety by thinking about happier events—his new girlfriend, an upcoming dance, a sports event—or anything else that will suppress his deep-seated fear of failure. Yet in the long run, he'd be better off to face the problem, get help, and work to improve his grade.

Denial involves some suppression, but instead of replacing the stressful thoughts with more benign ones, we change our interpretation of the situation to perceive it as less threatening. When a love relationship goes bad, we may remain in denial until our partner walks out on us—even though the signs of discontent are apparent to other people. Instead of paying attention to these signs, we may reinterpret our partner's negative behavior by making excuses for it, or blaming ourselves, or ignoring it. Our need to protect ourselves against separation and loss may prevent us from facing the problems in our relationships and, perhaps, finding solutions.

Denial seems to be a common weakness of Internet users, who feel a false sense of privacy when they make provocative comments on sites like Facebook, YouTube, and Twitter. A good example is the UCLA student who posted a three-minute tirade on YouTube about bad-mannered Asian students who use cell phones in the university library. Speaking alone to a computer in the privacy of her room, she was surely in denial that her rant would have any consequences, let alone cause the firestorm of condemnation it sparked, or the vitriolic charges of racial intolerance, even death threats. Her instant notoriety was so poisonous that she dropped out of school because of—as she put it—"the harassment of my family . . . the death threats and being ostracized from an entire community." Maybe an inexperienced college student can be forgiven a lapse in judgment, but how do you explain two congressmen falling into the same trap? First there was Democrat Rob Weiner, who tweeted lewd photos of himself to a college coed, then Republican Chris Lee, who sent flirtatious emails plus a shirtless photo to a woman he met on Craig's List. Both men resigned from Congress in the wake of their scandals. The apparent anonymity of the Internet seems to seduce even the most worldly people into denying that there may be consequences.

Albert Camus created an extreme case of denial and suppression in his existentialist novel *The Stranger*. The protagonist, Meursault, kills an Arab on an Algerian beach for no apparent reason and remains in denial about his own motivation, blaming it on the scorching heat of the sun instead. Thus, he reinterprets the situation to diminish his own responsibility and the psychological threat it entails. Later, in jail, he suppresses the anxiety one would expect him to feel about the upcoming trial and thinks instead about his bedroom at home. He spends literally hours recalling every crack in the wall, every chip in the paint, every item in the room—and successfully manages to avoid stress-provoking thoughts. Suppression and denial prevent him from devising his own best defense—that he shot the man in self-defense—a claim for which there is some evidence in the novel but which, of course, would undermine the existential theme.

People who remain in denial about life-threatening physical ailments run the risk of losing their lives or forfeiting the lives of others. A particularly troubling example is the AIDS "denialists," who claim that HIV is harmless, a belief that contradicts the scientifically proven fact—not theory—that HIV causes AIDS.[10] These people advocate against

Cartoon by Beattie/Creators Syndicate.

Instant denial.

---

[10]For more on this, see: Moore, John and Nattrass, Nicoli. "AIDS and South Africa: Deadly Quackery." *International Herald Tribune* 4 June 2006.

taking antiretroviral drugs because they think such drugs cause AIDS rather than curb it. If only a few people were affected, this wouldn't be an issue, but when the head of a country advocates this claptrap, thousands suffer. In the last decade, the president of South Africa, Thabo Mbeki, so firmly persisted in denying the cause and treatment of AIDS that his administration curbed access to antiviral drugs. As a result, only about a quarter of those needing treatment received it, despite generous assistance from foreign donors. To make matters worse, the South African health minister, who believed antiviral drugs were poison, promoted nutritional alternatives like lemons, garlic, and olives to treat HIV, thus using pseudoscience to provide worthless "cures," which ultimately resulted in the deaths of many South Africans. Why people persist in this form of denial despite widely publicized evidence to the contrary is both puzzling and troubling.

7. THE BENEFITS OF SELF-DECEPTION, WISHFUL THINKING, AND DENIAL

Our account of human beings as self-deceivers, as well as rational agents, has been objected to on several grounds, perhaps the most important being that such a harmful device could not have evolved and, if it did, would long since have been weeded out by natural selection.[11] There are at least two important responses to this objection. First, whatever any theory may say, it seems clear that human beings do in fact deceive themselves and do engage in wishful thinking that sometimes results in harmful behavior. Those who accept a theory of evolution and natural selection have to make their theory conform to this fact—they cannot deny the fact because of their theory. (One of the great virtues of science is that scientists are not permitted to engage in this kind of monkey business.)

The second response is that self-deception and wishful thinking do in fact provide important survival benefits as well as harms; it thus makes sense to conclude that they evolved because of these beneficial effects. Although these benefits are not yet clearly understood, we now are beginning to grasp how this side of human nature works.

One important function of self-deception is to reduce anxiety or stress, giving us greater ability to make decisions and to act when delay might bring on disaster. One of the authors of this text, for example, was in a serious auto accident a few years ago during which he felt no fear whatsoever. He thus was able to control his car during the crucial moments in a way that would have been impossible had he been paralyzed by conscious fear. (After the accident was over, of course, he pretty much fell apart.) Psychologists would say that his fear was repressed during the crucial moments.

Anxiety reduction also is crucial with respect to long-term dangers and potential failures. Scientists are beginning to understand the biological effects of long-term anxiety on the body, and they are not good, to say the least. Stress is related to reduced effectiveness of the immune system and perhaps also to problems with other important

---

[11]That the rational, intelligent side of our nature should have evolved seems quite natural, given its immense value in solving life's problems, and this idea was held even in the nineteenth century, for instance, by Charles Darwin and Charles Peirce, among many others.

body systems.[12] The relationship between anxiety or stress and belief systems is still not very well understood by psychologists, but this much seems to be true: Doubt, particularly doubt about important matters, produces anxiety in most people. Settling doubt and coming to some belief or other thus reduces anxiety and makes us feel better. So it isn't only the need to act, to do something, that sometimes leads us to premature or unwarranted beliefs. Even when there is nothing to be done right now, doubt may produce ongoing anxiety (sometimes referred to as *generalized anxiety*), and wishful thinking that eliminates this doubt may reduce the anxiety.

Self-deception also plays a positive role in life for those who tend to relive in memory the good experiences life has afforded them while tending to forget the bad ones. Why, years later, dwell on the bad? Why drag ourselves down in this way? (It's important, of course, to remember the mistakes one has made in order to make sure not to repeat them. The point is that nothing useful is accomplished by dwelling on them needlessly, as so many depressed people do.)

A widespread example of beneficial self-deception called the *placebo effect* occurs when people take dummy pills that they think are a form of medication but, in fact, are not. Because they expect the pills to make them well, they often do feel better even though the substance contains no medication whatsoever. Medical researchers have long understood the effect of placebos and regularly use them as a control in experiments to test the effectiveness of drugs. But a study published in the *Journal of the American Medical Association* (March 2008) showed that the cost of the pill as well as the pill itself raised patients' expectations. Investigators gave dummy pain pills to half of the 82 participants, who read that they cost $2.50 a dose. The other half read that the pills had been discounted to 10 cents each. Participants were asked to rate the pain caused by electric shocks to their wrists before and after taking the pills. Although all the pills had a strong placebo effect on both groups, 85 percent of those taking the expensive ones said that they experienced significant pain relief compared to 61 percent taking the cheaper ones—yet the pills taken by both groups were identical. Studies like this illustrate the extent to which the mind will trick the body into responding, and in this sense the self-deception is beneficial. People who take untested alternative medicines often experience similar placebo effects even though the drugs may be worthless. The danger is that they may be trying to cure serious ailments with bogus pills, and no amount of self-deception will do that.

In some countries, miracle potions are commonly accepted medications, though they may have little more than a placebo effect. A retired Tanzanian preacher concocted one such herbal remedy, hyping it as a cure for everything from AIDs to cancer to diabetes—all this and more for just 30 cents a cup.[13] It sold like hotcakes. Thousands of sick people

---

[12]For an excellent and very readable account of the relationship of self-deception to anxiety reduction and of how the unconscious mind selects what comes into consciousness, see: Goleman, Daniel. *Vital Lies, Simple Truths.* New York: Simon & Schuster, 1985. For a short account of one theory concerning the relationship between stress and the immune and endocrine systems, see the May 1987 *Scientific American,* pp. 68B–68D.

[13]Taken from a delightful article: Gettleman, Jeffrey. "Crowds Come Over Roads and by Helicopters for Tanzania's Cure-All Potion." *New York Times* 29 March 2011.

poured into his village, waiting in lines so long that some of them died in the process. Rich and poor came—even Tanzanian politicians, who flew into the bush by helicopter for a swig of the magic medicine. "It's all about faith," one woman said. "If you believe that this works, it works." And it probably does, if all you need is a placebo, but the benefits stop short of curing AIDs or cancer, or diabetes—way short.

Perhaps the classic case in which self-deception helps people feel better occurs when, in spite of medical evidence, the terminally ill deny the proximity of death, thus reducing the numbing effect of terrible fear. We all need defenses against the knowledge of the certainty of death, those close to it much more than the rest of us. Similarly, it may be useful to be able to deny the seriousness of ailments that are not life-threatening, as it was for Franklin D. Roosevelt, whose denial for some time of the permanence and debilitating nature of his paralysis may well have been an important reason that he was able to persevere and become president of the United States.

In some cases, however, there may be a serious difference of opinion concerning the benefits of the denial that death lurks nearby. It is notorious, for example, that most young men who find themselves in the lethal killing zones typical of modern wars are able to function even though terrified in a way that most of the rest of us can hardly imagine. They can fight (those who can—many cannot) in large part because they tend to see the flying bullets and exploding shells hitting the other guy, not themselves. Soldiers tell stories of the extreme surprise some individuals show when they realize that they have been hit and are dying. The people who send young men into battle rely on this ability of the young to deny consciously what in some sense they know all too well—that they may be the next one to get it. The obviously good function of this kind of self-deception is that it enables soldiers to fight for their country when outside forces threaten its existence. The not entirely good consequence is that tyrants and other megalomaniacal leaders find it easier to get the young to risk their lives in immoral or foolish endeavors.

8. THE PULL OF PSEUDOSCIENCE AND THE PARANORMAL

That scientists, particularly those in the "hard sciences," generally know what they're talking about is vouchsafed by the everyday miracles that science makes possible, from computers to automobiles, TV sets, electric lightbulbs, nylon, toilet paper, eyeglasses, insulin, and clean water, hot or cold, flowing out of kitchen faucets. But **pseudoscientific theories** continue to be accepted by a significant number of people in spite of the fact that they produce no positive results whatsoever. Why is that?

A 2007 Harris interactive poll showed that a large number of Americans believe in ghosts (41%), UFO's (35%), witches (31%), and astrology (29%). Why are they all so gullible? The answer lies in the strength of the various psychological mechanisms that we have been discussing in this chapter. Although science produces results, it doesn't always provide easy or satisfying answers to our problems. Instead, it often confirms what we would like very much to deny, including, unfortunately, the fact that we are not entirely rational animals; that the virtuous are not always rewarded, nor the guilty punished; that hard work is the fate of most of us; and that in the end we all die. (It also says nothing one way or the other about the possibility of life after death.)

Pseudoscience, on the other hand, while it often titillates with predictions of disasters others will experience, generally has rosy things to tell us about our own futures. It sometimes allays fears that it itself has generated—for instance, by transforming the fear that extraterrestrials lurk about by making them into benign cuddly creatures. It tends to be comforting, uplifting, optimistic. It often provides relatively easy solutions to our problems. Astrologers tell us that we, too, can be successful in business, provided, of course, that we schedule economic transactions on the "right" days. Fortune-tellers predict success in romance and marriage. Mediums claim to put us into contact with departed loved ones (implying the happy thought, by the way, that we too will survive death).

Nevertheless, it is bound to seem odd that pseudosciences are so widely believed, given that they are regularly proved worthless. Astrology, for example, has been disproved countless times over the centuries. Pliny the Elder (Roman scholar and naturalist, 23–79 CE), for instance, stated a simple yet devastating objection to astrology way back then when he said, "If a man's destiny is caused by the star under which he is born, then all men born under that star should have the same fortune. But masters and slaves and kings and beggars all are born under the same star." Can wishful thinking alone generate the considerable acceptance so many pseudosciences enjoy in the face of constant refutation? Whatever the answer to that question, it is clear that a pseudoscience like astrology retains much of its appeal in spite of crushing objections in part because charlatans have devised ways to make it seem plausible to the very suggestive (that includes most of us, in weak moments).

One weapon in the con artist's arsenal is what some psychologists call the "Barnum effect," after nineteenth-century circus magnate P. T. Barnum. Barnum is deservedly famous for remarking that "There's a sucker born every minute," but he also maintained that the secret of his immense success was in providing a little something for everyone. Con artists disguised as astrologers follow this advice very carefully. They word their horoscopes ambiguously, so that virtually everybody who wants to can see themselves in the descriptions under their sign. Here is part of a "typical Barnum profile":

> You have a great need for other people to like you and admire you. You have a tendency to be critical of yourself. You have a great deal of unused capacity, which you have not used to your advantage. While you have some personality weaknesses, you are generally able to compensate for them. . . .You pride yourself on being an independent thinker and do not accept others' statements without satisfactory proof.

In fact, this description fits relatively few people, but it does fit how most of us think of ourselves—or want to think of ourselves.

Extrasensory perception (telepathy, clairvoyance, precognition, and so forth) is another form of pseudoscience widely believed by the public. But, in fact, over a century of research fails to confirm the existence of ESP in any of its alleged forms. After reviewing a large body of research in this area for the National Research Council, a scientific committee concluded that "despite a 130-year record of scientific research on such matters our committee could find no scientific justification for the existence of phenomena such as extrasensory perception, mental telepathy, or 'mind over matter' exercises. . . .

Evaluation of the large body of the best available evidence simply does not support the contention that these phenomena exist."[14]

In the face of such findings, why do people continue to believe in ESP? We mentioned a few reasons a few pages back, but Thomas Gilovich, a cognitive psychologist at Cornell University, concludes (from surveys asking people to explain the origin of their beliefs) that personal experience also plays an important role. When by chance or coincidence people experience a run of good or bad luck they often attribute it to some special power. Gamblers who have streaks of luck at blackjack or roulette have trouble accepting the fact that the theory of probability predicts that streaks of luck are likely to occur every once in a while. They often become convinced that some special power is at work—that unseen forces are on their side—rather than accept the fact that coincidences are bound to happen now and then.

Con artists are pikers in the great sweep of things. They titillate, comfort, and do a small amount of harm, and that's about it. But the great mesmerizers, the Benito Mussolinis and Ruholla Khomeinis, who sell whole nations a bill of goods, are another matter. Here are a few pronouncements about mass propaganda by Adolf Hitler, an intuitive master at the game (culled from his writings by the Secular Humanist Bulletin, March 1988):

All propaganda must be popular and its intellectual level must be adjusted to the most limited intelligence among those it is addressed to.

All effective propaganda must be limited to a very few points and must harp on these slogans until the last member of the public understands what you want him to understand by your slogan. . . . [T]he masses are slow-moving, and they require a certain time before they are ready even to notice a thing, and only after the simplest ideas are repeated thousands of times will the masses finally remember them.

Propaganda's effect . . . must be aimed at the emotions and only to a very limited degree at the so-called intellect. [Italics added.]

The very first axiom of all propagandist activity: to wit, the basically subjective and one-sided attitude it must take toward every question it deals with. The function of propaganda is . . . not to weigh and ponder the rights of different people, but exclusively to emphasize the one right that it has set out to argue for. Its task is not to make an objective study of the truth, . . . its task is to serve our own right, always and unflinchingly.

Does this sound like the formula to which most political rhetoric in the United States today is tailored?

---

[14]*American Psychological Association Monitor,* January 1988—more recent evaluations come to the same conclusion.

Premonitions fall into the same category. A premonition is really a coincidence that occurs between someone's thoughts and actual events in the real world. A young man dreams about his ex-girlfriend, and lo and behold, she calls him the next day. If he thinks his dream is a premonition, he has forgotten for the moment the many times he has dreamed about her when she didn't call. After all, people frequently dream about ex-lovers, but rarely do they telephone the next day. When they do, it's coincidental. This element of chance applies as well to extraordinary premonitions that foretell an important event that really does occur. A woman has a dream that a passenger jet will crash in the Florida Everglades—and it does! Of what significance is this? The question to ask is whether such events occur more often than we would expect them to by chance. People have an unfortunate tendency to believe premonitions that come true and to forget those that don't. This, by the way, nicely illustrates the difference between pseudoscience and science. Pseudoscience pays attention to successes and ignores failures; science never ignores failures. It puts its hypotheses to severe tests, requiring independent repetition of observations and experiments rather than relying simply on coincidence and anecdote.

9. LACK OF A GOOD SENSE OF PROPORTION

The kinds of irrationality catalogued in this chapter so far—provincialism, self-deception, and so on—seem to have evolved primarily because they are advantageous in certain kinds of circumstances. Self-deception, as mentioned before, may reduce stress, and provincialism tends to increase group cohesiveness. But explanations as to why so many of us lack a good *sense of proportion* are much harder to come by.[15] In any case, there can be no doubt that on occasion we all lack a good sense of proportion when we make decisions and come to conclusions in everyday life. The trick is to learn how to minimize this natural impediment to cogent reasoning.

Prudence is one of the chief components of a good sense of proportion. In the sense intended here, prudence consists in being provident—of tempering what we do today to

---

[15]Part of the explanation lies, no doubt, in the benefits of the psychological mechanisms already discussed. But perhaps another part lies in two important facts about human evolution. The first is that behavior guided by intelligence is a later arrival on the scene than responses motivated purely by desires and emotions (something that is confirmed by what is known about the development of the brains of vertebrate animals—in particular, mammals). Strong emotions that appropriately guided behavior at much earlier times now sometimes skew rational thought and motivate responses that are less than optimal. The second relevant fact is that until quite recently, very little was known about what philosophers used to call the "secret powers" that move things, and a great deal that was "known" has turned out to be false. (Think only of medicine until about 150 years ago, when doctors used bloodletting to treat almost every ailment.) If we go back, say, just 10,000 or 20,000 years in human history—an eyeblink on the evolutionary time scale—we are back to a time when exceedingly few accurate general beliefs about cause-and-effect relationships can have been known. So it is only recently in the great sweep of things that it has slowly become increasingly beneficial to moderate the urges of immediate desire and strong emotions in terms of what intelligence can learn from experience. Perhaps, then, the lack of a better sense of proportion is partly explained as being due to a kind of "evolutionary lag."

maximize our overall, long-run interests. Of course, being prudent does not mean becoming a drudge, or a workaholic. It doesn't mean always putting off until tomorrow pleasures that could have been had today. But it does mean carefully weighing today's pleasures against long-term interests.

Note, though, that imprudence frequently is not a factor when people lack a sense of proportion. The impediments to cogent reasoning already discussed certainly play an important role here. A sense of loyalty, for example, sometimes clouds the perspective of even the most level-headed among us, leading us to exaggerate the wonders of our own society while neglecting its defects. And wishful thinking certainly plays an important role. People play state lotteries not just because they have little understanding of what it means to say the odds are a million- or a hundred thousand-to-one against winning the big prize, but also because of wishful thinking. ("This is my lucky day," or "I was born on 1/23/45, so 12345 is my lucky number.")

But there are plenty of cases, some of a much more serious nature, in which wishful thinking or self-deception plays little or no role. After the attack on the World Trade Center, for instance, Americans stopped flying just about everywhere. While this reaction was understandable, given the terrifying nature of the event, the odds against being killed in this way were millions-to-one. (Again, driving to work every day is much more life-threatening.) Many Americans refuse to fly commercial airplanes from one city to another even though driving is many times more dangerous. In fact, flying commercial airlines is just about the safest way to travel ever invented, yet lots of people, including one of the authors of this chapter on pseudoreasoning, have serious bouts with fear every time they fly.

In fact, failure to see things in proper perspective is one of the most serious errors in reasoning that most of us are guilty of. As might be expected, politicians frequently (one might say continually) take advantage of this tendency in our nature. They know that people can be diverted from important issues and problems by being given "bread and circuses," and that, for instance, the best time to announce unpopular measures is when the minds of masses of people are riveted on the private lives of celebrities like Lindsay Lohan or Britney Spears. Sometimes these measures slide under the radar when other, more riveting news hits the media. For instance, in 2007 when the subprime mortgage debacle surfaced and the stock market skittered around, President Bush vetoed a bill to expand health-care coverage

It often is difficult to know whether someone is irrationally self-deceived, or perhaps imprudent, rather than being completely rational. Take the case of professional boxers and football players. Do they deceive themselves about the likelihood of permanent and serious damage to their bodies? Are they being extremely imprudent? Or do they so value their professional life (and its financial rewards) that to them it is worth the pain and suffering likely at a later date? Some retired professional football players, for instance, say that they were foolish to take the pounding week after week that has left them walking wounded; others say it was worth it. Are the latter still deceiving themselves?

to include more children under the State Children's Health Insurance Program (SCHIP). The cost of this program—$60 billion over a five-year period—was a drop in the bucket compared to the staggering cost of the Iraq War at the time—$607 billion in direct funding, plus uncalculated billions in hidden costs. This, in itself, shows a skewed sense of proportion, but apparently members of Congress didn't get things in perspective either, because they failed to muster enough votes to override the president's veto, and the American people, sidetracked by other issues, paid the matter little attention.

SUMMARY OF CHAPTER 6

Human beings are not completely rational animals. There also is a nonrational component to our makeup that often interferes with our ability to argue or reason cogently.

1. Our reasoning sometimes is skewed from the truth because of *loyalty,* which inclines us to see our own society and its beliefs in a more favorable light than the evidence may warrant; because of *provincialism,* which tends to narrow our interests and knowledge of what goes on in the world; and because of the *herd instinct,* which makes it easy and natural for us to believe what most others in our society believe. *Example:* Failing to notice the undemocratic and nasty things our own government does on the international scene.

2. Loyalty and provincialism are related to *prejudice*—in particular, to prejudice against members of other groups, and to thinking in terms of unverified stereotypes. *Example:* The stereotype that was common in the United States until about the late 1950s, which pictured African-Americans as foot-shuffling, obsequious children. But believing bad things about others constitutes prejudice only when not justified by sufficient evidence.

   Prejudice against others often is conjoined with an overtolerance of the defects and foibles of one's own group and its members, and it may be reinforced by the need to find *scapegoats*—others who can be blamed for our own troubles and mistakes. *Example:* Blaming the Jews for the transgressions of others.

   Thinking in terms of stereotypes and scapegoats often stems from a *partisan mind-set*—viewing everything in terms of "us against them" or "my right opinions against your wrong ones." Good reasoners, by way of contrast, have minds open to the truth, wherever it may lead.

3. *Superstitions* often are supported by a small amount of evidence. What makes them superstitions is that we believe them on the basis of insufficient and, frequently, biased samples from which all negative evidence has been eliminated. *Example:* Overlooking the fact that good things sometimes happen on Friday the 13th and bad things on other days.

4. Beliefs acquired in the irrational ways just described generally result from *wishful thinking*—believing what we want to believe, no matter what the evidence—or from its variant, called *self-deception*—consciously believing what, at some deeper level, we know to be dubious. *Example:* British Prime Minister

Neville Chamberlain wishfully believing that the Munich agreement with Hitler had assured "peace in our time."

5. Two other important ways to cut the wishful thinking pie are *rationalization, suppression,* and *denial. Example:* Smoking cigarettes after being exposed to all sorts of evidence that they're bad for one's health. Rationalization often supports *procrastination*—putting off until tomorrow what ought to be done today. *Example:* Starting to write a term paper the day before it's due.

6. While we can't yet be sure why nonrational mechanisms have evolved, scientists are beginning to understand some of their beneficial effects. Loyalty and provincialism increase group cohesiveness when there is competition or strife with other groups. The herd instinct helps individuals to work well with others in their group. And self-deception frequently aids in the reduction of anxiety and stress, both of which can be harmful to health. Prolonged doubt about serious matters tends to produce stress and anxiety; coming to firm beliefs about these matters tends to combat depression and thus be good for one's physical well-being. *Example:* Denying the seriousness of a terminal illness, thereby reducing grief at the end of one's life.

7. *Pseudoscientific beliefs* are adopted, and endure, in spite of their failure to help us deal successfully with everyday problems, because of wishful thinking, self-deception, and similar psychological mechanisms. *Pseudoscience* is comforting and upbeat concerning our own welfare and the satisfaction of our deepest desires. *Example:* Seances that practitioners claim can put us into contact with deceased friends and relatives.

   But pseudosciences also gain widespread acceptance because charlatans have learned how to manipulate us in our unguarded or weak moments. *Example:* Alleged astrologers papering over the phoniness of their forecasts by larding them with "Barnum" profiles that tend to fit everybody. Note that the con artists who play on our weaknesses in this way are two-bit operators compared to such great political mesmerizers as Adolf Hitler, who expertly manipulate masses of their compatriots by clever and sophisticated appeals to the irrational side of the human psyche.

8. On occasion, most of us lack a good *sense of proportion,* a defect in reasoning that critical reasoners try to minimize. *Example:* Being persuaded by political rhetoric to pay more attention to relatively unimportant matters than to those that are more serious. Being *prudent,* in the sense of provident—acting so as to maximize long-run interests—is an important component of a good sense of proportion that we often lack. *Example:* Weighing today's small pleasure more highly than the long-run benefits of doing well on a final exam, thus not preparing until the last minute. But people often fail to see things in proper perspective for other reasons; for example, because of group loyalty or wishful thinking or because of other emotional interferences with cogent reasoning. *Example:* Being more afraid of small risks than of much bigger ones.

EXERCISE 6-1

1. How about this *Luann* cartoon?

Luann reprinted by permission of University Features Syndicate, Inc.

2. When France defied the United States and came out against the Iraq War in 2003, the same sort of stereotypes surfaced among some Americans as did at the end of World War II when the GIs liberated Paris: The French don't bathe, they're cowardly collaborators, their women are loose, and the like. Explain the psychological impediments involved and compare the political climates that gave rise to these attitudes.

3. Explain how this conversation between a student and a teacher (not quite verbatim) relates to topics discussed in this chapter:

   Student: I've come to your office to see about getting a B in this course.
   Teacher: But you're doing C work, the semester ends next week, and you missed two assignments. What makes you think you can get a B?
   Student: Well, I need to get a B to get into Berkeley [University of California at Berkeley] next fall.
   Teacher: But why didn't you come in sooner and talk to me about this and perhaps get help to do better work?
   Student: Yes. But I really need to get that B, or I can't get into Berkeley.

4. Do you believe that loyalty really does skew people's beliefs away from what the evidence will support? If so, support your belief with at least one example not mentioned in the text. If not, show that the examples given in the text are somehow mistaken.

5. Do human beings really have a herd instinct, or is that just true of cows and such? Defend your answer.

6. How does the text use the expression "belief provincialism"? Give some examples, other than those mentioned in the text, and explain why and how they fit the definition.

7. According to the text, what is wrong with categorizing, say, the French as great lovers, Germans as obedient automatons, and so on? After all, doesn't experience show that the members of a given group tend to be different from the members of other groups, as Greeks are different from Pakistanis, and Mexicans from Nigerians?

8. Give at least two examples of other people engaging in self-deception or wishful thinking, and explain why you think their actions fit the relevant descriptions provided in the text. Do you ever engage in this sort of funny business? Explain and defend your answer. (Hint: You do.)

9. What are some of the good consequences of wishful thinking and self-deception that are mentioned in the text? Explain. Can you think of others?

10. Critically evaluate the following argument. (Does it contain a correct use of induction?) "Several of my friends have been very lucky in life so far, and I've read of quite a few other lucky souls. So when I say that my lucky friends will continue to have good luck, I'm basing my conclusion on experience, not wishful thinking."

11. If you had been interviewed for the Harris poll discussed on page 145, would you have been among those expressing belief in at least one of the claims asked about by that poll? If so, explain. If not, you get a free ride on this question. (Note the temptation for those who would have been among the ones with the appropriate beliefs to engage in a tiny sort of "lie of silent assertion" by simply passing over this question!)

12. Carefully explain the so-called Barnum effect. How did the typical Barnum profile reprinted in this chapter fit you?

13. The box on page 147 lists some of the principles underlying Adolf Hitler's propaganda technique. Find at least two examples from the speeches of American presidents, members of the U.S. Congress, or Supreme Court justices that seem to be in accordance with these principles. Explain and defend your choices. (It's cheating to use examples that appear in this text.)

14. We all suffer to some extent from the impediments to rational thinking described in this chapter, the authors of this text not being exceptions. (Actually, one of us is an exception, but the other isn't.) Doesn't this textbook, for example, reflect the provincialism of its authors in some ways? If so, how? If not, why might some readers think otherwise? What about any other ways in which you think the text could be construed so as to indicate rational failures—of the kind discussed in this chapter—on the part of its authors? (Be brief!)

graft

a word for political corruption by payoff; a word that used to send shivers of fear and disgust, now a quaint relic that is never even heard anymore

because what used to be considered criminal is now considered normal government procedure, and so the need for fresh terminology.

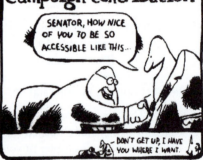

campaign contribution

SENATOR, HOW NICE OF YOU TO BE SO ACCESSIBLE LIKE THIS...

— DON'T GET UP, I HAVE YOU WHERE I WANT.

An important art of politicians is to find new names for institutions which under old names have become odious to the public.

—Talleyrand

7 Language

If concepts are not clear, words do not fit. If words do not fit, the day's work cannot be accomplished, morals and art do not flourish. If morals and art do not flourish, punishments are not just. If punishments are not just, the people do not know where to put hand or foot.

—Confucius, *Analects*, XIII: 3

When an idea is wanting, a word can always be found to take its place.

—Goethe

He who defines the terms wins the argument.

—Chinese proverb

Beware of and eschew pompous prolixity.

—Charles A. Beardsley

anguage is the indispensable tool used in formulating arguments. We all are familiar (or should be!) with the power of language when it is employed by fine writers of fiction—Shakespeare, Fielding, Austen, Conrad (to name just a few who wrote in the English language)—the list is very long. The principal point of literature classes is precisely to make this apparent. But good writing can be equally effective when used in the construction of argumentative essays and other argumentative passages. The trouble is that language can be used effectively in the service of fallacious as well as cogent arguments, deceiving the unwary or unknowing into accepting arguments they should reject.

1. COGNITIVE AND EMOTIVE MEANINGS

If the purpose of a sentence is to inform or to state a fact, some of its words must refer to things, events, or properties of one kind or another. These words must thus have what is commonly called **cognitive meaning**. (The sentences they compose also are said to have cognitive meaning.)

155

But most words also have **emotive meaning**, which means that they have positive or negative overtones. The emotive charges of some words are obvious. Think of the terms *wop, kike, nigger,* and *fag,* or the so-called four-letter words that rarely appear in text-books, even in this permissive age.

The words just mentioned have negative emotive charges. But lots of words have positive overtones. Examples are *freedom, love, democracy, springtime,* and *peace.* And plenty of others have either neutral or mixed emotive force. *Pencil, run,* and *river* tend to be neutral words. *Socialism, politician,* and *whiskey* get mixed reviews.

In fact, almost any word that is emotively positive for some people or in some contexts may be just the opposite for others. One person's meat often is indeed another's poison. Perhaps the paradigm case is the word *God,* which has one kind of overtone for true believers, another for agnostics, and still another for strident atheists. To the average person, the word *student* has positive connotations, but not to a landlord or landlady.

Terms that on first glance may appear to be emotively neutral often turn out to have at least modest emotive overtones. The terms *bureaucrat, government official,* and *public servant,* for instance, all refer to the same group of people and thus have approximately the same cognitive import, but their emotive meanings are quite different. Of the three, only *government official* comes close to being neutral in tone.

2. EMOTIVE MEANINGS AND PERSUASIVE USES OF LANGUAGE

The fact that expressions have emotive as well as cognitive meanings has not escaped the notice of con artists, advertisers, politicians, and others whose stock in trade is the manipulation of attitudes, desires, and beliefs. Over the years, they have learned how to use the emotive side of language to further their own ends.

One common way in which the emotive force of language can be used to con, as Talleyrand observed some time ago, is to mask the odious nature of an institution or practice by giving it a nice name rather than a more accurate, nasty one. Why call the Chinese dictatorship by an accurate name when it can be called the *People's Republic of China*? When Saddam Hussein took control of Iraq, why should he have fiddled with the increasingly inaccurate name *Republic of Iraq*? The ruling clique in Myanmar (formerly Burma) surely had ample reason to call its thugs who engaged in mass murder and other kinds of nasty business anything other than the *State Peace and Development Council.* In a slightly different vein, why call diluted beer *watered-down beer* when you can call it *lite*? Why should a minority political group call itself *The Moral Minority,* when it can puff itself up into *The Moral Majority*? (Note, by the way, the implication that the individuals in this group are more moral than other people.) And doesn't *Department of Defense* have a much sweeter ring to it than the original and more accurate name

> I am firm, you are obstinate, he is pigheaded.
> —Bertrand Russell's example of words having similar
> cognitive meanings but much different emotive senses

War Department? And how about the *Clear Skies Initiative,* Bushspeak for the set of pollution laws that dumb down the *Clean Air Act*?

The language of diplomacy is particularly prone to tricky manipulation, especially when it refers to provocative international issues. A good case in point was cited by William Safire in his column on language.[1] In 2006, when things were heating up between Israel and the new Hamas government in Palestine, the prime minister, Ehud Olmert, wanted to move 90,000 Israelis from West Bank villages into secure areas behind the antiterrorist fence under construction, but instead of using the word *retreat,* he wanted a synonym that would not suggest weakness for withdrawing, or imply that the new border was permanent. The Hebrew word chosen was *hitkansut,* or coming together (in a safe place), which seemed an appropriate choice for the Israelis, but the problem came with translating the term for the international community. After several false starts, Olmert and his aides decided on *realignment,* which suggests shifting of the lines to describe their withdrawal plan. Safire notes, "By adjusting the line of separation without seeking to establish a formal border, Israel's purpose is to minimize friction while retaining its historic claim on the land in dispute." Thus, the carefully chosen translation was an attempt to gain international support for establishing a firm line of separation from Palestine for the present, while leaving open the possibility of reclaiming the disputed land in the future. This type of language manipulation goes on all the time in diplomatic circles, where word choice is often critical in policy explanations.

In recent years, manipulative uses of language have been given a spate of emotively negative names, each with a slightly different connotation, including *doublespeak* (deliberately ambiguous or evasive language), *bureaucratese* (governmental doublespeak), *newspeak* (media doublespeak), *academese* (the academic variety), *legalese* (lawyer talk), *gobbledygook, bafflegab,* and *jargon.*

Take *militaryese.* The military at all times and places has devised expressions intended as much as possible to hide the fact that war is, to put it mildly, unvarnished hell. For example, the term *waterboarding* sounds more like a harmless water sport than what it really is, a brutal method of torture. Here are some more examples:

Comfort women	Women of conquered countries forced to work as prostitutes "servicing" soldiers (term used by the Japanese during World War II).
Preemptive action	Our side attacking first.
Battle fatigue	Insanity suffered as a result of the unbearable horrors and strains of battle.
Incursion	Invasion.
Collateral damage	People who are inadvertently killed or property that is inadvertently destroyed in warfare.
Ethnic cleansing	Driving out unwanted citizens of a country, burning their houses, and killing some along the way (as in Kosovo, 1999).

---

[1]Safire, William. "When Diplolingo Does the Job." *International Herald Tribune* 11 June 2006.

Enhanced interrogation technique	Torture.
Simulated drowning	Actual drowning that is interrupted.
Smart Bombs	Bombs.
Friendly fire	Shelling friendly villages or troops by mistake.
Servicing a target or visiting a site	Bombing a place flat (used during the Gulf War).
Information extraction	Torturing people into giving confessions.
Pacification center	Concentration camp (itself originally doublespeak).
Termination	Killing (also used by the CIA, where *termination with prejudice* means *assassination*).
Nuclear deterrent	Nuclear weapon.
Selective ordinance	Napalm (used to kill by incineration).
The Final Solution	Plan of the Nazis to murder all European Jews.

During World War II—one of the most awful of all wars—the expression *dehousing industrial workers* was used by the British and Americans to mean killing civilians, including women and children via *saturation* air raids. The indescribably horrible massive air raids on Germany and Japan that created incredible firestorms were said to result in *self-energized dislocation,* not widespread death by either incineration or asphyxiation. The term *war* itself has been euphemized into *conflict* or *operation.* Bush the elder waged "Operation Desert Shield"; Bush the younger, "Operation Iraqi Freedom." In the latter conflict, the term *war* was used to describe the War on Terrorism or the War for Peace (!), but not the Iraq War, until we were several years into the conflict. During that war, both sides manipulated terminology to suit their own bias. In the United States, the networks used the term *coalition forces* for what the Arab media called *occupation forces.* And when CNN reported that 16 "insurgents" were killed in an Iraqi uprising (May 7, 2004), the Arab media described them as "resistance fighters." George Orwell got it right when he said "If thought corrupts language, language can also corrupt thought." Few people would realize that the harmless terms cited above were devised to sugarcoat the truth, or create a bias, or mask sinister, even hideous practices—unless it were pointed out to them.

The military are amateurs, though, compared to a pro like the Libyan dictator Muammar Qaddafi, who stymied critics with his incredible doublespeak right up to the end. Before being deposed, he was widely considered a tyrant, yet he repeatedly claimed that the power was in the people, not in him. Decades ago, he gave up any official title. "I led the revolution in 1979 and went back to my tent." So when critics urged him to surrender power during the 2011 insurgency, he claimed that he already had. Qaddafi ruled Libya with an iron fist, micromanaging the smallest details, all the while double-talking a different story, that the country was governed by the people through local councils and a people's parliament. And for decades, Libyans were coerced into submission—until one day they weren't. And he was gone.

Much less dramatic examples of doublespeak are prevalent in other ways. The law has its own version—legalese, a hybrid of French, English, and Latin that baffles the average person. In plain English, a *writ* is a claim form, and a *plaintiff* is someone who makes a complaint against another party. Meetings with the judge *in camera* are just private meetings behind closed doors. Why all this turgid terminology? The principal reason is to ensure certainty, to protect clients by using phrases defined by statutes or case law. Using different expressions may raise doubts as to precisely what is meant. But why can't plain English accomplish the same thing? Another justification is that it's cheaper and less trouble to use archaic language than to rewrite everything. Maybe, but then again, lawyers might have to charge lower fees if legal documents were clear.

Of course, sometimes, doubletalk is just fuzzy thinking cloaked in garbled metaphors. Take, for example, Sarah Palin's reply to Sean Hannity when he asked her if Harry Reid should resign as senate majority leader. "He should step down," Palin said, "because I think he is driving a bus that is headed towards a train wreck." —which prompted comedian Lizz Winstead to quip, "Give her enough rope and she'll shoot herself." (True, the Palin example is a stretch for doubletalk, but it was too good to pass up.)

In recent years, it's possible that doublespeak in the business world has managed to surpass even that of militaryese in its deviousness. Well, maybe not. But consider these examples of euphemisms used when someone is fired:

> *bumped, decruited, dehired, deselected, destaffed, discontinued, disemployed,*
> *dislocated, downsized, excessed, involuntarily separated, nonretained, nonre-*
> *newed, severed, surplussed, transitioned, vocationally relocated.*[2]

Firing large numbers of workers is *corporate rightsizing,* by the way, and the place where you get *downsized* is sometimes called the *outplacement office.*

The term *reform* is tricky in the business world. For instance, whereas tort reform suggests that limiting damage awards in a court of law is good for us, what it really

---

Everyone knows that politics is fertile ground for doublespeak. All political parties use it when it suits their purposes. Here are a few examples noted in John Leo's article "Double Trouble Speak" (*U.S. News & World Report,* July 4, 2005).

Republican	**Democrat**
climate change	global warming
trial lawyer	personal injury lawyer
faith-based	religious
school choice	school vouchers
tax relief	tax cuts
illegal	undocumented
fetus	uterine contents
military difficulties	quagmire

---

[2]New York Times Service (8 March 1996); mentioned in the July 1996 issue of the *Quarterly Review of Doublespeak.*

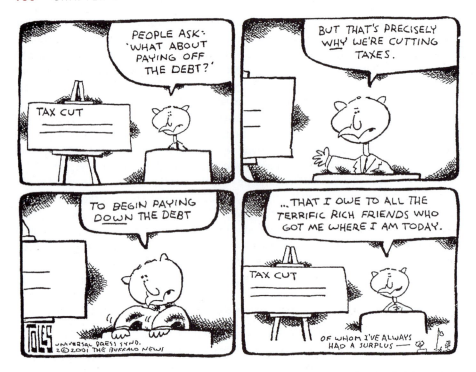

*A play on words that distorts paying off the national debt to mean paying down the debt
that this political character owes to his campaign contributors.*

means is that limiting the victim's right to sue is good for the profit margins of the corporations and people who may be at fault. A Doonesbury cartoon (November 20, 1999)
nails the deceptive nature of business language by satirizing the owners of start-up
companies that earn no money but make millions from IPOs (initial public offerings of
stock). One character says, "We'll probably walk away with a fortune. It's only the small
investors who get burned. It's called socializing the risk while privatizing the profit."

These examples illustrate the use of euphemistic language—locutions from which as
much negative emotive content as possible has been removed—and the replacement of
accurate names with more high-flown locutions. The point generally is to conceal or to
mislead, which could be one reason that this kind of talk has become so popular with
government officials, lawyers, military officers, doctors, and (alas) a large number of
academics. (Is this one reason why so many other [!] textbooks are so dull?)

Interestingly, class differences have always been mirrored euphemistically. Average
people *rent* apartments; the rich *lease* them. The nonrich talk of *social climbers;* social
climbers like to think of themselves as *upwardly mobile* or (more recently) *changing
course,* and not as *pushy* but rather as *emphatic.* The wealthy don't earn a *salary,* they
receive *compensation* or have an *income.*

In the field of education euphemisms abound (and why should we be different?). One college gives placement tests in *Student Success Workshops,* presumably to soften the blow to the many students who place in remedial (uh, developmental) classes. Teachers no longer *teach* but *facilitate* in *comfort zones* where *collaborative learning* occurs.

Then there is academic doublespeak, especially deadly when it comes in whole sentences or runs on for whole paragraphs. Here, for example, is a tiny snippet from Zellig Harris's well-known text *Structural Linguistics* that makes a simple idea seem more profound:

> Another consideration is the availability of simultaneity, in addition to successivity as a relation among linguistic elements.

This seems to mean (there is a certain amount of vagueness here) that we can do two things at once, like gesture while we talk (You didn't know that, did you?)

The deliberate use of euphemistic language has been going on at least since the beginning of recorded history, but it seems to have increased dramatically in recent years, perhaps because of the professionalization of most trades. Titled professionals want to sound objective and authoritative, not opinionated or biased. Also, controversial topics can be toned down when dressed in euphemistic language. For instance, to lessen its negative connotation, the term *abortion* comes in many guises nowadays: *effecting fetal demise, planned cessation of gestation, interrupted pregnancy, termination,* and *selective reduction.*

It's true that euphemisms can and often do serve useful, nonmanipulative functions. Circumlocutions used to replace offensive four-letter words are good examples. Using expressions like *put to sleep, passed gas,* and *for the mature figure* often is just a matter of politeness. Why shock or offend when we don't have to? Nevertheless, all too often euphemisms are used to further Machiavellian purposes. Indeed, the nastier something is, the greater the need to clothe it in neutral garb.

Doublespeak has become so common that we hardly notice it. Euphemisms slide past us without registering and soften our grasp of reality. When politicians "misspeak" rather than lie, we are less likely to hold them accountable. When the military "deploys troops" rather than invades a country, we are less alarmed. When mayors refer to neighborhoods with "substandard housing" rather than slums or ghettos, we are less likely to think of people living in poverty.[3] Doublespeak hoodwinks us into thinking wrong is right, dangerous situations are benign, poverty is nonexistent, and we are lulled into a deceptive calm. A misleading phrase here and there may not seem like much, but the cumulative effect is to erode our understanding of what is actually going on in the world. When doublespeak is a buffer between us and reality, we are more likely to be manipulated into mindless acceptance of half truths, distortions, and lies.

Of course, sometimes attempts to whitewash bad news are so obvious that the American public simply rolls its collective eyes. When a recession loomed in 2008, President Bush avoided the R word and talked, instead, about "economic challenges" and "uncertainties," as in ". . . we have a dynamic economy, but there are some uncertainties." It didn't take an economist to recognize the code language for recession. Given the sinking economy

---

[3]Examples are taken from *Doublespeak Defined,* by William Lutz, a perceptive compilation and commentary of misleading language.

> *The popularity of the writings of George Orwell is an important reason that dou-*
> *blespeak has received more than a usual amount of attention in recent years. In*
> *this excerpt from his 1948 classic "Politics and the English Language," he explains*
> *one reason why politicians favor this less-than-straightforward kind of rhetoric:*
>
> In our time, political speech and writing are largely the defence of the indefensi-
> ble.... Thus political language has to consist largely of euphemism, question beg-
> ging, and sheer cloudy vagueness. Defenceless villages are bombarded from the
> air, the inhabitants driven out into the countryside, the cattle machine-gunned, the
> huts set on fire with incendiary bullets: This is called *pacification.* Millions of
> peasants are robbed of their farms and sent trudging along the roads with no more
> than they can carry: This is called *transfer of population* or *rectification of*
> *frontiers....*
>
> The inflated style is itself a kind of euphemism. A mass of Latin words falls
> upon the facts like soft snow, blurring the outlines and covering up all the details.
> *The great enemy of clear language is insincerity. When there is a gap between*
> *one's real and one's declared aims, one turns as it were instinctively to long words*
> *and exhausted idioms, like a cuttlefish squirting out ink.* [These italics added.]

and the drain on their pocketbooks, most people fully understood what was going on, and
no amount of hedging could convince them otherwise. Unfortunately, many people have
trouble seeing through doublespeak until they are personally affected, and sometimes that
is too late.

Language in every field, whether it be politics, law, medicine, or any other, is sometimes inflated or obscure and often larded with *jargon.* There are several senses of this
term, one being nonsensical, incoherent, or meaningless talk; another, the specialized
language used by professionals when talking (or writing) to each other. The trouble is
that jargon intended in the professional sense can and often does turn out to be jargon in
the meaningless or incoherent sense, making vacuous or otherwise simple and easily
understood remarks appear to be profound.

We need to remember, though, that technical terms used by professional people generally do have an important function—namely, to ensure precision when it counts. Lawyers want contracts to be airtight. Doctors need to be sure they understand each other
when they talk about patient illnesses. It may be adequate for a layperson to talk, say,
about rapid or irregular heartbeats, but cardiologists need a more precise way of distinguishing the various kinds—distinguishing, for example, *supra ventricular tachycardia*
from *atrial fibrillation* or from the immediately life-threatening *ventricular fibrillation.*
Use of these technical expressions quickly conveys rather precise and absolutely vital
information from one doctor to another. Technical jargon used by people in the same
field is an essential form of communication, but when it deteriorates into incoherent or
meaningless verbiage, it is puzzling at best and incomprehensible at worst.

And when professional lingo is not translated into ordinary language for the average
person, it can be troubling, indeed. For example, doctors who tell patients they have a
malignant melanoma without clarifying the term, may leave them ignorant of the fact
that they have a form of skin cancer which quickly leads to death if untreated.

As the world changes, language inevitably changes with it. New words come into common use for things and procedures that didn't exist just a few years ago; old words take on new meanings. The computer age illustrates this nicely. We now talk glibly of an inanimate variety of mouse, of clipless clipboards, nonedible menus, floppy and hard discs, RAM, ROM, bytes and even megabytes, and glassless windows. We cut and paste without scissors or glue, and not only delete but also unerase. We surf the (dry) Net and zero in on spiderless web sites, navigating with a cursor.

Initially, these new locutions were used and understood primarily by computer nerds and functioned, as professionalese generally does, to exclude the uninitiated. But they quickly worked their way into the vocabularies of everyone who uses computers, even though much of what we do with them is word processing or game playing, not mathematical computation. So it goes.

Another common feature of jargon, by the way, is *padding*—adding significant-sounding sentences here and there that in fact say little or nothing. Here is an example typical of a common variety in psychological writings: "Although the effects of mental attitudes on bodily disease should not be exaggerated, neither should they be minimized." True. And here is an example of another type: "As soon as there are behaviors you can't generate, then there are responses you can't elicit." Yes. And another: "In order to achieve products, outputs, and outcomes through processes, inputs are required." Absolutely.

3. OTHER COMMON RHETORICAL DEVICES

Let's now look at a few of the many other rhetorical devices that are frequently used to manipulate the unwary or less knowledgeable. (This does not mean that these devices cannot be used in the service of truth and justice!)

Tone

Good writers or speakers try to choose the **tone** best suited to their audience, as students are taught to do in writing classes. Tone expresses attitudes or feelings—of compassion, anger, levity, humility, congeniality, and so on—and can be quite powerful when

Reprinted by permission of Stuart Hample.

employed properly in argumentative passages. Using the proper tone, even though doing so clearly plays to emotions, isn't like arguing fallaciously or from premises known to be false, but rather is just a matter of common sense; arguments aren't won by unnecessarily ruffling the other guy's feathers.

But tone can be employed for nefarious purposes, not just virtuous ones. Lawyers addressing juries are masters of the art, as are politicians addressing constituents. Success in politics requires knowing how to use the tone of "Mom and apple pie" rhetoric when addressing, say, families of soldiers returning from overseas duty, and humor when dealing with matters of a lighter nature. Here, for instance, is an excerpt from the veto by Adlai Stevenson, then governor of Illinois, of a bill to protect birds by restraining the roaming of cats:

> It is in the nature of cats to do a certain amount of unescorted roaming....That cats destroy some birds, I well know, but I believe this legislation would further but little the worthy cause to which its proponents give such unselfish effort. The problem of the cat versus the bird is as old as time. If we attempt to resolve it by legislation, who knows but what we may be called upon to take sides as well in the age-old problem of dog versus cat, bird versus bird, or even bird versus worm. In my opinion, the state of Illinois...already has enough to do without trying to control feline delinquency.

Just the right touch to put the quash on a bill that members of the legislature cared little about anyway. By using elevated language to explain his decision on a rather minor matter, and by carrying the consequences of the vetoed bill's logic to ridiculous lengths, Stevenson managed to undermine the opposition with gentle humor and without offending anyone. (Stevenson, by the way, was rightly famous for his ironic humor; witness his remark when accused of being an "egghead": "Eggheads of the world unite; all we have to lose are our yolks.")

Contrast the tone of the Stevenson veto with the following excerpt from the best-known speech by Winston Churchill, a master at the trade. It is taken from the end of an address to the British Parliament in the summer of 1940, during the darkest days of World War II, when the British expected to be invaded by German armies flush with recent and spectacular victories in France—a time when most observers believed Britain was about to be crushed by German military power:

> We shall not flag nor fail. We shall go on to the end. We shall fight...on the seas and oceans; we shall fight with growing confidence and growing strength in the air. We shall defend our island whatever the cost may be; we shall fight on beaches, landing grounds, in fields, in streets and on the hills. We shall never surrender and even if, which I do not for the moment believe, this island or a large part of it were subjugated and starving, then our empire beyond the seas, armed and guarded by the British fleet, will carry on the struggle until in God's good time the New World, with all its power and might, sets forth to the liberation and rescue of the Old.

The point of Churchill's rhetoric was to buck up the courage of the British people—to stiffen their resolve to fight in the face of terrible odds—and the tone of his speech, not to mention its content, accomplished exactly that. (Incidentally, Churchill's address was not recorded; the recording frequently heard of this momentous speech is by someone else, later.)

Slanting

Slanting is a form of misrepresentation. In one version, a true statement is made so as to imply or suggest something else (usually either false or not known to be true). For example, a defense lawyer may try to blunt damaging testimony by stating, "All this proves is that..." or "Since we willingly admit that...," implying that the testimony is of little importance when in fact it is quite damaging. Or an advertisement may say, "Try our best-quality knife, *only* $9.95," implying that the price is very low when in fact it may be just the ordinary price.

Slanting creeps into objective news reports, as in this example from a *Wall Street Journal* article (February 1, 2012) explaining super PAC donations to candidates. "In Iowa and Florida, the pro-Romney PAC unleashed a torrent of negative ads that helped dent Mr. Gingrich's poll numbers." The phrase "unleashed a torrent" suggests a virulent attack on an opponent, but the explanation of Gingrich's expenditures that followed is benign. "Mr. Gingrich's super PAC has spent a total of $4.4 million on ads, while his campaign has spent $2.7 million on ads." No mention here of *his* campaign's "torrent" of attack ads on Romney in Florida. A subtle slant, but one that creates a bias. Another example: In a *San Francisco Chronicle* article (October 29, 2003) about a White House press conference on the rebuilding of Iraq, the comment "Much of Bush's black-and-white view of the war persists" implies that the president habitually ignored not only the complexity of postwar problems in Iraq, but of all other issues he faced as well.

Slanting also can be accomplished by a careful selection of facts. (So slanting often invites the fallacy of suppressed evidence, discussed in Chapter 3.) For example, the authors of most U.S. history texts used in public schools select facts so as to sanitize American history as much as they can (given the general stricture against wandering too far from the straight and narrow). The point of public school history texts, after all, is not to produce disaffected citizens. Slanting, also, subtly promotes textbook biases. Now that multiculturalism has nudged out Eurocentrism, history books tend to romanticize Native Americans, for instance, and criticize the actions of white settlers. The word *massacre* is invariably used to describe whites attacking Native Americans but not when the situation is reversed and settlers are the victims of atrocities committed by Native Americans. (More said on these topics in Chapter 12.)

It's no secret that political parties slant information to favor their political bias. Under the second President Bush, for example, health information on government websites was subtly changed to reflect the administration's ideology. On the National Cancer Institute website, the statement that there was "no association between abortion and breast cancer" was changed to "the evidence is inconclusive." And the web site for the Center for Disease Control and Prevention used to explain that condoms could protect people effectively from HIV infection, but the revision claimed that "more research is needed."

Slanting sometimes goes under the name *suggestion* or, in some cases, the more pejorative name *innuendo*. The latter term might well be applied to the politician who responded to a statement by Dan Quayle, Vice President under the first President Bush:

Monroe C. Beardsley was one of the first to write a textbook dealing strictly with critical reasoning (as opposed to formal logic). In this excerpt from his book Thinking Straight, *he explains an example of* suggestion:

On November 30, 1968, the *New York Times* reported on the construction site for a new jetport in the Everglades, 40 miles from Miami:

> Populated now by deer, alligators, wild turkeys, and a tribe of Indians who annually perform a rite known as the Green Corn Dance, the tract could someday accommodate a super jetport twice the size of Kennedy International in New York and still have a one-mile buffer on every side to minimize intrusion in the lives of any eventual residents.

A more horrible example of suggestion could hardly be found. First, note that by putting the Indians in a list with deer, alligators, and wild turkeys, the writer suggests that they belong in the same category as these subhuman species. This impression is reinforced by the allusion to the "Green Corn Dance," which (since it is irrelevant to the rest of the story) can only suggest that this kind of silly superstitious activity sums up their lives. And the impression is driven home sharply at the end when we get to the need to "minimize intrusions on the lives of any eventual residents"—the Indians, of course, can hardly be counted as real residents.

—*Thinking Straight. 4th ed. Englewood Cliffs, N.J.: Prentice Hall, 1975.*

"Well, I admit he wasn't lying *this time*." The nice thing about slanting, so far as practitioners of the art are concerned, is that you can always deny that you implied or suggested what you in fact have implied or suggested.

Weasel Words

Weasel words (or phrases) are locutions that appear to make little or no change in the content of a statement while in fact sucking out all or most of its content. (Weasels often suck out the content of eggs without breaking their shells.) Typical is the use of the terms *may* or *may be,* as in this example from a student paper: "Economic success *may be* the explanation of male dominance over females" (italics added). Using the expression *may be* instead of the straightforward verb *is* protected the student from error by reducing the content of her statement close to zero. What she said is consistent with the economic success of males *not* being the reason for male dominance. By the way, note the assumption that males do dominate females in the last analysis, a contention some males (and females!) would deny. The term *arguably* is another weasel word frequently employed to spruce up weak arguments. The student quoted here might just as well have protected herself by stating that "Economic success *arguably* is the explanation for male dominance over females."

Weasel words are the stock and trade of most politicians when discussing controversial issues—and they can be subtle. For example, when President Obama went to Ohio in 2011 to spread the good news about the improved economy of the automobile industry, he had this to say on his weekly radio address: "Chrysler has repaid every dime and more of what it owes American taxpayers for their support during my presidency."[4] Literally this was true. Chrysler *did* repay the $8.5 billion that the Obama administration lent the corporation—but not the $4 billion loan from the Bush administration. Obama weaseled out of that one.

Fine-Print Disclaimers

Another common trick is to take back unobtrusively in the (usually) unread fine print what is claimed in the most easily read part of a document. Schlock insurance policies are notorious for their use of this device. They tout wonderful coverage in large type while taking it away in the fine print. When private property is damaged by earthquakes, tornadoes, or hurricanes, for instance, people usually think they are sufficiently insured against damage from natural disasters, but they often discover to their chagrin that upfront promises of replacement cash are severely limited in the fine print of their insurance policies.

Advertisers regularly use very small asterisks to direct readers to the bottom of ads, where they find out, say, that to get the "low-low" airline fare, tickets must be purchased 21 days in advance and cover a stay over at least one Saturday, and also learn that "other restrictions may apply" (note the weasel word *may,* hiding the fact that they do).

Fine-print disclaimers have become so odious that advertisers have begun to play on the fact with a bit of humor, announcing (as some Lexus auto commercials did) that their lawyers have gone into paroxysms of joy while writing the fine print that is then scrolled across the TV screen (very quickly, so it can't be read—but that's part of the humor).

A variation of the fine-print disclaimer is the sneaky stipulation buried in contracts. A blatant example of this fine-print finagling occurred in the case of a fellow named Jim Turner, who rented a car in Connecticut, but discovered when he returned it to the car rental company that he had been charged $450 because of a stipulation in the contract that "fined" the driver $150 every time the speed exceeded 79 miles per hour. His car had been tracked by satellite over seven states! Alas, poor Mr. Turner didn't read the fine print in the contract when the agent asked him to sign his initials by the X.

Another variation on the fine-print disclaimer gambit is the *reinterpretation ploy.* Having said what turns out to be unpopular, or perhaps offensive, the best strategy for a politician often is just to reinterpret the ill-advised remark. On one of the tapes released by Gennifer Flowers, Bill Clinton is heard making a remark that clearly implies he thought Mario Cuomo (then governor of New York) acted like a mafioso. When the tapes became public, an embarrassed Clinton apologized, which is the right thing to do when caught with…uh…one's pants down, but also stated that "I meant simply to imply that Governor Cuomo is a tough, worthy competitor," which was a clever, but somewhat shady, reinterpretation of his remarks.

Obfuscation

Dictionaries tell us that to *obfuscate* is "to be so confusing or opaque as to be difficult to perceive or understand" or "to render indistinct or dim." President Obama's press

---

[4]Cited in: Kessler, Glenn. "President Obama's Phony Accounting on the Auto Industry." *Washington Post* 6 June 2011.

secretary, Robert Gibbs, wins a prize for opacity in his response to a question about the administration's plan to release results of the bank stress tests used to determine the health of the banking system. (Press briefing, April 15, 2009):

> ... I think by May, early in May, you will see in a systematic and coordinated way some—the transparency of determining and showing to all involved some of the results of these stress tests.

Say what? Apparently all Gibbs could do was stumble around the issue to sidestep the fact that the health of the banking system was in such dire straights.

Let's stretch the definition of *obfuscation* a bit here to cover cases in which an issue or question has been *evaded* by *wandering from the point* or by snowing one's audience with an immense amount of detail in the hope that they either won't notice or at least won't press the point. For example, in the run-up to the 2008 election, ABC news anchor Charlie Gibson questioned Governor Sarah Palin about whether she had the national security credentials to serve as vice president, perhaps president of the country. He noted that she did command the Alaskan National Guard and that Alaska was close to Russia and then asked, "Are these sufficient credentials?" Palin replied:

> ... it [running the country] is about reform of government and about putting government back on the side of the people, and that has much to do with foreign policy and national security issues. Let me speak specifically about a credential that I do bring to the table, Charlie, and that's with the energy independence that I've been working on for these years as the governor of this state...

And off she went on her energy policy. Well, government reform is important, and so is putting government back on the side of the people, but Palin's response told us nothing about her national security credentials. And so she evaded the issue, then wandered from the point when she slid into her energy policy. One can hardly single her out, though, for what has become standard political obfuscation. Nowadays that's just common practice (as in *two wrongs*).

By the way, it needs to be said that not all wandering from the point constitutes obfuscation. We have to say this here because the many asides in this textbook ("Interestingly...", and "By the way..." for example) definitely are not intended as obfuscations, but merely as remarks about related or secondary matters that it is hoped the reader will find either interesting or informative.

4. LANGUAGE MANIPULATORS

People manipulate language for all sorts of reasons: to flatter, to impress, to persuade, to obfuscate, and to distort the truth—to name a few. Sometimes language manipulation is benign, but when it is done to benefit those in power, it can undermine the rights of others. Often the point of redefining language is to circumvent legal stipulations or to justify inequities—as noted below.

When the torture scandal at Abu Ghraib hit the news, officials in the Bush administration claimed it was the work of a few bad apples, but skeptics dug deeper and came up with the Justice Department's interpretation of existing laws banning torture abroad (posted on the *Washington Post* web site, June 14, 2004). In Section 2340 of the U.S. Criminal Code, torture is defined as any act "specifically intended to inflict severe physical or mental pain or suffering...upon another person within his custody or physical control." The Justice Department's legalistic explanation (written in June 2002) was that "mere" pain wasn't enough. "Physical pain amounting to torture must be equivalent in intensity to the pain accompanying serious physical injury, such as organ failure, impairment of bodily function, or even death."[5] This interpretation seems to make torture legal, unless it is extreme.

As for the fate of interrogators "who might arguably cross the line drawn in Section 2340" and be charged with torture—not to worry: They could claim they acted out of "necessity" or "self-defense," pleas that "would potentially alleviate criminal liability." In other words, they could get off the hook.

Those Who Control the Definitions...

Calling something by just the right name is crucial when you want to bend the law in your favor, influence public opinion, or justify funny business of one kind or another. For example, employers who want to pay employees less than the legal minimum wage or escape contractual obligations to provide health and other benefits to employees need only categorize them as *subcontractors* and arrange paperwork accordingly. Minimum wage laws in the United States apply to employees but not to subcontractors; union-brokered agreements concerning employee health insurance don't cover subcontractors.[6] Attempts at this kind of chicanery via definition occasionally have been overturned by the courts, but often they are successful.

The food industry is plagued with misleading labels initiated by special interest groups who change the meaning of words used to describe food. For example, in 2003 the House and Senate passed a huge federal spending bill with the last-minute provision that meat, poultry, and dairy products could be labeled "organic" even if the animals were fed partly or entirely nonorganic feed. This rider was added to the bill on behalf of Fieldale farms, which complained about the supply of organic feed (though organic farmers say that what is really at issue is the price, not the supply—which is sufficient). So when does organic mean organic?

Closer to home, college administrators manage to cope with shrinking budgets by hiring lots of cheap labor, often referred to as *adjunct faculty* to distinguish them from "tenure-track" professors. Teachers hired as adjunct faculty earn a good deal less per course than do their tenured colleagues, receive many fewer, if any, fringe benefits, and don't enjoy similar job security. This division of labor can be thought of as an academic analogue to the "downsizing" that goes on in the business world.

---

[5]Taken from: "Small Comfort." *Washington Post* 15 June 2004.
[6]While billionaire Bill Gates was becoming the richest person in the world, his Microsoft Corporation was using the subcontractor ploy to stiff over a thousand of his employees out of several perks other employees were entitled to. At one time or another, Microsoft has been embroiled in court battles over employee classification since 1990.

On a worldwide level, rich nations manage to undercut the labor force of poor ones by manipulating the language of international agreements to their advantage. Farm subsidies unfairly undercut the agricultural industry of developing countries, particularly in Africa, where most farmers are desperately poor, partly because they cannot compete with the subsidized products from the United States and European Union (EU). A world trade agreement was drawn up to prevent this situation from occurring, but the United States and the European Union managed to slide out of it by simply using different language for export subsidies. For instance, instead of violating the agreement with "trade-distorting" subsidies by paying farmers according to the amount they produce, the European Union gives them direct grants that have almost the same effect on the price of these crops as before but are now called "non-distorting" because grants are determined by the amount of land a farmer owns and how much the land produced in the past.[7] Thus the EU is able to undercut the labor force of developing countries without breaking the trade agreement.

Although the United States Constitution grants Congress the sole right to declare war, this has rarely deterred American presidents from waging war without obtaining any such declaration. As we noted earlier in the chapter, they have simply renamed their escapades or declared them not to be wars. Assuming the December 1990 congressional measure allowing President Bush (the elder) to carry out United Nations resolutions did indeed constitute a declaration of war, even though it didn't actually say we were declaring war, then the Gulf conflict is very likely the only legal war out of at least five fought by the United States since World War II.

How much can you squeeze out of a single word, like folks, *for example? A lot, according to Susan Anthony. In a trenchant analysis of the dumbing down of America, she explains how the ubiquitous use of* folks *is symptomatic of the erosion of cultural standards in this country.*

The word is everywhere, a plague spread by the President of the United States, television anchors, radio talk show hosts, preachers in megachurches, self-help gurus, and anyone else attempting to demonstrate his or her identification with ordinary, presumably wholesome American values. Only a few decades ago, Americans were addressed as people or, in the more distant past, ladies and gentlemen. Now we are all folks....[as in "our prayers go out to those folks" or "I've been in contact with our homeland security folks."]

The specific political use of folks...designed to make the speaker sound like one of the boys or girls, is symptomatic of a debasement in public speech inseparable from a more general erosion of American cultural standards....Look up any important presidential speech in the history of the United States before 1980 and you will not find one patronizing appeal to folks. Imagine: "We here highly resolve that these folks shall not have died in vain...and that government of the folks, by the folks, for the folks, shall not perish from the earth."

—*The Age of American Unreason.* New York: Pantheon, 2008. 3–4

---

[7]For more on this see the (London) *Guardian,* June 3, 2003.

In 2002, Congress gave President Bush (the younger) authorization to use the Armed Forces as he considered necessary to defend our country's national security against the threat of Iraq and to enforce the United Nations Security Council resolutions with regard to Iraq. Thus Congress gave Bush the authority to wage war on Iraq but managed to avoid a congressional declaration of war. This equivocation enabled Congress to pass the buck and avoid criticism if the war went badly.[8]

In the war in Afghanistan, the Bush administration classified as "enemy combatants" hundreds of suspected al Qaeda and Taliban fighters detained by the United States at Guantanamo Bay Naval Base. Had they been called "prisoners of war," they would have been entitled to release when the war was over, but as "enemy combatants," not only could they be detained indefinitely for questioning without charge, they couldn't challenge their imprisonment in court, nor were they entitled to any other constitutional rights. The case to reverse this decision was appealed for years until it finally worked its way up to the Supreme Court in 2008. In *Boumediene v. Bush,* the Court ruled that aliens detained as enemy combatants in Guantanamo have a constitutional right to challenge their detention in American courts. Will this ruling stand or will the term *enemy combatants* morph into another category that manages to slide past the law?

When President Obama took office, his administration immediately began rebranding military activities without necessarily changing the policies.[9] Cut from the vocabulary were favorites of the Bush administration like "surge," "enemy combatants," and "war on terror." As Senate majority leader Harry Reid said when Obama increased troop levels in Afghanistan, "Whatever you do, don't call it a surge." So tens of thousands of troops were sent to Afghanistan, but it wasn't a "surge." Captives were still held at Guantanamo Bay, but they weren't "enemy combatants." The War on Terror morphed into "overseas contingency operations." And the controversial U.S. Patriot Act (a euphemism if there ever was one) that allowed eavesdropping without warrant was renamed the Terrorist Surveillance Program. One of the first items on a new president's agenda is to revise the lexicon to make it seem as though it reflects a change in policy.

Sometimes common sense prevails, and redefinition backfires outside the courtroom. In 2008, when the biggest financial institutions were sliding into bankruptcy and the economy was in free fall, John McCain reassured the American people that the fundamentals of the economy were still good. That didn't play well with the liberals *or* the conservatives, or anyone else, for that matter. So McCain quickly revised his message and redefined *fundamentals* to mean the *workers*; not unemployment rates, nor trade statistics, nor any of the usual economic guideposts. Those hardworking Americans, the backbone of our country, were the fundamentals that were good. Well, no one would argue that the workers weren't good, but whether they were economic fundamentals was another matter. That redefinition unleashed a raft of satiric responses that eventually laughed it into oblivion.

When lesser known people manipulate language to their own ends, though, it often slips under the radar. Take, for instance, a German teenager, Helene Hegemann, who infused her best selling novel about clubbing and drugging in Berlin with passages lifted

---

[8]See: Dorf, Michael C. "Is the War on Iraq Lawful?" Web. 19 March 2003. http://writ.news .findlaw.com/dorf/20030319.html.
[9]See: Baker, Peter. "The Words Change, if Not the Policies." *New York Times* 3 April 2009.

from other writer's works. When her plagiarism was discovered, her response was to turn it on its head. "There's no such thing as originality anyway, just authenticity." (Whatever that means.) No apology given, despite the uproar it caused, and no consequences either. In fact, the book was nominated for a $20,000 fiction prize at the Leipzig Book Fair. By claiming that she didn't feel she was stealing "because she put all the material into a completely different and unique context," she managed to doubletalk her way out of blame. How many students could get away with that one?

When language is manipulated, it isn't always easy to determine whether there is some sort of sleight of hand going on. For years, the psychologist Thomas Szasz campaigned against the use of the expression *mental illness,* on grounds that there is no such thing as *mental* illness. Declaring John Hinckley "not guilty by reason of insanity" after his attempt to assassinate President Reagan was for Szasz just an extreme example of what happens when we take the analogy between physical illness and alleged mental illness seriously. (He did believe, however, that sometimes what is thought of as mental illness really is physical dysfunction.)

But Szasz is in the minority on this point, with the result, he claimed, that various kinds of serious abuses of civil rights occur. One is that close relatives of the "mentally ill" often are able to have them "hospitalized for treatment" against their will. Forcing people into institutions in this way is a practice some see as not unlike the one that used to be common in the Soviet Union of confining political opponents in "mental institutions." In a similar vein, Szasz argued, "we call self-starvation either *anorexia nervosa,* a *hunger strike,* a *suicide attempt,* or some other name, depending on how we want to respond."

Well, then, is Szasz right about this? A number of psychologists find his position modestly persuasive, while the majority do not. The reason for this split of opinion is that good arguments can be made on both sides of the issue, making it difficult to choose one over the other. Which choice we should make may well depend, as Szasz noted, on how we wish to deal with whatever circumstances our decisions affect. (Philosophy students might note the connection of this sort of case to the age-old conundrum about whether, when every part of an old ship has been replaced over the years by a new part, it is still the same ship; the answer, at least half of this writing team believes, is that it depends on who we wish to say "built" a ship repaired in this way, not on any truth written in the sky.)

Those Who Frame Public Policy

Redefining words is one way to influence public opinion; another is to use loaded language to evoke a worldview that persuades people to adopt policies—even if these policies go against their own interests. Over the past decade, George Lakoff, a professor

Conservative, n. A statesman who is enamored of existing evils, as distinguished from the Liberal, who wishes to replace them with others.

—**Ambrose Bierce** *(The Devil's Dictionary)*

of linguistics at the University of California, Berkeley, has become well known (and controversial) for developing a theory about the science and art of framing the debate that has attracted attention across the political spectrum.

Lakoff defines frames as "mental structures that shape the way we see the world. As a result they shape the goals we seek, the plans we make, the way we act, what counts as a good or bad outcome of our actions. In politics our frames shape our social policies and the institutions we form to carry out policies."[10]

We recognize frames through language, and since people usually make decisions about politics based on their values, the language creates the frame that evokes those values. Lakoff uses as an example the loaded phrase "tax relief," conjured up by Republicans to hype their campaign for tax cuts (a neutral, but accurate term). The notion of relief suggests that there is an affliction that must be removed. Those who remove the affliction are the good guys; those who oppose it, the bad guys. The "frame" taps into the voters' value systems, and they, in turn, buy into the idea. Meanwhile the media repeats the phrase over and over until it enters the political lexicon.

In recent budget battles, the term "tax relief" has continued to evolve in ever more creative ways. When Democrats proposed closing special interest loopholes in the tax code to regain billions of dollars lost to off-shore tax havens, house Republicans labeled it a "tax hike," vowing that such tax increases cannot pass in the House. Buried by this doubletalk is the fact that companies use these gimmicks to avoid paying taxes already levied on them—in no sense are they tax hikes. But the frame hoodwinks people into believing that they are. Other examples include the ominous sounding "death tax" and the emotionally charged "partial birth abortion," loaded phrases that nudge voters into supporting tax cuts and banning third-term abortions.

Democrats invented their own political frames. When Republicans threatened to eliminate the filibuster procedure that Democrats were using to prevent a quick confirmation of Bush-appointed judges, the Democrats framed their attack as an "abuse of power." Day after day they hammered away at the message that they were fighting for democracy against a Republican abuse of power that was not what our founders intended. This frame evoked the worldview that we value democracy and want to preserve it. Republicans were attempting to undermine democracy by eliminating the filibuster, an American birthright that is central to our republic. In fact, the filibuster is a parliamentary procedure (not a birthright) that is typically used to prevent the Senate majority from ending a debate. The Democrats were actually breaking tradition in using it to block the confirmation of an entire slate of judges. Nonetheless the public was persuaded, and Republicans backed down under pressure.[11] It's not surprising, though, that Republicans had no qualms about using this trick repeatedly to block the Democratic agenda once Barack Obama became president.

Whether or not we agree with Lakoff's theory, there is enough truth in it to make us wary of the way politicians use language to manipulate us to side with them on critical issues.

---

[10]Lakoff, George. *Don't Think of an Elephant.* White River Junction, Va.: Chelsea Green Publishing, 2004. xv.

[11]For more on this see: Bai, Matt. "The Framing Wars." *New York Times Magazine* 17 July 2005—an in-depth discussion of Lakoff's theory.

Psychologists use the term *framing effects* to describe similar phenomena that influence our decisions. For instance, weight-conscious people are more likely to eat hamburgers described as 90 percent lean rather than 10 percent fat, even though the amount of fat is the same in either case. Charities rake in more money when they urge donors to give pennies a day rather than dollars per year. People are more likely to spend money described as a bonus (because it is extra income and thus dispensable) and more likely to save money described as a rebate (because it implies a return on money spent within their income that should not be squandered). Politicians could have used this ploy to good effect in 2008 if they had coined the term *tax bonus* instead of *tax rebate* to describe money returned to people, so that they will spend it and thus stimulate the lagging economy.[12] And, of course, advertisers regularly rely on framing effects to manipulate consumers into buying their products.

5. LANGUAGE REVISION

Languages aren't artificial products constructed by "linguistic experts" in some laboratory or think tank. They are living, changing products of human intelligence designed to perform various functions, including not just communicating ideas from one person to another, but also issuing commands, asking questions, and certifying relationships

---

[12]See: Epley, Nicholas. "Rebate Psychology." *New York Times* 31 January 2008.

(as in wedding ceremonies). This being the case, languages tend to mirror the foibles, aspirations, loyalties, and (alas!) prejudices of those who speak them. English is no exception. Like all languages, English undergoes revision on a regular basis.

The Reform of Sexist Language

In the past 20 or 30 years, a minor revolution has taken place in the United States, as well as many other countries, in the attitudes of most people toward members of minority groups and women. Inevitably, this revolution has been mirrored in the linguistic practices of those caught up in it. The pejorative terms mentioned at the beginning of this chapter are not often heard in polite circles these days, and expressions like "free, white, and 21," common until about 50 years ago, are now as outdated as "23 skidoo."

But the most extensive linguistic changes of this kind have been those reflecting the changing attitudes of most people concerning relationships between men and women and the roles played by women in society. A large majority of previously common sexist locutions have disappeared from everyday speech. This linguistic change has occurred very quickly, as these things go, no doubt in part because of the persistent demands of women's rights advocates. But it also has happened quickly because of the swiftness with which attitudes toward women and their roles in society have changed, and because of the speed with which women have entered fields previously reserved primarily for men.

Not so long ago, when the overwhelming majority of those in high office were men, it may have made some sense to refer to these people as business*men* and congress*men*. But in this day and age, with increasing numbers of women taking on these roles, it makes much less sense. In addition, there is a general realization that these sexist terms imply not just that those holding these offices always are male, but also, and wrongly, that only males are supposed to, or are competent to, fill them. The old sexist language implies in subtle but persuasive ways that positions of power should be *manned,* not *personed* or *womaned,* and this in turn implies that only men are capable of holding these important positions. Thus, substituting nonsexist words for the old sexist terms puts women on an equal linguistic footing with men that not only reflects their growing equality but also helps make it possible. Our thoughts about the world—how it works and how it should work—always are framed in language; sexist locutions tend to introduce sexist thoughts into our minds.

So today, people who head committees or departments are generally called *chairs,* not *chairmen* ("I would like to address the chair about..." or "The chair has ruled that..."). Similarly, people who deliver the mail tend to get called *letter carriers,* not *mailmen*. We say *firefighter* instead of *fireman* and *police officer* rather than *policeman*. The term *man* and its many derivatives now often are replaced by *people, person,* and the like. Publishers don't cotton to manuscripts that contain locutions like "Of course, a *man* might be described as taking a..." when it would be more accurate to say "*Someone* might be described as taking a..." or to phrases like "even if *he* is willing to allow..." when what is meant is *he or she*.[13]

---

[13]Both of these examples are taken, alas, from a journal article coauthored back in the bad old days by the male coauthor of this text.

One of the more interesting language changes accompanying the feminist revolution has been the widespread use of the term *Ms.,* intended to serve when the marriage status of a woman is not considered relevant. The point of this change was to foster equal treatment of the sexes. Men, whether married or single, have always been referred to by the same term, *Mr.,* whereas women have had to be called either *Miss* or *Mrs.,* depending on their marital status. In magazine and newspaper articles the trend is to drop the title entirely and simply refer to women by their last names—the way men always have been. A similar, and perhaps much more significant change, is the fact that women nowadays don't always take on the last name of their mate, although, interestingly, they still usually do (while men rarely do). But even when women do adopt their husband's last name, they often also hang onto their own, so that, for example, we refer to Hillary *Rodham* Clinton, not just Hillary Clinton.

But an even more important language change may be the elimination of locutions like this one, once typical of the language encountered in all sorts of places, including public school history textbooks: "Pioneers moved west, taking their wives and children with them." That made all of the pioneers into men, while women and children were just accessories. A text written today would get it right and say something like "Pioneer families moved west."

On the other hand, things can get carried too far. It would be unnecessary, wouldn't it, for Germans to stop referring to their homeland as the *Fatherland,* or Englishmen— that is, citizens of England—to their *mother tongue*? What purpose would be served by replacing *Uncle Sam* with *Aunt Sarah*? And why worry about using the term *manhole* when talking about those round excisions in streets and avenues, as did the Public Works Departments of several American cities? (Would it be wrong to change biblical references to God from the *He* employed in the original versions to some more neutral term?) The term *humankind* seems an apt substitute for *mankind,* but somehow the "era of ordinary people" doesn't have the same ring as the "century of the common man."

In any case, the changes in linguistic style brought on by the feminist revolution have also raised questions of aesthetic taste—of what sounds right or wrong rolling off the tongue or when reading a book. The expression *her or his,* to take one example, rings false, perhaps because it calls attention to the avoidance of *his* (used to mean *his* or *her*) or of *his or her,* and thus detracts from what is being said. Good taste sometimes dictates other sorts of moves, for instance, employing plural rather than singular pronouns, thus saying things like, "when students read their textbooks…" rather than "when a student reads his textbook…" (That's one reason for the plethora of plural expressions that occur in this textbook. Note, by the way, that the term *congressperson* nowhere appears on these pages, although *member of Congress* is used quite often.)

Interestingly, no one seems overwrought by the fact that Liberty always is portrayed as a woman. (Think, for instance, of the Statue of Liberty in New York harbor.) Note also that, although there are lots of complaints about sexist terms like *waitress* and *actress,* no one seems bothered by the equally sexist term *widower.* Women still receive an award each year for best *actress.* And freshmen still are called *freshmen.* Ah, well.

PC (Politically Correct) Terminology

The revolution concerning gender rhetoric is part of a larger movement that also has dramatically changed the ways in which we speak of minorities. As attitudes have changed, language, inevitably, has followed suit.

The result is that certain locutions have become "in," while others are "out." Some are politically correct, some politically incorrect. Careers have been wrecked by publicly using expressions like "fat Jap" and "Nigra." It would be political suicide today to say publicly, as someone did in the 1970s, when then Governor Tribbitt (Delaware) hired a woman as his press secretary at $20,000 a year, "If he wants to pay $10,000 a mammary, that's his business." We aren't supposed to use phrases like *admitted homosexual* (because it implies that being a homosexual is bad) or *tidal wave of immigrants* (because of its negative implication concerning immigrants).

On the whole, of course, changes of this nature are all to the good and are applauded by just about everybody. But problems do arise, and it is quite possible that an excess of zeal causes some of them. One of the authors of this textbook, for example, received letters from students and teachers accusing him of race prejudice, or at least insensitivity, for having used the term *black* in the sixth edition of this textbook, on the grounds that the politically correct, nondenigrating, term for the minority in question is *African-American*.[14] But when the sixth edition was published, the politically correct term happened to be *black,* which earlier had replaced the term *Negro* (which, of course, happens to mean "black" in several romance languages).

Anyway, the academic world is particularly fertile ground for PC talk. For example, the University of Cincinnati Student Senate has declared their higher institution of learning "a Columbus-myth-free campus." (The allusion, in case you missed it, is to the fact that Columbus could not possibly have "discovered" America—Native Americans having been here for at least 10,000 years before Columbus was born.) At Stanford University students can be punished for violating speech codes designed to suppress racist, sexist, and homophobic speech that carries no legal penalty in the "real" world. An administrator at the University of California, Santa Cruz, was even wary of phrases like a "nip in the air" and "a chink in one's armor" because certain of these words could be construed as racial slurs in other contexts.

Sometimes the attempt to be PC defies all logic. The reading passages of the New York State Regents English exam were edited to delete anything that might make "any student feel ill at ease when taking the test." For example, all references to Judaism were cut from an excerpt from a work by Isaac Bashevis Singer about Jewish life in Europe! In one revision, for instance, "most Jewish women" was changed to "most women." For this PC passage, the New York State Regents were given the NCTE Doublespeak award for 2002.

---

[14]Whether this is or isn't the PC term, many members of the group—for example, African-American politicians on television and students in many college classes—often refer to themselves as *black*. (Interestingly, both of these terms conceal the fact that most of the people so labeled also are genetically part Caucasian—indeed, often primarily Caucasian—or part Asian. The point is that both of these labels are social-political, not scientific, referring to class, not race.)

Are we getting a bit overzealous in our, shall we say, *linguistic cleansing*? It no doubt is a good idea, now that the children of unwed parents are not looked down upon, to refer to them as *nonmarital children* rather than *bastards,* thus getting rid of the unfair opprobrium of that nasty term. And why not change the name of the Italian Welfare Agency to the *Italian-American Community Service Agency*?

But is there anything wrong with calling "mixed-breed" dogs *mongrels,* "visually impaired" people *blind,* or the "psychologically impacted" *insane*? Don't those who call the *Sports Illustrated* swimsuit issue *pornographic* rob that word of its legitimate meaning? (Is there a risk here that the door will be opened to wrongheaded legislation?) Was Newt Gingrich just being polite when he said President Clinton was "factually challenged" instead of calling him a liar? (Was he just trying to be cute, snide, or clever?) Anyway, was the First Amendment bruised when the University of Michigan punished students for having uttered "hate speech" when they aired their belief that homosexuality is a disease in classroom discussions? And didn't certain Native Americans make some kind of mistake when they demonstrated during the 1995 World Series against the "demeaning symbols" used by the beloved Cleveland Indians and the Atlanta Braves?

Although quibbling about the trivial use of PC language continues, the more serious issue of political correctness toward certain minority groups may be eroding. Now that immigration has once again heated up in the wake of the Great Recession, and multiculturalism has come under attack with the rise in Islamophobia after 9/11, PC has been winding down. In the debate over whether to change the Constitution to deny citizenship to children born in this country of immigrant parents, terms like *anchor babies* are now widely used as slurs—this one implying that illegal immigrants have babies here to improve the parents' chance of getting citizenship. No PC is evident there. The same goes for widespread attacks on Muslims, who are increasingly targeted by well-funded anti-Islamic groups peddling hate and fear on web sites and blogs. When slurs and hate speech filter into the national dialogue, PC collapses into prejudice and scapegoating—exactly what it was created to prevent.

Summary of Chapter 7

1. Most words have emotive meanings (in addition to cognitive meanings). Words like *oppression, kike,* and *bitch* have more or less negative emotive overtones; words like *spring, free,* and *satisfaction* have positive emotive overtones; and words like *socialism, marijuana,* and *God* have mixed overtones.

2. Con artists use the emotive side of language (1) to mask cognitive meaning by whipping up emotions so that reason is overlooked and (2) to dull the force of language so as to make acceptable what otherwise might not be. The latter purpose often is accomplished by means of *euphemisms* (less offensive or duller expressions used in place of more offensive or emotively charged locutions).

3. Common rhetorical devices often are used in a slippery manner. *Examples: Slanting* words and expressions ("All this proves is that…"); *weasel words* that suck out all or part of the meaning of a sentence ("Economic success may be…"); *fine-print disclaimers* that take back part of what was originally asserted ("Tickets must be purchased 30 days in advance, subject to availability…"); *obfuscation* that, for example, may mask failure to respond to questions (Sarah Palin wandering from the point of the question about whether she had the national security credentials to serve as vice president). Note that employing the right tone can be used to mask lack of cogent reasoning or content or to sway audiences via emotional appeals.

4. The meanings of words and expressions sometimes are changed so as either to get around or to take advantage of laws, rules, or customs. *Example:* Calling an employee a *subcontractor* to avoid paying a minimum wage or Social Security taxes. But it isn't always easy to determine whether terms have been used rightly or wrongly. *Example:* Psychologists disagree about whether it makes good sense to use the expression *mental illness,* because they disagree about whether the implied analogy to physical illness is useful or accurate. Loaded language can "frame" issues and thus influence the way we think about public policy. *Example:* Calling tax cuts "tax relief" or estate tax "death tax."

5. The social revolution that changed the roles played by women in society, as well as the attitudes of most Americans concerning male-female relationships, has resulted in matching linguistic changes. *Examples:* Replacing expressions in which the term *man* is used to refer to people in general by more neutral words such as *person;* using *Ms.* in some cases instead of *Miss* or *Mrs.;* not repeatedly using *his* to mean *his* or *her;* or switching to the plural form to avoid this use of *his.* (Note that when use of dechauvinized language may ring a bit false—*her or his* can sound somewhat forced—there always are aesthetically acceptable ways to avoid sexist locutions.) But do we go a bit too far when we start talking, say, about *personhole* covers?

6. The linguistic revolution that has replaced sexist language with locutions that are more congenial with today's attitudes and beliefs also has changed many of

the ways in which we refer to members of minorities and other groups, as well as to activities in several important areas of life. Using current lingo, we can say that some ways of speaking are *politically correct* (PC), others not. *Examples:* The terms *Native American, physically challenged,* and *Latino* are "in"; *Indian, crippled* (or *handicapped*), and *Hispanic* (used to refer, say, to Mexican-Americans) are "out." In some cases, the PC revolution may have gone a bit too far. *Example:* Objecting to the use of Indian symbols by baseball teams. But some PC language is eroding for the wrong reasons now that immigrants are coming under attack and Islamophobia is on the rise.

EXERCISE 7-1

In the run-up to the 2008 presidential elections, Barack Obama gave a speech, "A More Perfect Union," hailed by many people as one of the most important speeches on race and the American experience since those given by Martin Luther King. Evaluate this excerpt and explain why it might be effective, persuasive rhetoric. Consider the language (positive and negative), tone, examples, repetitions of words and phrases, choice of pronouns, and anything else you can think of. Conclude with a discussion of the worldview it reflects.

. . . [W]e have a choice in this country. We can accept a politics that breeds division, and conflict, and cynicism. We can tackle race only as spectacle—as we did in the O.J. trial—or in the wake of tragedy, as we did in the aftermath of Katrina—or as fodder for the nightly news....We can pounce on some gaffe by Hillary Clinton as evidence that she's playing the race card, or we can speculate on whether white men will all flock to John McCain in the general election re-gardless of his policies.

We can do that.

But if we do, I can tell you that in the next election, we'll be talking about some other distraction. And then another one....And nothing will change.

That is one option. Or, at this moment in the election, we can come together and say, "Not this time." This time we want to talk about the crumbling schools that are stealing the future of black children and white children and Asian children and Hispanic children and Native American children. This time we want to reject the cynicism that tells us that these kids can't learn: that these kids who don't look like us are somebody else's problem. The children of America are not those kids, they are our kids, and we will not let them fall behind in a 21st century economy. Not this time.

This time we want to talk about how the lines in the emergency room are filled with whites and blacks and Hispanics who do not have health care, who don't have the power on their own to overcome the special interests in Washington, but who can take them on if we do it together.

This time we want to talk about the shuttered mills that once provided a de-cent life for men and women of every race....This time we want to talk about the fact that the real problem is not that someone who doesn't look like you might take your job; it's that the corporation you work for will ship it overseas for nothing more than a profit....

I would not be running for president if I didn't believe with all my heart that this is what the vast majority of Americans want for the country. This union may never be perfect, but generation after generation has shown that it can always be perfected. And today, whenever I find myself feeling doubtful or cynical about this possibility, what gives me the most hope is the next generation—the young people whose attitudes and beliefs and openness to change have already made history in this election.

EXERCISE 7-2

1. Louisiana license plates feature the motto "Sportsman's Paradise." Is this sexist? Defend your answer.

2. Over the past decade, the term *illegal alien* has been euphemized as "undocumented worker" or even "guest without status." What is the point of these euphemisms, and who would be most likely to use them?

*3. Translate the following statement, found on the back of a Hallmark greeting card, into everyday lingo:

   Printed on recycled paper. Contains a minimum of 10% post-consumer and 40% pre-consumer material.

   Aside from the euphemistic use of language in this statement, is there something a bit sneaky going on here?

4. Here is a passage from a thankfully out-of-print edition of the United States history textbook *America: Its People and Values:*

   A friendly Indian named Squanto helped the colonists. He showed them how to plant corn and how to live in the wilderness. A soldier, Captain Miles Standish, taught the Pilgrims how to defend themselves against unfriendly Indians.

   How is language used to slant this account? In what other ways is it slanted? Rewrite the passage from the point of view of the "unfriendly Indians" (that is, Native Americans) in question.

5. Explain in plain English Annette Koloday's "reconceptualization" of the term *family* in this quote from her book *Failing the Future: A Dean Looks at Higher Education in the Twenty-First Century.* (This passage was nominated for the Doublespeak Award, *Quarterly Review of Doublespeak,* January 2002.)

   To conceptualize what I am calling the "family-friendly campus" means reconceptualizing what we include in the term family. The family in the twenty-first century will no longer be identified by blood ties, by legalized affiliations, by cohabitation, or by heterosexual arrangements.

   How, then, would you define *family*?

---

*Starred (*) items are answered in a section at the back of the book.

*6. Translate into plain English the following remark by Admiral Isaac C. Kidd when he was chief of navy matériel:

> We have gone with teams of competent contract people from Washington to outlying field activities to look over their books with them...to see in what areas there is susceptibility to improved capability to commit funds.

7. An animal rights organization wants to replace the term *pet owner* in San Francisco laws with the expression *pet guardian,* because the term *owner* implies that animals are property. Defend or challenge their view on this.

8. Several groups opposed to legal abortions, as well as a few state legislatures in recently enacted laws, refer to a fetus as an *intact child,* a *partially born infant,* or an *unborn child* (see, for example, the March–April 2000 edition of *Extra!*).
   a. What is the point of their use of these locutions instead of the medical term *fetus*?
   b. To which sections or topics of this chapter is this example relevant?

EXERCISE 7-3

1. Find at least one good example of an inappropriate name (for example, *subcontractor*) that is applied so that the law, a custom, or whatever deals with them differently, and explain the chicanery. (No, you aren't supposed to "find" the example in this textbook.)

2. Check your local newspaper, magazines, television programs, the Internet, or some such; find at least two examples of doublespeak or jargon, and translate them back into plain English.

3. Do the same with a particularly obtuse use (as opposed to a "mention") of academese from one of your textbooks (*definitely* not from this one!).

4. Do the same with respect to sexist locutions, but this time translate into PC language.

EXERCISE 7-4

*1. Each chapter in this text starts out with a few (hopefully) apt quotes. But doesn't one of the quotes that starts this language chapter use one of the devices railed against in this chapter? Which one might this be? If it doesn't, why doesn't it? If it does, wasn't it a mistake to use this quotation? Explain. (By the way, does a different one of these quotes commit the fallacy slippery slope?)

2. Previous editions of this text have been criticized by some for implying that in some cases the recent linguistic revolution has gone a bit overboard. This edition contains the question "Why worry about using the term *manhole* when talking about those round excisions in streets and avenues, as did the Public Works Departments of several American cities?" Should we worry? Why, or why not?

3. Do you think universities should develop speech codes designed to suppress racist, sexist, and homophobic speech on campus? Write an argument for or against this policy.

8 Evaluating Extended Arguments

The prejudice against careful analytic procedure is part of the human impatience with technique which arises from the fact that men are interested in results and would like to attain them without the painful toil which is the essence of our moral finitude.

—Morris R. Cohen

There is no expedient to which a man will not resort to avoid the real labor of thinking.

—Sir Joshua Reynolds

Our principal topic in this chapter is the evaluation of extended passages, or **essays**, that argue to a conclusion. Up to this point, we've considered mainly short arguments, and these primarily to illustrate fallacious reasoning or manipulative uses of language. But in daily life, we frequently encounter longer passages, generally containing several related arguments, offered in support of a thesis—the overall conclusion of the passage.

We should recall, however, that there are other kinds of persuasive essays in addition to the argumentative variety. Even simple description or narration often is used for this purpose. For example, in his essay "A Hanging," George Orwell argues with some force against capital punishment simply by graphically describing a hanging and one person's gut-wrenching response to it. (The ongoing abortion debate is studded with detailed descriptions of aborted fetuses.) And just explaining something may effectively persuade others to our point of view. An article on chlorofluorocarbons, for instance, may simply describe how these chemicals deplete the ozone layer, thus increasing our chances of getting skin cancer, and yet convince readers of the implied conclusion that the use of freon in refrigerators and other modern equipment should be stopped.

But our main concern in this chapter will be rhetoric in which there is an attempt to present reasons for conclusions. We need to remember, however, that a conclusion can be argued for in various ways. We may, for example, weigh the merits and demerits of a possible course of action, instead of just presenting favorable reasons. A **pro and con argument** of this kind can be very effective because it tends to answer questions or objections the reader or listener may have about the thesis being argued for. This also is why essays often provide a **refutation to counterarguments**, as in the case of politicians who, after arguing for their position, may then go on to say, "Now my opponent will no doubt respond _____; but I say _____," and then attempt to refute their opponent's objections. An essay may also argue for a course of action by showing that likely alternatives are less desirable, which means arguing by a **comparison of alternatives**.

Note, by the way, that a legitimate appeal to experts in a field may count as a reason for accepting their conclusions, even in the absence of an account of their reasoning processes. During World War II, for example, President Roosevelt accepted the conclusion of physicists Leo Szilard and Albert Einstein (conveyed to the president in a famous letter) that it was possible to build an atomic bomb, even though Roosevelt, like every other lay person, would have been unable to comprehend the reasoning behind their conclusion (which, no doubt, is why the two scientists didn't bother to provide it).

Finally, note that essay writers frequently employ more than one of the methods just mentioned. They first may argue, for instance, by a general comparison of alternatives and then, finding the alternative that seems to be the most attractive, zero in on it for a more careful analysis. Or they may provide reasons that support the essay's thesis and are in turn supported by expert opinion.

1. THE BASIC TASKS OF ESSAY EVALUATION

There are almost as many ways to evaluate extended passages as there are evaluators. What works best for one person may not work so well for others. And time and interest always need to be taken into account. Even so, there are guidelines that most people find of value, in particular, those who initially have a bit of trouble handling lengthy or complicated passages. (Most of the discussion that follows will deal with written passages, but applies also to those that are verbal.)

The next few sections of this chapter describe a method for evaluating essays when the topic being dealt with is of great importance and we have the time necessary to do a thorough job. In daily life, of course, these two conditions are not often met. But getting good at a method like the one described here is a good way to become adept at the quicker kinds of evaluations that we do frequently have to make in everyday life.

Find the Thesis and Keep It in Mind

The most important thing is to *locate the thesis*—the main conclusion of the argument. The thesis isn't always obvious because the passage may be poorly written, or because the thesis may be implied but not explicitly stated, or simply because the author may build up to it and reveal it only near the end of the work. The thesis is the point of an essay, so you have to keep it in mind to determine whether sufficient *reasons* are provided for accepting it. In many sports, the trick is to keep your eye on the ball; in evaluating extended passages, the trick is to keep your mind's eye on the thesis, so that you can better judge whether the reasons do, or don't, adequately support it.

Find the Reasons that Support the Thesis

Obviously, then, the next task after locating the thesis is to *find the reasons*—the *premises*—that are provided in support of the thesis. Again, this will be hard or easy depending on the author's style and competence. But it may also be hard because the reasons themselves are supported by reasons, so that the sheer complexity of an extended passage makes analysis difficult.

Typically, however, it isn't all that hard to see what the thesis of an essay is and to discover the principal reasons offered in its support. For example, a newspaper columnist arguing for the thesis that cigarettes should be made illegal supported his conclusion by pointing out that cigarette smoking kills millions of people; then supported that claim by presenting statistics concerning smoking and heart disease, cancer, and emphysema; and then claimed that anything so bad for us should be illegal. The logical structure of his essay thus was something like this:

> *Thesis:* Cigarettes should be made illegal.
> *Reasons:* 1. Cigarette smoking is deadly.
>   2. Anything so deadly should be illegal.
> *Support for 1:* Statistical proof linking smoking cigarettes with heart disease, cancer, and emphysema.

The columnist assumed (wrongly) that most people would accept his second reason without further justification.

Identify the Evidence

Effective extended arguments usually provide evidence, or support, for the reasons they present. That is, they provide reasons for believing their reasons. In the cigarette example, statistical evidence was cited in support of the claim that cigarette smoking is deadly. But many other sorts of evidence may be appealed to, including authoritative pronouncements, examples, personal experiences, generally accepted facts or common knowledge, and so on. In the Szilard/Einstein letter mentioned before, the evidence for the conclusion that an atomic bomb could be built was just the authority of the letter's authors. Someone might defend the claim that cigarette smoking is deadly simply by appealing to what by now is common knowledge—that it causes lung cancer, heart disease, and so on. A powerful argument against war might well contain specific examples of wars—for example, World War I—that produced incredible misery with little else to show for them.

In a sense, of course, all reasons or premises offered in support of a thesis constitute evidence in its favor. The important point here is that reasons themselves often need, and receive, supporting evidence. Indeed, good essay writers always support reasons in this way except when confident that readers will accept them without further argument.

Identify Responses to Likely Objections or Counterarguments

The sample essay concerning cigarette smoking did not discuss likely objections or counterarguments, but essays often do. The cigarette essay, for instance, might have raised and argued against the objection that we have a right to risk shortening our lives by smoking, or taking other sorts of risks, if we want to. If this objection had been included in the essay, then it would have been important to note and take account of it.

Skip Whatever Doesn't Argue for (or Against) the Thesis

People write essays to persuade other people. So they sometimes include irrelevant material if they think it will help them to persuade others. This kind of "flavoring" material makes reading more fun, but it shouldn't influence the assessment of an argument.

Add Relevant Information or Reasons

Everything needed to prove a thesis is *never* included in an essay, no matter how long it may be. There is no point in trying to prove things that are obvious or generally accepted. Good writers try to provide just the information their audiences will need in order to see the merit of the writer's point of view. For instance, someone writing about education for an audience of teachers doesn't need to prove that plenty of students graduate from high school today without having developed sufficient ability in reading, writing, and basic arithmetic. Every teacher knows that.

Of course, writers, being human, often fail to do the best job of supporting their theses. They often overlook important evidence, or they reason incorrectly to a conclusion that can be supported by better logic. Good critical thinkers try to evaluate the best version of an argument, adding material that its author may have neglected. By the same token, of course, good reasoners also bring to bear whatever negative evidence or reasons they may know about.

Consider Tone and Emotive Language

Although tone and emotive language are not part of the formal elements of argument, they are subtle manipulators that deserve attention, particularly when considering a strongly emotive topic or one that uses irony or humor to persuade. When Adlai Stevenson argued against a state Senate bill to restrain cats (quoted in Chapter 7), his droll exaggeration of the consequences was part of the persuasive power. The idea that the Senate might be "called upon to take sides in the age-old problem of dog versus cat, cat versus bird, or even bird versus worm" made the bill seem just plain silly and thus not worth passing.

One way to identify these hidden persuaders is to underline or circle the emotive words or humorous phrases and then see how they nudge the reader into agreeing with the writer's thesis. Becoming aware of these expressions helps us guard against their undue influence.

Come to an Evaluation

While evaluation is logically the last thing we need to do when dealing with an argumentative passage, good critical thinkers start evaluating from the word go. They keep in mind questions such as, Do I already accept this thesis? Does it fit well with what I already know and believe? If not, in what way is the argument fallacious and why? What sort of reasons or evidence might change my mind? And they continue to evaluate as they go along, bearing in mind questions such as, Is this reason acceptable without further justification? Does that reason really defend the thesis at hand? Do the facts alleged seem plausible, given my background beliefs? Has the writer forgotten a serious counterargument or omitted important counterevidence? Is the use of tone and emotive language unduly persuasive? It's true that a completely confident judgment about a work can't be reached until an essay has been thoroughly examined, but it still is useful to make provisional evaluations right from the start.

Successfully bringing relevant background information to bear clearly is the key to good evaluations, but other relevant thoughts often play an important role. We often simply don't know enough to come to a confident evaluation but still may be able to speculate intelligently by thinking about the right questions that need to be raised either for or against a particular thesis. For example, one of the important reasons often given in favor of laws requiring capital punishment for heinous crimes is that these laws will act as a deterrent—criminals may think more carefully before committing murder if they know conviction means death. This sounds like a very plausible reason given the strength of the urge most of us have to stay alive. But does it in fact work this way? Not knowing the answer may be a good reason for withholding judgment, or for seeking further information, or for at least only *provisionally* assuming that the threat of death deters criminals more than do lesser penalties. The point here is that coming to a justified evaluation requires us to think of what it would be useful to know that we don't as yet know—it requires us to raise the right sorts of questions. (Raising questions of this kind, of course, also serves as a guide to research that might have to be undertaken.)

When the entire structure of an extended argument has been figured out, its relevant passages will divide into those that are argued for within the essay and those that are not. The latter are the writer's basic *assumptions—starting points*—assumed without being justified. When evaluating an extended passage, you need to ask and answer three vital questions, corresponding to the three basic requirements of cogent reasoning (discussed in Chapter 1):

1. Are the writer's assumptions and stated reasons justified by what you already believe?

2. Do you know other relevant reasons or arguments? (If so, then you need to add them before coming to a final conclusion as to the essay's cogency.)

3. Do the reasons (plus any relevant material you may have added) justify acceptance of the thesis—that is, is the reasoning valid?

If an assumption or reason is not supported by your background beliefs, if you know of relevant information that refutes or casts doubt on the thesis, or if the reasoning is not completely valid (taking into account material you may have added), then clearly you should not be convinced by that particular extended argument. It may be, of course, that your background beliefs neither support nor conflict with an argument's assumptions or reasons, in which case you can't either accept or reject the argument's thesis; you need to withhold judgment or delve further into the matter.

A note of caution: It is common for some of the subsidiary arguments in a long essay to be cogent, while others are fallacious. When this is the case, reason dictates accepting only the untainted portions of the overall argument. But it would be wrong to automatically toss out the whole extended argument—wrong to reject the thesis of the essay—if that thesis can stand on the basis of the legitimate portions of the essay (along with relevant material you may have added from your background beliefs). This point often is characterized as one of *charity*—of being fair to the other side on an issue—but it also is an important requirement of good critical reasoning.

EXERCISE 8-1

Here are several short passages (taken from longer works). Reveal the structure of each passage, including reasons that support the thesis, reasons for the reasons, counterarguments, extraneous material, and so on, as in this simple example. (Remember, sometimes a reason or thesis may be implied.)

Example

Original passage (from an essay by Baruch Brody on the abortion issue): There is a continuity of development from the moment of conception on. There are constant changes in the foetal condition; the foetus is constantly acquiring new structure and characteristics, but there is no one state which is radically different from any other. Since this is so, there is no one stage in the process of foetal development after the moment of conception which could plausibly be picked out as the moment at which the foetus becomes a living human being. The moment of conception is, however, different in this respect. It marks the beginning of this continuous process of development and introduces something new which is radically discontinuous with what has come before it. Therefore, the moment of conception, and only it, is a plausible candidate for being that moment at which the foetus becomes a living human being.

Rewritten Passage

Reason (premise): After the moment of conception, there is a continuous development of the human fetus, with no one state being much different from the next. *Conclusion:* No moment after conception can be selected as the moment the fetus becomes a human being. (This conclusion then becomes a reason [premise] in the larger argument.)

Reason (premise): But the moment of conception introduces something radically different from what came before.

Conclusion (thesis): The moment of conception is the only plausible moment when the fetus becomes a human being.

1. Payday loan stores prey on low-income people and drive them into debt. There are now so many of them that they outnumber most fast-food franchises. Companies with names like EZ Money and Check Into Cash give two-week loans with no credit checks, but they charge huge fees. It's not uncommon for a company to charge a fee of $22 per two weeks for every $100 borrowed; at this rate a $500 loan would rack up an annual interest rate of 572 percent. Loan companies like this take advantage of poor people who are desperate to make ends meet from one paycheck to the next. Borrowers begin by taking out one loan to tide them over, and then another if they still run short, and then another. For example, one woman had to take out loans from four different companies and wound up paying $600 in finance fees alone for a debt of $1,300. Borrowers like this, who live on the margin as is, are driven deeper and deeper into debt by the loan shark practices of payday stores. This is little better than thievery and should be stopped. State governments should prohibit payday lending. It's bad enough that these borrowers are living on the edge. Loan companies that take advantage of them are

unconscionable. (Data taken from: Leland, John. "Payday Loans, Nonprofit Style, Emerge to Mixed Response." *New York Times* 28 August 2007.)

2. Excerpt from "The Case for Censorship," by Roger Kimball. *Wall Street Journal* 8 October 2000:

> . . . What's wrong with a little censorship? Until quite recently all sorts of things were censored in American society. There were very strict rules about what you could show on television and in movies, what you could describe in books and what you could reproduce in magazines. Were we worse off then?
> . . . There are plenty of reasons to support government censorship when it comes to depictions of sex and violence. For one thing, it would encourage the entertainment industry to turn out material that is richer erotically. . . . Another reason. . . is that it would help temper the extraordinary brutality of popular culture.
> . . . [Society] has an interest in protecting the moral sensibility of its citizens, especially the young. Freedom without morality degenerates into the servitude of libertinage. Which is why judicious government censorship is not the enemy of freedom but its guarantor.

*3. Thomas Paine, in his classic *The Age of Reason:*[1]

> Revelation is a communication of something which the person to whom that thing is revealed did not know before. For if I have done a thing, or seen it done, it needs no revelation to tell me I have done it or seen it, nor to enable me to tell it or to write it. Revelation, therefore, cannot be applied to anything done upon earth, of which man himself is the actor or the witness; and consequently, all the historical and anecdotal parts of the Bible, which is almost the whole of it, is not within the meaning and compass of the word "revelation," and therefore, is not the word of God.

4. An argument on gun laws: In response to outbreaks of violence on college campuses, gun advocates are lobbying colleges and universities to permit students to carry guns on campus. Although they insist that the gun-toting students will discourage mass killers and thus make campuses safer, they are wrong. Undergraduates are too young to handle firearms responsibly and are more likely to shoot each other in the heat of an argument than a mass murderer—a phenomenon as rare as a dodo bird. Even if a killer did show up and students tried to gun him or her down, the police would have a hard time sorting out the students from the gunman. Besides, there are fewer than 20 homicides on campus a year, so colleges would hardly be justified in giving thousands of students the right to tote guns.

5. Argument implied in this excerpt from the *International Herald Tribune* 2 July 2003 "Court Orders Removal of Monument to Ten Commandments" by Adam Liptak.

> The federal appeals court in Atlanta has ordered the chief justice of the Alabama Supreme Court to remove a monument engraved with the Ten

---

[1]Starred (*) items are answered in a section at the back of the book.

Commandments from the rotunda of his courthouse. The 11th U.S. Circuit Court of Appeals concluded the monument violates the First Amendment's prohibition on government establishment of religion. In its ruling Tuesday, the court was unusually blunt in responding to the assertion by Chief Justice Roy Moore in court papers in the case that he did not recognize the authority of the federal court in this matter. The appeals court compared Moore to those Southern governors [George Wallace and Ross Barnett] who attempted to defy court orders during an earlier era.

6. Philosopher John Locke, in his classic *The Second Treatise on Government:*

> Though the earth and all inferior creatures be common to all men, yet every man has a property in his own person; this nobody has any right to but himself. The labor of his body and the work of his hands, we may say, are properly his. Whatsoever then he removes out of the state that nature has provided and left it in, he has mixed his labor with, and joined to it something that is his own, and thereby makes it his property. It being by him removed from the common state nature has placed it in, it has by this labor something annexed to it that excluded the common right of other men. For this labor being the unquestionable property of the laborer, no man but he can have a right to what that is once joined to, at least where there is enough and as good left in common for others.

7. From an article on genetically engineered foods, by John B. Fagan:[2]

> Giant transnational companies are carrying out a dangerous global experiment by attempting to introduce large numbers of genetically engineered foods widely into our food supply. Because genetic manipulations can generate unanticipated harmful side-effects, and because genetically engineered foods are not tested sufficiently to eliminate those that are dangerous, this experiment not only jeopardizes the health of individuals, but could also lead to national health threats. . . . Tampering with the genetic code of food is reckless and poses a serious threat to life. It could easily upset the delicate balance between our physiology and the foods that we eat. There is already ample scientific justification for an immediate ban on genetically modified foods in order to safeguard our health.

8. Philosopher Sidney Hook, on recovering from a near-fatal stroke triggered by an angiogram used to diagnose heart disease:

> A few years ago, I lay at the point of death [following the stroke]. . . .At one point my heart stopped beating; just as I lost consciousness, it was thumped back into action again. In one of my lucid intervals during those days of agony, I asked my physician to discontinue all life-supporting services or show me how to do it. He refused. . . .

---

[2]Fagan, John B. "Genetically Engineered Food: A Serious Health Risk." Physicians and Scientists for Responsible Application of Science and Technology (PSRAST). Web. http://www.psrast.org/jfhealth.htm

A month later I was discharged from the hospital. In six months I regained the use of my limbs [and voice]. . . . My experience . . . has been cited as an argument against honoring requests of stricken patients to be gently eased out of their pain and life. I cannot agree. . . . As an octogenarian, there is a reasonable likelihood that I may suffer another "cardiovascular accident" or worse. . . . It seems to me that I have already paid my dues to death—indeed . . . I suffered enough to warrant dying several times over. Why run the risk of more?

Secondly, I dread imposing on my family and friends another grim round of misery similar to the one my first attack occasioned. My wife and children endured enough for one lifetime. . . .

EXERCISE 8-2

In general, we do not read poetry with the intent of constructing a summary and then evaluating for cogency. We read out of love for effective poetic expression. Nevertheless, it is a fact that poems often argue for a conclusion. Andrew Marvell's wonderful (one might say "Marvell-ous") poem "To His Coy Mistress" is a case in point. Clearly, there would be no point in constructing a detailed summary of this, or perhaps any, poem, citing every bit of support given for the reasons provided for its thesis. So in this case, after first reading the poem for the enjoyment of the experience, simply state in a general way and in your own words the poem's thesis; the reason, or reasons, provided in its support; and a rough idea of the support provided for the reason or reasons.

To His Coy Mistress

Had we but world enough, and time,
This coyness, Lady, were no crime.
We would sit down and think which way
To walk and pass our long love's day.
Thou by the Indian Ganges' side
Shouldst rubies find: I by the tide
Of Humber would complain. I would
Love you ten years before the Flood,
And you should, if you please, refuse
Till the conversion of the Jews.
My vegetable love would grow
Vaster than empires and more slow;
An hundred years would go to praise
Thine eyes and on thy forehead gaze;
Two hundred to adore each breast,
But thirty thousand to the rest;
An age at least to every part,
And the last age should show your heart.
For, Lady, you deserve this state,
Nor would I love at lower rate.

But at my back I always hear
Time's winged chariot hurrying near;
And yonder all before us lie
Deserts of vast eternity,
Thy beauty shall no more be found,
Nor, in thy marble vault, shall sound
My echoing song; then worms shall try
That long preserved virginity,
And your quaint honor turn to dust,
And into ashes all my lust;
The grave's a fine and private place,
But none, I think, do there embrace.

Now therefore, while the youthful hue
Sits on thy skin like morning dew,
And while thy willing soul transpires
At every pore with instant fires,
Now let us sport us while we may,
And now, like amorous birds of prey,
Rather at once our time devour
Than languish in his slow-chapped power.

Let us roll all our strength and all	Through the iron gate of life,
Our sweetness up into one ball,	Thus, though we cannot make our sun
And tear our pleasures with rough strife	Stand still, yet we will make him run.

EXERCISE 8-3

The Declaration of Independence contains a thesis and reasons supporting that thesis. Get a copy of that important document, and (1) determine what its thesis is, and (2) list the reasons provided in defense of that thesis. Is the argument inductive or deductive? What is the worldview?

2. THE MARGIN NOTE AND SUMMARY METHOD

The **margin note and summary method** is a good method to use when an evaluation has to be right. The idea behind this method is that a summary can be more easily worked with than the longer work from which it is drawn, provided the summary is *accurate.* (Making a summary helps us to remember things better and thus is a good study technique—one, in fact, that instructors often use when preparing class material.)

The margin note and summary method has four basic steps:

1. Read the material to be summarized.
2. Read it through again, this time marking the important passages with an indication of their content written in the margin. (The point of the first reading is to enable you to spot the important passages more accurately when you read through the material a second time. First readings often don't catch the drift.) Margin notes need not be full sentences or grammatically correct. They may contain abbreviations or whatever shorthand notes you care to employ.
3. Use the margin notes to construct a summary of the passage, indicating which statements are premises (reasons) and which conclusions, so that the structure of the passage's argument is laid bare.
4. Evaluate the essay by evaluating your summary, checking back and forth to be sure there are no significant differences between the essay and your summary.

Two things need to be remembered about the margin note and summary method. First, when we skip portions of a passage, we make a judgment that the passed-over material is relatively unimportant. It takes practice and skill to know what to include and what to omit, and even those with a good deal of experience may differ on such matters. (This does not mean, however, that anything goes!) Second, margin notes and summaries are shorthand devices; they should be briefer than the passages they summarize—if possible, a good deal briefer. The risk in this process, obviously, is falsification. We don't want to commit the straw man fallacy by making judgments about the shortened version that would not be valid for the original.

3. EXTENDED EVALUATION OF AN ARGUMENT

An exended evaluation examines an argument in some detail, using the critical thinking tools covered throughout this text. The first step is to summarize the article using the margin note method explained in the previous section. Then identify the thesis, the reasons and the main points of the argument. The next task is to determine whether the argument is convincing. Do the reasons really defend the thesis or are they fallacious? Is the evidence plausible? Has the writer included important counterarguments? Is the use of emotive language persuasive or manipulative? Is the worldview convincing? These are some of the questions to consider when evaluating arguments.

It is important to keep in mind that there is no such thing as a perfectly reasoned, totally convincing argument (though there are plenty of really bad ones out there). Even brilliant thinkers slip up once in a while or get carried away with their own rhetoric. A good analysis determines what is convincing and what is not, then comes to an overall evaluation of the argument.

Here is a condensed version of an argument on capital punishment by probably the most famous trial lawyer of the 20th century, Clarence Darrow, followed by an evaluation. One of Darrow's most celebrated cases was his defense of Richard Loeb and Nathan Leopold, two teenagers who pled guilty to kidnapping and murdering a 14-year-old boy. The prosecution was determined to hang the killers, but Darrow's brilliant 12-hour summation, an eloquent attack on the death penalty, was so effective that the presiding judge wept at its conclusion and gave Leopold and Loeb a life sentence instead of the death penalty. (An interesting footnote on Darrow is that no client of his was ever executed.) The following essay was published a few years after the trial. Although written in the first half of the 20th century, the arguments Darrow made are still used by abolitionists today. Given his legendary prowess in a court of law, one might think his arguments were airtight, but even the great Darrow lapsed into fallacious reasoning and used rhetorical tricks to persuade.

The Futility of the Death Penalty[3]

. . . It is my purpose in this article to prove, first, that capital punishment is no deterrent to crime; and second, that the state continues to kill its victims, not so much to defend society against them—for it could do that equally well by imprisonment—but to appease the mob's emotions of hatred and revenge. . . .

Behind the idea of capital punishment lie false training and crude views of human conduct. People do evil things, say the judges, lawyers, and preachers, because of depraved hearts. . . .

If crime were really the result of willful depravity, we should be ready to concede that capital punishment may serve as a deterrent to the criminally inclined. But it is hardly probable that the great majority of people refrain from killing their neighbors because they are afraid; they refrain because they never had the inclination. Human beings are creatures of habit; and, as a rule, they are not in

---

[3]Darrow, Clarence. "The Futility of the Death Penalty." *Verdicts Out of Control.* Eds. Arthur and Lila Weinberg. Chicago: Quadrangle Books, 1963. 225–234. This essay first appeared in *The Forum,* September 1928. By permission of the Estate of Clarence Darrow, all rights reserved.

the habit of killing. The circumstances that lead to killings are manifold, but in a particular individual the inducing cause is not easily found. In one case, homicide may have been induced by indigestion in the killer; in another, it may be traceable to some weakness inherited from a remote ancestor; but that it results from *something* tangible and understandable, if all the facts were known, must be plain to everyone who believes in cause and effect.

Of course, no one will be converted to this point of view by statistics of crime. In the first place, it is impossible to obtain reliable ones, and in the second place, the conditions to which they apply are never the same. But if one cares to analyze the figures, such as we have, it is easy to trace the more frequent causes of homicide. The greatest number of killings occur during attempted burglaries and robberies. The robber knows that penalties for burglary do not average more than five years in prison. He also knows that the penalty for murder is death or imprisonment. Faced with this alternative, what does the burglar do when he is detected and threatened with arrest? He shoots to kill. He deliberately takes the chance of death to save himself from a five-year term in prison. It is therefore as obvious as anything can be that fear of death has no effect in diminishing homicides of this kind, which are more numerous than any other type.

The next largest number of homicides may be classed as "sex murders." Quarrels between husbands and wives, disappointed love, or love too much requited cause many killings. They are the result of primal emotions so deep that the fear of death has not the slightest effect in preventing them. Spontaneous feelings overflow in criminal acts, and consequences do not count.

Then there are cases of sudden anger, uncontrollable rage. The fear of death never enters into such cases; if the anger is strong enough, consequences are not considered until too late. The old-fashioned stories of men deliberately plotting and committing murder in cold blood have little foundation in real life. Such killings are so rare that they need not concern us here. The point to be emphasized is that practically all homicides are manifestations of well-recognized human emotions, and it is perfectly plain that the fear of excessive punishment does not enter into them.

In addition to these personal forces which overwhelm weak men and lead them to commit murder, there are also many social and economic forces which must be listed among the causes of homicides, and human beings have even less control over these than over their own emotions. . . . the United States has gathered together people of every color from every nation in the world. Racial differences intensify social, religious, and industrial problems, and the confusion which attends this indiscriminate mixing of races and nationalities is one of the most fertile sources or crime.

Will capital punishment remedy these conditions? Of course it won't; but its advocates argue that the fear of this extreme penalty will hold the victims of adverse conditions in check. To this piece of sophistry, the continuance and increase of crime in our large cities is a sufficient answer. No, the plea that capital punishment acts as a deterrent to crime will not stand. The real reason why this barbarous practice persists in a so-called civilized world is that people still hold the primitive belief that the taking of one human life can be atoned for by taking another. It is the age-old obsession with punishment that keeps the official headsman busy plying his trade.

And it is precisely upon this point that I would build my case against capital punishment. Even if one grants that the idea of punishment is sound, crime calls for something more—for careful study, for an understanding of causes, for proper remedies. To attempt to abolish crime by killing the criminal is the easy and foolish way out of a serious situation. Unless a remedy deals with the conditions which foster crime, criminals will breed faster than the hangman can spring his trap. Capital punishment ignores the causes of crime and, like the methods of the witch doctor, it is not only ineffective as a remedy, but is positively vicious in at least two ways. In the first place, the spectacle of state executions feeds the basest passions of the mob. And in the second place, so long as the state rests content to deal with crime in this barbaric and futile manner, society will be lulled by a false sense of security, and effective methods of dealing with crime will be discouraged. . . .

. . . [W]hile capital punishment panders to the passions of the mob, no one takes the pains to understand the meaning of crime. People speak of crime or criminals as if the world were divided into the good and the bad. This is not true. . . .

Human conduct is by no means so simple as our moralists have led us to believe. There is no sharp line separating good actions from bad. The greed for money, the display of wealth, the despair of those who witness the display, the poverty, oppression, and hopelessness of the unfortunate—all these are factors which enter into human conduct and of which the world takes no account. Many people have learned no other profession but robbery and burglary. The processions moving steadily through our prisons to the gallows are in the main made up of these unfortunates. And how do we dare to consider ourselves civilized creatures when, ignoring the causes of crime, we rest content to mete out harsh punishments to the victims of conditions over which they have no control? . . .

Even now, are not all imaginative and humane people shocked at the spectacle of a killing by the state? . . . How can the state censure the cruelty of the man who—moved by strong passions, or acting to save his freedom, or influenced by weakness or fear—takes human life, when everyone knows that the state itself, after long premeditation and settled hatred, not only kills, but first tortures and bedevils its victims for weeks with the impending doom?

For the last hundred years the world has shown a gradual tendency to mitigate punishment. We are slowly learning that this way of controlling human beings is both cruel and ineffective. . . . There is no doubt whatever that the world is growing more humane and more sensitive and more understanding. The time will come when all people will view with horror the light way in which society and its courts of law now take human life; and when that time comes, the way will be clear to devise some better method of dealing with poverty and ignorance and their frequent byproducts, which we call crime.

Analysis

In "The Futility of the Death Penalty," Clarence Darrow argues against capital punishment because it is "no deterrent to crime" and it is the state's attempt "to appease the mob's emotions of hatred and revenge." His overall argument is valid and often persuasive, but he sometimes reasons fallaciously, and though he uses language effectively, he also uses it cleverly, to manipulate the reader. He is at his best, however, when he urges us to consider the humane world view at the heart of his argument.

Darrow's first premise, that capital punishment is no deterrent to crime, is hypothetical, based on common sense and his own background experience as a defense lawyer. Darrow himself concedes that "no one will be converted to this point of view by statistics of crime" partly because "it is impossible to obtain reliable ones." Although recent studies seem to provide some statistical corroboration that the death penalty is a deterrent, Darrow's reservations about crime statistics are just as relevant today as they were then. According to the Death Penalty Information Center, the homicide rate in states without the death penalty has been consistently lower than in states with the death penalty over a 20-year period from 1990 to 2009. However, these findings suggest the fallacy of questionable cause, since the states cited may have had a higher rate of murder to start with and may have instituted the death penalty to reduce the number of homicides.

Instead of using questionable statistics to make his point, Darrow reasons that most killers are not deterred by the death penalty when they kill in the heat of the moment—during attempted burglaries, in sex-related quarrels, or in cases of uncontrollable rage. Our own background beliefs would probably confirm his assumption that people aren't likely to think of the consequences under these circumstances. But he is guilty of suppressing evidence when he dismisses the idea of premeditation in his claim that "men deliberately plotting and committing murder in cold blood have little foundation in real life." Countless examples of premeditated murder could be used to refute this claim, but the most obvious in Darrow's case is the gruesome crime committed by his own clients, Leopold and Loeb, who systematically planned to commit the perfect crime to kidnap and murder their 14-year-old victim. His argument that a "great majority of people refrain from killing their neighbors . . . because they never had the inclination" probably applies to most people but doesn't take into account those who *do* have the inclination to kill and who *are* deterred by the fear of punishment.

There is some truth to his second premise that the state continues to kill its victims to appease the mob's emotions of hatred and revenge. Politicians do, indeed, pay attention to the attitudes their constituents have about capital punishment. In Texas, for instance, candidates who take a stand against the death penalty would have a hard time getting elected. But Darrow relies more on provocative rhetoric than reasoning to make his point. He argues that those who favor the death penalty are a " mob," incited by "hatred and revenge," and the state is a murderer in the questionable premise that "the state itself, after long premeditation and settled hatred, not only kills but first tortures and bedevils its victims for weeks with the impending doom." By presenting the criminal as the "victim," he transforms the entire legal process—from the interrogation, to the trial, sentencing, and appeals—into torturous treatment of the murderer, all of which evade the issue that a real victim is dead at the hands of a killer.

Darrow's argument is driven by highly emotive, often persuasive language, used to engage the reader in his crusade. His tone is characterized by compassion for the hapless killer and moral outrage at the harsh retribution exacted by the state. Capital punishment is condemned as a "barbarous practice," the "easy and foolish way out of a serious situation." Those who favor it are "moralists" with "crude" notions of human conduct, people with the "primitive belief" that executing the killer will atone for the murder. To counter these uncivilized tendencies in human nature, Darrow describes right-thinking people as "imaginative and humane," "shocked at the spectacle of killing by the state." This is an effective ploy to jar the reader into seeing the state in a different light—as a killer not far removed from the murderer it condemns. Less persuasive is the linguistic sleight-of-hand he reserves for the criminals, whom he repeatedly refers to as "victims"—of social forces, emotional drives, or biological quirks—implying that they commit crime through no fault of their own because of the questionable premise that their behavior is the result of "conditions over which they have no control."

Perhaps more than anything else, his argument stands or falls on his worldview, which encompasses his attitude toward the criminal class and the responsibility of society in dealing with it. Darrow's philosophy of determinism is evident throughout when he claims that homicides may be "traceable to some weakness inherited from a remote ancestor" or "the result of primal emotions" or "uncontrollable rage," or that criminals are "victims of conditions over which they have no control." Although it is true that we have no control over the environment we are born into or the genes we inherit, most of us believe that we not only can but should control our actions, despite the problems inherent in our background. A more compelling reason for abolishing capital punishment is rooted in his humane worldview that a civilized society should not sink to the level of the criminal, that it should resist the primitive urge to exact retribution, and that it should deal with criminals in a humane manner, by mitigating punishment and trying to remedy the conditions that foster crime. In this way, he appeals to our better natures and presents his most convincing argument.

EXERCISE 8-4

1. The above analysis of Darrow's argument is one person's evaluation and may not agree with your own. In what ways would you agree or disagree with it? Analyze the premises, reasoning, language, and worldview of Darrow's argument and come up with your own evaluation.

2. Find a two- to three-page argument in a magazine or on the Internet and evaluate it, using the critical thinking tools covered in the text.

4. DEALING WITH VALUE CLAIMS

By now, it should have become clear how often the reasons presented in favor of a thesis are at least in part about values, not facts. It is a *fact,* for example, that sugar sweetens coffee; it is a *value judgment* that sweetened coffee tastes better than unsweetened. It is a fact that the Earth goes around the sun once every 365 days or so; it is a value judgment that, other things being equal, those who give to the poor are better people than the Scrooges who don't. (Note the slanting word used in the previous sentence.)

When someone argues, say, that vacations are better taken in the spring, because spring is the best time of the year, that person uses a value judgment as a reason (premise) supporting the conclusion that vacations are best taken in the spring. (Note, by the way, that this conclusion is itself in part a value judgment, as are all conclusions that depend on at least one reason that is a value judgment.)

Value judgments typically are justified, or defended, in ways that are different from judgments about facts. Someone who claims, for example, that gold does not rust can support that claim by citing the fact that nothing made of gold has ever been observed to rust and that all attempts to rust gold have failed. But the person who says that gold makes beautiful jewelry has to cite a different sort of evidence—for example, that people generally like the look of gold jewelry. That is why many philosophers say that value judgments concern matters that are *subjective,* while judgments about alleged facts deal with matters that are *objective.*

The idea that values are subjective is captured nicely by the saying that beauty is in the eye of the beholder, and by the old precept that there is no disputing about taste. According to these maxims, the fact that some people like string beans, or Bach fugues, while others don't doesn't make those who do or those who don't wrong. By way of contrast, those who make a nonvalue, factual claim—for instance, that the Earth is flat (so-called "flat earthers")—are wrong; the rest of us who believe that it is spherical (well, extremely close to being spherical) are right. (Yes, there are people who still, in this day and age, believe that the Earth is flat. Recall the discussion of self-deception in Chapter 6.) Merely believing that something is a fact doesn't make it a fact; nor is such a belief justified in the absence of evidence (experience about something relevant) to support that belief.

It's true, of course, that lots of philosophers would argue against the idea that value judgments are by their nature subjective. Some would say, for example, that beauty is in the object, not just in the eye of the beholder, so that the person who doesn't see the beauty in beautiful objects is like someone who is color-blind. (One of the points of a philosophy course in which value judgments are discussed is precisely to deal with disagreements of this kind.)

Fortunately, when the value judgments relevant to an argument are about beauty, or taste, or other aesthetic matters, we generally can come to an evaluation without having to deal with underlying philosophical issues like the one about objectivity versus subjectivity. Suppose, for example, that some people in a community want to make uncovered auto junkyards illegal, on the grounds that they constitute an "eyesore." Voters don't need to decide whether being an eyesore is an objective or a subjective property to figure out how to vote. They can just find out whether most people find them to be ugly, or at least whether they themselves see junkyards as a good deal less than attractive. (There may, of course, be good reasons against banning open auto graveyards, but that is another matter.) The point is that, in these cases, we can appeal to something subjective—namely, whether we see junkyards as ugly or not—without answering the underlying questions about whether the ugliness of something is in the thing itself or merely in the eyes of the beholder.

But other sorts of value cases are more problematic, the prime case being *moral values*. If it is true that moral values are subjective, then claims about them can be justified simply by appealing to evidence that most people hold these values. Enslaving people and working them to death then become morally wrong just because virtually everyone finds this sort of behavior wrong or unfair. But if moral values are objective, judgments about them cannot be defended in this way. Subjective feelings become irrelevant if moral principles are objective—if there is something outside us, be it biblical commandments, natural rights, the greatest good for the greatest number, or whatever, that determines which actions are right and which wrong.[4] Thus, those who hold that moral standards are objective need to think carefully as to what sorts of justifications—appeal to cultural norms, natural rights, religious principles, or something else—they believe should count in assessing moral claims and whether these allegedly objective standards in turn can be justified without appeal to subjective values or standards.

The point here, however, is that when someone makes a moral value claim in an argument, it may be crucially important to find out what makes that person hold the value in question. Those who argue against legal abortions, for example, often present as their principal reason the claim that taking a human life is morally wrong; but if their justification is the biblical commandment "Thou shalt not kill," then those who do not accept the Bible as the ultimate authority on moral matters have not been given a persuasive reason for accepting this claim about the immorality of taking a human life.[5] Similarly, those who argue in favor of legalizing prostitution often claim that a woman has a right to use her body in any way that she sees fit; but if their justification is a theory of objective natural rights, then those who reject the idea of objective rights have not been given a satisfactory reason for being in favor of legal prostitution.

In any case, good critical reasoners accept premises that contain moral value judgments only if those judgments conform to their own moral standards. Socialists, for instance, sometimes argue that it is not just impractical but also immoral to allow (as is currently the case in the United States and some other industrial countries), and they use this claim as a reason for overturning, or at least modifying, the free enterprise system now in place in most industrial countries. Good critical reasoners accept or reject moral claims of this sort by seeing how they fit with the moral principles they already accept.

This does not mean, of course, that moral standards and values are exempt from challenge. Those who believe, say, that it always is morally wrong to violate legally enacted legislation may see the matter differently if laws are enacted forbidding the practice of their own religion, or forcing acceptance of another faith.

It also needs to be noted that there often are no simple principles—say, those like the Ten Commandments—to apply in determining moral right and wrong. It seems

---

[4]All of these, and many other allegedly objective factors, have been argued for, and against, by philosophers and theologians.

[5]Note that appeals to authorities such as the Bible can be tricky. With respect to the abortion case, for instance, it has been argued that the original Hebrew has been mistranslated and that what the commandment says is better translated as "Thou shalt not *murder*," so that the question remains as to whether abortion is murder—immoral killing. There also is the problem that most who deny the legitimacy of abortion believe certain kinds of killing are justified—for instance, in wartime or in self-defense; those who believe this would have to show why killing fetuses is not also sometimes justified.

morally right to many people that income should be proportionate to what one produces, a standard encapsulated in the idea that one should reap what one sows. According to this *principle of just desserts,* the fruits of a cooperative effort ought to be distributed according to the relative contributions of the various parties, whether in labor, capital, or whatever. But even supposing this idea is accepted, how are just desserts to be determined in actual cases? How do we compare, for instance, the efforts of a corporate chief executive officer who oversees the successful introduction of a new product with the engineers who designed and perfected that product, or with workers on the line who actually produce the goods? How do we compare the contributions of those who put up the money (stockholders) with those of company executives or production line employees?[6]

Finally, it is important to remember that those who go through life without carefully examining and questioning their moral principles run the same risk of mistake as do those who fail to acquire accurate factual beliefs about how things work in this complicated world of ours. This is true even if the subjectivist view of moral right and wrong is correct, for it still could well be that a person's unexamined feelings about this or that moral issue will fail to agree with how that individual might see the matter after giving it careful thought or after bringing to bear relevant background information. The first thought that virtually all of us have about infanticide, to take an interesting case, is that it always and everywhere is the worst sort of murder; but thinking carefully about the hard choices life presents to some parents has changed the minds of more than a few thinking and even compassionate individuals.[7]

EXERCISE 8-5

In a *New York Times* op-ed piece (16 April 2008), James Alan Fox argues that colleges and universities are creating an "unwarranted and unhealthy level of fear" by beefing up campus security with measures that might well be ineffective. Fox, a professor of criminal justice and law at Northeastern University, believes that colleges are overreacting to shootings at Virginia Tech and other institutions by developing security measures like lockdowns and mass notification "that not long ago would have been considered unnecessary, if not absurd." Lockdowns, or plans to seal off buildings to prevent a gunman from moving from one place to another, "may do little to prevent casualties . . . [since] almost all college shootings have taken place in one location." They have the added disadvantage of preventing a potential victim from fleeing the building that has been sealed off. Mass notification may be equally ineffective. Emergency sirens could be set off by other causes other than gunfire, and text message alerts on cell phones wouldn't reach a lecture hall full of students required to turn off cell phones. Professor Fox argues that security measures like these raise the level of student fear without providing reliable

---

[6]For more on this topic, see: Kahane, Howard. *Contract Ethics: Evolutionary Biology and the Moral Sentiments.* Lanham, Md.: Rowman & Littlefield, 1995.

[7]It sometimes happens that the only alternatives open to parents in poor societies, or societies in the throes of famine, are to do away with a newborn child so as to be able to keep their other children alive or else to see all of their offspring slowly starve to death.

protection. He does believe in taking sensible precautions, like having an adequate se-curity force and well trained staff members, but he thinks colleges have overreacted to violence on campus, creating fear and apprehension that undermine the "carefree atmosphere of campus life." Would you agree or disagree? Do some research on security measures at your campus and evaluate them for effectiveness.

EXERCISE 8-6

A while back (Exercise 8-1, number 5), you were asked to summarize excerpts from the writings of philosopher John Locke.

1. Indicate which of his assertions, if any, in his essay concern values, moral or nonmoral.

2. Use the summary of the article that you constructed before, along with your beliefs about any value statements the essay in question may contain, to come to an evaluation of Locke's view on the matter, indicating where you think his argu-ment is weak, where strong, and what your overall evaluation is, making sure, of course, to explain why you think so.

EXERCISE 8-7

From Hitler's *Mein Kampf*, a book in which he explained his philosophy and his goals for a "Thousand Year Reich":

Nation and Race
There are some truths which are so obvious that for this very reason they are not seen or at least not recognized by ordinary people. They sometimes pass by such truisms as though blind and are most astonished when someone suddenly discovers what everyone really ought to know. Columbus's eggs lie around by the hundreds of thousands, but Columbuses are met with less frequently. Thus men without exception wander about in the garden of Nature; they imagine that they know practically everything and with few exceptions pass blindly by one of the most patent principles of Nature's rule: the inner segregation of the spe-cies of all living beings on this earth. Even the most superficial observation shows that Nature's restricted form of propagation and increase is an almost rigid basic law of all the innumerable forms of expression of her vital urge. Ev-ery animal mates only with a member of the same species. The titmouse seeks the titmouse, the finch the finch, the stork the stork, the field mouse the field mouse, the dormouse the dormouse, the wolf the she-wolf, etc. . . . Any cross-ing of two beings not at exactly the same level produces a medium between the level of the two parents. This means: the offspring will probably stand higher than the racially lower parent, but not as high as the higher one. Consequently, it will later succumb in the struggle against the higher level. Such mating is contrary to the will of Nature for a higher breeding of all life. The precondition for this does not lie in associating superior and inferior, but in the total victory

of the former. The stronger must dominate and not blend with the weaker, thus sacrificing his own greatness. Only the born weakling can view this as cruel, but he after all is only a weak and limited man; for if this law did not prevail, any conceivable higher development of organic living beings would be unthinkable. The consequence of this urge toward racial purity, universally valid in Nature, is not only the sharp outward delimitation of the various races, but their uniform character in themselves. The fox is always a fox, the goose a goose, the tiger a tiger, etc., and the difference can lie at most in the varying measure of force, strength, intelligence, dexterity, endurance, etc., of the individual specimens. But you will never find a fox who in his inner attitude might, for example, show humanitarian tendencies toward geese, as similarly there is no cat with a friendly inclination toward mice.

Therefore, here, too, the struggle among themselves arises less from inner aversion than from hunger and love. In both cases, Nature looks on calmly, with satisfaction, in fact. In the struggle for daily bread all those who are weak and sickly or less determined succumb, while the struggle of the males for the female grants the right or opportunity to propagate only to the healthiest. And the struggle is always a means for improving a species' health and power of resistance and, therefore, a cause of its higher development. . . .

No more than Nature desires the mating of weaker with stronger individuals, even less does she desire the blending of a higher with a lower race, since, if she did, her whole work of higher breeding, over perhaps hundreds of thousands of years, might be ruined with one blow. Historical experience offers countless proofs of this. It shows with terrifying clarity that in every mingling of Aryan blood with that of lower peoples the result was the end of the cultured people. North America, whose population consists in by far the largest part of Germanic elements [Hitler classified the English as Germanic] who mixed but little with the lower colored peoples, shows a different humanity and culture from Central and South America, where the predominantly Latin immigrants often mixed with the aborigines on a large scale. By this one example, we can clearly and distinctly recognize the effect of racial mixture. The Germanic inhabitant of the American continent, who has remained racially pure and unmixed, rose to be master of the continent; he will remain the master as long as he does not fall a victim to defilement of the blood.[8]

1. Construct a summary of Hitler's arguments.

*2. Write an essay in which you critically evaluate these arguments (In this case, the friendly authors of this text provide a summary in the answer section at the back of the book, but not a critical evaluation. You should, of course, construct your own summary first and then compare it with the authors' summary at the back of the book.)

---

[8]From *Mein Kampf* by Adolf Hitler, translated by Ralph Manheim, pp. 284-287. Copyright © 1943, renewed 1971 by Houghton Mifflin Harcourt Publishing Company. Reprinted by permission of Houghton Mifflin Harcourt Publishing Company and The Random Group Limited.

EXERCISE 8-8

In the fall of 2003, Californians were asked to vote on Proposition 54, a measure that prohibits state and local governments from classifying any person by race, ethnicity, color, or national origin. Your task is too evaluate the argument for Proposition 54 and decide whether you would vote for or against it.

Argument in Favor of Proposition 54[9]

"What is your race?"

African-American? Mexican-American? Asian-American? White? Native American? Or, the mysterious "other?"

If you're like most Californians, you're getting tired of that question.

Californians are the most racially and ethnically diverse people in the world—and we are proud of it. We are also among the most independent; and we resent being classified, categorized, divided and subdivided based on our skin color and the origin of our ancestors.

When you're asked to check a government form with row after row of these rigid and silly little 'race' boxes, have you ever just wanted to say, "None of your business; now leave me alone?" Proposition 54 seeks to eliminate racial categorization, by the government, in all areas except medicine, health care and law enforcement.

The advocates of racial categorization maintain that you have no right to privacy concerning your ancestry and racial background. They see no problem if your employer or school officials label you AGAINST YOUR WILL often without telling you—or charge you with "racial fraud" if their "racial" definitions are different from yours.

Dare we forget the lessons of history?

Classification systems were invented to keep certain groups "in their place" and to deny them full rights. These schemes were not invented by the Civil Rights movement! They were anathema to it. In fact, former Supreme Court Justice Thurgood Marshall once said, "Distinctions by race are so evil, so arbitrary and invidious that a state bound to defend the equal protection of the laws must not involve them in any public sphere."

Throughout history, government-imposed racial classifications have been used to divide people. They have been used to set people against each other. The slave owners and segregationists of the American past knew it when they labeled European Jews a separate and inferior "race"; American judges knew it when they had to determine if Asians or part-Asians were white or nonwhite for the purposes of naturalization. Now, the advocates of racial categorization tell us that government-imposed racial categories will somehow yield the very opposite of what they were originally intended to do! They insult our intelligence!

---

[9]*California Statewide Special Election.* California Secretary of State Official Voter Information Guide. Web. http://voterguide.sos.ca.gov/past/2003/special/propositions/2-3-2-arguments.html.

The unrelenting daily racial categorization of people by the government is one of the most divisive forces in American society. It is constantly emphasizing our minor differences, in opposition to our better instincts that tell us to seek our common interests and common values.

It's time for a change!

The government should stop categorizing its citizens by color and ancestry, and create a society in which our children and grandchildren can just think of themselves as Americans and individuals.

The colorblind ideal—judging others by the content of their character rather than the color of their skin—is more than a dream in California; it is central to the definition of who we are as a people, because, in California, we don't just dream; we do what others dream of doing.

Vote "YES" on Proposition 54 (*www.racialprivacy.org*)!

Ward Connerly, *University of California Regent*
Martha Montelongo Myers, *Columnist*
Joe Hicks, *Human Relations Consultant*

1. Using the margin note and summary method, or whatever method works best for you, construct a summary of the excerpt, and then identify the thesis and the main premises.

2. Critically evaluate the article, using your summary as your guide, making sure that your evaluation accurately reflects the excerpt itself, as well as your summary.

3. Drawing on your background knowledge and beliefs, decide how you would vote on this issue and defend your decision.

5. EVALUATING IRONIC WORKS

Jonathan Swift, author of *Gulliver's Travels,* wrote a famous satire called "A Modest Proposal" in which he suggested that the Irish should raise babies to be eaten in order to solve the myriad problems confronting that famine-stricken land back in the 18th century.

But the point of his essay, of course, was completely other than that people should literally carry out the plan he proposed. He was, to be plain, using **irony**—that is, saying one thing, but meaning something entirely different. So when evaluating ironic works it is a mistake to take them literally; you need to evaluate them in terms of their underlying message. Swift's point was to force his British audience to face the mass starvation and misery in Ireland that British policies had produced; his ironic suggestions were intended to shock his audience into a recognition of what they were doing in Ireland.

Irony often is combined with humor or exaggeration to form a potent weapon in the hands of a master at the trade. Telling us what is true in a funny or exaggerated way makes it harder to deny than if it is put to us in a straightforward, serious manner. Ironic writing is particularly effective in penetrating the kinds of self-serving psychological defenses—denial, rationalization, and so on—that were discussed in Chapter 6.

EXERCISE 8-9

Today, political columnists such as Gail Collins and Maureen Dowd use a combination of irony and humor to make points about the current social/political scene. Here is an example, written in 1999 by the late and sadly missed Arthur (Art) Hoppe. It is just as relevant today as it was when written.

Our Deserving Rich

Let us pray that not a hand is laid on the $792 billion tax cut passed by the House when the Senate takes it up today. Never has a piece of legislation been so pure in its concept, so efficient in its means, so right on the mark.

As you may have read, the Republican measure passed by the House proposes giving 79 percent of the income-tax reductions to the richest one-fifth of our citizens and .03 percent to the poorest. The richest's take would average $4,592, while the poorest would haul in $15.

It is high time we recognized the tremendous contributions the rich have made to this great land of ours. Hitherto, we have punished them for their well-earned money. The harder they labor and the more they make, the more we penalize them financially. What sort of a message does this send to every little tad in the land?

At the same time, we have rewarded the poor for their inability to find well-paying jobs. The less money they make, the more we subsidize them with our taxpayer dollars. There can be no doubt that they take far more from us than they give.

Let's ask ourselves: What has poverty ever done for America? The answer is absolutely nothing. Do the poor endow the symphonies and operas that flood our souls with musical grandeur? Of course not. Do they build the museums that increase our knowledge of the world or the galleries where hang the masterpieces of human creativity? Do they donate vast acreages of untouched land as a heritage for generations yet unborn? Don't be silly.

How many poor people have adopted a highway or saved a baby harp seal? Their commitment to the environment is infinitesimal at best. Indeed, rather than devoting themselves to improving our surroundings, they go out of their way to make our cities and towns far less inviting.

Their ghetto tenements, their sleazy housing projects and their skid row hotels are a blight on the landscape. Generally speaking, their wardrobes are tasteless, if not downright appalling. And those who live in the country have a penchant for littering their yards with unsightly collectibles such as broken-down washing machines and rusted-out cars.

Contrast this utter disregard for our sensibilities with the care the rich lavish on their surroundings. How pleasant it is to stroll through a wealthy neighborhood, graced with high flower-bedecked walls, verdant hedges and stately cast-iron fences.

How pleasing to the eye is the sight of an immaculately tuxedoed man and his bejeweled wife in her haute couture gown stepping from a limousine to attend a culture-improving function. Never could a poor person hope to equal their gratifying splendor.

Yes, as we would say in the rosy Ronald Reagan days, "It's morning in Palm Beach."

So hail the Republicans! Let us take comfort in the adage that the rich will always be with us—at least as long as the Republicans are in power. As for the Democrats, they would foolishly squander our hard-won budget surplus on Social Security, Medicare and other give-aways to the less successful members of our society.

Let's admit that the Democrats were not totally defeated. In what was obviously a last minute compromise, the Republicans agreed to give the poor families that $15. I can't for the life of me think why. It will only encourage them.[10]

1. What is Hoppe's point—his unstated thesis?

2. Why does Hoppe bash the poor and praise the rich? What is the point of such questions as "What has poverty ever done for America?" or "Do the poor endow symphonies and operas that flood our souls with musical grandeur?"

3. In your opinion, is he on target or not? Explain.

4. Does he make you take account of something that you already knew or that you hadn't paid sufficient attention to or appreciated the significance of? If so, explain. If not, why not?

SUMMARY OF CHAPTER 8

Chapter 8 concerns the evaluation of extended arguments—essays.

1. Most types of essays are straightforwardly argumentative, but some—for instance, descriptive or explanatory essays—may mask their theses in one way or another. *Example:* Orwell's essay, "A Hanging."

2. Essays may argue by considering reasons *pro and con* a thesis, by providing a *refutation to counterarguments,* or by making a *comparison of alternatives,* as well as simply by presenting *reasons (premises)* in support of a *thesis.*

3. There are several guidelines to use in evaluating argumentative passages: (1) Find the thesis and keep it in mind as you read; (2) find the reasons (premises) that support the thesis, and (when there are any) the reasons for the reasons, and so on, taking into account the evidence presented; (3) identify responses to likely objections or counterarguments; (4) skip whatever doesn't support (or argue against) the thesis; (5) add relevant information, pro or con, that you may know of; (6) consider the tone and emotive language; and (7) come to an evaluation.

4. Coming to an evaluation consists primarily in asking and answering three questions, corresponding to the three basic requirements of cogent reasoning introduced in Chapter 1: (1) Are the writer's (or speaker's) assumptions and stated

---

[10]From Art Hoppe, "Our Deserving Rich," *San Francisco Chronicle,* July 28, 1999. © *San Francisco Chronicle.* Reprinted by permission.

reasons justified by what you already believe? (2) Do you know other relevant reasons or arguments? (If so, they need to be added to the mix.) (3) Do the reasons (plus any added material) justify acceptance of the thesis—that is, is the argument then valid?

5. The *margin note and summary method* is a useful way to clarify the main ideas of an essay before analyzing it. This method has four steps: (1) Read the material carefully; (2) read it again and add margin notes at the relevant spots in the essay; (3) construct a summary from the margin notes; and (4) evaluate the summary, making sure to bring relevant information to bear.

6. Reasons offered in support of a thesis may be about *facts* or about *values*. Claims about values typically are justified differently than those about facts. It often is said that facts are *objective*, values *subjective*. On this view, the shape of a gold ring, for example, is an objective fact about the ring itself; the beauty of the ring is "in the eye of the beholder." A contrary view is that values inhere in the valuable objects themselves, so that they too are objective. Among value claims, those about *moral* matters tend to be both controversial and important. If moral values are subjective, then moral claims can be justified by evidence that the writer or speaker, or most or even all people hold that value. But if moral right and wrong are objective facts, then how people feel about them is irrelevant, and something outside our feelings—for example, biblical commandments—need to be appealed to in order to justify a particular moral claim. So when one is evaluating arguments containing moral claims, it often is important to try to find out what makes the writer or speaker make such a claim and to then assess the claims in view of one's own moral standards, however one has arrived at them. Of course, one's own moral standards should not be exempt from challenge and improvement. Those who accept, say, the Ten Commandments need to see that they do not automatically answer all questions—they don't answer all economic ones, for example—and thus are in need at the very least of interpretation and perhaps also augmentation. Careful consideration of a standard may lead to a change of mind, say, about abortion or infanticide, in view of the dire situations some people find themselves in.

7. Ironic essays argue for a point indirectly and thus are not to be taken literally. (For example, Swift did not espouse the eating of Irish babies.) The point in irony is not to present reasons for a conclusion so much as to get readers to see something clearly that they may have overlooked, or not paid sufficient attention to, or defended against by some sort of self-serving self-deception. An honest evaluation of ironic writing requires us to determine whether, as implicitly claimed, we have overlooked or denied something important.

9 Writing Cogent (and Persuasive) Essays

There are no dull subjects. There are only dull writers.

—H. L. Mencken

He can compress the most words into the smallest idea of any man I ever met.

—Abraham Lincoln

Learn as much by writing as by reading.

—Lord Acton

A deluge of words and a drop of sense.

—John Ray

The discussion in Chapter 8 should make clear the essential contents of an argumentative essay: a thesis (grand conclusion) and reasons (premises) supporting the thesis. It also should be clear that in most cases the reasons themselves need to be supported by evidence or secondary reasons and that it often is useful to consider and refute likely objections.

But it should quickly become evident that writing a cogent and effective essay is much more difficult than summarizing and evaluating someone else's effort. Writing is character forming; it does indeed make evident the truth that writing is nature's way of letting us know how sloppy our initial thoughts on a topic often are. There are three reasons for writing essays, and one is without doubt that it is the very best way to sharpen sloppy thoughts into ideas that are clear, sensible, and well supported by good reasons and evidence. (The other two are to convince others and—obviously—to satisfy course or other requirements.)

1. THE WRITING PROCESS

Experienced writers tend to keep their basic goals firmly in mind as they write and, indeed, as they prepare to write. They usually develop a plan of attack designed to meet their goals, but they don't generally move relentlessly from one idea to the next. Rather, they frequently revise their original plans in the light of new evidence or ideas or in the face of unexpected difficulties. One task often interrupts another. (Interestingly, editing seems to have a higher priority with most experienced writers than any other writing task and tends to interrupt others at any time. Having used an inaccurate word, for example, writers tend to put aside whatever they are doing and search for one that is more precise.) The point is that for most people essay writing is a convoluted process, not a straightforward, linear one.[1] Skilled writers constantly rework their ideas as they plan and then write. The process itself leads to discovery, including, alas, the discovery of the inadequacy of our previous thoughts.

2. PREPARING TO WRITE

Students generally are asked to write short argumentative essays on specific topics—for instance, literacy in the United States, or legalizing marijuana. Suppose your assignment is to write an essay on the topic of regulating the possession of firearms.

The first task is to determine what the precise thesis of your essay will be. Gun regulation might involve restricting the carrying of handguns to specific places or perhaps only to specified individuals. Your thesis might be for, or against, the legal possession of automatic, quick-firing weapons, or it might focus just on handguns such as pistols.

Once you have provisionally decided on a thesis, your research and greater thought on the matter may well urge a change of mind, perhaps even a switch from pro to con, or vice versa. Unless a precise thesis is forced on you, say, by your instructor, the very process of thinking about the topic and investigating the evidence and the reasonings of others is likely to motivate you to revise your thesis in one way or another. Poor thinkers often decide on a thesis and hang on to it no matter what the evidence seems to indicate, as though changing one's mind indicates failure. Good thinkers realize that changing one's mind *for good reason* is the hallmark of intelligent thought. In the case of laws concerning firearms, for instance, evidence about the incredible destructive firepower of handheld automatic weapons such as Uzis might convince you to argue for the banning of these weapons.

After you have provisionally selected a thesis and have developed reasons and evidence in its favor, it often is useful to construct an outline of the essay that is to be the finished product. It's true, of course, that we all are different. Some people do better just starting out writing, doing research, and even altering their thesis as they go along rather than following the order suggested here. (Recall the earlier remark about writing being a convoluted process.) But most writers, in particular those with little experience, find it useful to do a good deal of preparation, including the construction of an outline, before starting to write the essay itself. (That is an important reason why essays written the night before they're due seldom get good grades—the fact that they are "off the top of the head" is obvious to instructors.) At the very least, an outline should include a provisional thesis and the principal reasons and

---

[1]There have been a very few exceptions to this rule, the philosopher Bertrand Russell, interestingly, being a case in point. His handwritten first drafts, with extremely few changes here and there, often were used by publishers to set final type. We ordinary writers can only examine these drafts with a sense of awe, not with the intent to acquire the knack ourselves.

supporting evidence expected to be presented in its favor. Outlines need not be written in grammatically correct or even whole sentences. Phrases and key words often are sufficient. But it is a good idea for inexperienced writers to state the thesis and principal reasons in complete sentences.

Calvin (of the Calvin and Hobbes duo) found it overly tedious having both to write an essay about bats and to do research on the topic, but research—diligent research—usually is essential. When doing research, take notes (including citations!) of pertinent evidence—statistics, examples, the opinions of experts, and so on. Regularly review what you have discovered in the light of your thoughts on the topic to see how the evidence supports, or undermines, your thesis or important reasons. If research undermines your thesis, it obviously needs revision (making the thesis narrower, perhaps) or a significant change in the reasons you intend to offer in its support. *Never simply ignore counterarguments or reasons!*

Some reasons involve legal matters that require us to review the law and interpretations of it. For instance, many arguments address issues that involve constitutional law (such as abortion, gun control, pornography, and so on). Because the Constitution often is used to support either side of an argument, it needs careful interpretation to be persuasive. For this reason, it's a good idea to research judicial opinion (the majority and dissenting opinions of high-court judges) in court cases addressing the issue you are writing about. Consulting expert opinion will help you understand the kind of careful deliberation needed in arguing complex legal matters.

Of course, you don't want to snow readers with a mountain of reasons or evidence. Plan to stick to your best reasons—those that reflect your most convincing evidence. Remember, though, that not all reasons are based on factual research or evidence. When relevant, moral convictions and standards, or beliefs about aesthetic or other values, constitute very good reasons indeed. For instance, the belief that taking the life of animals solely for our own purposes—for food or for furs—is morally wrong certainly is relevant to issues concerning the treatment of animals.

Finally, before starting to write an essay, make sure that its thesis follows logically from the reasons (premises) you intend to offer in its support. After all, validity—deductive or inductive—is an absolutely necessary condition of cogent argument. And reasons that do not genuinely support a thesis are useless.

3. WRITING THE ESSAY

Argumentative essays can be structured in several ways. One way is to present the opposition's argument in some detail, then refute it point by point, emphasizing your position as you go along. Another is to present reasons for and against a proposition, but wait until the end of the essay to draw conclusions that persuasively argue your position. Organizing arguments in these ways, however, can be tricky for students learning the craft. Too often the tendency is to drift off message or to present the opposition's argument so persuasively that it seems more convincing than your own. The best way for most students to structure an argument is to state the thesis in the introduction, present the reasons point by point in the body—taking care to refute the opposition when appropriate—and drive home the thesis at the end in an emphatic conclusion.

The Introduction

A good introduction engages the reader's attention and lays the groundwork for the essay's thesis, which usually is stated toward the end of the introduction but may be placed at the beginning. The point of the introduction is to start persuading readers to accept your thesis, perhaps before it is even stated. (Remember, you have two goals in mind. One is to write an essay that is cogent. The other is to persuade readers to accept your thesis. A perfectly cogent essay that is not well written may very well not convince many readers.) An essay can be introduced in all sorts of ways—with a quotation from an authoritative source, for instance, or a personal example that supports your position on the issue.

Once you capture the reader's attention, state the thesis and two or three major reasons in its support. Starting the essay in this way prepares the audience to read the body of the essay intelligently. Although it isn't necessary to include the main reasons after the thesis, doing so helps to keep both the writer and the reader on track.

The Body of an Essay

The body of an essay develops the reasons and evidence offered in support of the essay's thesis. How much support is needed depends on how resistant the intended audience is likely to be (or how much space is available to make your case). You don't want to hit people over the head with what they already believe or know. Support for each reason can take many forms (to be discussed in detail later in the chapter) but in brief, the reasons need to be persuasive, the evidence convincing and the explanations logical.

If the opposition has a reason you think important enough to address, then bring it up by all means and either refute it or concede that it may be right—but not right enough to sink your argument.

The Conclusion

The conclusion of an argumentative essay usually restates the thesis. If the essay is rather long or complicated, the main points may need to be summarized. But avoid the temptation to introduce new ides. The conclusion is the place to draw your argument to a close with an emphatic statement of your position on the issue.

Here, now is what an entire essay might look like. It is rather short as essays go, intended primarily to serve as an example, but it nevertheless does a satisfactory job of clearly presenting and defending a thesis. The topic was purposely chosen to provoke some controversy and invites an essay in rebuttal.

Why Bother With College?

Introduction, ending with thesis and reasons.

Is college worth it? Not according to 57% of Americans, who claim that our system of higher education fails to give students "good value for the money they and their families spend."[1] Times are tough and life is short, so why waste it on college when all you get for your money is a load of debt? A friend of mine graduated from state university last year, and he still cannot get the kind of job his anthropology major prepared him for. Instead, he works at McDonald's for $7.60 an hour and lives at home with his parents, buried under a $30,000 debt. That is not going to happen to me. I am halfway through my freshman year and plan to drop out. Going to college makes no sense economically and does little to prepare most students for the job market: It is too expensive, the job-related courses I should take don't interest me, and besides, practical experience in the business world is worth more than an academic education.

Reason #1, followed by supporting evidence: high cost of a college education and extensive student debt.

Most Americans agree that a college education costs too much. According to a Pew Research Center survey, 75% say college is too expensive for most people in this country, and the cost keeps going up.[2] Each year the College Board releases figures on the average cost of a higher education. In 2011–12, for example, in-state students in public colleges paid $17,131 for tuition, room, and board per year—and that reflects an 8.3% increase in tuition plus a 6% increase in room and board over the previous year.[3] That would be about $68,500 total if the cost stayed the same, but, of course, it won't. It has been spiraling up for years. The increase in tuition alone is 5.1% beyond inflation over the previous five years. As far as private colleges go, the $38,500 price tag per year is so far beyond my wallet that it doesn't compute.

Increasing costs for most students means deepening debt. According to Consumer Reports the average debt per student in 2011 was $22,900, up 47% from the previous decade, taking inflation into account.[4] That is a lot of money. Many college grads have trouble getting jobs to begin with or wind up working for

[1] "Is College Worth It?" *The Pew Research Center.* 15 May 2011. 4 April 2012.
[2] Id.
[3] "New College Board Trends Reports Price of College Continues to Rise Nationally." *College Board.* 25 October 2011. Web. http://press.collegeboard.org/releases/2011.
[4] "2011 College Grads Have Highest Average Debt to Date." *Consumer Reports.Org.* 16 May 2011. Web. http:/news.consumerreports.org/money/2011/05/2011-college-grads-have-highest-average-debt-to-date.html.

minimum wage in jobs they are vastly overqualified for—like my friend, for example, whose salary before taxes is $15,200. With that paltry paycheck he can't afford to pay down his debt. And since he will probably have to retrain for work in another field, he will run up an even bigger debt. College was a waste of time for him.

Reason #2, followed by a list of hot careers that don't interest the writer.

Another major drawback is that the courses designed to prepare students for success in the job market don't interest me. According to a College Board report, the hottest careers from 2008-2018 for graduates with bachelor degrees are in education, accounting and computers.[5] Elementary, middle, and high school teachers are right up there along with accountants, auditors, and computer analysts. None of these fields interests me. What I really want is a liberal arts major, but that won't prepare me for the job market. In fact, only 56% of all graduates in the class of 2010 got any jobs at all, and those who did earned a median starting salary of $27,000, down 10% from graduates in 2006–7.[6] These depressing statistics don't motivate me to stay in school.

Concession to the opposite side, which the writer then refutes.

I admit that there are a few advantages to getting a college education. It would expand my knowledge, develop my communication skills and probably make me into a well-rounded person. If I took more English classes, I would write better, and a philosophy course would help me reason more clearly. A few classes in history wouldn't hurt either, to give me a better perspective on current affairs. But these are all things I can learn on my own without the exorbitant cost of college—knowledge is free at the local library after all. Another advantage widely touted for getting a degree is that college grads earn more money than high school grads. However, an economist for the Brookings Institute once argued that the numbers are skewed because smarter kids are more likely to go to college to begin with. It stands to reason that if these smart, ambitious kids decided to go into business rather than college, they would have a good chance of succeeding on the job as well.

Reason #3, with an explanation of practical experience gained on the job, and examples of college dropouts who succeeded brilliantly in business.

A college education may provide academic grounding, but it doesn't give the practical experience that the business world does. It doesn't teach you the skills

[5]"Hottest Careers for College Graduates." *College Board.* 29 March 2012. http://www. collegeboard.com/student/csearch/majors_careers/236.html.
[6]Rampell, Catherine. "Many With New College Degree Find the Job Market Humbling." *New York Times* 18 May 2011. Web. http://www.nytimes.com/2011/05/19/business/economy/19grads.html

you need in the job market—like how to sell a product or how to develop a business network. You learn skills like this by going to work. Maybe you fail some of the time, but that is another practical lesson to be learned—how to turn business failures into success stories. Failure in college is a stain on your transcript, but not in business. Besides, a bachelor's degree really isn't necessary to succeed in business. Two titans of our times, Steve Jobs and Bill Gates, were college dropouts. So was Mark Zukerberg, the Facebook CEO. In fact, 15% of the Forbes 400 richest people in the country are either college dropouts or high school graduates.[7] Only 5.3% have PhDs. Of course, I'm no Steve Jobs, but I could learn to be a pretty good entrepreneur with a small business of my own. President Obama was right when he told Congress, "Everyone here knows that small businesses are where most new jobs begin." The sooner I get there, the better.

Conclusion that emphatically restates the thesis.

Going to college is fine for students who have the money and the time. I have neither. The price tag is too high and the payoff too paltry. Given my financial situation, it makes more sense to gain practical experience in the workplace where I am earning money, not giving it away to an academic institution. Since far more professions require on-the-job training than classroom learning, it stands to reason that someone with ambition and brains can succeed.

[7]"Billionaire University: Education of the Forbes 400." *Forbes.com*. 16 January 2012. Web. http://www.forbes.com/forbes/2012/0116/leaderboard-education-billionaires-forbes-400-university.html

4. SUPPORTING REASONS EFFECTIVELY

Perhaps the most difficult part of writing an argument is to provide convincing evidence. It's not enough to have sensible reasons to begin with. You need to convince the reader that those reasons are worth believing. Here are a few guidelines.

Provide Concrete Evidence

When possible, provide evidence that is specific. Use examples, cite statistics, compare or contrast relevant material, and draw on factual information. Reasons are more likely to be convincing when they can be verified by specific information than when they are explained in terms of generalities.

Specific information of this kind is usually drawn from these three sources:

1. *Personal experiences:* Suppose your thesis is that the food served at school should be improved. In this instance, you, yourself, have had personal experiences that can be used to support your position. Every time you have eaten lunch in the cafeteria, the food has been terrible: The bread is hard as a rock, and the spaghetti tastes like rubber. Citing these personal experiences

provides good support for your reasons, though usually other kinds of evidence are needed as well.

2. *The experiences of others:* When using this type of evidence, you need to make sure that their information is accurate. You know what your own experiences are, but judgment is required in evaluating what others claim has happened to them. (Sad, but true.)

3. *Authoritative sources:* These include such sources as reference books, journals, and people who have extensive knowledge about a subject—experts. But here, too, judgment must be used. Reputable encyclopedias, dictionaries, and handbooks on specific subjects can usually be relied on with respect to bare facts or matters that are not politically controversial. You have to be more careful with magazines, newspapers, television programs, and particularly the Internet because people can put anything online they want to and claim to be authorities when they aren't.

Note this important point: *Authoritative sources must always be credited,* either in a footnote or in the text itself. And direct quotations must always be indicated by the use of quotation marks. Using someone else's material without acknowledging the source constitutes **plagiarism,** an extremely serious offense.

Provide Transitions

A good essay obviously has to have a logical structure, but you also want to write so that one thought flows into another—so that the logical structure of your essays is easy to follow. Transition terms and expressions highlight the flow of an essay, helping readers to know what to expect next—to know which expressions serve as reasons and which as conclusions and, in general, how things hang together. Note the use in the sample essay of the words *but, however, instead, besides, of course* and the expressions *for example, another advantage is,* and *it stands to reason that.*

Think Your Position through Carefully

Having to write so as to convince others—much more than speaking extemporaneously—is an excellent way to get clear in your own mind as to where the truth lies. Writing a good argumentative essay requires mental discipline—the ability to see through the natural tendency to hang on to opinions once formed, even in the light of their inadequacy—to root out inconsistencies and fuzzy beliefs, and to arrange thoughts into a coherent whole.

Consider Your Audience

Writers who seriously intend to influence others have to keep their audience firmly in mind. It's all too easy to forget the audience as we sit alone at a desk scribbling away

> The plural of anecdote is not evidence.
>
> —Bill Lockyer, Attorney
> General of California

Block Those Metaphors!

Metaphor is a time-honored linguistic device. In the hands of careful writers, it often can express ideas swiftly and more effectively than more literal language. The trouble is that writers often go overboard in their enthusiasm for this linguistic tool. Here is an example from the writings of Guy Gugliotta in the Washington Post *(carried as one of the* New Yorker's *occasional metaphoric overkill items):*

There was no time, Acting Chairman Matthew F. McHugh (D-N.Y.) said last week, and the committee was tired of stoking public outrage with fortnightly gobbets of scandal. It decided to publish everything it had left, warts and all.

Now everyone is tarred with the same ugly brush, and the myth that forever simmers in the public consciousness—that the House shelters 435 parasitic, fat-cat deadbeats—has received another shot of adrenalin.

This little snippet also illustrates another writing no-no: the use of obscure words few readers can be expected to understand. Or did you know what gobbet means without having to look it up?

(well, these days also tapping away). But experienced writers learn that they must always write with the intended readers in mind. Past failures—having had manuscripts rejected, severely criticized, or simply passed over by others—motivate them to figure out who they are writing for and how best to engage the interest of that particular audience.

One way to develop a sense of audience is to have one immediately at hand. Much has been written about the importance of writing with an audience in mind, but this advice needs to be augmented by actually having others respond to your work. In college, papers are usually directed to an audience of one—the teacher who evaluates your work and provides valuable advice intended to improve your writing ability.

However, what do you do in the hazy prewriting stage when you have the glimmer of an idea but aren't sure whether it will work, or when you have thought of a thesis and reasons but don't know whether they are convincing? In this stage of the writing process, it is helpful to try your ideas out on other people. Their feedback will give you a sense of audience response. Some teachers divide their classes into response groups so that students can discuss their ideas and read drafts aloud to each other. Some schools have tutors who can act as an audience. The point is to use whatever resources happen to be available so as to become accustomed to addressing a real audience.

Here are some questions to ask about the audience:

1. What is your intended audience?
2. What are their worldviews and background beliefs?
3. What tone is appropriate?

Think of how different your approach would be if you were arguing for gun control either to a group of mothers or to a local gun owners' organization. Most likely their

Reprinted by permission of Paul Miller

worldviews and background beliefs would differ considerably, and undoubtedly the gun owners would be harder to convince than the mothers. Once you have the audience firmly in mind, you can begin to see what reasoning and evidence would be most likely to persuade and what tone would be appropriate.

Rewrite! Rewrite! Rewrite!

The difficulty of arranging thoughts coherently is an important reason why rewriting almost always is necessary. When writing a critical essay, we often realize that our thoughts aren't as focused or penetrating as we supposed. The writing process itself constitutes an important part of the reasoning process.

That's why most writers, definitely including the authors of this text, construct the first draft of an essay as a learning, or thinking, device. They do the best job they can on the first draft and then critically evaluate it as they would an opponent's essay. The next draft then can take account of what has been learned, perhaps by introducing new reasons and arguments that aren't open to the criticisms made of the first draft.

But one thing is clear. Only a few of the very best writers can construct a really good critical essay in one draft. Writers like philosopher Bertrand Russell (recall that his manuscripts often showed only a word or two changed here and there to mark the transition from first to final draft) are extremely rare in this world. The rest of us have to write at least two drafts, usually more, to get our thoughts into good order and to express them so they can be easily understood by others. And you shouldn't be surprised to find out that learning to do this well takes . . . practice, practice, practice. (The good news here is that computers, those marvelous "word processors," make the task of seemingly endless revision a good deal easier for many—but not all!—writers.)

If the need to practice, practice, practice has been mentioned, can lots of exercise chores be far behind? Here are a whole bunch of exercises—just how many you will need to sweat over is up to your instructor.

Good Writers Respect Their Audience

F. L. Lucas, once fellow and lecturer at King's College, Cambridge University, stressed the writer's obligation to readers in his essay "What Is Style?" from which this excerpt is drawn:*

The writer should respect his readers; therefore [he should behave with] courtesy. . . . From this follow several other basic principles of style. Clarity is one. For it is boorish to make your reader rack his brains to understand. One should aim at being impossible to misunderstand—though men's capacity for misunderstanding approaches infinity. Hence Molière and Po Chüi tried their work on their cooks; and Swift on his men-servants—"which, if they did not comprehend, he would alter and amend, until they understood it perfectly." Our bureaucrats and pundits, unfortunately, are less considerate.

Brevity is another basic principle. For it is boorish, also, to waste your reader's time. People who would not dream of stealing a penny of one's money turn not a hair at stealing hours of one's life. But that does not make them less exasperating. Therefore, there is no excuse for the sort of writer who takes as long as a marching army corps to pass a certain point. Besides, brevity is often more effective; . . . And because one is particularly apt to waste words on preambles before coming to the substance, there was sense in the Scots professor who always asked his pupils—"Did ye remember to tear up that fir-r-st page?"

*Holiday magazine, March 1960

EXERCISE 9-1

One good way to get practice in writing well is to critique poor writing. Here is a tiny (142 words) tongue-in-cheek essay from the delightful book *Ordinary Money* by Louis B. Jones (New York: Viking, 1990). For many years, Jones was a reader for freshmen English and other college writing courses. As a warm-up exercise, explain the various writing bloopers, of the kind that might move your instructor to make negative margin comments—blunders that Jones constructed into his little "student-written" essay (described by one of the book's characters as "complete bull___, but Ohrbach [the instructor] never notices"):

The comparison/contrast of the Greeks and Romans is a very important comparison/contrast. Since the beginning of time, people have pondered this question. In the hustle-bustle world of today, the comparison/contrast of the Greeks and Romans is very important and relevant. For example, the Romans were after the Greeks and therefore they had a more technology-oriented advancement. For example, they had plumbing and flush toilets and they had lead in the pipes which made everybody gradually insane. For example, Caligula, which caused the Decline and Fall of the Roman Empire. Another comparison/contrast of the Greeks and Romans is, the Greeks were very sane. For example, Plato and other world-famous philosophers pondered the greatest question of all time. Plato believed that everything was ideal. This is still true today. . . .

Student Essay Bon Mots

Here are a few extreme examples from student essays to serve as a reminder that good writing requires care and—yes—extensive revision. (Our thanks to English students at Knowname College.)

The elementary school I first attended was racial towards minorities.
(Poorly expressed thought.)

Women have sat on the back burner long enough.
(Unfortunate figure of speech.)

She was a rabid typist.
(Malapropism.)

Secondly, the American school system is more loose, thus encouraging students to be creative rather than Japanese.
(Faulty comparison.)

Every day at 4:00 thousands of people evacuate on their jobs.
(Poor choice of words and construction.)

The octopus of communism spread its testacles over the continent.
(Really!)

Do punctual errors count?
(Yes, they do.)

He resorts to name calling and puts himself on a peddle stool.
(What a motor-mouth.)

A broader view also prevents the student from charging blindly into a brick wall of unconceptuality.
(Block that metaphor!)

I have a fool-time job.
(Freudian slip?)

The vowels we made at the alter.
(Double display of ignorance.)

I am in favor of capital punishment particularly in cases of murder and rape and aggravated napping, child or otherwise.
(Unintended humor.)

And here are a few gems culled from Jaime O'Neill's article "The Goal Is Garbage In, Writers Out" (*San Francisco Chronicle* 4 September 2005):

"I believe in my second amendment that is the right to bare arms."
"I have this udder glow of happiness."
"I placed a reef on my grandmothers' grave."
"My ex-best friend is so stuck on herself. She's like a pre-Madonna."
"I was in the mist of studying when my cell phone rang."

Ah, well, everyone can't go to the head of the class in this doggy dog world. But at least we all can have self-of-steam.

EXERCISE 9-2

Here are many issues that should be of some interest to college students. Select one and, bearing in mind the writing suggestions just discussed, write an essay (about 1,000 to 1,500 words), taking one side or the other of the issue. Then write a critical analysis in reply to your own essay (as though you were a competent—and fair!—opponent attacking your position). And then rewrite your original essay to try to take account of your own criticisms. Think of your fellow students, not your instructor, as your audience. Pick a topic that will let you show how well you can reason about a complicated issue. Do not pick an issue that you think has an obviously right solution to it. For example, do not select number 10 if all you are going to say is that of course we should not offer abstinence-only sex education, because we all have the right to learn about contraception. Every issue is more complicated than that, and there always are serious pros and cons to consider. This is a difficult and very important assignment; it absolutely cannot be done satisfactorily the night before it is due—if for no other reason than that a certain amount of research very likely is in order. (Your instructor definitely and without doubt will quickly tell when reading your essay if it's a last-minute concoction.)

1. Should speech codes be instituted in colleges and universities to fight racism on campus?

2. Should illegal aliens be allowed to get driver's licenses?

3. Should affirmative action with respect to the education or employment of women and minorities be the law of the land? (If you write on this topic, you must carefully explain what you mean by "affirmative action," and you should restrict your topic either to education or to employment.)

4. Should colleges and universities support big-time football and basketball teams?

5. Should colleges and universities permit teachers and students to carry guns on campus?

6. Are the salaries paid to movie stars and sports stars too high? If so, what should be done about this? If not, rebut those who would argue otherwise. In either case, support the side of the issue that you chose.

7. Should stem cells from embryos be used in medical research?

8. Should the Supreme Court have ruled that all or part of the Affordable Health Care Act is constitutional?

9. Should alleged terrorists be read their Miranda rights to remain silent and to have an attorney present during questioning —before they are interrogated?

10. Should high school courses in human sexuality offer abstinence-only sex education and eliminate discussion of contraception?

11. Should homosexual couples enjoy the same legal benefits as heterosexual married couples?

12. Should voters be required to show government-issued photo IDs in order to vote at the polls?

13. Florida now has a Stand Your Ground law that lets a person use deadly force if he or she believes it is necessary to prevent death or great bodily harm to himself or herself or someone else. Under these circumstances, the person using force cannot be prosecuted. Once you have researched the law and understand the particulars, write an argument for or against it.

14. Increasingly colleges and universities are encouraging students to take unpaid internships for academic credit at for-profit companies, even when the companies use the students to replace regular employees rather than give them on-the-job experience that internships are meant to provide. Argue for or against his practice.

15. Current law penalizes people who distribute to minors "harmful matter," like pornography, alcohol and cigarettes, but it doesn't restrict the sale of graphically violent and first-person shooter video games (where the player advances the game by killing). Should legislation be enacted to prohibit the sale of these games to minors?

16. In recent years, some pharmacists have refused to fill prescriptions for birth control pills or devices, arguing that their religious or moral beliefs prevented them from doing so. Should pharmacists have the legal right to refuse this service?

17. As of spring 2001, discoverers of human genes are allowed to patent their discoveries, so that, for instance, certain tests for a propensity to breast cancer cannot be conducted on your genes without paying a royalty to the patent holder. The principal argument in favor of gene patenting is that allowing it dramatically increases the incentive to discover such genes. Should we allow human genes to be patented?

18. Most scientists believe that increased use of fossil fuels (coal, oil, and so on) is leading to increases in global warming that will have adverse effects such as raised sea levels and the inundation of low-lying coastal areas. But some scientists deny this is true, and a very few argue that the good effects of global warming will outweigh the bad ones. Take sides in this debate.

EXERCISE 9-3

1. In recent years, many European and Middle Eastern governments have debated whether to forbid people from wearing certain types of Islamic dress like the niqab, a face veil with slits for the eyes, and the burqa, a garment that covers the entire body from head to toe. The French parliament has overwhelmingly approved banning the niqab and the burqa, the Dutch have enacted a burqa ban, and the Turks have banned Muslim head scarfs at university. Those in favor of the ban argue that wearing Islamic garb is degrading to women and presents a security risk because it masks a person's identity. Those opposed maintain that it is a violation of religious freedom and stigmatizes Islamic people.

   Much has been written about this issue in recent years that can easily be researched in periodicals and on the Internet. Examine the reasons given on both sides and write an argument for or against a full or partial ban of Islamic dress. Include persuasive evidence to support your reason.

2. Online courses have become so popular that 30% of all college students took these courses in 2010, and the number is growing. These courses work well for students who live far from a campus or have jobs and cannot attend regularly scheduled classes. They offer everything a conventional classroom provides except live participation. But some educators worry that the virtual classroom is no substitute for the real thing. They argue that electronic conversations can't match classroom discussions where students are stimulated by the spontaneous exchange of ideas and by professors who are better able to clarify and channel discussions in person than online.

   Interview students who have studied online and professors who have taught these courses. Use the evidence you gather, along with current research on the subject, to support an argument for or against taking courses online.

3. Hip-hop has been controversial for decades. It has a reputation for using bad language, for glorifying sexism, racism, and crime, and for popularizing an anti-snitch attitude that discourages cooperation with the police. Critics of the genre argue for censoring hip-hop, but advocates of free speech believe that rappers have the right to say whatever they want. Although the media usually bleep out offensive remarks, the recording industry does not.

   Write an essay arguing for or against the recording industry censoring bad language and offensive attitudes expressed in hip-hop.

4. In the ongoing debate about the rights of alleged terrorists imprisoned in United States territory, the main issue is whether those prisoners, classified as enemy combatants, should be detained indefinitely without a writ of habeas corpus. This constitutional right allows prisoners to ask the court to determine whether they are being lawfully imprisoned. When the Supreme Court ruled in 2008 (*Boumediene v. Bush*) that enemy combatants held in U.S. territory are entitled to this right, it ruled against the Bush administration policy that disallowed it. However, there continues to be much controversy over the issue.

   Examine the literature on this subject, particularly rulings and dissents of the Supreme Court and lower courts. Then write an argument defending the position you find most convincing.

5. A Florida technology company has developed a computer ID chip that could be implanted inside the body. The implant, about the size of a grain of rice, can be encoded with a wide range of information—everything from secret codes to sensitive medical data. Such a device would be invaluable to the medical community for giving emergency workers access to an unconscious patient's medical history, but it raises questions about privacy rights. Lee Tren, a senior attorney for a privacy advocacy group, cautioned that ". . . you always have to think about what the device will be used for tomorrow. . . . At first a device is used for applications we all agree are good, but then it slowly is used for more than it was intended."

   Write an argument either defending or rejecting the use of embedded ID chips.

6. Here are brief arguments for and against public colleges and universities soliciting private funding from corporations and wealthy benefactors. Take a

stand on this issue and write an argument defending your position. Good sources of information might be professors, department chairs, and deans in your own school.

An argument for soliciting private dollars is that state and federal budget cuts have been so severe in the past decade that public schools have had to look to the private sector for funding in order to ensure a high-quality education, to do cutting-edge research, to replace outdated equipment, and to upgrade deteriorating buildings.

The opposition argues that private funding transforms public schools into appendages of private industry, preoccupies the faculty with fund-raising instead of teaching, pits one department against another, and undermines the curriculum through corporate influence.

7. DDT, once used to control malaria-bearing mosquitoes, has been banned for decades because of its harmful effect on animals and humans. Fish-eating birds, in particular, were threatened with extinction from eating fish that had concentrated DDT in their tissues. But humans eating contaminated fish were afflicted as well, accumulating DDT in their systems and passing it onto their babies through breast milk. Since the chemical has been banned, however, malaria rates in developing countries have soared, and a movement is underway to start spraying houses in these countries to protect people from mosquitoes carrying the disease.

Do some research on this subject and write an argument for or against using DDT in developing countries to prevent the spread of malaria.

8. In recent years, Wikileaks has released confidential State Department material on an unprecedented scale to selected media sources like the *New York Times* and the *Guardian*. Wikileaks justifies these disclosures on the grounds that they hold the government more accountable and thus improve our foreign policy. But those who disagree argue that secrecy is essential to foreign relations and that leaks in confidential information will damage our diplomatic relations and thus our foreign policy will suffer.

Argue for or against the WikiLeaks practice of disclosing confidential State Department material.

EXERCISE 9-4

In 2011, *Newsweek* ran an article titled "Texting Makes Us Stupid," by Niall Ferguson (September 19) claiming that young people read and write a lot of text messages, but not many read books. According to a National Endowment for the Arts survey, only 50.7% of Americans ages 18–24 read a book not required in school, down 9% from 20 years ago. And English teachers regularly complain that students lapse into text message short cuts in writing assignments.

Is there any truth to the claim that texting contributes to illiteracy in this country? Ask other students and teachers what their opinions are and do research on recent literacy surveys. Then write an argument for or against the notion that "texting makes us stupid."

EXERCISE 9-5

The tragic shootings at Virginia Tech in 2007 by a psychotic student raised questions about the way colleges and universities deal with mentally ill students. Warning signs of Cho Seung Hui's troubled mental state surfaced well over a year before the killings. Mental health officials knew of his suicidal tendencies, two women students complained to the police about annoying contacts initiated by Cho, and several English teachers informed university officials about his deeply disturbing writing, full of violent images, persecution, and anger. Yet the university was limited in taking action by federal privacy and antidiscrimination laws. Colleges and universities are restricted by the disabilities act from screening prospective students for mental health problems. They cannot put a student on involuntary medical leave on the grounds of mental illness, nor can they notify parents of their child's mental condition or release medical records without the student's consent. Although these laws are designed to curtail discrimination and the invasion of privacy, they make it harder to detect seriously disturbed students like Cho and to take the steps necessary to prevent violent behavior.

Consider the complex issues involved and write an argument for or against amending laws that restrict colleges and universities from dealing with students who have serious mental illness.

EXERCISE 9-6

We live at a time when surveillance technology is so advanced that we can easily be spotted in public places by video cameras, or tracked by GPS devices, or identified by software with face recognition. In fact, the former head of public policy at Google, Andrew McLauglin, said at a Stanford conference in 2007 that he expected public and private agencies to request Google to post live, online surveillance fields worldwide within a decade. Alarmed at the increasing scope of public surveillance, privacy rights advocates argue that this invasion of our privacy violates the Fourth Amendment, which prohibits unreasonable search and seizure. But their opponents claim that we have no reason to expect privacy when we are in public places; rather we should welcome surveillance technologies, because they prevent and discourage crime as well as provide evidence for criminal investigations.

Examine these and other reasons as well as the evidence on either side of the issue. Then write an argument on the position you find most convincing.

EXERCISE 9-7

In a bitterly contested case, *Citizens United v. Federal Election Commission*, the Supreme Court made a landmark ruling that the government may not prohibit political spending by corporations or unions in elections. Although banned from giving money directly to candidates, they are not restricted from making unlimited contributions to independent political committees (later dubbed super PACs). The case was decided on First Amendment grounds with the majority arguing that political expenditures are a form of speech, and since corporations are made up of individuals, they are entitled to the same free speech protection as individual citizens. In defense of the ruling, Justice Anthony Kennedy wrote, "If the First Amendment has any force, it prohibits Congress from fining or jailing citizens, or associations of citizens, for simply engaging in political speech." The dissenting opinion argued that the Court's ruling threatened to corrupt democracy by allowing corporate money to flood the political system. As Justice John Paul Stevens wrote, "A democracy cannot function effectively when its constituent members believe laws are being bought and sold."

Review the First Amendment. Then look up the majority opinion written by Justice Kennedy and the dissent by Justice Stevens. Examine their arguments carefully and decide which ones are the most convincing. Write an argument for or against the Court's ruling using your own reasons and evidence as well as those of the justices. And remember to cite sources.

EXERCISE 9-8

In a very well-known, often-reprinted lecture, "The Idea of a University," Cardinal John Henry Newman (1801–1890) argued that the principal work of the university is to provide a liberal education, not merely, or even primarily, professional training. He said that a liberal education

> gives a man a clear conscious view of his own opinions and judgments, a truth in developing them, an eloquence in expressing them, and a force in urging them. . . . it prepares him to fill any post with credit and to master any subject with civility.

Do you agree with Cardinal Newman's assessment of a liberal education and agree that the primary job of a university (or college) is to provide such an education? Write an essay defending your opinion.

EXERCISE 9-9

High-tech cheating has increased dramatically now that almost all students have access to the Internet. Some examples: Seventy-eight students at Dartmouth College were caught copying online answers to homework assignments; 150 students from two classes at the University of California, Berkeley, were caught plagiarizing papers from the Internet; and 30 engineering students at Northeastern University were caught gaining access to each other's online homework assignments.

It has been suggested that this new wave of cheating is due in part to there being a relatively low risk of detection and even more to the lenient nature of punishments when caught. In view of this and the fact that cheaters do harm to those who do not cheat, would you approve expulsion from college for first-time proven cheaters? Or flunking the course? Or suspension for one semester? Defend your answer.[2]

---

[2] See the article by Ted Wallach, *San Francisco Chronicle* 14 August 2000.

SUMMARY OF CHAPTER 9

The essential contents of an argumentative essay are a *thesis* and *reasons (premises)* supporting the thesis. Usually, reasons need to be supported in turn by evidence or secondary reasons.

1. Experienced writers tend to keep their basic goals in mind as they prepare to write, developing a plan of attack to meet those goals, revising their original plans in the light of new evidence or unexpected difficulties. But they don't generally write in a linear fashion; writing tends to be a convoluted process.

2. The first task when preparing to write is to determine precisely what your thesis will be. Later, of course, you may change your mind, perhaps by narrowing the topic or zeroing in on it more carefully. While preparing to write and during the writing process itself, changing one's mind for good reasons is the hallmark of intelligent thought.

   After selecting a thesis and developing your principal reasons in its support, you may find it useful to construct an outline of the proposed finished product. When doing the generally inevitable research, be sure to take notes, including reference citations. If research undermines your thesis or reasons, you must revise. Never simply ignore counterarguments or reasons. Before starting to write, make sure your thesis follows logically from the reasons you intend to offer in its support.

3. Argumentative essays typically divide into three parts. The *introduction* generally states and lays the groundwork for the thesis, either before or after stating it explicitly. The *body* of the essay should contain the reasons and evidence, perhaps also reasons in support of the reasons. It is likely to be more convincing if it contains examples. If counterarguments are to be discussed, the right time to do so is in the body of an essay; and similarly for comparing or contrasting with other ideas. The *conclusion* of your essay may restate the thesis or perhaps provide a short summary of the essay's most important points.

4. The point of writing an argumentative essay is to persuade readers to accept your thesis. To do so, effective writers provide convincing reasons and supporting evidence. They also keep the reader firmly in mind by considering the background beliefs of their audience and the appropriate tone to take given that audience.

5. Good writers also try to achieve a natural flow by providing readers with transition words and expressions such as *but, although, for instance,* and *nevertheless.*

   But (note the transition word), however well planned an essay may be, rewriting almost certainly will be necessary. A first draft may thus serve as a learning device, so that later drafts can take account of what has been learned.

6. Think your position through carefully and revise the essay as you reexamine your ideas. (You may find that your ideas change in the writing process itself.) Write and rewrite until your essay says just what you want it to say.

10 Advertising: Selling the Product

The ads of our times are the richest and most faithful daily reflection that any society ever made of its entire range of activities.

—Marshall McLuhan

Advertising is legalized lying.

—H. G. Wells

Doing business without advertising is like winking at a girl in the dark. You know what you are doing, but nobody else does.

—Stuart Henderson Britt

Would you persuade, speak of interest, not reason.

—Ben Franklin

Advertising persuades people to buy things that they don't need with money they ain't got.

—Will Rogers

Advertising is what you do when you can't go see somebody. That's all it is.

—Fairfax Cone (ad executive)

A dvertising is so obviously useful that it's surprising it has such a bad name. Ads tell us what is new and what is available, where, when, and for how much. They tell us about a product's (alleged) quality and specifications. All for free, except for the effort of reading or paying attention.

Yet there are legitimate gripes about advertising. Ads don't tell us about product defects. They often mislead, either via exaggeration or, occasionally, downright lies. And because some products are advertised more heavily or more effectively than others, ads tend to skew our choices in unreasonable ways.

It also has been argued that advertising increases the costs of goods to consumers. It isn't uncommon for a quarter, or even a third, of the price of an item to be due to advertising costs, and critics have argued that this constitutes a tremendous waste.

But this charge is misleading. Advertising does cost a great deal of money, and this expense has to be factored into the costs of finished goods. Nevertheless, advertising greatly reduces the prices of those goods in the marketplace compared to what they would cost were advertising abolished or greatly restricted. It does so because it lowers production costs by making mass production profitable, thus enabling producers to obtain a mass market. In short, advertisers advertise because it reduces the costs of *selling goods*. It is not an accident that virtually all businesses advertise; they do so because they don't know of a better or cheaper way to sell their products. Those who argue otherwise generally forget that if a company doesn't advertise, it will have to increase other selling costs, especially sales commissions. (Advertising also has been objected to on the grounds that it gives an unfair advantage to large organizations when they compete against smaller ones, but objections of this kind raise issues best left unexplored here—for example, about the desirability of large versus small businesses.)

It is worth noting, though, that advertising techniques and markets have changed dramatically over the past 40 years. In 1965, companies poured most of their advertising dollars into the three major TV networks: ABC, NBC, and CBS, the market that reached 80 percent of the prime target audience—the 18- to 49-year-olds. Today, most Americans have more than a hundred channels to choose from and the hi-tech tools to mute or bypass ads altogether. Since fewer people read newspapers and magazines (once major marketing outlets) and more turn to the Internet for information and entertainment, the advertising industry has had to reach far broader and much more complex markets than ever before. But advertisers are nothing if not inventive. So over the years, ad agencies have metamorphosed into marketing companies that hawk their products through public relations promotions, in-store displays, and direct mail gimmicks. They use product placement, show ads in movie theaters, and inundate the Internet with pop-up ads and TV commercials that stream on (and on and on) to websites like YouTube and Facebook, giving them an eternal shelf life. But no matter how glitzy or numerous the innovations are, the bottom line is that they still manipulate consumer attitudes about beauty, status, relationships, and sex, using age-old gimmicks to sell us the goods.[1]

1. PROMISE AND IDENTIFICATION ADVERTISEMENTS

Virtually all ads are one or another (or both) of two basic kinds. **Promise advertisements** promise to satisfy desires or allay fears. All you have to do is buy the product advertised (remove bad body odor by using Old Spice deodorant; enjoy life more by driving a Ford Explorer). Most promise ads provide "reasons why" the product will do the job or do it better than competitors (Kleenex tissues are softer; a bowl of Total cereal has more vitamins and minerals). Then there are ads that promise to satisfy our bodily needs, like the taglines for Snickers candy bars, "When you're hungry, reach for a Snickers" or "Hungry, why wait?" The implication is that Snickers is a food that will satisfy hunger when, in fact, the only food value is in a few peanuts—the rest is sugar, chocolate, nougat, and caramel—none of which will ward off hunger for long. But this immensely successful campaign boosted sales 3½ percent, no small amount for the best-selling candy bar in the world.

---

[1]For more on the changing world of advertising, see: Auletta, Ken. "The New Pitch." *The New Yorker* 28 March 2005.

> *Promise, large promise, is the soul of advertising.*
>
> —Samuel Johnson

Identification advertisements sell the product by getting us to identify with the product. They are a kind of promise ad, since they promise that somehow or other you will be better off using the product. But the promise is made indirectly through identification with respected institutions or individuals (or occasionally simply by fostering identification with the product directly, as in the case of some Pepsi commercials). We all tend to identify with our own group and with those whom we respect—people who are famous, rich, accomplished, unusually brave, or powerful. Identification ads take advantage of this very human trait. Celebrity ads work precisely because we identify with the famous people they feature and thus with the products they tout; we become like them in some small way by using L'Oreal make-up (Beyonce), by wearing Armani clothes (Rafael Nadal) or by reading a good book (Oprah Winfrey).

Identification ads—indeed, all ads—work for another interesting reason. When people shop, say, in a supermarket, they tend to purchase products whose brand names are familiar to them. Few of us, for example, will buy a brand of toothpaste we have never heard of or never seen advertised; we buy a brand we recognize even though we know no other "reason why" we should buy that brand and not a competing one. (When was the last time you chose an unadvertised product rather than an advertised competing product?)

Among identification ad campaigns, celebrity ads have the strongest consumer appeal. Now that the lives of celebrities are chronicled around the clock on websites, in tabloids, and on television, people are eager to wear the same clothes, drink the same beer, and drive the same cars as their idols. When Nicole Kidman pumped new life into the aging Chanel No. 5, women ran out and bought it. (Sales went up 30 percent after she signed on.) Adidas seemed trendier when Dave Beckham hawked them; American Express cards more appealing when Kate Winslet pitched them; and chic, expensive handbags more desirable when Gwyneth Paltrow clutched a Coach bag. Nothing sells like celebrity. Consumers live vicariously through big stars and identify with the products they endorse.

2. THINGS TO WATCH OUT FOR IN ADVERTISEMENTS

The good news about advertising, you will recall, is that it often provides true and useful information about products and entertains us with humor, storytelling, or just nice scenes or sentiments. Time enjoyably spent is time not completely wasted. *Classic Examples*: The Budweiser Christmas TV commercials featuring their magnificent Clydesdales in winter scenes; Jockey shorts's tagline—"The Best Seat in Town," Volkswagen's "Relieves Gas Pain" and Taco Bell's "Think Outside the Bun." Or the Billy Graham billboard ad:

> You're born.
> You suffer.
> You die.
> Fortunately, there's a loophole.

The bad news about advertising stems from the increasing ability of advertising geniuses—and some of them, alas, *are* geniuses—to manipulate audiences via sophisticated psychological ploys. Everyone realizes how others are conned by advertising, but most of us think that we somehow are exceptions. Young people, including college students, often deny that they are influenced by advertising. They typically say that they don't wear designer jeans or Adidas shoes because of advertising but rather that they just "like" these products, self-deceptively ignoring the effect of advertising on their preferences. In fact, *no one* is immune to the influence of advertisements. (A Madison Avenue bigwig owned up to this when he said, "Even I fall for the stuff.") So we all are faced with the problem of how best to use advertising without being used. One way is to become familiar with the advertising devices and gimmicks used to appeal to our weaknesses, prejudices, and emotions unguided by intelligence. No doubt we'll still get taken now and then, but perhaps less often and with less seriously harmful consequences.

Ads Invite Us to Reason Fallaciously

We've already noted that ads often feature celebrity endorsements to manipulate us into buying the product. They thus invite us to commit the fallacy appeal to authority. We don't stop to think whether Jeremy Lin really does prefer Coca-Cola to Pepsi, or whether he just gets paid to say he does. Anyway, what difference would it make to you if he didn't drink soft drinks at all? (*Consumer Reports* taste tests, by the way, show hardly anyone can distinguish between Pepsi and Coke. Can Jeremy Lin? Can you? Hint: In several actual classroom tests conducted by one of the authors of this text over a period of years, students consistently failed to distinguish their favorite brands of beer from competing brands.)

In the case of Jeremy Lin advertising Coke, it seems obvious that he is no authority on the taste of soft drinks, which, anyway, certainly are a matter of individual preference. But some celebrity ads are different, sports endorsements being a case in point. Before the sex scandal shattered the image of Tiger Woods, he dominated the golf scene and was thought to be one of the greatest golfers of all time. So his endorsement of Nike's Tour Accuracy golf balls carried great weight with golf duffers intent on improving their scores. But in fact Woods doesn't use these ordinary golf balls in tournaments. Instead, he hits custom-made balls not available to the general public (as do, by the way, some other pro golfers who endorse other brands).

After the scandal erupted, Woods's advertising appeal evaporated, confirming multiple studies showing that most successful celebrity endorsements depend on a tight fit between the celebrity and the product. In Woods's case, the fit was intensified. Not only was he an iconic golfer, he was the embodiment of ideal virtues. A genius at the game, he appeared to be hard working, dedicated, disciplined, and tough-minded—an ethical, reliable man. In other words, his virtues as well as his prowess persuaded consumers to buy the sports products he endorsed. And that, of course, is the best sell of all. Consumers are inclined to trust a virtuous celebrity—even though he isn't virtuous and doesn't use the product he is hawking. So for a while no one has used the slogan "Go on. Be a Tiger." But his image is beginning to rebound, particularly overseas, so we are in for another wave of Tiger endorsements.

Anyway, moving on to a related topic, it should be clear by now that ads generally are designed to invite us to overlook their *suppression of evidence.* They tell us the good features of products but always hide their product's warts. (Why should they do otherwise?) Cigarette ads contain probably the most obvious examples of this fallacy, given what we know about the lethal effects of smoking. When R.J. Reynolds Tobacco launched a feminine version of Camels called Camel No. 9, you can be sure the ads made no mention of the fact that far more women die of lung cancer today than breast cancer. Instead, they played up the feminine appeal of the cigarette, giving it a name that evokes images of perfumes like Chanel No. 19 and packaging it in pink and green floral boxes labeled "light and luscious." Getting women to identify with a brand that has long played to male smokers has put Camels in competition with its biggest competitor for the female market, Virginia Slims, whose classic slogan, "You've come a long way, baby," ironically reflected the fact that women, indeed, have come a long way—in catching up with male mortality rates for lung cancer.

> *There is an art to making whole lies out of half truths.*
> —Christy Mathewson (baseball hall of fame pitcher who was paid to endorse Tuxedo pipe tobacco)

Advertising audiences also are invited to make *faulty* or *invidious comparisons. Examples:* Pizza Hut ads that compared their delivery service with dingbat pizza parlors that don't deliver at all, ignoring their true competitors, such as Domino's Pizza, that do; Wisk ads that claim their product is more powerful than Tide, so you need to use less, making it seem that it costs less to use Wisk than Tide, which is not true (figure out why).

Some ads, though, use fallacious reasoning humorously and aren't meant to be taken seriously. A good example is this BMW ad: "Doctors say increased activity slows the aging process. Coincidentally, BMW drivers are ten years younger than other luxury car drivers." This humorous use of cause and effect was not an example of *questionable cause* because it was not intended to be taken literally. Nor was this clever blurb for American Coach Lines, "If men were meant to fly, God would have lowered the fares." Nonetheless, both ads are intended to manipulate prospective customers into buying the products.

Advertisements Pound Home Slogans and Meaningless Jargon

In fact, ads run through the entire range of fallacies, challenging theorists to invent pigeonholes into which to put them all. How, for instance, should we categorize the fallacious reasoning that leads people to be swayed by endlessly repeated, mostly empty slogans? *Classic Examples:* "Because I'm Worth it" (L'Oreal); "Think Different" (Apple—with the "ly" dropped at Steve Job's insistence); "You can be sure of Shell"; "A Diamond is Forever" (DeBeers). And so on, *ad* infinitum (heh, heh).

Slogans run the range from the modestly informative ("Miller Light: Great taste, less filling") to the somewhat suggestive ("Chevrolet. Like a rock") to the completely irrelevant ("Nike: Just do it"). In general, they work because they are repeated endlessly, so that they become ingrained in our minds. In the days before television, which is primarily a visual medium, singing commercials did the job on radio. There can be very few people over 70, for example, who could not at the drop of a hat sing the Rinso soap flakes jingle they heard belted out on radio countless times lo these many years ago: "Rinso white, Rinso bright; happy little washday song!"

The most brilliant propaganda must confine itself to a few points and repeat them over and over.

—Adolf Hitler

Calvin & Hobbes © Watterson. Reprinted with permission of Universal Press Syndicate. All rights reserved.

Slogans that tout products as "the official" something or other are an interesting special case. In 2004, for example, Tylenol advertised itself as "The official supplier of pain relief products for the 2004 U.S. Olympic team" (accompanied by pictures of athletes with massive, rippling muscles, presumably injury prone). Puffs of this kind generally imply something that is false. The Tylenol slogan implied that Olympic athletes preferred this brand to others, or that Tylenol was better than any other painkiller. But you can bet your life that if they were in real pain, they would take something stronger, like Vicodin. In fact, becoming official whatever merely means paying for the privilege of being identified with a name. Tylenol paid through the nose to be identified with the Olympic Games, as did other official Olympic sponsors, like Coca-Cola, Chevrolet, and Budweiser. Another wrinkle on the "official" gambit is the naming of sports arenas and stadiums after companies that buy this privilege (Coors, Minute Maid, AT&T, and so on).

Ads Play on Weaknesses, Emotions, Prejudices, and Fears

Particular kinds of advertisements sell some products more easily than they do others. Those that play on weaknesses or fears are a case in point, one reason so many TV commercials are of this nature. *Examples:* Ads for, deodorants, mouthwashes, hair restorers, and hair colorers; and so on. Some of these ads do have the virtue of being informative (Just for Men does darken gray hair), but in many cases the product doesn't do the job advertised (Aquafresh does very little if anything for bad breath, since most bad breath originates elsewhere; it does, though, kill some mouth bacteria). In many other cases, the advertised product doesn't do the job any better than competing products (Mylanta isn't any better at counteracting stomach acidity than Maalox, Gelusil, or several other brands; Energizer and Duracell batteries are equally good).

Calvin & Hobbes © Watterson. Reprinted with permission of Universal Press Syndicate. All rights reserved.

Ads Employ Sneaky Rhetoric, Photos and Layouts

In particular, *weasel words* are quite common in advertising. When an ad says the product "*fights* bad breath," it's wise to assume it doesn't *cure* bad breath, because if it did, the ad would make this stronger, less weaselly claim. Similar remarks apply to claims such as "*helps* control dandruff with regular use," "gets dishes *virtually* spotless," and so on.

We also need to watch out for sneaky uses of *comparative* and *evaluative* terms, like *good, better,* and (best of all) *best.* The term *best* at best translates into "tied for first with all other leading brands." The "lowest fare to Europe" may turn out to be the standard fare every airline charges. And when an ad says "No one sells ___ for less," you can be pretty sure others sell for the same price. And then there is that wonderful term *free,* itself perfectly unsneaky, but so often used to lure the gullible (all of us in weak moments) into thinking they're getting something for nothing.

But these kinds of ads aren't as sneaky as fine print disclaimers that let the manufacturer off the hook. The dietary supplement industry, for example, makes a huge profit hyping health products in ads that don't exactly say they treat a condition but make claims that lead people to believe they do. Fine print disclaimers do little to dissuade consumers—instead, they provide regulatory loopholes for the manufacturer. For instance, an ad claiming a product is an "amazing new joint health supplement" that is "clinically shown to quickly improve mobility and joint comfort" doesn't really say it treats arthritis but suggests it does.[2] Then the fine print disclaimer lets the manufacturer off easy when it says in tiny print, "This statement has not been evaluated by the Food and Drug Administration. This product is not intended to diagnose, treat, cure or prevent any disease." A wary consumer would be wise to check out those "clinical trials," by the way, to see if they have been published in legitimate scientific journals or are just the marketing ploys of health care hucksters.

Misleading language is just one of the sneak factors in ads. Photos are even more deceptive. Take, for instance, ads for diet pills endorsed by celebrities air-brushed to a size 2 or cruise ads with photo-shopped landscapes. Then there are the food ads that "enhance" products to look believably scrumptious, but are in fact really inedible.[3] In mouthwatering photos of luscious meals, for example, the spaghetti is actually glued to the fork to keep it in place, the ice cubes in frosty drinks are acrylic imitations, and the ice cream smothered in syrup is a slab of lard doused with Karo syrup. More subtle deceptions are the visual cues that tweak our brains into Pavlovian responses when we watch chocolate syrup streaming over caramel candy with the sexy voice-over "Chocolate." It is safe to say that nothing ever tastes as good as it looks in the ad.

> **Deliberate deception:** A Charles Schwab commercial shows a satisfied couple talking about their successful investments with the brokerage firm. Then a three-second statement appears on the screen with about ten lines of print, starting with the information that the people telling their story were real customers of Schwab. But only a speed reader could get to the end fast enough to read the sentence revealing that the customers were paid for their testimonials.

Finally there is the layout. When does an ad not look like an ad? When it's laid out like a news article—as it was, for instance, when the *Los Angeles Times* ran a front page ad for an NBC drama, *Southland*, that was framed as a news report.[4] The only sign of its real intent was an NBC logo with the label "advertisement" in small print. Another issue ran a four-page ad for the movie *The Soloist* laid out in the form of a news article in the entertainment section. A case could be made that the struggling *Times* was desperate for money, given the recent massive cuts to its newsroom, and maybe an occasional lapse is forgivable in marketing something as trivial as entertainment. (Still, 100 reporters signed a letter of protest.) Marketing entertainment as news may not be a serious deception, but framing a sales pitch that way for fraudulent herbal remedies, say, most certainly would be.

---

[2]From an informative article about diet supplements: "The Bad News About Products, Too Good to Be True." *Tuft's University Health and Nutrition Letter* September 2009.

[3]Taken from an interesting article on the tricks of the trade in food ads: Segal, David. "Grilled Chicken, That Temperamental Star." *New York Times* 9 October 2011.

[4]See: "in Advertisers We Trust." *Extra!* May 2010.

All of us come from someplace else.

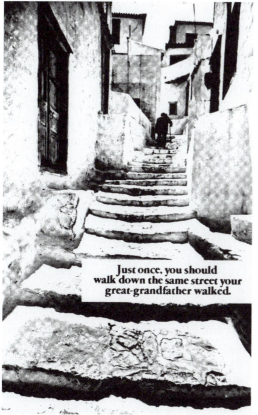

Just once, you should walk down the same street your great-grandfather walked.

Picture this if you will.

A man who's spent all his life in the United States gets on a plane, crosses a great ocean, lands.

He walks the same streets his family walked centuries ago.

He sees his name, which is rare in America, filling three pages in a phone book.

He speaks haltingly the language he wishes he had learned better as a child.

As America's airline to the world, Pan Am does a lot of things.

We help business travelers make meetings on the other side of the world. Our planes take goods to and from six continents. We take vacationers just about anywhere they want to go.

But nothing we do seems to have as much meaning as when we help somebody discover the second heritage that every American has.

America's airline to the world.

See your travel agent.

Courtesy of Pan American World Airways, Inc.

Advertising tends to concentrate on marginal needs, desires, and fears at the expense of many more important ones. Indeed, a frequently heard charge against advertising is that it increases the already strong tendency of people in industrial countries to become preoccupied with buying and consuming goods. (Note the humorous bumper sticker WHEN THE GOING GETS TOUGH, THE TOUGH GO SHOPPING.) *Occasionally, however, an ad comes along that reminds us of what (for most of us) are much more important values, even though we tend to forget them in the hustle and bustle of everyday life. This Pan Am ad is one of those rare ads that tend to push us in the right direction. Yes! If we can afford it (and more of us could if we spent less on lesser needs), just once, we should walk down the same street our great-grandfather walked. (Pan Am went belly up in the early 1990s, but for other reasons.)*

Ads Draw on Trendy Issues in the News

Issues that grip the country are fertile ground for advertisers, who use them to play on our fears and desires. For instance, mounting concern over the obesity epidemic has inspired a glut of low-fat, low-sugar, low-salt, low-carb products. McDonald's is pushing McVeggie Burgers and McGriddles (cheese, eggs, and meat wrapped in pancakes). Kraft Foods is marketing a new version of "Lunchables" called Fun Fuels, made with fruit, meat, grain, and dairy products. And Hershey's has launched sugar-free chocolates with slogans like "Your recommended daily allowance of indulgence."

Weight-loss ads aimed at fat-conscious consumers have been making such exaggerated claims lately that the Federal Trade Commission released a guide in 2003 to help consumers spot deceptive ads for phony weight-loss products. You'd think people would be skeptical of slogans like "lose weight without diet or exercise," but apparently not. P. T. Barnum got it right when he said there's a sucker born every minute.

Some ads were understandable, perhaps. Given the drastic drop in air travel after the terrorist attack, United Airlines had good reason to launch a major ad campaign. The documentary style ads featured interviews with United employees making patriotic comments like "We're Americans and this is not gonna beat us down," and "We took the blow but we're gonna get up." The ads received mixed reviews, and though they might have boosted United's image, they didn't sell tickets—air travel was down for two years after the attack.

Ads Whitewash Corporate Imagery

Whenever an ad sells a company's image instead of a product, you have got to wonder what is going on. With the popularity of environmental issues on the rise, corporations that have a major impact on the environment have sponsored an increasing number of "green" ads. DuPont's classic "seal-slapping" ad captures the flavor of these eco-friendly spots. This one features a scenic shoreline with dolphins diving, penguins waddling, sea lions clapping (you get the idea)—all to the melodic strains of Beethoven's "Ode to Joy." Just visible on the horizon is an oil tanker. The voiceover tells us "recently DuPont announced that its energy unit would pioneer the use of new double-hulled tankers in order to safeguard the environment." Not long after the ad appeared—with its happy sea creatures cavorting in an eco-friendly environment—the EPA issued a report that DuPont was far and away the largest emitter of toxic waste.

GE launched an "eco imagination" campaign designed to remake the company's image as a leader in clean technology. The dancing elephant ad, a charmer that was top rated in viewer surveys, showed a computer-generated elephant dancing through a rain forest to "Singin' in the Rain." (Never mind that elephants don't live in rain forests.) The dancing elephant cavorts past a bunch of beaming monkeys, toucans, and flamingos—a bucolic scene intended to show us that GE's low-emission products benefit the environment. "Technology that's in step with nature," the voiceover intones. Judging from an

Ad Track survey, this spot was one of the most engaging ads in 2005, and GE was well on its way to transforming its image.

Ubiquitous Ads and Sensory Overload

Marketers are nothing if not resourceful. What with conventional reading material and TV watching on the wane, they can no longer count on reaching consumers through established media like magazines, newspapers and TV. Instead they are taking a scattershot approach, plastering ads all over the place.[5] Microsoft advertised on tray tables in U.S. Airways planes; Geico on subway turnstiles; Continental Airlines on Chinese food cartons and pizza boxes; Perry Ellis on shirt boxes and hanging bags at dry cleaners. And how about this for a mini-marketing gem: CBS was stamping the names of CBS television shows on supermarket eggs. Then there are the video screens that have appeared in taxicabs and elevators, ostensibly to provide news but heavily larded with ads. Ads are even projected on the sides of buildings, and old-fashioned billboards are being converted into digital screens that change messages throughout the day.

Given this marketing barrage, it is a wonder that consumers haven't reached a saturation point. According to Yankelovich, a marketing research firm, 30 years ago people in cities could see up to 2,000 ads a day. Now they see up to 5,000—that's 2½ times as many. In addition, consumers are regularly blitzed with spam e-mail, Internet pop-ups, and repetitive cell phone messages plugging the company's services. A growing number of people are offended by this onslaught, and that worries marketers— sort of—but not enough to deter them from trying even more ingenious ways to hawk their wares.

Puffery Is Legal, but Not Deceptive Advertising

Finally, it's worth noting that what is called "puffery"—generalized, vague, or exaggerated claims, particularly when asserted humorously—is legal. *Example:* The claim by BMW to be "The Ultimate Driving Machine." (Litigation does very occasionally arise concerning borderline cases.) However, ads can overstep legal boundaries and make fraudulent claims. The cigarette industry, in particular, has come under fire for deceptive advertising. For example, in spring 2003, Philip Morris was found guilty of consumer fraud in its ads for "light" cigarettes. Judge Nicholas Byron ruled that the company intentionally misled the public into thinking that Marlboro Lights and Cambridge Lights were "less harmful or safer than their regular counterparts" and ordered the company to pay $10.8 billion to the plaintiffs. This case is one of several lawsuits brought against cigarette companies in recent years.

---

[5]Examples taken from: "Anywhere the Eye Can See, It's Now Likely to See an Ad." *New York Times* 15 January 2007.

EXERCISE 10-1

Here are several advertising snippets (usually including the main ploy). Evaluate each of them for honesty, cogency, and the like, and point out uses of the various kinds of gimmicks and devices (humor, jargon, etc.) discussed in the text.

1. Woman in a cigarette ad: "Until I find a real man, I'll settle for a real smoke."

*2. Burger King sign: "10 FREE French Fry Certificates for only $1.00."

3. Calvert Gin ad: "Dry, Drier, Driest, Crisp."

4. Ad for a car: "You can love it without getting your heart broken."

5. Apple ad: "Think different."

*6. Part of a Nike commercial: "You don't win silver; you lose gold."

7. Ad for Swiss Mocha: "Drift into a Chocolate Daydream."

8. Ad for presidential coins: "Every reader of this newspaper who beats the order deadline will still get one of the last never-circulated Golden Presidential Dollar Coins free with each sealed vault tube at just twenty-eight dollars plus shipping."

9. Budweiser commercial: A rooster very carefully crosses the road and then goes into a tavern where they serve Budweiser. A guy watching this then says to his buddy, "Well, I guess that answers that question." (Hint: This ad is a particular favorite of at least one of the authors of this text.)

*10. The principal part of a newspaper ad sponsored by the U.S. Council for Coconut Research/Information featuring a photo of Martin Agronsky: "The truth told by a famous U.S. television personality: Whoever says coconut oil's 'poisoning' America isn't supported by facts. . . . In fact, an on-going medical study in a Boston hospital has turned out some strong evidence that the 'fatty acids' of coconut oil could be beneficial to human health. America's intake of coconut oil fats is a lot less than what you think. The FDA [Food and Drug Administration] commissioner testified recently before the U.S. Congress that less than 1.5% of U.S. total fat intake is made up of coconut oil. . . ."

11. Newspaper ad for the Massachusetts State Lottery: "There's a good chance you could win the Numbers Game today. Just ask the 12,000 people who won yesterday. . . . The only thing that's hard to do is lose. When this many people win, how can you lose?"

12. Notice on the package of Elizabeth Arden Ceramide Time Complex Capsules: "Take your skin back in time to the future of a younger tomorrow."

---

*Starred (*) items are answered in a section at the back of the book.

EXERCISE 10-2

1. Apple ads have been among the most successful in the history of advertising. Examine a wide range of these ads on the Internet, starting with the text-heavy spots in the 1970s, followed by the strong, visual ads in later years that have almost no text except taglines like "Think different." How does the evolution of these ads reflect new generations of consumers? Explain the appeal of an early ad and a later one. In what ways are they promise and/or identification ads? What ploys do they use to sell Apple products? Are there any fallacies involved? An entire generation of consumers seems to have loved these ads. Why?

2. How about the following excerpts (paraphrased) from a *Wall Street Journal* commercial:

    Twenty-five years ago, two very similar young men graduated from the same college and started work at the same company. Returning to college for their 25th reunion, they still were much alike—happily married, three children, and so on—but one was manager of a small department in the company, the other was the company's president.

    The difference that made the difference was in what each of these two men knew and how they made use of that knowledge: one read the *Wall Street Journal;* the other did not.

*3. Here is a United Airlines TV commercial (used by permission of Leo Burnett Co.):

    Ben (the boss, addressing his sales force): I got a phone call this morning from one of our oldest customers. He fired us. After 20 years. He fired us. He said he didn't know us anymore. I think I know why. We used to do business with a handshake—face to face. Now it's a phone call and a fax—get back to you later. With another fax probably. Well folks, something's gotta change. That's why we're gonna get out with a little face-to-face chat with every customer we have.
    Salesman: But Ben, that's gotta be over 200 cities.
    Ben: I don't care. Edward, Ryan, Nicholas . . .
    Voiceover: If you're the kind of business that still believes personal service deserves a lot more than lip service, . . . welcome to United. That's the way we've been doing business for over 60 years.
    Salesman: Ben, where're you going?
    Ben: To visit that old friend who fired us this morning.
    Voiceover: United. Come fly the friendly skies.

    Do you think this was a successful commercial? Why, or why not? Is this primarily a promise or an identification ad?

4. A letter from a travel company included this note on the envelope: "Lowest Fare Advertised on Holland America Guaranteed." Assume, as is likely, that this ad for Holland America (a large cruise ship company) is true. Is there something about this blurb that should make you suspect that the rates quoted are not the lowest you can get? Explain.

5. One of the classic ads in the Pepsi–Coke advertising competition is set some time in the distant future and shows a teacher taking his students to an archeological site containing artifacts from the late twentieth century. He explains the various objects while his students drink cans of Pepsi. One of them holds up a bedraggled Coke bottle and asks the teacher what it is, to which the teacher responds, after much puzzled thought, "I've no idea." A great commercial (why? what is its pulling power?), it brings to mind the way in which ordinary items from a time and place can reveal a great deal to discerning investigators (doing the archeological equivalent of reading between the lines).

6. Advertisements, if you can believe Marshall McLuhan, contain a treasure trove of clues about our times. If you were an investigator who came across records containing most of today's advertisements a thousand years hence, what might you learn from them about life in the early twenty-first century? Explain.

EXERCISE 10-3

1. Create a magazine ad for a product: (1) Decide which product it will be, (2) decide on an intended audience for your ad, and (3) design the picture and the copy. Use the ad to make a sales pitch to the class. Then ask students why they would or wouldn't buy the product, based on your ad, and analyze the ad's appeal, or lack of same. (Doing this will make you better appreciate the creative ability of professionals in the advertising business.)

2. Compare two ads for the same or similar products in magazines with very different audiences (for instance, *Vogue* and *Time* magazine or *Sports Illustrated*). Explain how the intended audience influenced the ad design and sales pitch.

3. THE UP SIDE OF ADS

Although most ads hawk consumer goods, a few actually attempt to educate us or warn us against harmful activities. Partnership for a Drug-Free America has aired a series of ads aimed at combating drug use in this country. The ads, targeting young people as well as parents, focus on the harmful effects of drugs ranging from Ecstasy to marijuana to alcohol. For example, one set of TV spots focuses on embarrassing or disturbing moments that teen drug users experience as a result of their habit. One ad shows a girl trying to conceal a drug-induced nosebleed that starts suddenly in class. Another features a boy inadvertently dropping a drug packet on the counter of a fast-food restaurant. A more shocking series of ads appeals to the vanity of teens by running photographs of young adults who are long-term users in fashionable but grotesque poses that highlight the disfiguring effects of methamphetamines. For instance, under the caption "Body by Crystal Meth" a young man stands, hand on hips, revealing a skeletal body ravaged by drugs. Ads aimed at parents urge them to monitor their kids' activities and social life. They feature parents asking questions like "Where are you going after school?" or "What are your plans after soccer?" Companion ads show older, grateful teens who realize in hindsight that all those irritating questions their parents asked managed to deter them from using drugs. Clearly the message is that parents should be involved in their kids' lives by asking questions and by knowing what they do, whom they hang out with, and where they go. We can only hope that all the advertising devices and gimmicks used so effectively to market goods and services will be just as successful at discouraging drug use among teens.

Public service announcements crafted like ads are another strategy used to publicize wrongdoings and bring about change. In an effort to ferret out insider trading on Wall Street, the FBI ran a one-minute video featuring Michael Douglas, well known for playing the criminal financier Gordon Gekko—whose mantra was "greed is good"—in the film *Wall Street*. In the video, Douglas drives home the message that insider trading is illegal. "The movie was fiction, but the problem is real," he says. By using a mega-watt celebrity like Douglas, the FBI hoped to bring the crime to the attention of the public and encourage whistle-blowers to report illegal activity in the financial world.

4. MARKETING STRATEGIES

Although the advertising professionals are exceedingly good at their business, they are forced by increasing competition between advertisers, coupled with increased consumer sophistication, to do a good deal of market research. That is why, these days, there is an immense amount of research behind every successful advertising campaign. One way for consumers to defend themselves against the ad campaigns that result from sophisticated market research is to become familiar with methods advertisers use to market their products.

Eric Clark notes, in *The Want Makers*,[6] that "virtually nothing appears from a major advertiser or agency until it has been opinion-polled, test-marketed or copy-tested, submitted on the way to panels of consumers whose words have been turned into statistical tables or analyzed by psychologists." Most large agencies have research staffs of their own, in addition to using specialist agencies such as the A. C. Nielsen Company.

Types of research vary, depending on the method in favor at any given time, but roughly they can be divided into *qualitative research*—getting into people's heads to find out their thoughts and feelings—and *quantitative research*—gathering information by observation, experimentation, and surveys.

Qualitative research grew out of Freud's theory that unconscious motivations often influence behavior. The underlying assumption, already stressed here, is that people make many decisions irrationally and often are not even aware of their reasons for making them. So researchers try to figure out how people really feel about products, not just how one might suppose they would feel. For example, on the basis of interviews with 300 mothers about how they fed their babies, researchers concluded the mothers were more concerned that feedings should be convenient and enjoyable for *themselves* rather than for their children, even though the mothers said their baby's satisfaction was paramount. The resulting successful marketing ploy was merely to mention that babies would enjoy being fed the food but to stress that feeding time would be shortened.

---

[6]Some of what follows is summarized from this fascinating book.

Since all of us are motivated by unconscious desires at some time or other, these marketing techniques make it more difficult for us to make rational decisions about the products we buy (including political products, to be discussed shortly). We need to be more careful about what we buy and ask ourselves some commonsense questions before plunking down our money. Do we really need the product? Can we afford it? How does it compare with other similar products? Are we being conned—perhaps overly motivated—by advertising?

These questions are especially relevant when we are tempted to believe in a product's claim even though there isn't a shred of evidence to support it. For instance, in an all-out effort to sell toning shoes (the latest craze in athletic gear), marketers claim that the shoes help burn calories and tone leg muscles, glutes, and core.[7] To glamorize the product, ads show a man ignoring a woman in clunky shoes as he ogles another one wearing Truebalance, while the voiceover says "Burn calories and activate muscles. The toning shoe that doesn't look like one." You can't help wonder why people fall for this stuff. But they do, despite studies by the American Council of Exercise to the contrary. Of the three brands tested, it found "no evidence to support the claims that the shoes will help wearers exercise intensely, burn more calories, or improve muscle strength and tone." Although the study was highlighted on NPR and ran in several newspapers, it didn't deter consumers from buying the shoes. As one marketer said, ". . . Americans love a silver bullet. [They say] 'All I have to do is walk around and I'll be more fit.' " A good example of the magical thinking advertisers tap into when they take into account unconscious motivations.

The quantitative approach to research has come a long way since the days when researchers asked people on the street what brand of soap or cereal they preferred. When you buy goods at most stores these days, the bar codes that are read at the checkout counter provide the retailer with a good deal of information concerning price, item purchased, and so on, that can be stored in computers; market researchers are now tapping into this information to find out what products people actually buy, not what they say they will buy. They are keeping track of the purchases made by carefully selected families, linking this information with further data concerning family income, number of children, and TV programs watched, including special test commercials. The result is that these marketing gurus can identify the ads that effectively sold the targeted products and plan large-scale ad campaigns accordingly. The currently popular "shopping cards" that claim to give discounts to customers on certain products are really intended to provide information on customer shopping habits that is analyzed and then sold to marketing companies. In many stores, sales clerks ask shoppers for their ZIP codes, which are fed into a marketing program (called PRIZM) that gathers consumer information. This program is advertised to marketers in *Advertising Age* as "the targeting tool that turns birds of a feather into sitting ducks." Perhaps an appropriate slogan these days would be that eternal vigilance is the price of economic solvency.

---

[7]See: New man, Andrew Adam. "Studies May Not Matter if Consumers Want to Believe the Marketing." *New York Times* 20 September 2010.

The object of all this research is not necessarily the low-income consumer but the more affluent. As Michael Schudson points out in *Advertising: The Uneasy Persuasion,* marketers are more interested in people with $100,000 to spend on nonessential goods than those with $1,000. The consequence is that consumer choices are often top-heavy in luxury items. Schudson argues that this tendency sometimes works to reduce the spectrum of goods available to people with modest incomes. The example he gives is the transformation of the automobile. "More and more extras become standard equipment in automobiles and other products, and the low-income consumer has no choice but to go deeper into debt to pay for the simplest model, now weighted with superfluous 'standard' equipment." (In fairness, we need to note that used cars do cost less than new ones, although prices for used, ah . . . "pre-owned" cars, also reflect the fancy equipment—electric windows and doors and the like—that they, too, are loaded with.)

Luxury used to be for the happy few, but now it is hawked to the mass of consumers. Even ordinary products are hyped with inflated language to give them luxury status. James B. Twitchell comments on this trend in "Luxe Populi," San Francisco Chronicle, May 20, 2007.

. . . [T]he consumers of the new luxury have a sense of entitlement that transcends social class, a conviction that the finest things are their birthright. Never mind that they may have been born into a family whose ancestral estate is a tract house in the suburbs, near the mall, not paid for, and whose family crest was downloaded from the Internet. Ditto the signet ring design. Language reflects this hijacking. Words such as *gourmet, premium, boutique, chic, accessory* and *classic* have loosened from their elite moorings and now describe such top-of-category items as popcorn, hamburgers, discount brokers, shampoo, scarves, ice cream and trailer parks.

There are psychological consequences to targeting the affluent as well. Fed a steady diet of ads for upscale goods, low-income consumers begin to crave luxuries beyond their wallets. How many people can afford a Rolex watch, a BMW X3, or diamonds from Tiffany? But they can fantasize about luxury items in classy ads—and maybe then max out their credit cards.

Even the best-targeted ads, however (fortunately?), often miss their mark because people have become more adept at tuning them out. Increasingly sophisticated technology allows just about everyone to zap commercials with remote controls, or skip ads altogether with digital video recorders. We may not be outfoxing advertisers as much as we think, though, when we fast-forward commercials to get to the main attraction. The assumption has always been that ads have no effect when played at high speed, but recent research suggests that they do, indeed, engage us. Experiments done by NBC show that viewers are just as involved in speeded up commercials as they are when they slow down and watch the program that follows. Not only that, but viewers who have already seen an ad in slow time tend to register the same emotional response when they speed through it again in fast time.[8]

Advertisers also have to contend with the growing popularity of less-well-advertised generic products, and with the escalation of price wars that squeeze profit margins and advertising budgets. In response to this trend, advertisers regularly try new strategies. For the past decade, marketing money has shifted away from conventional media and into nonmedia sectors, such as sales promotions, public relations, direct mail, catalog marketing, and trade promotions. Think, for instance, of the avalanche of junk mail just about everybody gets these days. At least consumers inundated by telemarketing sales pitches can now block the calls by entering their names in the do-not-call registry.

The Shopping Mall as Marketing Tool

Theatricality, illusion, pretense, manipulation, and artifice are the essence of the mall setting. The shopper must buy . . . Every possible design tool is aimed at behavioral control, to make the shopper visit more often, stay longer, and buy more. Pathways are contrived to require her to walk past the maximum number of shopping outlets en route to the planned destination, tempting her to suspend judgment and yield to impulse. Attention-getting banners, vivid signs, dramatic lighting, seductive color schemes, lush plantings, upbeat music, and soothing sounds provide intense sensations, alternately stimulating and relaxing the visitor until she is freed from normal restraints and caught up in the mood of buying.

—Rifkind, Carole. "America's Fantasy Urbanism: The Waxing of the Mall and the Waning of Civility." *Dumbing down : essays on the strip mining of American culture.* Eds. Katharine Washburn and John F. Thornton. New York: W. W. Norton & Co., 1997. 261. ;

Databased marketing is another of the current advertising concepts. As Stan Rapp and Thomas L. Collins point out in their book *Beyond Maxi Marketing,* advertisers are reducing their concentration on mass marketing in favor of more focused, less wasteful, individualized marketing strategies, using precisely targeted database programs. For example, a Tennessee department store chain's database identified 1,400 customers who purchased clothes by high-fashion designers such as Anne Klein and Liz Claiborne only when they were on sale, and then notified these customers when designer clothes went on sale, increasing two-day sale receipts on these items by 97 percent. Personalized marketing is much more likely to appeal to consumers than is mass marketing, making it harder to resist.

---

[8]For more on this see: Story, Louise. "Engaging at Any Speed? Commercials Put to Test." *New York Times* 3 July 2007.

Drug manufacturers have come up with a new marketing ploy in recent years that has physicians and the FDA worried. Instead of advertising prescription drugs to doctors only, as has been the practice in the past, drug companies are marketing directly to consumers. Probably the most widely hyped product is Viagra, but all manner of drugs are hawked to the public for treating everything from depression to heart disease. It comes as no surprise that patients are now insisting that doctors prescribe the pills advertised on TV, and are often unwilling to consider alternative treatments. One unfortunate consequence, noted in the *New England Journal of Medicine,* is that "demand by patients is the most common reason offered by physicians for inappropriate prescribing." Increasing concern about the adverse effects of advertising drugs has prompted the American Medical Association to study the potential problems of this type of advertising and the FDA to increase its surveillance of pharmaceutical ads.

When all else fails, marketers can always change the look and shape of a product to seduce consumers into buying it. In days gone by, companies rarely changed their product packaging. Kleenex came in square or rectangular boxes, Pepsi redesigned its cans only ten times in 100 years.[9] But nowadays, marketers are turning packages into three-dimensional ads that lure buyers to their products as they stroll down store aisles. Kleenex has come out with bright oval cartons, Coors Lite bottles turn blue when chilled, Pepsi is changing the graffiti-like design of its cans every few weeks (to attract the younger generation, with its alarmingly short attention span), and Evian is packaging water in elegant, swan-necked bottles. (The wildly successful marketing of bottled water is ironic, not to mention illogical, given the fact that most tap water in this country is as good or better than bottled water.) Other ploys include soda cans that emit a sweet-smelling spray when you pop the top, and packages with tiny, embedded speakers that talk to you when you walk by. Talking boxes. Ah, the wonders of consumerism.

Strategies for hawking products work so well that it is no wonder the Army is using them to recruit officers.[10] With the economy on the skids, young people have signed up for military service in droves, despite the wars in progress—but not the college graduates who would qualify for officer training programs. To boost its shrinking supply of officers, the Army has created classic identification and promise ads showing famous generals like George Washington, Douglas MacArthur, and Colin Powell with a voice-over announcing "Officers in the U.S. Army can rise to any challenge. Can you?" Other ads link achievement in the Army with success in the business world by running ministories of CEO's who were once Army officers. The obvious ploy here is to set up identification with these super stars followed by the promise, however improbable, that the Army is a pathway to achieving that status. This emphasis on the promise is the result of marketing research showing that when "Army strong" music introduced a commercial, college students were turned off, but with the promise of super stardom, they were engaged. Yes, the Army does the same kind of research that big business does. As one general put it, the goal isn't just to recruit officers, but to do a better job of marketing the "product" to young Americans.

---

[9]Examples are taken from: Story, Louise. "Product Packages Now Shout to Grab Your Fickle Attention." *New York Times* 10 August 2007.

[10]For more on this see: Quenqua, Douglas. "With Enough Soldiers, The Army Is Looking For a Few Good Officers." *New York Times* 3 August 2009.

Advertising to Children

Targeting children has become a tricky business for advertisers. Consumer advocates have become more vocal about the evils of marketing to kids, and regulators have pressured various industries to soft-pedal their ads.[11] Given the rise in childhood obesity, food marketers, in particular, have come under fire, with the result that some companies, like Coca-Cola and Hershey, have actually agreed not to advertise to children. But marketers are nothing if not creative, and though they proceed with caution, they have developed strategies to bypass regulations with ads that don't look like ads at all. Instead they are framed as games or contests or events that "engage with" kids rather than sell directly to them. So you have magazines like *Sports Illustrated Kids* inventing such programs as "Sports Dad of the Year," sponsored by Wendy's, or design-your-own games for Goldfish, the Pepperidge Farm cracker. This subtle sell may seem innocuous, but not to those opposed to commercials for kids, who worry that children are brainwashed into identifying with the brand. Of course publishers in favor of ads for kids (for obvious reasons) dismiss these concerns with the argument that children have to get used to the commercial world they live in—and the earlier the better. Really? Tell that to a mother in the supermarket who is battling her kid for the box of Cocoa Puffs he just yanked off the shelf.

Advertising on the Internet

The days when the Internet was exclusively, or even primarily, noncommercial are now long-since over. A growing number of businesses are advertising their products on home pages on the World Wide Web. Users can click on to a commercial and read about and order the product in one fell swoop. Quick, easy, and tempting.

Because of mounting evidence that TV ads are less effective than they used to be, marketers are reaching a wider audience by integrating the Internet and television into their ad campaigns. One ploy is for networks to sell ad packages that combine Internet space with TV commercials. Some of the glossiest, most engaging Super Bowl ads run by the TV broadcaster on game day have been made available on websites like espn.com, nfl.com, and video.google.com. And now that social media have become so popular, these commercials run Ad Meter apps on sites like Facebook.com for people to view and evaluate—and, of course, send on to their friends. So the ads run over and over again. What a godsend to marketers that is! All they have to do is set the ad in motion to have it blogged and tweeted around the Internet. (It's no wonder they want more bang for their buck, though, with Super Bowl commercials costing $3 million for 30 seconds, as of 2011.)

In fact, social media are now a major force in marketing products. Nielson surveys show that 60 percent of consumers who research products on line learn about specific brands through social networking sites, three out of five create their own reviews, and women especially share their likes and dislikes with others. Since most people using social media are likely to trust recommendations of friends and family, they are naturally influenced by the opinions of these trusted sources. In this way, social networking sites

---

[11]Clifford, Stephanie. "A Fine Line When Ads and Children Mix." *New York Times* 15 February 2010.

promote products by word of mouth—an ingenious way for marketers to launch low-cost advertising campaigns that go on and on and on—like the Energizer bunny.

The consumer doesn't fare as well as the advertisers, though. The downside of social networking is that every click or swipe is captured in vast data banks on sites like Facebook. All the "like" buttons, the shared links, the songs streamed, the games played—everything, in fact, is silently filed away for future use. This is the treasure trove that marketers tap into when they want to match products to consumer preferences.

And then there are the privacy issues at stake when these sophisticated ad systems vacuum up information on Internet users. As early as 1999, *60 Minutes* ran a segment (November 19) on how advertising networks use tracking devices that allow them to record, *without our knowledge,* where we surf the Internet, thereby collecting data about our interests, shopping tastes, and even our medical concerns. With this information, they develop a profile of us that enables them to personalize ads that come up on our screen. The more data we give them, the more complete their profile. To entice users to give personal information, Internet ad companies such as Double Click offer an array of personalized services. For instance, when we tell them our travel plans, they can let us know whether our plane is delayed or give us the weather forecast or provide an entertainment guide for the city we are visiting.

Perhaps the most questionable feature of this kind of practice is that the information we give Internet companies can be, and often is, shared with "offline" companies as well, and can be obtained by employers or insurance companies doing background checks. So far there are no regulations governing the Internet. Savvy users give fake names and information to guard against invasion of privacy, but most people surfing the net do not. So users beware. You don't get something for nothing. The data you provide is the price you pay for Internet access.

Stealth Marketing on Blogs and Social Networks

By now, savvy consumers have figured out that blogs and social Web sites are teeming with fake positive reviews of products and services. Many companies give free merchandise to bloggers and consumers touting products, or pay them for their promotions. This practice has become so prevalent that the Federal Trade Commission (FTC) has tightened its guidelines, requiring advertisers as well as bloggers to disclose any payments or freebies given for reviewing products. The National Advertising Review Council, a watchdog for self-regulation in advertising, investigates fraudulent blogs that try to gull consumers into buying products with fake reviews.[12] For example, it found that one company selling supplements like diet pills was running blogs that claimed to be independent product review sites, but in fact were paying reviewers to promote their products under "Customer Choice Awards." Another company ran a "Prostate Health Blog" that was little more than an advertisement for their prostate supplement, Prostalex Plus. In each instance the advertising council recommended that paid-for endorsements be disclosed and that certain claims be omitted. Both companies complied, but they didn't

---

[12]Clifford, Stephanie. "Notice Those Ads Blogs? Regulators Do Too." *New York Times* 11 August 2009.

have to. FTC guidelines are not binding. True, violations can lead to lawsuits, but not necessarily.

Even more toxic are the fake news sites that emerge when consumers click on an ad (often with an endorsement attributed to a celebrity who did not endorse the product).[13] The fake news site reports that the product really works, then invites you to click on a link offering a free trial, which requires credit or debit card information. If you are lucky, it will cost nothing more than shipping charges for the free sample of a product hyped by a paid-for endorsement. If you are unlucky and haven't read the fine print (who reads that stuff?) you will wind up being charged large sums weekly or monthly until the scammers are caught. This, of course, is the worst-case scenario, but buyers beware, the Internet is a haven for con artists who flood cyberspace with their scams.

The Justice Department has become increasingly aggressive in regulating illegal Web activity. Recently it cracked down on Google, fining the company $500 million for knowingly showing ads for Canadian pharmacies that have been filling orders for controlled substances like Ritalin and Oxicontin without requiring prescriptions. Although Google had no part in creating the ads, it is considered liable for illegal advertising on their website. But even when search engine companies try to track down illegal ads (as Google claims it does), these rogue pharmacies manage to slip under the radar, only to surface again with a different name. The government's answer is to be more vigilant. But as a lawyer for Google said, policing the Internet for illegal activity is "an ongoing, escalating cat-and-mouse game." If *they* can't do it, what hope does the consumer have?

EXERCISE 10-4

1. Find an ad that has strong emotional appeal for you and try to figure out why you find it so engaging. Once you have done so, decide whether you would purchase the product, and explain your decision. (Be honest. Think carefully about it. No off-the-top-of-the-head goody-goody.)

2. Go through a bunch of ads on some kind of product that interests you—cars, cosmetics, sports gear, whatever—and choose the one you would like to buy based on what you are told in these ads. Then do some research in *Consumer Reports, Consumers Digest,* or any one of several publications that specialize in product comparisons. On the basis of your research, decide whether you would still purchase the item you selected. Explain your decision.

3. Visit a shopping mall and examine the ploys used to seduce people into buying products. Consider subtle as well as obvious marketing devices and explain why you might be tempted to buy them.

---

[13]Baker, Pam. "Online Ad Scams, Part I: Tip for a Tiny Belly and Other Snake Oil." *Ecommerce Tactics* 16 September 2011. Web. http://www.ecommercetactics.com/2011/online-ad-scams-part-1-tip-for-a-tiny-belly-and-other-snake-oil/

4. Here is part of a comment made by John Kasson: "Advertising . . . has become . . . a way of telling us not just what we should buy but how we should live, how we should associate the advertised objects with ourselves."

Is Kasson right? Or do ads primarily appeal to already-existing desires and life-styles? It is obvious, for example, that we cannot have a desire to play computer games like Nintendo before they exist, but do most ads touting products merely tell us about new ways to satisfy old desires, or do they create new ones, or per-haps just strengthen existing desires so that we spend more on them than we should? Do ads, say, for designer jeans and other fashion clothes just reinforce existing preferences? (Defend your answer.)

5. In his book, *Business Civilization in Decline,* Robert Heilbroner claims that ad-vertising is "the single most value-destroying activity of a business civilization." Would you agree or disagree with this statement? Write an argument defending your position.

6. Imagine that you live in another country (or on another planet, for that matter) and know nothing about the United States except what you see in ads. What values and attitudes do you think Americans might have? Support your response by using ads as evidence.

7. As Internet use increases, marketing companies devise devious ways to reach potential customers, like targeting people's preferences by tracking their activi-ties as they surf the net. These surveillance techniques have raised ethical ques-tions about Web users' rights to privacy. Advertisers argue that people benefit from online targeting because they see more relevant ads, but privacy advocates worry that the increasing surveillance of Web activities is an invasion of their right to privacy. Write an argument for or against government regulation of on-line advertising.

5. POLITICAL ADVERTISING

By now, just about everybody knows that political candidates and issues are marketed in pretty much the same way as breakfast foods and laundry detergents. This means that appeals to reason are scarce, while emotional appeals are rampant.

In the very old days, only candidates for local office could reach more than a tiny fraction of their prospective constituents—via "whistle stop" campaigns in which they made speeches before small audiences and "pressed the flesh." Billboards, lawn signs, newspaper ads, posters, patriotic bunting, and that sort of thing were extremely impor-tant parts of any successful campaign.

But the average voter never heard the actual voices of candidates running for high office or, except for some presidential candidates, ever saw their pictures or photo-graphs. Political parties and platforms thus loomed much larger than they do today. Charisma didn't travel very widely.

Things began to change early in the 20th century with the introduction of electronic and other scientific devices, starting with methods for printing pictures in newspapers and continuing with the widespread ownership of radios. Franklin Roosevelt was the first president to fully understand and gain significant political advantage from the miracle of radio; his "fireside chats" were an immensely successful public relations instrument, and his voice was instantly recognized by virtually everyone in America in those days.

But the changes in political rhetoric and tactics that came after World War II dwarfed those that preceded it. A large increase in the number of primary elections reduced the power of political parties and party "bosses" and, much more important, television brought candidates and their pitches into living rooms across the nation. Political campaigns were changed forever (as was pretty much everything else—but remember the saying that "The more things change, the more they remain the same"). Within a few years, image makers, which means advertising experts, reigned supreme.

The first presidential candidate to make full and effective use of the new medium was Dwight D. Eisenhower. His successful 1952 campaign against Adlai Stevenson featured short television commercials like the following example, part of a series of TV spots in which General Eisenhower read from letters sent in by "citizens" asking questions that Eisenhower then "answered":

> *Citizen:* Mr. Eisenhower, what about the high cost of living?
> *General Eisenhower:* My wife, Mamie, worries about the same thing. I tell her it's our job to change that on November 14.[14]

No need for Eisenhower to tell viewers *how* he planned to change it.

Of course, Eisenhower conveyed an almost perfect image—war hero and father figure—and most people therefore strongly identified with him. War heroes, father figures, and candidates with charisma, like John Kennedy, are very hard to beat. When Kennedy ran for office, his father, whose connections in Hollywood dated back to the 1920s, hired film professionals experienced in using effective film production techniques, to hype the candidate as a symbolic role model—a strong, courageous hero— and to capitalize on his undoubted glamorous appeal. Nowadays, candidates who project a less appealing image can, and frequently do, overcome their handicaps by hiring image makers to attractively tailor their campaigns *and their personalities.*

Image makers have honed their craft in recent years. They have learned, for example, that negative ads attacking one's opponent can be dynamite. Mudslinging isn't new, of course. John Adams was labeled a closet monarchist, Thomas Jefferson was derided because he didn't enlist in 1775 (!), and Abe Lincoln was dubbed "Honest Ape." And in one of the most vicious presidential campaigns in history, John Quincy Adams was accused of pimping for the Czar of Russia. But that was nothing compared to the mud slung at his opponent, Andrew Jackson, who was called a murderer, a drunk, a bigamist and—get this—a cannibal. The charge? He massacred a village of peaceful Indians, had a dozen bodies dressed to barbeque, and ate them for breakfast the next morning! So when we lament the onslaught of negative ads, let us not forget that our political history is steeped in mudslinging. The difference is that television and the Internet have brought it to a far wider audience, and thus made it more

---

[14] Ogilvy, David. *Confessions of an Advertising Man.* New York: Atheneum, 1963. Ogilvy quotes Eisenhower as moaning between takes, "To think that an old soldier should come to this." Note that the device used is a promise to satisfy a strong desire (for lower prices) without providing a single reason for believing that the promise would be kept.

Negative campaigning has been honed to a fine art. Just about every political campaign involves people who are opposition researchers, a polite term for political hitmen (or women). Here is a description of the process by one such fellow who finally became so demoralized by the whole business that he dropped out and wrote a book about it:

Step I: The political hitmen dig up the dirt.

Step II: The dirt is then given to the pollsters, who through sophisticated polling can determine which pieces of dirt are the most damaging in the minds of the voters.

Step III: The pollsters give their results to the media advertising folks, who put the most damaging two or three negative issues into the TV, radio, and direct-mail pieces that do their best to rip their political opponent into shreds.

—Marks, Steven. *Confessions of a Political Hitman.* Naperville, Ill: Sourcebooks, Inc., 2007.

That final step only hints at the warped genius of ad writers who transform pages of research into 30- or 60-second spots that crucify the opposition in sound bites the public can easily grasp and often believe.

Orthodontics and the hair dryer have become vital to the achievement of political power.

—**Len Deighton**

---

effective. One of the first TV spots to use this technique to full effect—the 1964 "Daisy/Girl/Peace" spot—also is probably the most famous of all political TV commercials. It ran just once as a paid advertisement, but received so much comment that it was broadcast several times as a news item. (It was once believed that this commercial was never run again because of a public outcry against it, but in fact the original plan was to run it just once and then to garner free repeat TV coverage, which is exactly what happened.)

The spot starts by showing a very young girl picking petals from a daisy while counting, "1, 2, 3, 4, 5, 7, 6, 6, 8, 9, 9," at which point there is the voiceover of a man counting, "10, 9, 8, 7, 6, 5, 4, 3, 2, 1, 0," followed by the blast of an atomic bomb on the screen and the voice of President Lyndon Johnson saying, "These are the stakes—to make a world in which all God's children can live—or to go into the dark. We must either love each other or we must die." Then another voiceover: "Vote President Johnson on November 3rd. The stakes are too high for you to stay home."

The point of this commercial was to picture Johnson's opponent, Republican Senator Barry Goldwater, as an extreme hawk all too willing to push the button, while Johnson is portrayed as a responsible "peace" candidate. Is it an accident that this best-known of all political spots also is one of the most vicious, inaccurate, and unfair? Fortunately, it sank into the quagmire of history, where it belonged.

For the next few decades, Congress enacted various campaign-finance reforms to regulate campaign spending and limit the influence of wealthy people or interest groups on elections. Electioneers struggled to bend reform laws—not too hard to do, since money, like water, finds ways to trickle in. As restrictions eased through various court cases, political actions groups (PACs) thrived by bundling contributions (to comply with legal restrictions on donations). The law required that they be independent of candidates' official campaigns, but in fact, they functioned as arms of campaigns, with money and clout to influence elections.

PACs are in the business of running primarily negative ads. One, with the innocuous title of National Security PAC, came up with a lulu during the 1988 presidential campaign between George H. W. Bush and Michael Dukakis. Probably the second-most-notorious ad in modern history (after the Daisy ad), the Willy Horton ad featured a mug shot of Horton, an African-American convicted murderer who escaped from a Massachusetts prison while out on a weekend furlough pass. He later raped a white woman and stabbed her fiancé. The ad played on voter anxieties about race and crime and was widely criticized for its racist content, but it helped demolish Michael Dukakis, who supported the furlough act when he was governor of Massachusetts.

In retrospect, however, those were the good old days, when negative ads were used but didn't dominate campaigns. In 2010, though, the Supreme Court lifted restrictions even more drastically in *Citizens United v. Federal Election Commission*, when it ruled that corporations, unions and individuals could contribute to Super PACs without limit as long as they didn't fund candidates directly. Then, as night follows day, unprecedented sums of money poured into political campaigns and negative ads went viral.

President Obama launched his campaign with an all-out assault on Mitt Romney's record as chief executive of Bain Capital, his private equity firm. In one scathing ad, steelworker Joe Soptic implied that Mitt Romney was somehow responsible for his wife's death from cancer because Soptic lost his health insurance when Bain Capital shut down the steel mill he worked for. He said Romney didn't know what his firm did to workers, and ended with this zinger: "And furthermore, I do not think Romney is concerned." Like most negative ads, this one is factually questionable. The steel mill closed two years after Romney said he left Bain, and Soptic's wife died five years later.

Then there were a spate of ads claiming Romney would leave "Medicare dismantled" and "Social Security privatized," and ads taking his offhand remarks out of context, like this doozy that slipped out in an unguarded moment. "I like being able to fire people." He was actually referring to insurance companies that didn't do a good job, but what adman cares about that? As one media consultant (known as Murphy the Mudslinger) said, "I've been doing this since the early eighties. The standards have dropped lower and lower, as to what's allowed. There is less accountability now because of the outside groups [Super PACs]." [15] They may have sunk low, but not as low as the cannibalism attacks—not yet.

---

[15]Quoted in a very good article on negative advertising: May, Janet. "Attack Dog." *The New Yorker* 13 and 20 February 2012.

Interestingly, attack ads aimed at President Obama weren't as searing, not because of compassionate conservatism, but because focus groups wouldn't buy into them.[16] Political hucksters are no different than the ones who hawk cosmetics and detergents when it comes to market research. They tried out various ploys on focus groups across the country and discovered that middle-of-the-road voters didn't respond well to arguments that Obama lacked integrity or that he was a rabid partisan with liberal policies that would sink the country. What they did respond to was the claims that government was spending recklessly despite major budget problems, that their children would face economic hardship, and that the change Obama promised for the better never happened. So those were the issues that drove the marketing campaigns early on. One ad, for instance, shows a woman getting out of bed in the middle of the night to look at her sleeping children. "Lately," she says, "I worry a lot about my kids. What's their future going to be like?" This one scored big in focus groups. As the campaign heated up, a deadlier round of attacks hit the airways, like the ad drawn from Hillary Clinton's 2008 arsenal of campaign ads when she was competing against Obama for the presidential nomination. This one shows her lashing out at him for lavishing "millions of dollars perpetuating falsehoods." A stealth bomb if there ever was one—coming from Clinton, who became Obama's Secretary of State and is currently his ally.

Hitler's henchman, Joseph Goebbels, summed up the Nazi position on negative advertising: "The propaganda which produces the desired results is good and all other propaganda is bad. . . . Therefore, it is beside the point to say your propaganda is too crude, too mean, too brutal, or too unfair, for all this does not matter. Propaganda is always a means to an end."

Obvious political smears are the tip of the iceberg, though, in undermining political opponents. Less obvious techniques involve the visuals and the pacing. For example, an editor can make a candidate look less attractive by cropping the photo and going tighter on the face or by draining the color to black and white and reducing the action to slow motion. Editors have enormous power. They can—and do—manipulate every element of an ad in ways so subtle that most viewers have no idea that they, themselves, are being manipulated.

You can fool some of the people all of the time, and those are the ones you need to concentrate on.

—George W. Bush, quoting Robert Strauss (in a spoof) at the 2001 Gridiron Dinner

---

[16]From Peters, Jeremy W. "Subtler Entry From Masters of Attack Ads." *New York Times* 23 May 2012.

Most people are eternally taken in by the myth and rhetoric of democracy. . . . What we have now is an increasingly uneducated public—especially in what used to be called civics—dealing with evermore complex issues with which they are unequipped to knowledgeably deal. . . . We have a population ripe for manipulation by powerful public relation firms and political consultants who are expert in sound bites and seductive imagery.

—Brechin, Gray. Imperial San Francisco:
Urban Power, Earthly Ruin. Berkeley:
University of California Press, 1999.

Although voters have complained repeatedly about negative ads, the media continue to run them—because they work. If this were the best of all worlds, people would study the candidates' records and vote rationally on the basis of their credentials; instead, too may people sit mesmerized in front of their television sets or computers, passively absorbing the sound bites they get from infotainment and its ubiquitous commercials—including negative political ads. It's no wonder campaigns resort to using these ads. They actually grab the viewers' attention in ways that information about the candidates' records almost never does. So when we complain about the onslaught of negative ads, let's remember that political campaigns would never waste money on them if there weren't a receptive audience ready to absorb their messages.

As must be evident by now, political campaigns are indistinguishable from advertising campaigns. In fact, one of the most successful factors in selling a product, brand recognition, is just as effective in marketing a candidate, but in politics the brand name is a recognizable family name of a politician whose father, uncle, or husband has served in public office. Most recently there was George Bush, the father, then Bill Clinton, then George Bush the son, then Hillary Clinton, the wife, who lost the first time she ran for the office of president but may run again. Voters recognize the family name and feel comfortable with it much as they do with brands like Ivory soap or Campbell's soup. This tendency to favor candidates with dynastic names has deep roots in American politics. Before the Bushes and the Clintons, the Kennedys dominated the dynastic field, with John, the president, then Bobby and Teddy, the senators, and a raft of their offspring in Congress and state governments. Before them was Teddy Roosevelt and his distant cousin Franklin Delano Roosevelt, and so on, all the way back to John Adams, the second president, and his son John Quincy Adams, the fourth president. It seems that voters

I'm not an old hand at politics. But I am now seasoned enough to have learned that the hardest thing about any political campaign is how to win without proving that you are unworthy of winning.

—Adlai Stevenson (1956)
What one candidate learned from two (failed) runs at the presidency.

often put more stock in the family names of prominent politicians than they do in the candidate's qualifications, a fact not lost on political advertisers.

Of course, most candidates don't bear the name of a famous forebear and have to market other attributes. One of the most important ploys in marketing candidates is image making, and one of the most effective formats for candidates to sharpen their image is presidential debates. The presidential debates provide candidates with the largest audiences they will be able to advertise to during a whole election campaign. (Nowadays, of course, a tradition has been established so that candidates pretty much are forced to debate or lose face.) Political debates are hardly a new idea—think of the famous debates between Abraham Lincoln and Stephen Douglas. But the first presidential debates, between Richard Nixon and John Kennedy, did not take place until 1960. Kennedy is generally seen as the winner because he exhibited "vigor" and youth and exuded great charisma, whereas Nixon appeared to be overcautious and a bit sneaky. (Nixon later complained that his makeup was incorrectly applied—a very important point.) The debates generally are credited with being the crucial factor in Kennedy's extremely narrow victory (we pass over the controversy concerning alleged chicanery in counting votes in Texas and Illinois), but not because his proposals and comments were any better than those of Nixon.

In all of the presidential debates so far, just as in the Nixon–Kennedy debates, it has been *image,* not reasoning or displays of intelligence or character, that has determined the winners. The 1988 debates between the first George Bush and Michael Dukakis illustrate this nicely. When Dukakis failed to respond with instant outrage to CNN commentator Bernard Shaw's famous question about what Dukakis would do if his wife were raped, his chances of winning the election pretty much flew out the window.

Mitt Romney's strong showing in the first 2012 debate literally turned the narrative of the presidential race around. Lagging at the polls until then, he came across as confident, intelligent, and articulate–in short, presidential–and his poll numbers shot up. In contrast, Barack Obama seemed lackluster, even tired, bemused by Romney at times, annoyed and condescending at others. Stylistically Romney was clearly the winner, but Obama changed that perception in the next two debates when he went on the offensive, defending his record and making spirited attacks against Romney on everything from taxes to jobs to foreign affairs. Although the media paid some attention to the candidates' positions on the issues, far more coverage went to the image they projected. A reinvigorated Obama built on the momentum he gained in the debates and went on to victory.

Election Polls—A Special Case

Finally, no account of campaign rhetoric could be complete without mention of the role of polls in elections. No serious candidates for high office these days would open their mouths without having first tested the wind via polls. Whatever may be the case after they have won, when running for election, smart candidates make their pitches conform to what the polls indicate about voter sentiments and prejudices. During campaigns, at any rate, successful politicians generally are followers, not leaders. They waffle because they have to in order to get elected. It's always better to tell voters what they want to hear, not what the candidate genuinely intends to do if elected.

Polls tell candidates how to advertise; their media experts build campaigns in terms of what they learn from polls; blind advertising bit the dust a long time ago. In the 2012 campaign, for example, the polls gave advertisers information they needed to market their candidates to the undecided voters who were considered so important in the campaign. To reach these voters, advertisers focused their efforts on ten or so swing states that could decide the election. As the campaigns heated up, some voters in these states got more than a dozen robocalls a day that pounded away at poll-driven issues like the ailing economy, the failing housing market, and the health care law. But those who lived in the big states (like California, Texas, and New York) where the vote was predictable saw much less advertising for the candidates.

Well, then, if virtually all political rhetoric is guided by expediency, why pay attention to it? If we can expect candidates to waffle, even to lie, why hear them out? The answer is that even waffling and lies can tell those of us who read between the lines a great deal about how candidates may perform if elected to office: Which sorts of lies they tell and what kinds of campaign promises they make tell us something about which groups and positions a candidate is likely to favor if elected. The promises made by Barack Obama and his advocates during the presidential campaign were different from those made by Mitt Romney and his advocates, because different constituencies were being appealed to.

Nevertheless, it is true in the political arena at least as much as anywhere else that actions speak louder than words. It has to be true that a candidate's past performance is almost always a better guide to future performance than is his or her political rhetoric. Smart viewers of the political scene always evaluate current political advertising in the light of past performance. So a sensible evaluation of political rhetoric requires us to bring to bear good background information (nothing new here). (The other key ingredient, aside from background information is, of course, the desire and attempt to be intellectually honest—to set aside prejudices of all kinds and come to fair, cogent evaluations.)

Noncampaign "Campaign" Rhetoric

Politicians don't just campaign via advertisements or after they have thrown their hats into the ring. Image building is a day-in, day-out task—indeed, in terms of time spent, perhaps a successful politician's principal task. Of course, for those holding high office, particularly for the leader of a nation, image building often coincides with ceremonial duties. For instance, when George W. Bush referred to the War on Terrorism as a crusade at one point, he was photographed with all manner of religious figures from fundamentalist Christian delegates at the Southern Baptist convention to the pope in the Vatican. Candidates challenging incumbents don't have the opportunity to improve their images via ceremonial activities, one reason incumbents are hard to unseat.

Incumbents also have an advantage when it comes to garnering media coverage via press conferences. President Roosevelt was perhaps the first American president to exploit this kind of image-building opportunity, but the technique was perfected by President Kennedy, who, unlike Roosevelt, had television at his beck and call. Since Kennedy's time, presidential news conferences have generally been scheduled so as to gain the president free exposure on evening TV news programs. Because presidents are coached beforehand, they have ready-made "answers" to all likely questions, and they rarely are forced into on-the-spot improvisations.

Typical politician at work.
Reprinted by permission of Paul Miller.

Further Developments

Many years ago, virtually all political advertising was for candidates running for office. But with the advent of ballot initiatives and referendums—propositions put before voters for their direct decision—*issue advertising* entered the scene, and during the past few years it has become an extremely important kind of political advertising, because voters in many states and localities now are regularly asked to decide all kinds of controversial issues. Interested parties now spend millions advertising their views on these measures. The U.S. Chamber of Commerce, for example, ran an anti-Obamacare ad in Missouri claiming the health care act will kill jobs. "Call Claire McCaskill [Missouri senator]," the voiceover intones, "and tell her Missouri doesn't need government-run health care." Ads like this generate floods of letters and calls to elected representatives.

Even wars are marketed to the public. The first Gulf War, generally thought to be the first war tailored for the mass media, was "branded" "Operation Desert Shield" much the way brand names are given to toothpaste or cereal. The second war, "Operation Iraqi Freedom," was promoted by state-of-the-art marketing techniques that launched the "conflict" (not the war) with "shock and awe" (instead of bombing), wrapped it in patriotism and morality (stressing good versus evil), and downplayed the ugly realities with euphemisms like "decapitation strategy " (for kill Saddam Hussein). War propaganda has a long history, of course, but current marketing savvy has raised it to new heights (or sunk it to new depths, depending on your point of view). We can only roll our eyes at the Alice-in-Wonderland approach to marketing wars displayed by Andrew Card (the second Bush's chief of staff) when he told the *New York Times* that the administration had waited until after Labor Day (2002) to make its case for military action in Iraq because "from a marketing point of view you don't introduce new products in August."

Telephone and Internet Advertising

The great increase in negative telephone advertising that has occurred in the past few years is one of the more unfortunate recent developments in political advertising. The device itself is old, perhaps first being used on a large scale in 1946, when Richard Nixon first ran for Congress. A typical call in that telephone campaign went like this: "This is a friend of yours, but I can't tell you who I am. Did you know that Jerry Voorhis [Nixon's incumbent opponent] is a communist?" (Click.) Nothing much changes. Nowadays robocalls are standard procedures in political campaigns, and bugged voters regularly in 2012—particularly in swing states.

Although television still draws most of the money spent on political advertising, online marketing has increased dramatically. By analyzing data on the browsing habits of millions of computer users, campaign strategists identify voters most likely to side with their candidate. Republicans, for instance, targeted political conservatives who needed more persuasion to vote for Mitt Romney. Democrats ran a Hollywood-style documentary about Obama on YouTube, allowing viewers to donate money, volunteer their services, and post Facebook comments while on the site. Nowadays every click of the mouse or swipe of the finger gives marketers another piece of information about us—our magazine subscriptions, our charitable and political contributions, our health care purchases, and our consumer preferences—all of which are fodder for political campaigns. [17]

The upshot of all these various ways to advertise is that the 30-second TV spots that played the major role in elections to high office during the previous 45 years or so have now become just one of several important devices used to influence the electorate (although still the most important). In 2012, tens of millions of Americans tuned in to at least one presidential debate, and at least that many heard candidates give their spiels on TV talk shows. What this electronic age has in store for us next is an interesting and exceedingly important question, to which politicians and their media masters would very much like to know the answer. (So should we, so as to better defend ourselves against deceptive or emotively driven advertising.)

SUMMARY OF CHAPTER 10

1. Most ads can be divided into either of two groups. *Promise ads* promise to satisfy desires or allay fears. *Example:* Use Old Spice deodorant and get rid of body odor. *identification ads* sell the product by getting us to identify with the product. *Example:* The Virginia Slims cigarette ads, "You've come a long way, baby," tailored to specific audiences.

---

[17]See Peters, Jeremy W. "With Video, Obama Looks to Expand Campaign's Reach Through Social Media." *New York Times* 15 March 2012, and Peters, Jeremy W. "As TV Viewing Habits Change, Political Ads Follow Would-Be Voters Online." *New York Times* 2 April 2012—two articles that explore political inroads into the Internet.

2. Although ads provide us with useful information about products, often in an entertaining way, they also are designed to manipulate us via sophisticated ploys.

   a. They invite us to reason fallaciously. *Example:* Appeals to the authority of famous figures such as golf star Tiger Woods.

   b. They employ repetitive slogans and meaningless jargon. *Example:* "Nike: Just do it."

   c. They play on our weaknesses, prejudices, and fears. *Example:* The "ring around the collar" TV commercials.

   d. They use sneaky rhetoric, including fine-print disclaimers and weasel words. *Examples:* Using the word *free* when the product isn't free; weaselly expressions like "fights bad breath."

   e. Ads draw on trendy issues. *Example:* The low-fat, low-sugar, low-salt, low-carb ads aimed at overweight Americans.

   f. They whitewash corporate imagery. *Example:* GE's "Singin' in the Rain" commercial designed to transform GE's image into an eco-friendly company.

3. Although most ads hawk consumer goods, a few actually attempt to educate us and warn us against harmful activities. *Example:* The ads aimed at combating drug use in this country.

4. Old marketing techniques have been updated with new wrinkles, including new qualitative and quantitative procedures. *Example:* The Tennessee department store direct-mail ads based on in-store records of specific customer purchases. Targeting children has become tricky because of new regulations, but marketers manage to slide under the radar with ads that don't look like ads. *Example:* Design your own games for Goldfish ®, the Pepperidge Farm cracker.

5. Advertising on the Internet has increased and moved into the social media where consumers go to research and evaluate products. The downside is that advertising networks collect data on our Internet activity—without our knowledge—and use it for their own purposes.
   As Internet marketing grows, so does fraudulent marketing on blogs and the social media.

6. Political candidates and issues are sold in pretty much the same way as any other products.

   a. In the age of television, elections are won or lost via exposure on the tube, whether in debates, paid 30-second TV spots, press conferences, or whatever. And it is *image,* not rationality, that often wins in this arena. Increasingly, image makers have focused on negative advertising. Although mudslinging has long been a part of our political history, attack ads are far more extensive and effective than ever before. *Examples:* The Daisy/Girl/Peace TV spot that portrayed Barry Goldwater as too trigger-happy to be trusted with the nuclear bomb button; the Willy Horton ads that helped sink Michael Dukakis.

b. It also should be noted that the campaign rhetoric of candidates running for high office generally is guided by the results of polls. It's always safer to tell voters what they want to hear, not what candidates intend to do if elected. That is why we can expect candidates to lie, exaggerate, or otherwise distort when necessary to curry the favor of voters. (But savvy voters still can learn from political rhetoric by reading between the lines and paying attention to past performance, so as to figure out what candidates are likely to do if elected.)

c. Politicians in a democracy "campaign" virtually all of the time, not just when actually running for office. They always have to be intent on projecting the right *image* to the voters, and once in office, they have several standard ways of doing this. One is by performing the ceremonial duties of their office well; another is by holding press conferences.

d. Views on issues now are advertised just like candidates. The point is to influence voter preferences and thus legislation that is before Congress or state or local legislatures. *Examples:* the anti-Obamacare ad sponsored by the Chamber of Commerce.

e. The Internet has become increasingly important in marketing politicians. Not only do campaign strategists advertise their candidates online, but by analyzing the browsing habits of millions of users they are able to target people open to political persuasion.

EXERCISE 10-5

Write two letters to one of your senators or representatives in Washington, D.C., in one taking a short, strong stand on an issue of importance to you, in the other taking an equally strong but different stand (completely opposite, if possible) on the same issue. Compare the two replies that you get. (Remember that you can't expect instantaneous replies.) Send each letter from a different address and use different names (because some members of Congress keep track on computers).

EXERCISE 10-6

Examine a political commercial for the visual effects, the pacing, and other nonverbal elements, and analyze how they either enhance a candidate's image or undermine it (in a negative ad).

EXERCISE 10-7

These days, the mass media (in particular, newspapers and magazines) spend a modest amount of time and effort covering and evaluating the political advertisements, especially TV spots, of candidates for high office. Look into some of this reporting; then (1) present and explain the content of at least two such analyses of advertisements for candidates in your state or locality; and (2) evaluate their accuracy and cogency.

EXERCISE 10-8

Recall Len Deighton's remark quoted on page 255 about straight teeth and blow-dried hair and consider what Andy Rooney had to say in his syndicated column (August 5, 1996) about what he called a candidate's "X-Factor"—what makes a person likeable. Rooney noted that Eisenhower, Kennedy, and Reagan had it, whereas Johnson, Nixon, and Bush (the elder) did not, and he speculated that if Dole lost the 1996 election, it wouldn't be "because of any one stand he took on an issue. The loser will be the one who, for some unfathomable reason, appears least attractive [he meant in the sense of being likeable] to the American public. Never mind the issues."

Rooney meant to imply that the X-Factor goes much deeper than what can be manipulated by makeup artists. Do you agree? Is Rooney right that being liked by voters is frequently more important than differences over issues or past records in determining who wins elections? Do you think personality was crucial in the victory of George W. Bush over Al Gore and John Kerry? What about Barack Obama and Mitt Romney? Defend your opinions.

EXERCISE 10-9

In an article with the provocative title "Nuke 'Em" (*New York* magazine, June 25, 2012), Frank Rich argues that negative advertising is an essential part of political campaigns. Although he concedes that it is universally deplored, he defends it as powerful marketing that must be used in campaigns. "The president, any president," he writes, "should go negative early, often, and without apology if the goal is victory." Except for a few notorious examples, he claims attack ads are soon forgotten. What matters is not the mudslinging, but the victory—winning the presidency. In other words, the end justifies the means.

Do some research on the way negative advertising influences presidential campaigns. Then write an argument for or against using it.

Drawing by David Levine. Copyright © 1975 NYREV, Inc.
Reprinted by permission from *The New York Review of Books*.

In this drawing, David Levine pictures the television-viewing audience as contented sheep. Do you agree?

11 Managing the News

When covering the Capitol, the first thing to remember is that every government is run by liars.

—I. F. Stone

Freedom of the press is guaranteed only to those who own one.

—A. J. Liebling

Has any reader found perfect accuracy in the newspaper account of any event of which he himself had inside knowledge?

—Edward Verrall Lucas

Journalists separate the wheat from the chaff . . . and then print the chaff.

—Adlai Stevenson

And if all others accepted the lie which the party imposed—if all records told the same tale—then the lie passed into history and became the truth.

—George Orwell, 1984

I really look with commiseration over the great body of my fellow citizens who, reading newspapers, live and die in the belief that they have known something of what has been passing in the world during their time.

—Harry S Truman

The Press, like the public, has room in its brain for only one story at a time.

—E. L. Doctorow

People who read tabloids deserve to be lied to.

—Jerry Seinfeld

If Abraham Lincoln wanted to make a point today, he would deliver the Gettysburg Sound Bite.

—Bob Greene

The news media have been going through a huge transformation comparable to what it went through with the advent of television. For the past several years, Project for Excellence in Journalism[1] has been tracking and analyzing significant

---

[1]For a detailed analysis of emerging trends see "The State of the News Media; An Annual Report on American Journalism 2011–2012." *Project for Excellence in Journalism.* Web. http://www.journalism.org/

trends and changes in the industry. Technological advances like the Internet have created new ways for people to access the news, and as a result, traditional news outlets have been shrinking. The newspaper industry has declined 43 percent since 2000 because of the steep drop in circulation and advertising revenues. Fifteen papers a year went out of business from 2006–2011, and scores more have had to reduce their print schedule. One notable victim was the New Orleans newspaper *the Times-Picayune*, which carried on heroically during Hurricane Katrina. Dozens of staff members rode out the storm in the newspaper's offices, filing stories on the Internet until they were forced to evacuate to another site, where they continued posting updates on conditions in the city. This is the kind of stuff that wins Pulitzers, (which, in fact, it did), but alas, the once-mighty paper has had to reduce its print version to three days a week.

There is a glimmer of hope in all this gloom, though. More news outlets have moved successfully to digital subscriptions, rather than simply giving the news away online, and network and cable news audiences have grown somewhat in 2011 after a decade of decline. One online news source that has done exceptionally well in recent years is *Bloomberg News*, a publication geared mainly to financial markets, but loaded with national and international news. While most media outlets are downsizing, *Bloomberg* is snapping up some of the best journalists in the business from top-rated newspapers across the country.

Bloomberg News is an exception, though. For most of the news industry, economics is still a major problem. For the past century, advertising has been the main source of revenue, but with the growth of advertising on the Internet and the shift of classified ads to free sites like Craigslist, income from these sources is drying up—the industry has lost more than half its ad revenue since 2006. As a consequence, major investors are reluctant to finance newsrooms adequately and large cuts in staff are inevitable. Now that most people are getting the news online, particularly on mobile devices (used by 27 percent of the population), advertisers are following the audience. This change in news venues is a mixed blessing. The good news is that more people than ever have access to the news. The bad news is that a handful of technology giants are consolidating their power to control as much of the digital world as they can by devising the operating systems, browsers, e-mail services, and so on—all of which provide detailed personal information about Internet users (more about this later in the chapter). Then there is the worrisome possibility that these Internet giants will acquire major news companies and be in a position to control the content.

In the past, Internet companies did not hire their own reporters to generate news, but instead aggregated news previously developed in newsrooms around the country. Now, however, they are financing traditional news organizations to produce original news content online. Yahoo has funded ABC to produce most of its news videos, for instance, and Facebook has linked up with the *Washington Post*, the *Wall Street Journal,* and other publications. These ties have produced some badly needed income for traditional newsrooms, but the question remains whether these technology companies will aggressively attempt to monopolize the industry.

New trends in journalism require us to be even more vigilant in thinking critically about the way the news is managed and presented to the public. Although there is more and better news out there than ever before in history, not all of the more is better. The trick is to know how to separate the wheat from the chaff and, thinking of the remark, above, by Adlai Stevenson, concentrating on the wheat. (Another bit of bad news is that masses of people pay more attention to news schlock than to news pearls.)

1. THE MEDIA AND THE POWER OF MONEY

In France, the expression is *cherchez la femme* ("look for the woman"). In America, at any rate, and perhaps in France and just about everywhere, a more apt expression would be "follow the money."

The Power of the People

The one overriding fact about all news sources is that they are businesses. They exist to make money. They sell a product and we buy it. Or we don't, in which case they go out of business. This means that we, the viewers of television programs, listeners to the radio, and readers of newspapers and magazines, have the most important say as to what sorts of news stories are reported in the mass media and how they are presented. That is why, for instance, the mass media so often play up relatively unimportant events while slighting more important ones—most people tend to be more interested in certain kinds of relatively trivial goings-on than in extremely important events. A case in point is the low priority often given to foreign news (unless, of course, the United States is involved, as in the Afghanistan War, or a major upheaval occurs, like the Arab Spring). Since the news is now driven by ratings and foreign news ranks low in public interest, overseas coverage has been in decline. Now that revenues in the news industry are falling, foreign news is hit even harder. Since 1998, 18 newspapers and two chains have shut down all of their overseas bureaus. So what we get in the media instead of international news are more sensational new stories, reality shows, celebrity gossip, and a host of other trivial news that audiences seem to thrive on.

Since large audiences also tend to be quite provincial, the mass media concentrate on national affairs and home-grown celebrities, slighting news events from other countries. Similarly, because they are more interested in light-hearted material, human-interest stories, and fantasy than in hardheaded reality, human interest also tends to crowd out more important matters. For instance, during the week when *the New York Times* reported that as al-Qaeda was building a hub for terrorist operations in the mountainous tribal area of north Pakistan, the mass media was obsessing over Britney Spears's sheared head and Jennifer Aniston's nose job.

As mentioned in Chapter 6, large numbers of people are superstitious or believe in pseudosciences of one kind or another, and we all are wishful thinkers to some degree. That is why many TV programs feature so many more pseudoscience programs than they do those concerning genuine science. It is particularly troubling when popular TV personalities feature dubious medical advice and pseudoscientific claims. Oprah Winfrey, for instance, is oddly taken in by the scientific claptrap of celebrities and doctors with questionable credentials. She was impressed when film star Elke Sommers gushed over the benefits of estrogen, growth hormones, and vitamin supplements; she promoted actress Jenny McCarthy's scientifically discredited claim that vaccinations cause autism; she featured a New Age physician who uses tarot cards to help diagnose illnesses. These bizarre enthusiasms could be dismissed if she weren't such an influential role model for millions of women, but given her immense stature, they give credence to bogus, sometimes dangerous, claims.

Comedy Central's Stephen Colbert skewered the media in this satiric send-up at the annual White House Correspondent's dinner (quoted in Extra! Update *June 2006).*

Here's how it works: The president makes decisions. He's the decider. The press secretary announces those decisions, and you people of the press type those decisions down. Make, announce, type. Just put 'em through a spell check and go home. Get to know your family again. Make love to your wife. Write that novel you got kicking around in your head. You know, the one about the intrepid Washington reporter with the courage to stand up to the administration. You know—fiction!.

Needless to say, the press was not amused.

It's also true that the mass media pander to the extremely short attention spans of so many people in their mass audiences.

Shorter and shorter sound bites have become the mainstay of all network daily news programs. In 1968, sound bites lasted a mere 40 seconds on average. By 1988, they had shrunk to an average of 10 seconds. Nothing, absolutely nothing, of any consequence can be dealt with in 40 seconds, much less in 10. The current trend is even worse. News coverage of election campaigns from 1992–2004 used significantly more image bites than sound bites. Nowadays we watch candidates more than we listen to them. It is true, though, that the news on PBS is presented in modestly larger and somewhat more sophisticated chunks, but PBS audiences are minuscule compared to those of the major networks. (Some news programs on NPR—National Public Radio—tend to be a bit more detailed and sophisticated and are the best source of news on the radio or TV.)

The Power of Advertisers

The media are beholden not just to the people, but also to advertisers. Advertising revenue is the most important source of income for virtually all newspapers and magazines, and also the principal source for television stations and TV networks. Since money translates into power, the media must cater to the interests of advertisers as well as to those of the general public. Commenting on this fact years ago, H. G. Wells, in his classic *Outline of History,* remarked:

> [T]hose fathers of America thought also that they had but to leave the Press free, and everyone would live in the light. They did not realize that a free press could develop a sort of constitutional venality due to its relations with advertisers, and that large newspaper proprietors could become buccaneers of opinion and insensate wreckers of good beginnings.

Wells would not be a bit surprised at the way things have been going on the tube. For several years, the main problem with advertising was that it was drying up. Recently, however, all the news media except print journalism have made financial gains since the steep losses in 2008-2009. Revenues increased for both cable news and network news, but the biggest increase by far was in online advertising, which shot up 23 percent in 2011 compared to 2010.[2]

Online advertising has become more complicated for the news industry now that digital news relies on technology companies like Google or Facebook or YouTube to attract their audiences. These new players not only get a cut of the revenue, they usually control the most important information—data about the audience, which means that they can target advertising to suit individual users. Because these companies have the technology to recognize the tastes and preferences of users, advertisers have more power than ever before in persuading people to buy their products. It also means that the news industry has less control of its future now that it increasingly relies on technology companies who understand the audience best and can deliver the news consumers want as well as attract advertising revenues.

In order to increase advertising revenue and to maintain their autonomy, news organizations will have to make more effective use of digital advertising to survive. To do this, they may well resort to the lucrative business of gathering consumer data, just as the technology companies are doing. This raises the question of whether they will violate the trust of their audience. Because advertisers have always been important to the media, the issue now isn't just that advertisers may have undue influence, but that they are fed data on consumers that may seriously undermine their privacy.

Online advertising is just one of many ways advertisers make their power felt. Now that the 30-second commercial doesn't have the appeal it used to, they are using subtle ploys, like product placement and "news releases." One company, Citizens Bank, persuaded the venerable *Philadelphia Inquirer* to let it sponsor (that is, pay for) a column emblazoned with their green Citizens Bank banner. Although the *Inquirer's* editor had qualms about renting out editorial space to an advertiser, he promised that the newspaper staff would have "complete independent control" of the column. Well, maybe.

---

[2]This section includes more information from the 2012 report by the Project for Excellence in Journalism.

Other ways the media cater to advertisers is by suppressing news that reflects badly on them or their products, and by touting advertisers' products free as "news" items. When an editor for *The Pioneer Press* (publisher of many papers in suburban Chicago) ran a review critical of a restaurant that advertised in the *Press,* she was told by higher-ups that the paper was "not in the business of bashing business." A while later, a favorable review of the same restaurant was written by someone in the marketing division—not a journalist (*Extra!,* May/June 2004).

The Power of Government

Government has the right and often the power to regulate business activity. It thus can harass a news agency by being strict about the rules it sets up (it usually isn't) and the licenses it requires. The mere threat of government action has a "chilling" effect on the media. It is true, of course, that the U.S. Constitution guarantees freedom of the press as one of several freedoms necessary to make a representative government function. And various Supreme Court decisions provide added protection for the press. For instance, our laws protect journalists against libel suits, particularly by government workers, and against government censoring in advance anything the media want to report, except certain kinds of classified information. But more important, the media are free to advocate controversial, even dangerous ideas, like overthrowing the government—a freedom allowed in almost no other country. Despite these legal protections, the government has ways of restricting the freedom of the press, and has done so with increasing regularity since September 11, 2001.

Just about every administration tries to muzzle the media in one way or another, and the Obama administration is no exception. For instance, in 2009, Congress proposed a national shield law that allowed reporters to protect confidential sources that provided information vital to important news stories. Before subpoenaing a journalist to reveal these sources, prosecutors would be required under the bill to use every other method possible to find the source of the information. So many journalists had been subpoenaed after 2001 (and four were jailed for refusing to reveal sources) that advocates for reporters lobbied congress to pass this national shield law. But the Obama administration responded with major revisions that watered down the bill. One such provision was that journalists would not be allowed to protect sources of news items that might cause "significant" harm to national security. However, the judges who determined whether indeed the information was harmful would be "instructed to be deferential to the administrative opinion." Thus the bill would offer little protection and eventually was scrapped.

But government censorship doesn't end with classified information. Administrations can, and often do, suppress information that doesn't conform to their political agenda. For example, when Dr. Richard Carmona, the former surgeon general in the Bush administration, testified before a congressional oversight committee in 2007, he made the startling revelation that political appointees censored his speeches and prevented him from expressing his views on comprehensive sex education, emergency contraception, and the science on stem cell research, among other things. Two other former surgeon generals testified as well about the political interference of presidents they served under, but nothing approached the constraints placed on Dr. Carmona, who not only had to manipulate scientific information to suit the political landscape, but was ordered to mention President Bush's name three times on every page of his reports!

Governments have other ways of managing the news. One way is to censor material alleged to be obscene, which is not covered by the First Amendment. The problem comes in trying to determine legally what is obscene. The FCC sidesteps this issue by levying fines and revoking licenses, not by censoring material. In recent years, the FCC has raised its fines considerably for obscenity and indecency. CBS was fined $550,000 after Janet Jackson's breast was famously bared during her halftime Super Bowl performance in 2004 with Justin Timberlake (who euphemistically called it a "wardrobe malfunction"). Although this incident did not literally involve "speech," the public outrage it sparked, along with other similar incidents, spurred the FCC to set a stricter standard for determining indecent behavior and obscene language. This issue has been in and out of the courts since Jackson's bared-nipple debacle. Public outcry grew louder when celebrities let fly coarse comments, as Nicole Ritchie did at an awards ceremony aired by Fox, and when a seven-second bare buttocks scene aired on ABC's *NYPD Blue*. Complaints over these "fleeting expletives" (FCC talk for spur-of-the-moment obscenities) convinced the FCC to ramp up its fines to $325,000 an episode. The case bounced back and forth in the courts until the Supreme Court finally ruled in 2012 against the FCC on the grounds that the incidents occurred before the FCC put its new policy in place, and thus Fox and ABC weren't given fair notice. But this narrow ruling didn't address the First Amendment issue of regulating indecency in the media, and the issue will probably surface again.

Government officials also can, and do, manipulate the news by playing favorites among reporters, leaking only to those news people who play ball in return. Since leaks are such a large source of media information (see the discussion of news-gathering practices a few pages forward), reporters have to think twice before crossing their government informants. Similarly, reporters have to be careful in press conferences not to ask embarrassing questions or follow-up questions; those who are too brash or persistent don't get called on in future. In the early days of the Iraq War, two reporters from the Knight Ridder chain wrote a series of articles expressing skepticism that weapons of mass destruction were the real reason for going to war. Their analyses never ran in the mainstream media, which was pro-war at that time, but *Editor and Publisher* (May 23, 2007) reported that the Pentagon spotted the articles and barred the reporters from the defense secretary's plane for "at least three years" because of their critical coverage.

Although many items leaked to the media are on target, the fact that their sources can be concealed gives government officials a good deal of power. They can rig stories to serve their own interest without being accountable. But if sensitive material is leaked that the government does not want released, it can, and often does, threaten reporters with criminal prosecution unless they reveal their sources. If reporters comply, however, they lose their credibility and their sources dry up, so they almost always refuse to cooperate. But failure to do so may result in their being subpoenaed to reveal their sources. If they refuse, they may be convicted. With a jail threat hanging over their heads, reporters may be deterred from using controversial, confidential sources.

Another way the government manages the news is by issuing prepackaged reports that can be slipped into 90-second slots in the local news. Presidents Bush and Obama both used this ploy to get their messages out or to put a positive spin on the news, packaging it as though it came from traditional reporting. The Bush administration hyped all kinds of policies from regime change in Iraq to Medicare reform, often featuring government officials with scripted answers to scripted questions without any critical overview or comments. This covert propaganda, broadcast around the country without citing government as its source, is on the rise now that the news media are on the skids, and news staffs are shrinking.

Of course, no U.S. government agencies have censoring powers that are anywhere near those regularly exercised in quite a few foreign countries. In China, Myanmar (Burma), Liberia, and many other countries, news media rarely are allowed to criticize governmental policies or actions. Middle East governments were especially repressive during the Arab revolts. At the start of the uprising in Egypt, TV viewers around the world saw thousands of protesters pouring into Tahrir Square in Cairo and thousands more fleeing the country.[3] But state-controlled TV showed life proceeding as usual, with pictures of the steady traffic flow over a Cairo bridge and empty streets below office buildings. When the uprising intensified, state TV linked the protests to lawlessness, reporting that thousands of criminals were released from jails and neighborhoods were overrun by looters. Regular newscasts assured viewers that the government was in charge, quelling the insurgents and restoring order. Predictably the government attempted to muzzle other media sources by cutting off Internet service and shutting down Al Jazeera.

Worse still, reporters in dangerous countries are often threatened, even murdered, in the line of duty. From the start of the Iraq War to 2011, 530 journalists and media support workers were killed on duty as a result of hostile action, according the Committee to Protect Journalists (CPJ). Many of these deaths are murders that go unpunished. The CPJ website gives descriptions of abductions and deaths, citing in grizzly detail the signs of torture (like body bruises and broken fingers), gunshot wounds, and beheadings. A quick look at this website is enough to deter any aspiring journalist from working as a foreign correspondent in hostile territory.

The Power of the Media

The media are not simply beholden to the three powerful groups just discussed. They themselves are a genuinely separate power faction. This is particularly true of the mass media: television, radio, major newspapers and magazines, and so forth. Investigative reporters can, and sometimes do, unearth governmental chicanery as well as stories not in the best interests of advertisers, although we have gone to some pains to show why they often hesitate.

This doesn't mean that the media constitute a monolithic, organized group but, rather, that individual mass media organizations have a certain amount of power and that, taken as a whole, the mass media have great power and frequently common interests. Cases such as *the Washington Post* Watergate exposés, which set in motion events that drove Richard Nixon from office, are well known. Going back even further to the Vietnam War, the press turned the tide of public opinion when journalists began reporting that the chaos and destruction they witnessed on the battlefield was nothing like the official

---

[3]Fahim, Kareem. "State TV Offers Murky Window into Power Shift, with Few Protesters in Sight." *New York Times* 1 February 2011.

upbeat version. This may seem like ancient history, but it set an important precedent that continues to this day (with notable exceptions, like the media's failure to question the Bush administration's rationale for the Iraq War).[4]

During and after World War II, the press rarely questioned the judgment or truthfulness of our military leaders, but as the Vietnam War churned on, journalists became disillusioned with the war and its leaders when they saw what was really happening on the ground. They wrote about it forcefully and photographed it graphically. These reports were so upsetting that President Kennedy tried to persuade certain major newspapers to pull outspoken reporters out of Saigon. (Presidents Nixon and Johnson used similar tactics.) Future administrations learned from this experience that if they let journalists roam the battlefields unescorted, the news coverage might be very bad indeed, so they herded reporters into supervised "pools" during the Gulf War and embedded them in military units during the Iraq War.

But controlling access to the action in Iraq and imposing other official restraints didn't succeed in muzzling the media once they got over their initial patriotic fervor. Just as they had in Vietnam, reporters started filing gritty dispatches about car bombings, assassinations, rampant militias, and failed politics. And just as previous administrations had tried to control the press in Vietnam, the Bush administration fought back, excluding some reporters from official briefings, refusing others the chance to embed, classifying a mountain of material as top secret, and serving up its own optimistic version of the war. The media didn't cave in, however, and became probably the single most influential force in turning Americans against the war. For better or for worse, the media wields immense power in swaying public opinion.

A recent example of the power that media can exert is the 2010 publication of the whistle-blowing WikiLeaks material by *the New York Times*. The difference between this publication and previous ones is the sheer scale of information released—a whopping 250,000 confidential government documents that ranged from secret military reports to impolitic comments by U.S. diplomats in foreign countries. Although WikiLeaks had been publishing leaks for several years, it only gradually made its way into mainstream media. But it hit the big time in 2010 when the *Times*, *Der Spiegel* in Germany, and the *Guardian* in England simultaneously published reports of secret military operations in Afghanistan after hundreds of hours spent analyzing and confirming the documents.[5] When the WikiLeaks material hit the newsstands, it stunned the country and gave Americans who were already weary of the war more reason to call for an end to it.

Often, though, the news media tend to report the same stories while ignoring others that may never come to light unless some publication chips away at them for years

---

[4]For more on this see Filkins, Dexter. "A Skeptical Vietnam Voice Still Echoes in the Fog of Iraq." *New York Times* 25 April 2007.

[5]Before releasing the material, the *Times* showed it to the State Department to identify any confidential sources that might compromise national security, and then edited out the information, a procedure commonly followed by responsible news organizations when dealing with major leaks. But that doesn't mean the government managed to censor the publication. The editorial staff decided what material it would publish. As might be expected, the Obama administration opposed it and tried to undercut the leak about military operations in Afghanistan, but to little avail.

before they catch fire (as happened when the *Washington Post* exposed the Watergate scandal). A recent example is the way the *Guardian* has investigated Rupert Murdoch's British tabloid, the *News of the World*, for illegal phone hacking to get sensational stories. For decades, Murdoch, arguably the most powerful media mogul in history, has wielded immense power over British politicians by using his tabloids as a bully pulpit to punish or reward them. In recent years, he has expanded his empire to the United States, where News Corporation, his U.S. company, took control of the *Wall Street Journal* and Fox News, outlets that have given him more power to influence American politics than any other single person in the media.

Like the biblical David pelting stones at Goliath, the *Guardian* doggedly followed leads for years on phone-hacking reporters who tapped into conversations of celebrities and the royal family. The public found this salacious gossip amusing but inconsequential until the *Guardian* broke the news that hackers had tapped the cell phones of a murdered 13-year-old and the families of soldiers who died in Iraq and Afghanistan. Soon after, *the New York Times* and *Vanity Fair* jumped on the story and suddenly it had legs. The usual denials and cover-ups surfaced, like News Corp. laying the blame on a "few rotten apples" and the editor of the *News of the World* claiming she knew nothing, absolutely nothing about the phone hacking that had been going on under her nose for years. When Murdoch was questioned by members of Parliament, he said was shocked, yes shocked! at the illegal activity endemic in his organization.

The press kept digging and gradually revealed that the scope of the phone tapping was far greater than anyone imagined—thousands of phones were hacked. Prominent politicians were hand-in-glove with Murdoch, and some senior officers in Scotland Yard had a cozy relationship with editors of the *News of the World*. As one revelation led to another, Murdoch decided to shut down the tabloid, not so much to eliminate a rogue newspaper as to buy time to repair the damage. This story continues to unfold in Great Britain and the United States.

Of course, one media giant's power has to compete with that of the others. CBS's power to determine what will be shown on its network programs is held in check by the identical power wielded by NBC, ABC, Fox, CNN, and the rest of its competitors, not to mention competitors in the print media, just as the power of one politician may be reduced by the power of others and by the power of the media. Vive le competition!

> Have you ever noticed that the heads of labor unions frequently are referred to as "union bosses" but that expressions like "big business bosses" or "the boss of XYZ corporation" are almost never used in the mass media? Big business bosses go under nice labels like "CEO" and "President."

Every country has its own influential media, of course. A good case in point, given our current involvement in the Mideast, is the increasing importance of the media in the Arab world. Probably the most influential network in that area is Al-Jazeera, established in 1996 by the British-educated, progressive emir of Qatar. The network reaches over

35 million people and is reputed to have as much power as *the New York Times*. With its nonstop coverage of the protests that swept through the Arab world, it has been a major influence in galvanizing popular rage against Middle East dictators. Because it has trumpeted the common struggle against oppression of people throughout the region, it has become a lightning rod for political factions in the Middle East. When it covered the uprisings in Tunisia, Lebanon, and Egypt, reporters were either harassed or driven out of the country, but through local contacts Al Jazeera managed to broadcast grainy cell phone pictures of police violence. Middle East factions weren't the only ones that wanted Al Jazeera muzzled; Western governments have been deeply suspicious of the motives behind its sympathetic coverage of Hezbollah and Hamas and of its tendency to broadcast Arab anger at Israel. Since all this ferment makes for riveting television, Al Jazeera's continuous coverage of Arab protests, often shared with other media outlets, has had a profound influence as the "Arab Spring" unfolded before our eyes.

The Power of Big Business

The days are long gone when most business in countries like the United States was conducted by individuals or small organizations. "Ma and pa" stores have given way to Walmarts and Safeways. Individual doctors hanging out their shingles have been replaced by group practices and HMOs. Most family farms have been replaced by huge agribusinesses. These days, virtually all industries are controlled by large corporations—in particular, by huge multinational conglomerates. Large corporations, individually and collectively, thus have great power, which they exercise almost exclusively in the interests of maximizing their own profits.

Corporate power affects the dissemination of news in two ways: first, by getting the viewpoints of big business reported favorably in the mass media; second, by preventing conflicting viewpoints from being reported or stressed. This censoring power of large corporations stems in part from their power as advertisers (a point already discussed). Large corporations, after all, are by far the largest advertisers in the mass media. But it also stems from the power money has in the political arena (a point to be discussed later). When the mass media cooperate with political power, they thus indirectly also cooperate with large corporate interests. Furthermore, the mass media themselves have become controlled in large part by very large media conglomerates, which often are parts of even larger corporate structures (a point also to be discussed shortly). In general, the interests of media conglomerates coincide with those of other large businesses—for example, in favoring lower wages for low-level employees—so that the mass media tend to have a built-in bias in favor of big business. (Interestingly, many conservative commentators regularly accuse the media of having a left-wing bias.)

The result is that news and opinion in the mass media tend to be skewed strongly to the interests of the rich rather than ordinary citizens or the poor. Ordinary people, of course, also have great power in determining how the mass media portray the world—they can switch channels or otherwise tune out. They also can go to non-mass media news and opinion sources (yes, these will be discussed shortly), but most people do not do so, one reason being that the average person does not understand how the news is slanted in the interests of those with great political power.[6] (Another reason is that large numbers of people—in particular, those in the lower half of the economic pecking order—tend to concentrate on their own personal lives and problems and to be inattentive when it comes to the important economic and political issues of the wider community, even though a good deal of what happens in their lives is seriously influenced by what happens in the broader social arena.)

Most big city dailies have "business" sections that report the goings-on of large corporations and of the various financial markets—almost exclusively from the point of view of investors and other large money interests. But no daily newspapers have labor sections or report on business from the point of view of individual workers or, except on occasion, organized labor. Similarly, several business news programs are aired on TV during the day (when MSNBC is devoted almost exclusively to stock market goings-on), but no labor programs or programs regularly reporting from the point of view of ordinary workers. (But consider the fact that a majority of daytime TV audiences prefer to watch the soaps, sports news, and sitcom reruns. How then could a labor channel be a paying proposition?).

However, when the economy slides into a recession and people lose their jobs, foreclosures multiply and retirement funds dwindle, the media pay attention. Until 2011, labor union stories had been underreported for decades—a reflection of the decline in power of organized labor since its heyday from 1955 to 1967. But as the Great Recession lingered on and state budgets dwindled, unions suddenly leapt into the news when the governor of Wisconsin, decided to cut bargaining rights and benefits to public workers to close gaps in the state budget—a measure later supported by the state Supreme Court. No one expected this isolated incident to spark the kind of national attention it got. But times were tough and workers throughout the country were threatened with reduced benefits or job loss, so the massive response to this action forced the media to address union issues at length.

The result was a public debate on the plight of organized labor. Pro-union advocates argued that the slow slide of workers out of the middle class was partly the result of

---

David Halberstam (one of the most respected journalists in recent years) on the importance of investigative reporting:

You have to keep digging, keep asking questions, because otherwise you'll be seduced or brainwashed into the idea that it's somehow a great privilege, an honor, to report the lies they've [those in power] been feeding you.

—Quoted in Herbert, Bob. "Working the Truth Beat." *New York Times* 30 April 2007.

---

[6]The idea is widespread in America that there are no social classes in the land of the free and the home of the brave. The truth in this idea is that in every generation some individuals move from lower into higher economic classes, even occasionally into the highest. The falsehood in this idea is that most of those born into rich families remain rich, and most of those born into average- or lower-income households never become rich. Class membership in large industrial democracies is not carved in stone in the way it was in the monarchies of old, but this surely does not mean that there are any truly classless societies on this planet, other than in tiny hunting-and-gathering groups.

dwindling union membership in the private sector. (Only one in 15 workers now belong to unions, compared to one in four in the 1960s.) Although organized labor is strong in the public sector (one in three government workers are unionized) the argument was that all unions were threatened nationwide now that a dangerous precedent had been set when they were stripped of bargaining rights in Wisconsin. Antiunion forces were quick to point out union abuses like blatant increases in overtime pay, unreasonable job protection, and crippling retirement benefits that threaten to undermine corporate budgets. Articles on both sides appeared, not only in editorial and business sections, but on the front page as well—unprecedented coverage of union issues.

Another segment of society usually given short shrift in the media is the plight of poor people in our country. According to the U.S. Census Bureau, in 2010, 46.2 million Americans lived below the federal poverty line, defined as $22,314 for a family of four—the highest number of poverty stricken people in 52 years. Until recently, however, coverage of poverty was a blip on the radar except during holidays and times of disaster (like Hurricane Katrina). But as the recession deepened and millions of people slid into poverty, the media addressed the issue. Stories about housing foreclosures, job losses, food banks, and homeless people cropped up on a regular basis. The poor population, once centered in urban areas, spread to the suburbs—long considered the bastion of the prosperous middle class—straining the resources of local government to provide social welfare. When poverty becomes that widespread, the media pay attention, particularly in an election year.

Power Tends to Cooperate with Power

Although the interests of big business and government often coincide with those of the media, sometimes they do not. Scandals may sell newspapers and increase TV news audiences, but they also tend to sink political careers. What is bad for Microsoft may be good for CNN.

In a majority of cases, however, it's better for the various power factions to cooperate rather than to fight. That is why, for instance, reporters covering the White House quickly learn which sorts of questions can be asked at presidential press conferences, how far follow-up queries can go, what sorts of editorial comments they can make in news reports, and the like. Journalists who don't play the game, who persist in challenging the standard self-serving replies to their questions, don't get called upon in the future. Columnists who tear into an administration in Washington with a great deal of gusto are less likely to receive leaks or other tidbits.

Of course, when the interests of politicians or big business moguls happen to coincide with those of the masses, coverage of interesting or important events will be automatic, perhaps even large-scale. This is especially true in times of war, particularly when the war is not our war, but another country's, and our government is not threatened by the media, but may stand to benefit from it. The protests that roiled the Middle East are a good example. This is the kind of ongoing story the media loves. Starting with the overthrow of the autocratic Tunisian government that sparked insurgencies in countries like Egypt, then Libya, then Syria—the revolts galvanized the press into action and gave our government the chance to express righteous indignation at oppressive Middle East regimes. When Egyptian strongman Hosni Mubarak brutalized protestors in bloody assaults, Secretary of State Hillary Clinton called on the Egyptian army to protect protestors and to hold accountable those responsible for the attacks. What a relief it must have been that the media was focused on the carnage in other countries rather than the bombing of civilians in Iraq and Afghanistan. When reporters were beaten and cameras were smashed in Tahrir Square, White House spokesman Robert Gibbs said the harassment was "completely unacceptable," and came down hard on the Mubarak government for its brutality. Of course, the fact that Egypt was getting annual American aid to the tune of $1.5 billion lent a certain ambiguity to those statements. Still, the media provided a mouthpiece for our government to criticize oppressive regimes, as befits a democracy, and the interests of both the media and the government converged in those riveting events.

News as Entertainment

For all the reasons discussed so far, the news has increasingly become a source of entertainment more than an information source. Because money is the bottom line, because vested interests like big business and government shape the news to their advantage, and because the public wants entertainment more than information, news items tend to morph into Hollywood action stories. A good example is the saga of Jessica Lynch that dominated human-interest stories during the Iraq War. True, her story was hard to beat, crafted as it was into a hair-raising thriller. Small town girl joins the Army, winds up in Iraq where she is injured in battle, suffers multiple fractures, and becomes a prisoner of war. Freed in a rescue mission eerily filmed by the military, she becomes a national hero, receives the Purple Heart, the Bronze Star, and the POW medal, and lands a million-dollar book deal. The public lapped up her story, despite the inconsistencies that surfaced. No, she really didn't empty her gun firing on Iraqi soldiers as was originally reported. Her gun was jammed and she fell on her knees in prayer. Her captors tried to return her to the Americans before the rescue mission, but were fired on by U.S. troops who mistook them for invaders. Her story unfolded in the media like a riveting sitcom, transforming her into a symbol of the war, which to her credit, she apparently found embarrassing and wrongheaded.

Years later, in her testimony before the House Oversight and Government Reform Committee in 2007, she said, "the story of little girl Rambo from the hills who went down fighting" was untrue. She never fired a shot. When the committee chair asked if she was aware that her rescue was put off a day so that arrangements could be made to videotape the event, she said she didn't hear about it until much later. "I'm still confused as to why they chose to lie and make me a legend," she said, "when the real heroics of my fellow soldiers that day were, in fact, legendary."[7] One reason, of course, was to hype battlefield heroism and play up the war. But another reason was that the American people wanted a hero—and they got one in Jessica Lynch, however manufactured the story was. Stories like this, played up by the media and skewed by vested interests, glamorized the war and overshadowed the day-to-day activities.

At least campaign coverage and the Jessica Lynch story are connected to hard-core news about elections or wars, albeit with excessive hype, but much of the news nowadays has drifted downward to infotainment.[8]

---

[7]Quoted in "Lynch Calls Tales of Her Heroics Lies." *San Francisco Chronicle* 23 April 2007.
[8]See "The News Merchant," *Atlantic* September 2010, for an excellent article on agents who broker tabloid news.

Tabloid television has been on the rise ever since 24-hour news channels emerged in the 1980s. To maximize profit, Cable producers made use of increasingly sophisticated methods of tracking viewer preferences in content and time slots. The result is a mishmash of hardcore news and tabloid fodder. Over the years, sensational coverage of cases like the O.J. Simpson murder trial and the tragic death of six-year-old Jon Benet Ramsey have skyrocketed cable ratings and boosted profits. Nowadays the demand for salacious stories is so great the networks vie for a first crack at them. This competition has spawned a tier of middlemen—network bookers, who chase after stories about strangled coeds, kidnapped children, serial murderers, and a whole range of bloody, tragic cases. They then broker deals between the networks and the newsworthy people. This, by the way, enables networks to claim that they don't pay sources directly for news, a practice long considered corrupting because it undermines the credibility of the source. Instead they pay the agent, a sleight of hand that barely masks the negotiation. If this descent into tabloid journalism is unsettling, though, we have to remember that the networks are responding to the will of the people. They give viewers what they want.

An important lesson to be leaned from what has been said so far in this chapter is that the news, as presented to us by the mass media, tends to misdirect our attention away from important, underlying, day-to-day occurrences and trends in favor of "breaking news" (assassination of a foreign leader, Super Bowl coverage), "human interest" stories, particularly celebrity coverage, and what the powerful want to tell us.

It hasn't always been this way. In the years before media mergers and increasing demands that news divisions show a profit, the coverage of celebrities was a small part of mainstream news. *Extra!* (October 1997) reported that Elvis Presley's death in 1977 was covered in 29 minutes over the following five weekdays. When John Lennon was killed in 1980, his murder received 50 minutes over the same period of time. But coverage of Princess Diana's death in 1997 totaled 197 minutes on nightly newscasts over a five-weekday period—almost two-thirds of all nightly news coverage in the first week of September 1997. Fast forward to 2009, when Michael Jackson died—60 percent of the news coverage was devoted to his life story and death compared to 10 percent coverage of the bloody protests in Iran over disputed elections (according to an analysis by Project for Excellence in Journalism). Of course, the public's fascination with human-interest stories doesn't always result in celebrity news drowning out other more important items, but, in fact, it often works that way. As far as the Michael Jackson story goes, what catastrophe would be big enough to grab the public's attention away from that one? Another 9/11?

2. NEWS-GATHERING METHODS ARE DESIGNED TO SAVE MONEY

The all-important fact about the mass media, as we have been at pains to point out, is that they are in business to make money, not lose it. When they regularly spend more money gathering the news than they take in, they go out of business. One result is that true investigative reporting tends to get slighted, because it is so very expensive in time, effort, and thus money. More "efficient" news-gathering techniques are used whenever possible, even though spending greater amounts of money might produce more accurate accounts, not to mention dredge up dirt the powerful are trying to hide. Media people generally do try to be careful in what they report, so as not to leave themselves open to libel charges, and (in most cases) because of a desire to adhere to professional ethics. But they rarely get to dig below the surface.

The principal way in which news is gathered is through established "beats." The major wire services, television networks, and a few top newspapers and magazines routinely assign reporters to cover the major news-developing institutions—the White House, Congress, and so on. At the local level, they cover city hall, the police, and the like. Roving reporters are assigned to cover breaking stories in business, medicine, and so on, by interviewing interested parties—representatives of large corporations giving press conferences, "experts" in relevant fields, union leaders.[9] In effect, then, *most news is given to reporters by government officials or by others who have or represent power or wealth.* Further, as a condition of interviewing officials, reporters often have to show them drafts of the articles for quote approvals, which gives the interviewed officials veto power over what statements can be included. The news thus is bound to reflect established interests much more than those of the general public, given that it is the rich and powerful who have the means to call press conferences, provide video footage, or issue fancy press releases or control the quotable material.[10]

Pete Hamil, on the trend of journalists to degenerate into gossip hounds:

[Reporters in the 1950s] were conscious of their limitations; they knew that they never once had turned out an absolutely perfect newspaper, because the newspaper was put out by human beings. But in their separate ways, they tried very hard never to write anything that would bring the newspaper shame. They would be appalled at the slovenly way the word "tabloid" is now used. [*Tabloid* describes the shape of the page, not the content.] They didn't pay whores for stories. They didn't sniff around the private lives of politicians like agents from the vice squad. Even in large groups, on major stories, the photographers didn't behave like a writhing, snarling, mindless centipede, all legs and Leicas, falling upon some poor witness like an instrument of punishment. Somehow, they found ways to get the story without behaving like thugs or louts.

—Hamil, Pete. *News Is a Verb.* New York: Random House, 1998.

---

[9]Experts can be found on every side of virtually all issues. Which experts are consulted depends on the way in which a story is to be slanted, and that, of course, usually is determined by the various factors we have been considering in this chapter.

[10]An important exception to this rule is that ordinary people often are interviewed to impart "human interest" to stories that otherwise reflect the opinions and viewpoints of power or money. Another exception is the coverage of local news events such as fires—reporters actually go to the scene and interview those affected by the event.

That is an important reason why *very few important news stories in the mass media result from true investigative reporting!* It's much easier, quicker, and cheaper to interview heads of government agencies or representatives of big business than it is to find out what actually is going on by tedious digging. (It's also safer; recall the discussion a while back about the power of government and why power tends to cooperate with power.)

Anyway, there is a bit of good news on the topic of true investigative reporting. In recent years, newspapers, and occasionally TV and radio programs, have been recycling items from non-mass media magazines and from the major newspapers (which have set up syndicates for this purpose to compete with feature syndicates). Reprinting someone else's investigative efforts is a good deal cheaper than digging on one's own. So items from *The Washington Monthly, The Atlantic, The New Republic, The National Review,* and other non-mass media publications, as well as from *the New York Times, the Washington Post,* and *the Los Angeles Times,* appear now and then in local rags and on network news programs.

3. NEWS REPORTING: THEORY AND PRACTICE

People don't often stand back and look carefully at what they're doing from a wider perspective; they don't often theorize about their activities. On the whole, media workers do so more than most, but their theories frequently are self-serving.

News Reporting Is Supposed to Be Objective, Not Subjective

Until well into the twentieth century American journalists covered the news from politically biased points of view, following the eighteenth- and nineteenth-century models that date back to the American Revolution. Alexander Hamilton took full advantage of the freedom of the press set forth in the Bill of Rights to expound his Federalist philosophy and attack his opponents in the Republican Party (not to be confused with the current political party). He, in turn, was vilified in opposition newspapers by such stalwarts as John Adams and James Madison. But in the early part of the twentieth century, journalism evolved into a more politically independent profession and attempted to report unbiased news, relegating opinion-based articles to the editorial pages. (Many European countries, though, still use the partisan model. In England, for example, the *Guardian* tends to champion liberal causes, the *Times*, conservative ones.)

However, both conservatives and liberals claim that the other side dominates the news. In the 1970s, to offset what conservatives believed was a liberal bias in the press, they launched magazines like the *National Review* and *Commentary* to get their message out and begin to influence news coverage. Later, conservative think tanks and television networks emerged, along with talk shows hosted by right wingers like Rush Limbaugh and Laura Ingraham. Liberals were slower to respond, maybe because the media did seem more liberal until the late 1970s. But gradually liberal think tanks sprang up, as did news programs and political comedy shows like *The Daily Show* and *The Colbert Report* that skewered the opposition on both sides and began to influence a more youthful audience than the more traditional programs did.

But even news coverage that strives to be unbiased cannot be completely objective. Reports of facts generally depend on somebody's judgment that they are facts. A reporter must reason to the facts, or at least report someone else's reasoning to the facts, just as one reasons to anything else. Facts are not like fruit on trees, to be plucked at one's leisure.

The idea that media hands should not make value judgments is foolish. They *must* make value judgments, if only about which items are important enough to be featured, which should be mentioned only briefly, and which should be tossed into the round file (where most items that go over Associated Press wires end up). The point is that *editing,* one of the chief tasks performed by media workers, requires value judgments about the relative importance of events.

In any case, theory is one thing; practice, another. Practice is driven primarily by the various forces we have been at pains to describe and only to a small extent by abstract theory. The theory of objectivity serves as a convenient cover under which this can be done. Its cash value is that reporters are motivated to stay within the narrow, middle-of-the-road social consensus when they make judgments or draw conclusions. So one effect of the theory of objectivity is to discourage the reporting of nonestablishment or nonconsensus points of view, satisfying instead the desires of media audiences, advertisers, and others who have great power. Objectivity turns into not rocking the boat.

It's also true, and worth noting, that journalists often confuse objectivity with its close relative—being evenhanded. It has become common practice, for example, for the major networks to present rebuttal from the "other side" when they carry major presidential addresses, so that both major parties get their say. Comments about the truth of whatever is at issue tend to get lost—they would be considered value judgments anyway and so would not satisfy the criteria of the theory of objective reporting.

Robert Caro, journalist and biographer, told this anecdote about the advice an editor gave him when he was assigned his first story on the paper. Caro was just a copy boy then, but because all the other reporters were busy, the editor asked him to cover a controversial development at City Hall. This brief piece of advice embodies the basic principles of good journalism.

"OK, here's what you do," the editor said, "You go down to City Hall and listen for a while until you think you know what's going on. After the meeting, talk to whoever is opposing this plan to find out why. Then you go to the developer to get his side of the story. If you're confused, go back to the opponents and ask more questions. Keep going back and forth until you've figured out the story. Got it?"

—Quoted in "Read All About It—But Where Exactly?" *San Francisco Chronicle* 17 June 2007; a perceptive evaluation of the current state of journalism.

Note, by the way, how the expression "other side" masks the fact that there are *many* sides to most issues and that the viewpoints championed by the two major political parties often run the range only from A to B. During the 2012 presidential campaign, for example, the mass media were more or less "evenhanded" in their coverage of Democratic and Republican candidates, but they did very little reporting concerning candidates of the Green, Reform, Libertarian, and other "minor" parties. Even this attempt at evenhandedness is giving way to one-sided coverage on some TV news programs. Now that the public's interest in the news media is on the wane, cable TV outlets are experimenting with ways to build audience appeal by replacing conventional newscasts with opinion-based coverage. Fox News has done this for years, of course, but now MSNBC has a string of liberal news programs like *The Ed Show* and *Hard Ball with Chris Matthews*.

News Is Supposed to Be Separated from Analysis and In-Depth Reporting

The theory of objectivity requires that facts be reported separately from conclusions or evaluations (which are thought of as "subjective"). But this separation of news from analysis further aggravates a defect already in evidence in most media reporting: *the failure to tie what happens to any explanation as to why it happened and why it is important.*

For instance, in 1998, when Hurricane Mitch wreaked havoc in Honduras, Guatemala, and Nicaragua, the mass media reported horrendous destruction and a large number of deaths. But they failed to explain *why* the destruction was so great. To do that, they needed to explain how the Central American policies of the United Fruit Company and of the United States in the 1950s and 1960s led to intense deforestation that undermined the landscape. They failed to stress the important point that this deforestation, undertaken to replace local farmers with large-scale agriculture, was a major part of the cause of the massive flooding and landslides that resulted when Hurricane Mitch hit. See, for example, *Counterpunch,* November 1–15, 1998—a left-wing, non-mass media publication—or many good histories of Central America. Moral: To know what is really going on, you can't rely on the mass media.

Typically, when covering a story, a reporter consults those directly involved or affected by it. Writing, say, about civil service employee salaries, a reporter would very likely interview civil servants who, naturally, will say that their salaries are lower than for comparable jobs in industry, and critics who, having raised the issue, can be expected to say that the salaries in question are higher than in the nongovernment business world. In fact, this routine has been gone through several times in recent years. Most reporters, of course, have no idea which side is right—they don't know enough about the topic to make an intelligent judgment. They don't know, for example, whether civil service job specifications truly describe what happens on the job day to day. How could they, given that the topic they investigated the week before might have been water pollution in Pennsylvania, while next week's topic will be job flight to Mexico?

Although the theory of objective news reporting often tends to deter journalists from saying what they believe or even know to be true, as just described, it doesn't absolutely forbid the mixing of news with evaluation or analysis. In fact, reporters have a modest amount of freedom to spout off, at least when no toes of the powerful are being stepped on. Nevertheless, the impossibility of being experts on every topic they must investigate, coupled with the need to seem authoritative, whether they know what they are talking about or not, often produces rather mixed results. For example, the journalists embedded with the troops during the Iraq and Afghanistan wars reported a piece of the action as they experienced it, but they had no concept of the big picture. And since much reporting was instantaneous, aired on television or radio as it was happening, they had no time to sort through the information and give it context. As a result, the audience got a slice of the battle but little evaluation or analysis that would come from mature deliberation over time.

> Thoughtfully written analysis is out, "live pops" are in. . . . Hire lookers, not writers. Do powder-puff, not probing, interviews. Stay away from controversial subjects. Kiss a___, move with the mass, and for heaven and the ratings' sake don't make anybody mad. . . . Make nice, not news.
>
> —Dan Rather (of CBS's *Evening News*)

The Opinions of the "Right" Authorities Take Precedence

Since the reporters who gather the news are not usually experts in the fields they have to cover, they must, and do, seek out expert opinion. The trouble is that experts can be found on all sides of virtually every issue that is even mildly controversial. Which experts they consult thus becomes crucially important, and usually is determined by just a very few factors.

Perhaps the most important consideration is whether an expert's opinions might be unpopular either with the intended audience or with advertisers or other power groups. Experts with views that might raise too many hackles tend to be overlooked (or, sometimes, used as foils). Mainstream experts dominate the field. These days, for example, positions on race, gender differences, pollution problems, and so on, generally have to stay within bounds set by the concern to be "politically correct" (PC). There is, of course, still a great deal of racism in America, as in most other countries, but there also is an "official line" on the matter. Racism is definitely not PC.

During the 2008 presidential primaries, when racial attitudes were increasingly discussed, anyone who even hinted at racism was roundly criticized. The media shredded Bill Clinton for comparing Barack Obama's win in the South Carolina primary to Jesse Jackson's campaign in the South in 1984 and 1988 (implying that Obama would go no further than Jackson), and later they pounced on Hillary Clinton for citing evidence that "Senator Obama's support among working, hard-working Americans, white Americans is weakening again." Both of these comments, though mild, were perceived as racial slurs, and for awhile public sentiment turned against the Clintons—an ironic reversal considering that Bill Clinton had once been so supportive of blacks and appreciated by them that he was sometimes called the first black president. The experts called in to comment on Clinton's remarks and other racial issues were often black journalists and politicians who gave mainly white audiences insightful perspectives on how these issues were viewed in African-American communities.

Not all experts are trustworthy, however. When personal interest conflicts with public duty, ethical attitudes can disintegrate. This is exactly what happened when a group of high-ranking military officers were recruited by the Pentagon to sell the Iraq War to the American public. *The New York Times* ran a devastating, well-researched exposé of how these retired military experts became purveyors of Pentagon propaganda.[11] The article charted their activities in detail from the run-up to the war through the 2008 surge. Dubbed "key influentials" by the Pentagon, these military analysts were well-decorated, authoritative commentators who framed the way the audience should interpret the war. They didn't simply give objective descriptions of warfare in the battle zones or explain the capabilities of military hardware; they passed on the administration's ideology and helped establish its priorities. True, many of them believed that the war was justified, and since they had devoted their lives to the military, were understandably reluctant to criticize it. Nonetheless, there were powerful incentives for them to play along. Some were defense lobbyists, others were involved with helping companies win military contracts, and still others were board members of military contractors. What their willing participation gave them was access to power and influence and the opportunity for lucrative business deals. Eventually the Pentagon recruited over 75 retired officers, although some became disenchanted over time, and others were only briefly involved. Most of them appeared on Fox News and to a lesser extent on NBC, CNN, and other stations.

Thus, viewers who thought they were getting an objective analysis of the war were really getting a sell job. When journalists in Iraq began filing reports about the rise of insurgencies, the shortage of armor, the corruption of Iraqi security forces, and so on, the counterforce was the military analysts, briefed with Pentagon talking points, who assured the public that all was well. And the Pentagon monitored their media appearances, taking them to task if they criticized the war effort even mildly.

Meanwhile, the networks not only remained in the dark about the extensive interaction between the Pentagon and the military analysts, but they didn't seem to know that some analysts had business relationships with the Pentagon that could create conflicts of interest. And so the public was hoodwinked.

For two years *the New York Times* battled with the Defense Department, finally suing it successfully to gain access to 8,000 pages of documents describing the interaction between the Pentagon and the military analysts. So the news finally came out that these so-called experts were little more than shills for the Pentagon. This story, by the way, is journalism at its best—a trenchant analysis of government corruption, well substantiated by evidence.

Self-Censorship

The theory that news reporting should be objective does not require that all of the news, even all of the very important news, be reported. During wartime, for example, national

---

[11]See Barstow, David. "Message Machine: Behind TV Analysts, Pentagon's Hidden Hand." *New York Times* 20 April 2008.

security takes precedence. When United States troops were poised to invade Afghanistan in 2001, the media knew a full day in advance the exact time that the strikes would begin, but virtually no major media organization reported this information in the news. Even in peacetime, the media sometimes voluntarily suppress news out of a sense of duty. Perhaps the most famous instance of this kind occurred during John Kennedy's time as president, when *the New York Times* decided not to print reliable information about the impending attack on Cuba by U.S.-trained forces intent on overthrowing Fidel Castro.[12]

Another important reason for media censorship has to do with the power of media audiences to switch channels or to not buy a newspaper. Television, in particular, has to be sensitive to its audience, because its product comes into living rooms with such immediacy (and children may be watching). The way in which Elvis Presley was allowed to appear on an Ed Sullivan TV show in 1956 is a classic example; Elvis was shown only from the waist up so that TV audiences wouldn't be exposed to his pelvic gyrations. (That sounds silly today, but what may or may not be objectionable differs considerably from one time to another.) Another famous case occurred in 1952 when Lucille Ball became pregnant and the story line of the *I Love Lucy* show was adjusted accordingly: The TV Lucy could be said on camera to be "expecting" and *enceinte* (French for "pregnant"), but the word *pregnant* could not be used. Even in the 1950s, this sort of censorship seemed ridiculous to lots of people, but media moguls considered it to be a very serious matter; too many viewers were likely to be offended by use of the term *pregnant.*

Times change, of course, so that in the 1990s, when TV's Murphy Brown was allowed to be an unwed mother, only a slight fuss was made about referring to her as pregnant. But media self-censorship still is with us, as it always will be. It's just that standards and the topics subject to censorship change. Back in the 1950s, a program about homosexuals would have been unthinkable—absolutely out of the question—so much so that the lack of such programs hardly could be considered to constitute self-censorship. Gays simply did not exist as far as television was concerned. But today they do, yet programs featuring gays sometimes are censored by one segment of the media or other. When Ellen DeGeneres's character "came out" on the sitcom *Ellen,* several stations refused to carry the episode.

But those who see self-censorhip as automatically evil might consider the right of individuals to privacy in their nonpublic life. At what point does one draw the line? A person in the public eye is still, after all, entitled to a private life. Anyway, things are not as bad here as in, say, England, where the press hounded Princess Diana up to her death and continues to cover every move of her sons Prince William and Prince Harry.

In days long gone, the media felt more constrained in its reporting of the private lives of important public figures. It was well known to some in the press, for example, that both before and after his marriage—as a congressman, senator, and president—John Kennedy was quite a lady's man. But the media, on the whole, chose not to divulge this feature of his private life. In those days, matters of this kind were usually passed over, even though they would have found an eager audience. With the advent of the Internet,

---

[12]The invasion turned into a fiasco that was terribly embarrassing to the Kennedy administration. Kennedy himself is alleged later to have had the chutzpah to take the *Times* to task for this self-censorship on grounds that publication of the story by the *Times* might have resulted in the aborting of that ill-fated venture!

One of the most prevalent sources of "experts" is the think tanks that the media have used in recent years. It's a good idea to know the political orientation of these groups so that you can critically evaluate their analyses of the issues. Here are the most widely quoted think tanks (cited in Extra! *June 2012) and the ideological shift in network coverage over the years in the study.*

Citations of Think Tanks in Media

Think Tank Orientation	Political	2011	2010	2009	2008
			(rank in parentheses)		
1 Brookings Institution	Centrist	2,475	2,432 (1)	2,370 (1)	2,271 (1)
2 Heritage Foundation	Conservative	1,540	1.260 (2)	1,227 (2)	971 (3)
3 American Enterprise Institute	Conservative	1,312	1,022 (3)	946 (6)	1,026 (2)
4 Council on Foreign Relations	Centrist	1,090	954 (5)	1,083 (3)	951 (4)
5 Center for American Progress	Center-Left	896	898 (6)	949 (5)	730 (7)
6 Kaiser Family Foundation	Centrist	866	1,001 (4)	1,061 (4)	584 (10)
7 Cato Institute	Conservative/ Libertarian	754	724 (7)	705 (7t)	601 (9)
8 Center for Strategic and International Studies	Conservative	749	636 (8)	705 (7t)	778 (5)
9 Carnegie Endowment For International Peace	Centrist	613	336 (15)	421 (13)	300 (16)
10 Economic Policy Institute	Progressive	602	574 (10)	529 (11)	606 (8)
11 Center on Budget and Policy Priorities	Progressive	599	455 (12)	410 (14)	335 (15)
12 Urban Institute	Center-Left	542	451 (13)	535 (10)	527 (11)
13 RAND Corporation	Centrist	525	625 (9)	656 (9)	761 (6)
14 New America Foundation	Centrist	484	475 (11)	528 (12)	349 (14)
15 Hoover Institution	Conservative	436	310 (16)	272 (17)	299 (17)
16 Institute for International Economics	Centrist	293	219 (22)	271 (18)	277 (21)
17 Alan Guttmacher Institute	Center-Left	272	–	–	–
18 Washington Institute for Near East Policy	Center-Right	268	–	–	–
19 Aspen Institute	Centrist	266	179 (24)	–	–
20 Woodrow Wilson International Center for Scholars	Centrist	252	–	–	177 (24)

(Continues)

21 Center for Politics	Centrist	247	296 (18)	–	371 (12)
22 Center for Economic and Policy Research	Progressive	244	282 (19)	304 (16)	350 (13)
23 Manhattan Institute	Conservative	241	259 (21)	235 (21)	286 (18)
24 Public Policy Institute of California	Centrist	212	351 (14)	245 (20)	279 (20)
25 Center for a New American Security	Centrist	189	185 (23)	183 (23)	–
Center for Immigration Studies	Conservative	–	301 (17)	248 (19)	281 (19)
Electronic Privacy Information Center	Progressive	–	275 (20)	–	–
Commonwealth Fund	Centrist	–	174 (25)	313 (15)	193 (25)
Inter-American Dialogue	Centrist	–	–	188 (22)	204 (24)
Lexington Institute	Conservative	–	–	171 (25)	235 (22)
Joint Center for Political and Economic Studies	Progressive	–	–	–	206 (23)

Number and Percentage of Media Citations by Ideology

	2011		2010		2009		2008	
Conservative or Center-Right	5,300	33	4,512	31	4,509	31	4,477	33
Centrist	7,512	47	7,227	49	7,496	51	6,540	47
Progressive or Center-Left	3,155	20	2,935	20	2,727	19	2,754	20
Total	15,967	100%	14,674	100%	14,732	100%	13,771	100%

Percentages may not add up to 100 percent due to rounding.
Source: Nexis database on major U.S. newspapers and selected US radio and TV transcripts.

though, the media no longer have the power to suppress details about the private lives of politicians and celebrities. Gossipy web blogs and provocative cell phone photos crop up on Facebook, YouTube, and other social networks, eroding the line between public and private lives. As intimate details about public figures flood the Internet, the public no longer seems to take notice of information that once was off limits—a radical shift in attitude.

There comes a point, though, when knowledge about a person's sex life may, in some cases, be relevant to character and thus to potential performance as a public figure. Take the case of John Edwards. When he was a candidate for the Democratic presidential nomination in 2008, a sensational story hit the tabloids alleging that he was having an

Last year, 300,000 Americans were arrested for smoking an herb that Queen Victoria used regularly for menstrual cramps.

It's a fact

The herb, of course, is *cannabis sativa*. Otherwise known as marijuana, pot, grass, hemp, boo, mary-jane, ganja—the nicknames are legion.

So are the people who smoke it.

By all reckoning, it's fast becoming the new national pastime. Twenty-six million smokers, by some accounts—lots more by others. Whatever the estimate, a staggeringly high percentage of the population become potential criminals simply by being in possession of it. And the numbers are increasing.

For years, we've been told that marijuana leads to madness, sex-crimes, hard-drug usage and even occasional warts.

Pure Victorian poppycock.

In 1894, The Indian Hemp Commission reported marijuana to be relatively harmless. A fact that has been substantiated time and again in study after study.

Including, most recently, by the President's own Commission. This report stands as an indictment of the pot laws themselves.

And that's why more and more legislators are turning on to the fact that the present marijuana laws are as archaic as dear old Victoria's code of morality. And that they must be changed. Recently, the state of Oregon did, in fact, de-criminalize marijuana. Successfully.

Other states are beginning to move in that direction. They must be encouraged.

NORML has been and is educating the legislators, working in the courts and with the lawmakers to change the laws. We're doing our best but still, we need help. Yours.

Used with permission of NORML.

Ad censorship. NORML marijuana ad rejected by Time *and* Newsweek, *accepted by* Playboy.

affair with filmmaker Rielle Hunter. He adamantly denied it. But once the mainstream media picked up the story and began to question his political future, the pressure mounted—and then it soared when he confessed to the affair but claimed he wasn't the father of her child. Then he admitted he was the father. As evidence began to pile up suggesting he was using campaign money to cover up his affair, he was hauled into court on six felony charges. The judge declared a mistrial when the jury acquitted him on one of the counts but was undecided on the others. Long before the trial, however, the public saw sexual hypocrisy and crass attempts to cover it up as relevant to his political integrity.

EXERCISE 11-1

In April 2007, two days after a psychotic student, Cho Seung Hui, went on a tragic rampage killing 33 people at Virginia Tech, NBC received a package in the mail from the killer that included an 1,800-word diatribe, along with photos and videos of himself making threats and waving guns and other weapons. NBC aired portions of the material on the *Nightly News* that were quickly picked up by other networks, newspapers, and the Internet. The ethical issues raised by releasing this footage were widely debated. Although NBC took care to edit out disturbing content, it was criticized in some quarters for its insensitive handling of the material and for doing precisely what the psychotic killer intended—getting his deranged message out to the public. But others argued for full disclosure and criticized the network's arbitrary editing.

Write an essay or debate the question whether NBC should have suppressed the material altogether or released all the footage uncensored. Or should it have done exactly what it did—aired an edited version?

4. DEVICES USED TO SLANT THE NEWS

So far, we have been considering why the media slant the news and how that affects story selection. Now let's take a brief look at a few of the many devices used to accomplish this task. (The examples are taken primarily from newspapers and magazines, but television and radio have their analogs.)

Stories Can Be Played Up or Down

Breaking news of immense interest, like the killing of Osama bin Laden, for instance, is always played up in the news. Reports of the risky mission carried out in the dead of night by the elite Navy Seals riveted the entire nation. Gory photos of mangled bodies in blood-soaked rooms flickered across TV screens as commentators described the stealthy assault on the bin Laden compound. This is the stuff that newsrooms love. And the secrecy of the mission, hidden even from the Pakistan government, made it all the more tantalizing. But not all news is that compelling. Often stories are played up because of audience interest or media bias. If the interest isn't there, the story may be buried by placing it on page 59 or by packing the undesirable material toward the end of an otherwise acceptable story.

Of course, the most obvious way to bury the news is simply to ignore it. Bad news becomes no news when the media doesn't cover it. Project Censored, a media watchdog, noted in their 2012 report that one of the least-reported stories in 2011 was that the U.S. military had developed software to create fake online personas that behave like real people on the social media, in order to spread American propaganda in the Mid-East. These fake people, who have convincing histories and backgrounds of their own, are apparently weapons of psychological warfare used to encounter the online presence of al-Qaeda and other extremists resisting American presence in the Middle East. We are assured that it would be unlawful to unleash these fake people in U.S. social media, so it's not going to happen here—we hope.

Other, less dramatic omissions occur as well. For instance, newspapers often inform readers about which movies are drawing the largest audiences, which records are selling best, and so on. But *the New York Times,* for obscure reasons of its own, routinely excludes religious books (Bibles and so forth) and "romance" (Harlequin) paperbacks from its lists of best-selling books, even though together these two kinds of publications account for a very large slice of the book market.

Misleading, Sensational, or Opinionated Headlines Can Be Used

Many more people read the headlines on stories than read the accounts that follow. So even if an account itself is accurate, a misleading or sensational headline (generally not written by whoever wrote the news report itself) distorts the news for many readers. For example, a *Los Angeles Times* headline (June 16, 2010)—

"Debate Grows Over Afghanistan Drawdown Plan"

—implied that opposing points of view would be given on whether the U.S. should pull out of Afghanistan.[13] But the article's sources were U.S. military officials and John McCain—all of whom had serious reservations about a withdrawal timeline. No mention was made of the opposing position held by 53 percent of the American public at the time, who thought the war wasn't worth fighting. So the "debate" in the headline was no debate but the opinion of promilitary sources on one side of the issue.

---

[13]Cited in *Extra!* August 2010.

Here is a misleading headline from the *Daily Beast* about the Senate vote on President Obama's jobs bill in 2011.[14]

"Obama Loses Big on Jobs Bill"

Well, no, Obama didn't lose big. Although the vote of 50 to 49 was short of the 60 needed to end the filibuster, a simple majority would have passed the bill without it. This headline makes it seem like an abysmal failure, when in fact, more senators voted for the bill than against it. Here is another less egregious example in *the New York Times*—a paper that should know better.

"Obama's Jobs Bill Fails in Senate in First Legislative Test"

No, it didn't fail. It was blocked on procedural grounds but could later be called up for reconsideration. A more accurate headline appeared on BBC online.

"Obama Jobs Bill Blocked in Senate"

The first headline took advantage of the ignorance of many people that 60 votes are not required to pass the bill but are necessary to end the filibuster that had been used to squelch it.

Images Can Slant the News

Image has been important in American politics ever since George Washington refused a crown and declined a third term as president because he didn't want to create the wrong image. Abraham Lincoln played up his image as a rail-splitting back woodsman reared in a log cabin in the Illinois wilderness. But in those days news traveled slowly and photography was either nonexistent (in Washington's time) or in its infant stages (in Lincoln's). With the advent of television, visual images began to dominate the scene. Starting with John F. Kennedy and his photogenic family, the emphasis on visual imagery began to increase. Kennedy's impressive showing against Nixon in the presidential debates was due more to his handsome, debonair image than to the content of the debates. (People who listened to the debates rather than watched them on TV considered two out of three a draw.) Today image triumphs over content for most people.[15]

Now that photos can be transmitted instantaneously around the world, the power of imagery has enormous impact internationally as well as nationally. Knowing full well the effect of disturbing pictures on the public, the second Bush administration refused to allow coverage of the flag-draped coffins that were returned from Iraq to Dover Air Force Base, Delaware. But provocative photos tend to slip through the cracks no matter how carefully they are guarded. (The coffin footage eventually surfaced.) The most notorious example was the graphic photos of U.S. soldiers abusing and humiliating Iraqi prisoners at Abu Ghraib. The *60 Minutes II* airing of this footage sent shock waves around the world. Americans were horrified, Iraqis were alienated, and the popularity of the Bush administration plummeted in the polls. The Arab media were quick to respond. Although some of the coverage was evenhanded, media outlets opposed to U.S. intervention used the photos to inflame anti-American feelings. In the case of Abu Ghraib, the image was the story.

---

[14]Fallow, James. "A Modest Proposal. Call Obstruction What It Is." *Atlantic Monthly* October 2012.
[15]For more on this see Wahl, Richard C. "The Triumph of the Image." *Columbia Review of Journalism* November/December 2003.

As the wars dragged on, the Department of Defense tightened regulations on publishing information about U.S. battlefield casualties, ruling that "names, videos, identifiable written and oral descriptions or identifiable photographs of wounded service members will not be released without service members' prior consent."[16] Hardly likely, is it? Since U.S. news organizations depended on embedded reporters and photographers for coverage of the wars, they had to cooperate with the military or be denied access. But without these graphic photos, the public had no visual grasp of the ravages of war on our troops. It is worth noting, though, that the media raised almost no objections to the new regulations, and, in fact, did some self-censorship of war coverage in ways that skewed our perception. For instance, when they ran photos of dead or dying Afghans or Iraqis, they typically portrayed victims of attacks by their own countrymen, not by U.S. troops, thus revealing the damage Afghans and Iranians did to each other and not the harm we did. In an age when people rely more and more heavily on visual imagery for the news, it is no exaggeration to say that photos have far greater impact than the written word.

Follow-up Stories Can Be Omitted or Played Down

Follow-up stories rarely make headlines, primarily for three reasons. The first is that they are more difficult to obtain than breaking news stories. It takes much less time and effort to record the fact that a bank has failed than to follow up details of an ensuing court case against its directors. The second is that the public (and media) conception of "news" is what is new, and follow-up stories are just more of the same, or just plain humdrum.

Breaking news is often sensationalized, but follow-up stories usually aren't sexy enough to grab the audience's interest, so the media ignore them. For example, from August to October 2010, the media ran a story that electrified the public about 33 Chilean miners trapped in a coal mine in San Jose, Chile. Their drama unfolded in painstaking detail, covering their special diets and exercise routine, the rescue efforts of engineers and drill operators, and the families and friends camped out above ground anxiously waiting for their return. When a half-mile shaft was finally constructed through solid rock and the rescue was imminent, the entire world cheered as they struggled to the surface. They had endured underground longer than survivors of any other mine accident, and they were rewarded with acclaim and showered with gifts—like motor bikes from Kawasaki, and $15,000 each from a Chilean businessman. But that was the end of the story. Everyone assumed that they lived happily ever after, and no follow-up stories appeared to contradict this perception. A year later, though, on the anniversary of the rescue, a few scattered articles in papers such as *the New York Times* and the *Guardian*, mention that most of the miners had returned to poverty, and some were worse off, suffering from psychological and physical trauma after the ordeal. Little was made of their tragedy and most people thought they continued to thrive.

One reason for the paucity of follow-up stories is that most of us have short attention spans. Except for "ongoing" stories—wars providing the best examples—people tend to tire of any topic quickly (the truth behind Andy Warhol's remark "In the future, everyone will be

---

[16]Quoted in Arnow, Pat. "From Self-Censorship to Official Censorship." *Extra!* March/April 2007, an enlightening article on the muzzling of news coverage in the Iraq/Afghan wars.

world-famous for 15 minutes"). When bored, it's all too easy to flip the switch to another channel or to put down the newspaper and instead watch Oprah do her thing on the tube.

Well, no one can be in favor of boredom. The problem is that in the vast majority of cases it is the time-consuming details that make all the difference. Ten-second news sound bites aren't all that different from "Chevrolet—the heartbeat of America" or "Magnavox—smart, very smart." Short and easily remembered usually drives out long and complicated. That may well be the chief reason relevant background information and follow-up tend to be in short supply on TV news programs.

Occasionally, though, the media makes a concerted effort to follow through on old stories. One example is the *Lincoln Journal Star* in Nebraska, whose editor, Peter Salter, decided to fill in the Monday edition (traditionally thin on news) with follow-ups on old stories in their files.[17] Reporters took turns writing about any item of interest in the papers archives and came up with a wide range of topics. The column, called "Epilogue," covered such items as a woman who had half her brain removed surgically ten years earlier (she lost the use of the right side of her body but learned to walk and talk again), and a man jailed five years previously for impregnating and marrying a thirteen-year old (they were still married and had three children). The stories were so popular that they consistently made the front page, and they were so unusual that the *Columbia Journalism Review* awarded the paper a "laurel" for doing systematic follow-up on stories, a rare practice in journalism.

Points of View Can Be Conveyed via Cartoons and Comic Strips

According to the old saying, a picture is worth a thousand words, which may account for the ability of cartoons and comic strips to effectively—graphically—make a point. In any case, it most certainly accounts for the large number of these pertinent cartoons that have been reprinted in this particular textbook. A clever practitioner of the cartoonist's art can puncture prejudices and force us to open our eyes to unpleasant truths in a way that few others can match.

The *Doonesbury* strip, crafted by Garry Trudeau, deserves special mention here because it has been in the forefront of a minor trend on newspaper comic pages to feature strips that at least occasionally touch on social or political issues rather than just tickling the funny bone. A classic cartoon and a particular favorite of the authors of this text (one of whom is a UCLA alum) is the 1994 *Doonesbury* series that poked fun at the hiring of junk bond ex-con Michael Milken to teach a business course at UCLA. In one panel, Milken is pictured saying, "Who is Professor Milken, the genius who created a new world of financial instruments? Well, I'm many things, of course. But most of all, I'm a survivor. After a 98-count indictment and a 6-count plea bargain, I'm still here—and with $1 billion to show for it!" after which students repeat his code: "Greed works! Crime pays! Everybody does it!" In another strip, Milken states what must certainly be his actual opinion on the matter: that government attempts at regulation are a joke and government employees no match for "a true visionary and his defense team." Students are shown booing the student who has the temerity to ask a pertinent question: "As the

---

[17]Fenwick, Alexandra. "Darts and Laurels." *Columbia Journalism Review* September/October 2010.

key player of the greatest criminal conspiracy in the history of finance, do you think justice was served by your brief stay in a country club prison?" Interesting, isn't it, that this cartoon is just as relevant today as it was when it first appeared.

Unfortunately, this ability of comic strips to graphically make a point sometimes results in their being censored. *Doonesbury,* of course, bites the dust now and then. But even normally nonpolitical strips occasionally get the axe. For example, when a young boy in the *For Better or for Worse* comic strip summoned the courage to tell his parents that he was gay, the resulting furor came as a shock to the strip's creator, Lynn Johnston. The series of strips on this theme ran for just 10 days but was censored during that time in 40 papers, with 20 more canceling the strip outright. In Memphis, Tennessee, to cite just one city, about 2,000 readers canceled their subscriptions to the *Commercial Appeal* because that paper ran the strips they objected to. Johnston was flooded with mail, both pro and con, and stung by the anger and hate some letters exhibited. She wrote the series, she said, because several friends had died from AIDS, and one of her closest gay friends recently had been robbed and killed. "He was nothing more than a wonderful person and a good friend to me," she said. "My intent was to show that Lawrence [the gay boy in the strip] was different but that he's still the kid next door, still a member of the community, someone who should be judged on his moral character, not his genetic code."[18]

Boondocks © Aaron McGruder. Reprinted with permission of Universal Press Syndicate. All rights reserved.

Aaron McGruder's Boondocks *sometimes gets in trouble for its political satire.* Extra! *(December 2001) noted that this strip along with several others were pulled from some newspapers after September 11 because it was critical of U.S. foreign policy.*

In the United States, controversial cartoons may be censored or criticized, but they don't galvanize people into committing violent protests as they sometimes do in other countries. Cartoons featuring the Prophet Muhammad have incited violent protests from Islamists for almost a decade. When a Danish newspaper printed cartoons caricaturing Muhammad a few years ago, a group of fundamentalist Muslim clerics urged Middle Eastern embassies to demand a meeting with the Danish prime minister. He refused, and the protests escalated

---

[18]See, for instance, the *San Francisco Examiner* 25 April 1993.

into violence. Hundreds of Iraqis demanded an apology from the European Union, Palestinians stormed through European buildings in Gaza, burning German and Danish flags, and thousands of Syrians torched the Danish and Norwegian embassies in Damascus. More recently, a French satirical weekly newspaper released a cartoon cover on the Internet of an upcoming issue that featured Muhammad in a turban saying "100 lashes if you don't die laughing!" French Muslims were incensed. Hours before the issue was published an arson fire swept through the Paris office of the newspaper, gutting the interior. No cartoon in this country has ever come close to inciting protests on that level.

5. TELEVISION AND THE INTERNET

For the last half of the twentieth century, television was by far the most important mass medium. More households own television sets than bathtubs and showers. (Interesting facts: The average number of TVs per household is 2.5, and 31 percent of Americans own four or more TVs.) It would be hard to overestimate the effects of television on everyday life. (One thinks, for a parallel, of the ways in which the automobile has transformed the world.)

Consider, for instance, the ways in which news reporting has helped break down prejudices. It was a very important event indeed the first time a woman, Barbara Walters, read the evening news to us on national TV, and an equally important event the first time an African-American, Max Robinson, did so. In recent years, the number of TV commentators with diverse backgrounds has grown. When Barack Obama and Hillary Clinton vied for the Democratic presidential nomination, race and gender issues dominated campaign coverage as never before. To address these issues, cable news stations brought in seasoned minority analysts who hadn't had much exposure in the mainstream media. TV exposure also influenced the public's attitude about homosexuality. Although gay newscasters had long kept their sexual orientation under wraps, all that changed when news anchors like Anderson Cooper publicly acknowledged being gay.

But perhaps the most graphic illustration of television's power to change the world is in its effect on the nature of war and associated diplomacy. It is a commonplace today that television shortened American involvement in the war in Vietnam through its living-room coverage, but insufficient notice has yet been taken of the way in which TV influenced the conduct of the Gulf War, the Iraq War, and the war in Afghanistan. The American government and its coalition allies were exceedingly careful to reduce the number of casualties, not just of their own forces but also of enemy civilians, in a way that (in the long history of warfare) has rarely, if ever before, been true. Compare that, for instance, with the American and British record of mass bombings of civilians in World War II, when television was not peeking over every general's shoulder.

Even sitcoms and the other prime-time entertainment programs sometimes have positive effects—in addition to providing entertainment—a case in point being their role in reducing ethnic and gender prejudice, one of the great improvements that has taken place in the United States (and most other democratic nations) since World War II. African-Americans are portrayed as middle-class workers, not just as janitors or (the very expression is odious) cotton pickers, and women as business executives, not just housewives.

Television is the first truly democratic culture—the first culture available to everybody and entirely governed by what people want. The most terrifying thing is what people do want.

—Clive Barker

When we think of the mass media, it's important to remember that at least one third of American adults are or come close to being functionally illiterate. For them, and for many others, a picture is worth more than a thousand words. So for the mass of people, by default, television is the best news source. (Note, by the way, that it's much easier to become a couch potato and endlessly watch the tube than it is, say, to search the Internet for interesting material.)

But capturing and informing this kind of mass audience requires extremely tight editing (matched in print only by advertisements). The average attention span is short, and comprehension limited. TV does a better job than the other media in editing the news so that it can be understood, somewhat, by most Americans. However, a recent trend in cluttering the screen with multiple images tends to undermine otherwise concise editing. Even the most focused viewer gets distracted by split-screen pictures with headlines underneath and crawling commentary at the bottom.

The Internet

For the past several years, the audience growth in Internet news has outpaced growth in any other news source—not surprising, now that three-quarters of U.S. adults own laptops or desktop computers and 44 percent own smart phones. The advantages of using the Internet are obvious. It can be, and often is, more up-to-date than the best reference books; it allows people everywhere to read some of the best newspapers and magazines in the land; and it often is more readily available than books or other print media. The world of online journalism continues to expand. Just about all of the major media outlets have Internet access, including broadcast networks, cable networks, newspapers, and news magazines. In addition, Google News provides access to English-language news sites around the world. An outgrowth of the Google search engine, Google News draws on stories from 4,000 news sites, updating items on a second-by-second basis.

The Internet offers an unparalleled opportunity for the average person to express his or her views on blogs or on conventional news media sites that encourage audience participation. An increasing number of web-based sites are experimenting with news coverage from outside the profession. Global Voices, for example, mixes professional editors with volunteer "citizen reporters" from all over the world. In some respects, the Internet is the new town crier, giving citizens a voice in the democratic process. This was nowhere more evident than in the Arab uprisings that swept through the Middle East. A wide range of people, some from remote areas, came together in the social media to advocate rebellion against corrupt regimes and to organize demonstrations. Digital technology enabled activists to bypass state-controlled media and get their messages to the outside world. And they were riveting. Cell-phone images flashed across the media of horrifying scenes, like the ones of Syrian soldiers using children as human shields, or Egyptian soldiers stripping and beating a woman protestor. The Internet, social media, and mobile phones gave people unprecedented ability to organize, record, and transmit information about protest movements around the world.

For Web users who want an in-depth look at the news, the Internet has the capability of offering extensive links to background sources like archived material and related stories, interviews, or photographs. In this way, it provides much more information than a newspaper or magazine article. For instance, when *the New York Times* ran an article revealing that President Obama personally oversaw drone attacks on top terrorists, the online version was studded with links to related sources.[19] With a flick of the finger, readers could access Obama's counterterrorism record, the legal case for killing America citizens who are al-Qaeda operatives, Obama's speech defending his policies, and editorials questioning the power of presidents to make such attacks. This deep background fleshed out the report on a very controversial subject in ways that a newspaper or magazine article could never do, giving Web users a chance to examine related sources and judge for themselves the morality and legality at issue.

Although the Internet is a wonderful source of information, the downside is that it spawns so much more schlock than even the TV networks do. It takes a rather sophisticated Web browser to separate the wheat from the chaff. Of course, this is always a problem; the point is that it becomes more urgent to be able to do this well when surfing the web. (Instructors regularly tear their hair out when students turn in papers based on second-rate Internet sources.) The Internet is now inundated with bloggers and citizen reporters, and though they sometimes have more expertise in a particular field than career journalists, they often express strong biases that professionals try to avoid in straight news reporting.

Another major downside is the privacy issue that makes Internet users increasingly uneasy. Since most of us access the Internet through search engines like Google or Yahoo, we provide a stream of personal information about ourselves without giving

---

[19]Becker, Jo and Shank, Scott. "Secret 'Kill List' Proves a Test of Obama's Principles and Will." *New York Times* 29 May 2012.

our consent. Online newspapers and other businesses store information on us to use in their marketing departments and often share this data with other companies. By tracking online activity on Web pages, e-mails, social networking sites, and business sites, they compile enough data on us to create a pretty detailed profile of our interests, preferences, and other personal information. If this were just used for marketing purposes it might be relatively harmless, but plenty of sensitive information is collected about our health or finances, for instance, that could be used against us if it fell into the wrong hands.[20]

6. The Non-Mass Media to the Rescue

The mass media are a reasonably good source of information about breaking stories—speeches made by important officials, fluctuations in the Dow, bills passed by Congress (but not about a bill's value or who benefits and who is harmed!), and so on. Television does these stories rather well, at least when it can get good visuals. But for detailed,

---

Todd Oppenheimer, a seasoned journalist, on the limitations of "citizen journalists" who report news on the Internet:

. . . [I]t's one thing (a good idea) to use citizen journalists for material from the field, such as on-the-scene accounts from a Hurricane Katrina, or soldier diaries from the trenches of Iraq. It's quite another (a bad idea) to expect amateurs to figure out who is telling the truth about Iraq, or which priests have committed pedophilia. Stories in this later category obviously require skill in a host of exacting tasks, such as interviewing evasive sources, understanding how and where bureaucracies hide evidence and writing a narrative that is compelling yet properly sourced.

. . . In every field, standards are devised and continually refined by the profession's senior members. These masters earn their wisdom through years of challenging, often painful experiences. Their duty is to pass on their lessons to up-and-comers, who should serve some demanding period of apprenticeship. This is how every profession achieves its high ideals. In the media's case, those standards involve strong writing, fairness and independence, thoroughness and accuracy, ethics and astute judgment.

—From "Read All About It—But
Where Exactly?" *San Francisco Chronicle*
17 October 2007; an insightful article
about the current state of journalism

---

[20]For much more information about Internet privacy issues and ways to protect yourself, see "Fact Sheet 18:Using the Internet Safely." *Privacy Rights Clearinghouse.* Web. (www.privacyrights .org/fs/18)

sophisticated, in-depth accounts, and for analysis that doesn't just parrot what powerful people are saying, the non-mass media are indispensable.

The commercial networks do feature several rather good investigative, in-depth programs—namely *60 Minutes, Nightline,* and *20/20.* But PBS, the Public Broadcasting Service, is the best everyday television news—best without doubt, for in-depth reporting and analysis on programs like *The News Hour, Charlie Rose* (for penetrating interviews on a wide range of topics) and *Bill Moyers Journal* (for news analysis). Indeed, in most ways, PBS is perhaps the brightest spot on the television spectrum. But those viewers who are on cable, which means most people, can also click on the Discovery Channel, The National Geographic Channel, Arts and Entertainment, C-Span, and, of course, CNN, which still gives its viewers a reasonably well-balanced account of the news. Then there are the two NBC news channels, the Fox News Channel, and for science, Nova (PBS), an excellent, high-level program that examines cutting edge issues in science.

Nevertheless, TV still easily is eclipsed by the few good daily newspapers and especially by small-circulation magazines and journals. The mass media, even the big-city newspapers, generally focus on what is current, in the air, neglecting the underlying forces that ultimately determine what will be big news at a later date.

In addition, they often cover important stories that slide under the radar. For example, *Extra!,* a media watchdog that evaluates news coverage, reported on the mass media's failure to cover adequately the starting testimony on wiretapping by former Deputy General James Comey in May 2007.[21] The story is not only gripping but reveals a disturbing behind-the-scenes attempt to ambush the Justice Department. When U.S. Attorney General John Ashcroft was hospitalized for gall bladder surgery in 2004, Comey, as acting attorney general, refused to sign an extension of the controversial wiretapping program partly because it was considered illegal by the Justice Department's legal counsel. In a scene right out of a film noir, the White House chief of staff at the time, Andrew Card, and counsel Alberto Gonzales hurried to Ashcroft's bedside to persuade the very sick man to overturn Comey's ruling. Meanwhile Comey and FBI Director Robert Mueller got wind of the ambush and rushed to the hospital to intervene. But Ashcroft rallied his strength, rose to the occasion, and dramatically quashed the attempt. The media could have had a field day with this sensational, important story, but they didn't. Although *the New York Times* and *Newsweek* mentioned it in 2006, Comey's testimony before the Senate Judiciary Committee a year later got little notice except from a *Washington Post* editorial critical of the president for proceeding with a program that the Justice Department itself considered illegal. As *Extra!* points out, this significant scandal never even appeared in most of the mass media. This is the type of revelation that the non-mass media bring to our attention. (See an annotated list of publications at the end of the book for examples, and for some thoughts by the authors of this text concerning some of these important information sources.)

Finding out what is really going on, however, isn't so much a matter of mass versus non-mass media as it is of learning how to be selective—learning how to separate pearls from schlock. Those interested in science, for example, would do well to avoid

---

[21]Hart, Peter. "Illegal Yes—But Not Newsworthy." *Extra! Update* June 2007.

newsstand magazines that pander to the appetite so many people have for stories about ESP and other matters on the edge of legitimate science and that try to sensationalize science to increase sales. (Will stories about "close encounters of the third kind" ever go away?)

The point is that the non-mass media contain lots more pearls per square inch and are, on the whole, a good deal more sophisticated in their discussions of what is going on in the world than are newspapers, TV, and even mass-sales books. Best-selling books—for instance those concerning politics, economics, and the like—often are shallow or sensationalist.

Of particular note are the self-serving memoirs of "distinguished statesmen," such as Dick Cheney, that are often little more than bald-faced attempts to rewrite history in their favor. Presidential memoirs, supposedly written by former presidents, are perhaps the most self-serving of these tomes. *Example:* Ronald Reagan's *An American Life* (Simon & Schuster, 1990), apparently written by Robert Lindsey (whom Reagan credits by saying "Robert Lindsey, a talented writer, was with me every step of the way"). Also, Bill Clinton's, *My Life* (Knopf, 2004), written in longhand by Clinton himself, he claimed, played up his triumphs and played down his failures (as do most presidential memoirs), George W. Bush's *Decision Points* cherry-picked his successes and skipped passed his failures (though he did admit that he has a "sickening feeling" over the failure to find weapons of mass destruction in Iraq).

We should note, by the way, that National Public Radio (NPR) does a better job of presenting the news and analysis than does any television channel or most other radio outlets. Some examples of their regular programs are *All Things Considered, Talk of the Nation, BBC World News, Fresh Air, Science Friday,* and *As It Happens,* an excellent Canadian news program broadcast widely in the United States. There is even at least one major network entertainment program, *Law and Order,* that provides a good deal of information about how the legal system really works, as opposed to how it is supposed to work in addition to straight entertainment. Although this long running series was cancelled after twenty years in 2010, it is available in reruns and worth watching.

7. RECENT DEVELOPMENTS

During the past 30 years or so, dramatic changes have been taking place in the news business. Perhaps the most important of these is the ever-increasing concentration of media ownership, and thus power, in fewer and fewer hands.

The first and much smaller concentration of media power occurred way back in the late nineteenth century with the development of newspaper chains—the most important, perhaps, being the one put together by William Randolph Hearst and fictionalized in the movie classic *Citizen Kane.* The power of these early media magnates is illustrated in that film by a scene in which a journalist sent to Cuba in 1898 reports back that there is no sign of war in Cuba, only to be told that Kane (Hearst) would supply the war. (The scene is a takeoff on what is held by some to be true: that the United States's involvement in the Spanish-American War was in large part due to the Hearst publications' sensationalistic journalism. More likely, though, it was just one of many factors leading to that one-sided, unprovoked, war.)

The power of the Hearst media empire was illustrated again in 1941 when Hearst forced RKO, the producer of *Citizen Kane,* not to show that film in its theaters nationwide. The threat was to refuse ads listing any RKO theater offerings in Hearst's many newspapers around the country, which would have caused RKO a tremendous financial loss.

This blacklisting of *Citizen Kane* nicely illustrates the great censorship potential of concentrated media power. But back in those days, all big cities had more than one newspaper so that no small group or individuals could effectively control the newspaper business. (It was not until the 1950s that television usurped the role of newspapers as the principal news source for a growing majority of people in the United States and Canada.)

> The founders of this country believed a free and rambunctious press was essential to the protection of our freedoms. They couldn't envision the rise of giant mega-media conglomerates whose interests converge with state power to produce a conspiracy against the people. I think they would be aghast at how this union of media and government has produced the very kind of imperial power against which they rebelled.
>
> —Moyers, Bill. "On Media and Democracy."
> *Nation* 15 December 2003

Today's media conglomerates are a good deal more worrisome than were the newspaper chains of old, because they concentrate power into an extremely few hands in all of the major news media—television, radio, mass-circulation magazines and newspapers and the Internet. Independent newspapers still exist in some cities and towns, but their number shrinks every year, and most big cities now are down to just one daily paper, usually owned by a large and powerful chain. So today, a single individual may control quite a few TV outlets as well as newspapers and magazines, as does, for example, Rupert Murdoch (the Fox TV network, the *Wall Street Journal,* and many other newspapers, including the prestigious *London Times,* and magazines worldwide).

Equally troubling is the fact that the giant media empires have multiple business interests outside the news media world that provide enormous opportunity for product sales and promotion. The ruling principle of these megacorporations is the bottom line, not the best possible dissemination of news. Here is a list of some of the holdings of the top three of these huge media giants:

- **Walt Disney** owns ABC (*ABC Network News*, *Prime Time Live*), 80 percent of ESPN, dozens of radio stations, Walt Disney Pictures (including Pixar animation), Hyperion Books, Disney Publishing Worldwide, Disney Interactive Media Group, and Disney Music Group. Then, of course, there are Disneyland, Disney World, and a host of other theme parks, plus hundreds of Disney Stores selling Disney products.

- **Time Warner** owns HBO, Turner Broadcasting System (CNN, TNT, TBS and other networks), Warner Brothers Entertainment, Time-Life International Books, more than 20 imprints (including Little Brown), and dozens of online sites. It has over 100 magazines (including *Time*, *Fortune*, *Sports Illustrated*, *Money*, and *People*), Time Warner Investments Group, and Time Warner Global Media Group.
- **News Corporation** is Rupert Murdoch's international conglomerate (called News International in Great Britain), with lots of U.S. holdings: Fox television network and close to 200 affiliates around the world, 20th Century Fox, Harper Collins Publishers, the *Wall Street Journal*, *New York Post*, and *London Times*, as well as a few dozen newspapers and book companies in the United States, Great Britain, and Australia.

Then there are gigantic newspaper corporations like Gannett, Tribune, and the New York Times; book publishers like Bertlesman, Pearson, and Hachette, and Internet giants like Google and Yahoo.

Well, then, why should the rest of us care about this concentration of media power into fewer and fewer hands? Doesn't size, after all, yield efficiency? Aren't large news companies better able to afford large staffs of reporters gathering news items around the world? The answer to both of these questions may well be yes. But three other nagging questions immediately arise. Will being *able to afford* larger staffs automatically translate in practice into larger staffs? Will greater efficiency generally translate into better news reporting or simply into greater profits? Will media moguls resist the temptation to further their own interests, including the interests of their own nonnews subsidiaries, at the expense of news quality and fair evaluation? The answer to all of these questions, unfortunately, seems to be *no*.

Item: When cartoonist Dan Wasserman made edgy fun of the Boston Museum of Fine Arts (MFA) and Bank of America (a massive corporate contributor), the *Boston Globe* literally stopped the presses to pull the editorial cartoon scheduled to run on the day that the opening of the MFA's new wing was to be celebrated.[22] In the run-up to the opening, the *Globe* had covered the MFA expansion at length and in depth—including a 56-page magazine commemorating the event with a full-page ad from Bank of America. Why was the cartoon pulled? Because it showed an MFA exhibition of all the houses Bank of America foreclosed on!

Since megacorporations are profit driven and risk averse, one consequence of their dominating the industry is that the quality of programming has gone down in recent years, so instead of getting high-caliber, innovative sitcoms like the Mary Tyler Moore productions in the 1970s, for example, we get reality TV—cheap thrills that cost a fraction of a good sitcom to produce. Even more important, though, is that big media have the ability to limit the free exchange of ideas and thus undermine democracy. Because they are able to control the news, they can (and do) limit the range of information and debate from diverse sources, slant the news to their advantage, and kill stories that threaten their own interests.[23]

---

[22]Kennedy, Dan. "What Was Missing from Today's *Boston Globe*." *Media Nation* 14 November 2010.
[23]For more on this see Turner, Ted. "My Beef with Big Media." *The Washington Monthly* July–August 2004. Turner focuses in particular on the way big media increasingly shut out independent entrepreneurs with diverse points of view but not enough cash or clout to compete with the big guys.

Item: When *Frontline* showed a documentary "Hand of God," their PBS affiliate in Brownsville, Texas, KMBH, claimed it didn't get the video feed in time to air the program in January 2007. But critics, knowing the station was owned by the Roman Catholic diocese of Brownsville, suspected the real reason was that the documentary dealt with child molestations by Catholic priests.

Another disturbing issue closely connected to the concentration of media power in a few companies is the cozy relationship between media giants and corporate America. Project Censored did a study of media interlocks with big corporations and found that all 118 board members of the 10 largest media companies sat on boards of 288 national and international corporations.[24] Not only that, but eight out of 10 of these media companies had board memberships in common with each other. *The Washington Post* and NBC, for instance, both had board members with seats on J.P. Morgan and Coca-Cola. The *New York Times* and Gannett had members with seats on Pepsi.

---

[24]For a full discussion and list of overlaps between media giants and corporations see Phillips, Peter. "Big Media Interlocks with Corporate America." *Project Censored.* Web. 2 May 2010. http://www.projectcensored.org/

These interlocking connections raise obvious conflicts of interest. How likely is a network or newspaper to play down or ignore news stories harmful to companies with close ties? Very likely. And how tempting would it be to play up the products and images of these companies? Tempting, indeed. Take, for example, an NBC *Today* show (April 30, 2007) that featured Matt Lauer making glowing comments about Boeing aircraft in a segment shot at their Everett, Washington, factory. His "full disclosure" that Boeing is owned by NBC's parent company, General Electric, was a blip on the screen compared to the footage given to the favorable coverage of Boeing's 777s. Viewers were assured that the planes would make flying more comfortable, safer, and cost effective and would boost the U.S. economy. Not only that, employees loved making this "great product." The sign-off, "If it ain't Boeing, we ain't going," added the final touch. With news stories like this, "why bother with commercials?"[25]

An Afterword

All is not lost, though. While it is true that media giants can have a corrupting influence and the public's demand for sensationalism can fuel the gutter press, it is also true that good journalism still exists and continues to have a significant effect on our collective understanding and attitudes. As Ben Bradlee, legendary editor of the *Washington Post* wrote, "There is much to criticize about the press, but not before recognizing a ringing truth: the best of the American press is an extraordinary daily example of industry, honesty, conscience, and courage, driven by a desire to inform and interest readers."[26]

Over the past 50 years, the media have exposed significant wrongdoings, sometimes at considerable risk. Think back to two blockbusters—the Pentagon Papers and the Watergate scandal. When *the New York Times* published excerpts of the Pentagon Papers revealing that the Johnson and Kennedy administrations had systematically lied to the public and Congress about starting and expanding the war in Southeast Asia, it blew the lid off the Vietnam War. Then along came the Watergate scandal, painstakingly unearthed over two years by *the Washington Post*, which culminated in the resignation of President Nixon under threat of impeachment. Explosive stories like these require the kind of courage and sense of mission to expose deception in government that represents the best in journalism.

While these iconic stories have gained lasting fame, thousands of others have appeared in the national and local media, revealing not only corruption and deception in government and business (think of the ongoing coverage of bank scandals in the current recession), but stories about the bravery of everyday citizens (like the U.S. Airways pilot who landed a jet safely in the Hudson river) or news about the plight of regions where disaster strikes (like the *Times Picayune's* valiant reports of conditions in New Orleans as Hurricane Katrina battered the city and flooded the newspaper offices). At their best, the news media are an invaluable source of information and analysis. While there is much to criticize, there is also much to praise.

---

[25]Example from "Fear & Favor 2007." *Extra!* March/April 2008.
[26]From *A Good Life*, Ben Bradlee's autobiography, an absorbing insider account of journalism in the last half of the twentieth century.

SUMMARY OF CHAPTER 11

1. The news media have been going through a huge transformation. Technological advances like the Internet have created new ways for people to access the news, and as a result, traditional news outlets have been shrinking. These new trends in journalism require us to be even more vigilant in thinking critically about the ways the news is managed and presented to the public. The one overriding fact about all news sources is that they are businesses intent on making money. So they have to satisfy their audiences, advertisers and governments.

   They cater to their audiences by simplifying the news to make it more easily understood—by breaking news items into small sound bites that stay within the average attention span in length and by arranging coverage of news so as to conform to audience interests and prejudices.

   The media cater to advertisers by suppressing news that reflects badly on them or their products and by touting advertisers' products free as "news" items. *Example:* the *Pioneer Press* quashing a review critical of a restaurant that advertised in the paper.

   The media also has to take account of the power of government to harass them by rescinding licenses, restricting access to government records, censoring information that doesn't conform to their political agenda, playing favorites in the dissemination of news, and fining networks for broadcasting indecent material. *Example:* the half-million-dollar fine slapped on CBS for airing Janet Jackson's indecent exposure during her halftime Super Bowl performance. The media often give in to this power of government by treading more carefully in criticizing government actions. *Example:* reporters at press conferences who are careful not to ask overly pointed follow-up questions. Another way the government manages the news is by inserting into newscasts prepackaged reports that get their message out or put a positive spin on the news. (Note that the power of government to censor is much greater in many other countries than in the United States and in some other industrial democracies.)

   But the mass media have a good deal of power of their own, stemming from their ability to expose and publicize whatever they care to. *Famous example: The Washington Post*'s dogged exposé of the Watergate scandal that forced President Nixon to resign in disgrace.

   The business world—in particular, very large corporations—have a large say in the dissemination of news. They often use this power, first, to suppress stories unfavorable to their own narrow interests and, second, to get favorable stories included in media presentations. This power of big business stems from its power as advertisers (to withdraw advertising), from its ability to influence politicians and governments (principally through "campaign contributions") and from its ownership of a good deal of the mass media.

   Of course, in practice the media tend to try to satisfy all of the various power factions and not to needlessly throw their weight around. It almost always is more profitable to cooperate with power than to fight it. *Example:* Politicians and the media cooperating to produce sound bites: The pols get exposure and the media get cheap footage to show on the evening news. Unfortunately, the news has increasingly become a source of entertainment more than information, playing up human interest stories like the saga of Jessica Lynch at the expense of hard news.

Since the bottom line is, as they say, the bottom line, news-gathering methods tend to be designed to save money, which means that regular beats are set up to gather the news from those able to regularly supply it (the rich and powerful and the government). True investigative reporting is very costly and thus relatively less common than a mere gathering of the news from other sources. *Example:* the regular attendance at presidential press conferences as compared to the amount of journalistic digging below the surface.

2. For reasons already mentioned, the media tend to misdirect audience attention away from important, underlying issues and events to human interest stories. In doing this, they tend to take advantage of the average person's lack of a good sense of proportion. *Example:* playing up celebrity scandals and playing down or ignoring serious issues.

3. The media's theory of objectivity, to which lip service is widely paid, requires that news stories be separated from speculations, judgments, evaluations, and the like, which are considered to be subjective. But this theory is off the mark. Facts don't just lie around waiting to be picked up; reporters must reason to the facts. Similarly, decisions as to what will be covered and what will not depend in part on value judgments, so that news and evaluations cannot be completely separated.

In practice, however, the theory of objectivity simply keeps the media from straying too far in their judgments and evaluations from the mainstream social consensus. *Example:* Their attempts to be objective by being "evenhanded" merely result in our hearing what the Democrats have to say as compared to the Republicans.

Because the theory of objectivity says that news reporting must be separated from judgments, speculation, and background information, the mass media tend to be short on explanations as to why things happen as they do. Of course, reporters cannot be expected to be experts on every topic they cover. But they still want to appear to be authoritative—to appear to know what they are talking about whether they do or don't.

The media generally want to play it safe when featuring expert opinion. They want to satisfy all relevant power factions, if possible. So they tend to consult establishment figures, including media bigwigs, and not to annoy their audiences. The result often is silly pontificating. *Example:* the political correctness of almost all political discussion on TV.

Note that the media sometimes act as self-censors, either out of patriotic intent (as in wartime), or in order to placate their audiences or advertisers, or to avoid the possibility of libel. *Example:* showing Elvis Presley doing his stuff only from the waist up on the old Ed Sullivan TV show.

4. The media need to slant the news can be accomplished in quite a few different ways: playing a story up or down, using a misleading or sensational headline, omitting or playing down follow-up stories, using (or not using) emotive language, using suggestive photos and other imagery, and using cartoons to convey a point of view. *Example:* underreporting the massive displacement of the Iraqi people during the Iraq War.

5. Television is the town crier, certifier, and grapevine. It is the chief medium on which political contests are fought and news about major events such as wars is disseminated.

   The result is that the television industry has greater power than the other media and indeed can and does influence the course of events in the world on which it reports. *Example:* the way in which TV coverage of the Iraq War influenced the public to support it early on and turn against it as coverage became negative.

   Even prime-time television entertainment sometimes has positive features. *Example:* It has helped to break down prejudices against ethnic and religious groups and women—portraying blacks and women in important jobs in the business community. Note also the positive effects of employing African-Americans and women on TV news programs. (TV also is superior in explaining the news to ordinary people on the street.)

6. For the past several years, the audience growth in Internet news has outpaced growth in any other news source. It offers an unparalleled opportunity to access the news, obtain useful information, and participate in public discourse. But because of all the schlock on the Web, we have to be vigilant in thinking critically about the way the news is reported or managed. *Example*: "citizen reporters" or bloggers expressing strong bias or misrepresenting the news. Another issue of concern is the breach of privacy that occurs when search engines like Google or Yahoo routinely collect data on us without our consent.

7. Although the mass media are a modestly good source of breaking news, smaller-scale outlets are much better at analysis, at supplying background information, and at investigative reporting.

   PBS is a relatively good source of news, generally better than most mass media outlets, in particular in providing background information and analysis. But lots of small-circulation magazines are significantly better than PBS and CNN, being crafted so as to appeal to more sophisticated audiences. *Example: The Washington Monthly* coverage of politics.

   But the point is selectivity, not mass versus non-mass media. This is true not only with respect to television, newspapers, radio, and magazines, but also to books. Popular books tend to be lighter weight than some that are less popular, because mass audiences tend to be rather unsophisticated. *Example: Discover* and *Omni* magazines, which hoke up science in the attempt to make it interesting to a mass audience. (Note that presidential memoirs and those of other high government officials tend to be particularly shoddy products. *Example:* President Bush cherry-picking his successes in *Decision Points.*

8. The intense concentration of media power in the hands of giant conglomerates is one of the more ominous recent developments in the media business. *Example:* Walt Disney owning ABC, dozens of radio stations, hundreds of Disney stores, and so forth. Although size theoretically can yield efficiency and better news coverage, in general it hasn't worked that way so far.

EXERCISE 11-2

When Barack Obama was campaigning for the presidential nomination, CBS News.com received so many ugly remarks about the senator that the network decided to block all comments on its stories about him out of concern for the latent racism and the safety of the candidate. (Obama had been assigned Secret Service protection the previous week.) But CBS allowed comments on stories about all the other candidates. The network was criticized for denying him the publicity and for suppressing useful discussion about the candidate. Do you think CBS made the right decision?

EXERCISE 11-3

1. Evaluate the coverage in your local newspaper of a particular event or issue of national importance, with respect to (1) objectivity, (2) original versus second-hand reporting, (3) use of headlines, (4) establishment or mainstream point of view compared to minority opinions, and (5) any other matters discussed in this chapter.

2. Do the same for a recent issue of *Time, Newsweek, U.S. News & World Report,* or one of the online magazines such as *Salon.*

3. Do the same for an ABC, NBC, or CBS national evening news program.

4. Get a recent copy of *The Economist,* a British news magazine that widely circulates in the United States and Canada. Select a story in it about a particular event, and compare how it is handled with the way it is dealt with in one of the major American news magazines.

5. Compare news reporting on the BBC world news program carried on National Public Radio (NPR) with news reporting on any network TV or radio station. Which is better, and why?

6. Watch several episodes of *Grey's Anatomy* or *House* and explain how doctors and the medical industry are portrayed. Be sure to explain how their portrayal is similar to and different (if it is) from the real medical world. Do you think these programs influence how viewers tend to see doctors and medical care?

7. How are the elderly and teenagers portrayed on network TV programs, both in news stories and, especially, in popular entertainment programs? Back up your conclusions with details. How about women as compared to men?

8. Check the front page of a single issue of your local newspaper and determine as best you can the sources of their stories. (In the case of wire stories—Associated Press, Reuters, and the like—try to determine their sources.) How many of these stories are based primarily on a single handout or speech, how many were compiled from several such sources, and how many from reporters going out and finding for themselves what is going on?

9. Read through a single issue of three non-mass media magazines, one liberal (for instance, *The Nation*), one conservative (say, *The National Review*), and one libertarian (for example, *Reason*). Are their points of view evident? How do you think they compare to mass media magazines such as *Time* or *Newsweek* or to network national TV news programs?

10. How do you think the news would be presented to us if the federal government controlled and managed the mass media? Be specific and defend your answer with some thoughtful analysis.

11. Suppose that you owned a local television station or newspaper, or a whole television network. Would you report the news any differently from the way that the outlets in your area do now? If so, how, and why? If not, why not? (Assume that, although you may be rich, you can't withstand losses forever. And be realistic, not goody-goody.)

12. Many more women are working in the mass media today than in the old days, but fewer women than men rise to the top. Do you think the fact that men hold so many of the top positions in the mass media and thus make most of the important policy decisions seriously influences work conditions and news content in ways that would be different if women were equally represented in news media high management? If so, how? If not, why not?

13. For the energetic: Go to the library or the Internet and dig through back issues of some mass media publication and evaluate its coverage over time of some important, underlying, or long-term national issue or problem (for example, under- and unemployment, crime, pollution). Defend your evaluation.

14. Also for the energetic: Write your own news story about a personal event that truthfully makes you look bad. Write it as though it were to appear in your local or school newspaper, including headlines and the rest. Now rewrite the story to show your part in it in the best light possible without actually lying. Compare the two. Was this little exercise educational? (Answer: Very definitely, if you did it well.)

15. Examine the photographs accompanying a news story and explain how they slant the news.

16. The thrust of the discussion about the recent intense concentration of media power into fewer and fewer hands was that on the whole this is bad for the effective dissemination of the news. We noted, for example, that the chief concern of these large corporations is the bottom line, not the best presentation of the news. But isn't it possible, perhaps even likely, that these megacorporations will find that the highest profits are obtained by best satisfying their audiences, thus putting all of us (collectively) into the driver's seat—being given the sort of news coverage we most prefer? And if so, isn't that all to the good? So why worry about the concentration of media power that has been taking place lately?

By Handelsman, from *The New Yorker*. Reprinted by permission of Tribune Media Services.

"Do your owners treat you well? Mine are very kind."

This New Yorker drawing depicts what many critics claim is the principal problem with the political process in industrial democracies like the United States today—politicians are beholden to fat-cat contributors who provide most of the cash required to campaign successfully for high office. (By the way, what do you think are the chances that a social studies text containing this cartoon would be adopted by your school?)

12 Textbooks: Managing Worldviews

Not to know what has happened before one was born is always to be a child.

—Cicero

A high school teacher, after all, is a person deputized by the rest of us to explain to the young what sort of world they are living in and to defend, if possible, the part their elders are playing in it.

—Emile Capouya

A child educated only at school is an uneducated child.

—George Santayana

The less people know about how sausages and laws are made, the better they'll sleep at night.

—Otto von Bismarck

Germany has taught me that an uncritical view of the national past generated an equally subservient acceptance of the present.

—Hans Schmitt (who grew up in Nazi Germany)

If a nation expects to be ignorant and free, . . . it expects what never was and never will be.

—Thomas Jefferson

Public schools are one of the earliest sources of information about the world that most of us are exposed to. Although we take our schools for granted nowadays, public education was a new idea when our country declared independence in the eighteenth century.[1] Our founding fathers were deeply concerned about the stability of their newly formed republic, a fragile type of government that had never been tried on such a large scale before. They were afraid that the country would self-destruct, as the Roman Empire did, from the strife of internal factions and power-hungry citizens. One way to prevent that catastrophe, they believed, was to educate our young people to be good citizens in schools available to everyone—rich and poor. The obvious reason for

---

[1]From the introduction to Hirsch, E.D. Jr. *The Making of Americans*. New Haven: Yale University Press, 2009.

doing this was to make students competent in essential subjects like English and math, but the main one was to insure that citizens pledged their allegiance to the republic (not to individual factions) and to preserve the democratic ideals set forth by the founders. They were convinced that the way to do this was through compulsory education—but that took decades to evolve. Not until 1852 did the first state, Massachusetts, require everyone to go to school. Earlier than that, though, in 1825, the New York legislature provided funding for common textbooks that included the study of the English language, arithmetic, and history. As might be expected, the history text was the main tool used to create loyal citizens, committed to the common good.

Textbooks have come a long way since then, but history, civics, and social studies texts have a similar, though not so obvious purpose, to maintain student pride in America. As much as possible our leaders are pictured as better than human, all dressed up—minus their flaws—and our history is often distorted to maximize our virtues and minimize our faults. Since worldviews about our country are instilled at a young age, it is important to have a good idea about the accuracy of what we have been told while growing up.

One way to get an idea about this is to examine typical textbooks used in public school classrooms. Most teachers, after all, tend to coordinate classroom instruction with textbook content. This is particularly true in history courses, where the textbook is often the backbone of the curriculum. Since most history teachers in middle and high school haven't majored or minored in the subject, they tend to rely heavily on the content of the textbook. In some countries, like Japan and Singapore, where teachers are usually experts in history, they can supplement national curriculum guides with their own materials and can instruct students from their knowledge of the field. But since many teachers in the United States get their information from the same source as their students, it is critical to evaluate the quality of the average history textbook in this country. So let's discuss, first, the ways in which history texts tell high school students about the history of the United States.

1. HIGH SCHOOL HISTORY TEXTBOOKS

Textbooks don't stay the same for very long. Ups and downs in quality and content are bound to occur every so often.

The Good News

The good news is that since about 1960, the quality of high school history textbooks has improved in many significant ways. The first of these improvements was in the portrayal of African-Americans. Blacks had been close to invisible in texts published before that time. They were mentioned, of course, with respect to slavery and its elimination via the Emancipation Proclamation, and reference generally was made to two "token" Negroes, Booker T. Washington and George Washington Carver. But by sometime in the 1970s, virtually all history and civics texts had been revised to include more, and fairer, material about African-Americans and their place in American history and everyday affairs.

Improved treatment of other minority groups and of women quickly (as these things go) followed, reflecting changing attitudes and roles in the body politic. In older textbooks no mention was made of the atrocities committed by European explorers against Native Americans or of their later subjugation by the government. Today, virtually every high school history textbook mentions the "Trail of Tears" (the forced move of the Cherokee Indians from their homeland in the South to the Oklahoma territory), the illegal incarceration of loyal Japanese citizens in concentration camps during World War II, and so on.

Coupled with the improved treatment of minority groups has come a moderately large step toward objectivity in the portrayal of the darker side of American history. Imperialistic interference in the affairs of other countries—for example, of the so-called "banana republics"[2] of Central and South America—sometimes is hinted at (although the nasty details are never gone into in any depth).

> He that reads and grows no wiser seldom suspects his own deficiency, but complains of hard words and obscure sentences, and asks why books are written which cannot be understood.
>
> **—Samuel Johnson**

The Bad News

Oh, yes—the bad news.

History Texts Are Dull and Overly Long   Public high school history books, as virtually all junior and senior high school textbooks, are exceedingly dull and full of misleading verbiage, so that only the brightest and most diligent students who do a good amount of reading between the lines are apt to learn much from them about the true history of their country. Very little in these texts is likely to raise student interest in these matters. Part of the problem is that textbooks cover far too much material, compressing it in brief passages that squeeze out the juicy details, lobotomize the personalities, and suck the life out of the stories. Most of the better-selling high school history textbooks run to more than 1,000 pages (and weigh 7½ pounds) with endless "learning aids," exercise questions, special features, and gorgeous graphics, but no riveting accounts of dramatic events in American history that capture a student's imagination.

Students are snowed by an avalanche of facts ladled out one after another in a monotonous style devoid of what English teachers call "voice" or "tone"—not surprising, since almost all these books are written by multiple authors. The groupthink that results weakens their views, blurs their differences, and reduces the text to a dull mass of information, not to mention trivia. Names that even professional historians would not always be able to identify—for example, of some of the failed early nineteenth-century vice-presidential candidates—pile up one after the other as details are described concerning the election of 1816, the election of 1820, the election of 1824 . . . Interesting topics have

---

[2]The expression derives from the way in which the United Fruit Company dominated the political affairs of many of these countries for many years.

the guts wrung out of them. Even accounts of the good features of the American social system tend to fall flat.

Overly long books, overstuffed with facts, facts, facts, are not just dull, dull, dull. They're also heavy, heavy, heavy, often weighing more than six pounds. Students now carry these books home with them in backpacks, homework assignments being a regular feature of today's educational system (as opposed to the one in effect when the authors of this text attended high school—we're talking ancient history here).

The result is that backaches and strained back muscles have become all too common these days among public school students. One third of the students in a study by researchers at Simmons College in Boston said that their backs hurt so much that they had missed whole school days, or had missed physical education classes, or had needed to visit their doctor.

So the overstuffed texts in use today not only fail to increase student comprehension but also harm student health.*

*See, for instance, "Weighty Backpacks Straining Schoolkids." *San Francisco Chronicle* 14 February 2001, 1.

That detailed facts spewed out one after another don't easily become part of the working knowledge of students is supported by all sorts of surveys (in which, for instance, students identified J. Edgar Hoover as a nineteenth-century president, Jefferson Davis as a guitar player, and Socrates as an Indian chief). But students also don't seem to grasp the general, or approximate, kinds of knowledge that are more important than a mountain of trivia. It's more important, for example, that students know the approximate size and population of their country rather than precise statistics on this matter, and the evidence indicates that the ideas of most students concerning these important matters are either way off the mark or nonexistent.

To be fair, though, Americans have never had a solid grasp of their history. Proficiency studies going back to 1915–16 showed that Texas students confused Thomas Jefferson with Jefferson Davis and had trouble distinguishing 1492 from 1776. There wasn't much improvement by 1943 when only 6 percent of 7,000 college freshman could name the thirteen colonies.[3] Fast forward to 2011, when a Maris poll revealed that only 58 percent of Americans knew the year the country's independence was declared, and 25 percent didn't know what country we gained independence from! But just because we've always been historically challenged is no reason we should continue to be.

Since textbooks are the main way that students and many teachers get information about our history, they can be revised to engage the reader's interest and to drive home major historical events without bogging down in trivia. Then maybe history will be more meaningful to readers, and they will be more likely to retain factual information.

---

[3]Statistics taken from Paumgarten, Nick. "Report Card, Anyone?" *New Yorker* 27 June 2011.

History Texts Have Been Dumbed Down   Another part of the bad news is that in the past several years, a great many textbooks have been dumbed down with respect to vocabulary and sentence construction, although a few more linguistically sophisticated texts still are available. Dumbed-down texts shortchange students in several ways. One is the failure to stretch the already low student reading abilities that have led some educators to prefer the dumbed-down texts. Another results from the difficulty in presenting any complicated material using just simplified linguistic structures, forcing authors to oversimplify inherently complicated material.

One of the really annoying features of today's texts is the inane questions they sometimes ask students ("What evidence does this photo give of the depth of their poverty?"—under a photo that clearly shows the extreme poverty of the people pictured) or the allegedly "critical thinking" sidebars ("What kind of president do you think Americans were looking for after Watergate and the Nixon resignation?"). Not much critical thinking is needed to answer these make-work questions.

History Texts Have Gone Overboard on Multiculturalism   Still another part of the bad news is that history textbooks in recent years have reflected a general tendency to carry good, worthwhile improvements too far. If minorities and women were once seriously neglected in public school history texts, they now receive attention that distorts the history of the United States. History texts, in current lingo, have become *politically correct* and *multicultural*. (Recall the discussion in Chapter 1 concerning these trends.)

Noted historians and scholars who review textbooks have criticized this trend in both U.S. and world history texts.[4] For example, in one widely used U.S. history textbook, Native American cultures are discussed in 10 pages, the West African backgrounds of slaves get six pages, but the European background of white settlers rate no more than five pages—a gross distortion of actual fact.[5] The same book makes pretty much equal mention of immigrants from Europe, Asia, the West Indies, and Mexico a century ago, but has no discussion of the significant Jewish immigration in that same period.

Similar distortions occur in world histories. In an effort to avoid ethnocentrism, they pay the same attention and respect to all cultures, past and present, promoting a cultural relativism that misleads students into thinking that all cultures are equally important. Further, they tend to harshly criticize shortcomings in Western cultures but ignore or skirt them in other cultures. For example, one popular history text is critical of sexist attitudes in the medieval Catholic Church, but not of discrimination against women in Islamic societies.[6] In fact, since September 11, 2001, textbooks have handled the Islamic culture with kid gloves. No mention is made of the brutal treatment of hundreds of thousands of "comfort" women and sex slaves in Korea, China, the Philippines, and Taiwan. In an effort to avoid offending people from any one culture, textbooks like these distort history by suppressing evidence.

---

[4]See *A Consumer's Guide to High School History Textbooks*. Washington, D.C.: Thomas B. Fordham Institute, 2004—an excellent source for textbook reviews. The books discussed here are two of a dozen reviewed by a panel of historians.
[5]*The Americans.* Boston: McDougal Littel, 2003.
[6]*Connections to Today.* Saddle River, N.J.: Prentice Hall, 2003.

American History Is Distorted But arguably the most serious defect in today's history and social studies textbooks is that they still tend to distort American history and how the social–political system actually works in the United States, even if the distortion is less than in the past. Although those who ultimately decide what sorts of textbooks will be adopted surely do not intend to adopt books that stray too far from the truth, they haven't lost sight of our Founding Fathers' intent to create loyal citizens. To do this textbooks conjure up examples of democracy at work. One of the myths that regularly appears in history books is that America is a classless society that provides economic and social mobility for people who want to improve their lot in life. The American Dream, after all, is based on the notion that this is the land of opportunity, and some people do, indeed, improve their fortunes considerably. Yet the vast majority remain in the class they were born into. A 2011 Pew study (by the Economic Mobility Project) found that 62 percent of Americans reared in families in the top fifth of income stay in the top two-fifths, and 65 percent of those from the bottom fifth stay in the bottom two-fifths. In fact, there is less economic mobility in the United States than in most English-speaking countries, including Western Europe and Canada. Other studies have shown that social class is a pretty reliable predictor of a person's health, work, and economic status. As far as education goes, social class predicts the rate of college attendance better than any other factor, and even correlates strongly with SAT scores. These findings sometimes make their way into the news, particularly during the long recession, but they don't filter into textbooks.

Not only is our social structure distorted, our leaders tend to be pictured as better than human, all dressed up and minus their flaws (except, of course, for a very few Benedict Arnolds whose transgressions can't be papered over). Take the way in which Theodore Roosevelt, affectionately referred to as Teddy (the teddy bear was named after him), is spruced up in virtually all public school texts. Typically, he is portrayed as an energetic, hard-driving, exuberant, brave, trust-busting conservationist, reformer, and progressive, who was against monopolistic big business—a great man deserving of his place on Mount Rushmore.[7]

And perhaps he was. But no textbooks the authors of this text have ever seen, or even heard of, tell students about another side of good-old Teddy. They don't describe him as a bloodthirsty bigot who, though unusually brave, reveled in the slaughter he personally engaged in and witnessed during the Spanish-American War; a man who expressed pleasure after 30 men had been shot to death in the Civil War draft riots ("an admirable object lesson to the remainder"); a man who justified slaughtering Indians on the grounds that their lives were only "a few degrees less meaningful, squalid, and ferocious than that of the wild beasts," and who said that "All the great masterful races have been fighting races. . . . No triumph of peace is quite so great as the supreme triumph of war." Not exactly a teddy bear, this Teddy Roosevelt. (History texts also falsely pump up the part played by Roosevelt's Rough Riders in the famous charge up San Juan Hill in Cuba during the Spanish-American War at the expense of the black American soldiers, who did the most effective fighting.)

---

[7]But Roosevelt's role in the machinations that went on before construction of the Panama Canal, now seen as definitely not politically correct, sometimes are mentioned as a minus, whereas his role in the building of the canal previously was cited as one of his more glorious achievements.

The soul of historical research is debate, but that sense of uncertainty and contingency seldom finds its way into textbooks. By its nature, the textbook must pretend that its condensation of events and its presentation of their meaning are correct. In reality, every textbook has a point of view, despite a façade of neutrality; the authors and editors select some interpretations and reject others, choose certain events as important and ignore others as unimportant. Even when they insert sidebars with point and counterpoint on a few issues, they give the false impression that all other issues are settled when they are not. The pretense of objectivity and authority is, at bottom, just that: a pretense.

—Diane Ravitch
The Language Police

Embarrassing Facts and Topics Are Omitted or Played Down Although outright lying is frowned upon, the writers of public school textbooks have other devices at their disposal enabling them to satisfy the various kinds of social and political demands made on them. The most commonly employed of these devices is the complete omission of embarrassing historical events or facts. For example, most of the CIA "dirty tricks" and other sorts of interferences in the internal affairs of several foreign countries over the years get passed over. (Interestingly, the "Irangate" scandal that occurred during President Reagan's administration usually is mentioned.) Similarly, although all textbooks expend dozens of pages on World War II, most omit reference to the terrible firestorm bombing of Tokyo that killed more people than either of the atomic bombs we dropped on Japan, and they frequently fail to mention the deliberate policy of the American and British air forces to bomb German civilians, mostly women and children, as a way of breaking down German will to continue fighting.

Embarrassing events also sometimes are papered over by carefully controlled emphasis, especially by simply expending relatively little space on a topic. For example, most history textbooks these days, unlike those of times past, do tell readers about the war that occurred between American troops and Philippine guerrillas intent on gaining independence after the United States annexed the Philippine Islands at the end of the Spanish-American War, but they do so quickly, thus masking the extreme nastiness of the way in which the Filipinos were subjugated. The war with Spain gets relatively lots of space in most texts; the war against Filipino patriots extremely little, even though many more deaths and much greater destruction resulted from the war to force the Philippine people to knuckle under than from the war against Spain (itself quite a blot on the American escutcheon).

These devices are very hard for uninformed or unsophisticated readers to see through, particularly because we all want very much to believe in the greatness of our own society and tend to see national warts only after a good deal of experience has forced us to do so.

As might be expected, the role of the United States in patriotic wars such as World War II is puffed up and cleansed. But it might also be supposed that the suffering and dying of American fighting troops would be explained in a way that would let students understand the extent of their sacrifices and the terror they endured, as they did, for instance, on June 6, 1944 (D-Day), when several thousand American troops lost their lives on the beaches of Normandy, in France. After all, this would show how brave and self-sacrificing American troops have been. But telling students about this would require explaining what modern warfare really is like: about what it means to advance into concentrated machine gun fire that is certain to mow down most of those who find themselves in this terrible and terrifying circumstance; about flying on bombing missions with the knowledge that sooner or later most bombers in your unit are likely to be shot down and their occupants killed; about suddenly being covered with the splattered brains of a buddy who has just been hit by an unseen sniper; about the last moments of men drowning on submarines; about incinerated tank crews or the soldiers blasted into thousands of tiny pieces by enemy shelling. (Back in high school did you notice the total omission of pictures of dead American soldiers in history textbooks or of anything that graphically conveys the true horror of modern warfare?)

A Typical High School History Textbook

This textbook, America: Pathways to the Present, *contains 1,187 huge, double-columned, 8½ by 12-inch pages, chock-full of teaching devices (graphs, critical thinking questions, and so on)*. As might be imagined, this text is also chock-full of facts about American history ladled out one after another in a deadly flat tone of voice. Here, for example, is a short excerpt from this book's account of the presidential election of 1880:*

As the 1880 presidential election approached, the Republican party was split into three factions. The Stalwarts, followers of Senator Conklin, defended the spoils system. The Half-breeds, who followed Maine senator James G. Blaine, hoped to reform the spoils system while remaining loyal to the party. Independents opposed the spoils system altogether. James A. Garfield, a congressman from Ohio, won the party's presidential nomination. Garfield was linked to the Half-breeds. To balance the ticket, the Republicans chose as their vice-presidential candidate Chester A. Arthur, the New York Stalwart whom Hayes had fired two years earlier.

In the 1880 election Garfield won a narrow victory over the Democratic candidate, General Winfield S. Hancock . . . [*ad infinitum*].

Fascinating. But how many students ever remember even the tiniest bit of this dreary account?

*Cayton, Andrew R. L., Perry, Elisabeth Israels, and Winkler, Allan M. *America: Pathways to the Present.* New York: Prentice Hall, 2000. This textbook is reviewed in *The Textbook Letter* March–April 1999, the premier journal dealing with junior and senior high school textbooks.

> Who controls the past controls the future; who controls the present controls the past.
>
> —**George Orwell (*1984*)**

Violence in current wars is whitewashed in the same way. For example, in the 2007 edition of *The Americans* (an 11th-grade history cited earlier), no pictures of dead soldiers appear in the two-page account of the Iraq War, and no mention is made of the death toll, particularly of Iraqis. In fact, the only deaths cited are attributed to "insurgents or rebels engaged in acts of violence that killed thousands, including many Americans." Deaths caused by Americans are not discussed. The entire account glosses over the real reasons for the war and the ploys used to sell it to the American people, but 11th graders—some of whom would soon go off to war—weren't considered old enough to process this information.

As far as Afghanistan goes, few textbooks give the history of our country's involvement with the Taliban before the War on Terrorism. As James W. Loewan pointed out in his trenchant analysis of bias in history texts, only one of the six American history books he reviewed mentioned that the CIA supported the Islamic fundamentalists in their battle with the Afghan communist government.[8] (The U.S. had a similar history in Iraq. It helped Saddam Hussein gain power in the 1960s and continued to support him when he invaded Iran in 1980.) Supported by American advisors and armed with weapons from the CIA, the fundamentalists took control of the Afghan government, then proceeded to shelter Osama bin Laden and his training camps for terrorists who eventually bombed the World Trade Center, which became our reason for going to war with Afghanistan. But none of this is revealed in most high school history textbooks.

In fact, history textbooks tend to portray our country as peacekeepers around the world, as though our vast armed forces are stationed in 144 countries for altruistic reasons, not for economic or political power. Left out are the multinational interests we protect in oil-rich countries. Instead, our textbooks emphasize the new technologies and products we provide to backward nations. The American way, after all, is to improve living standards in other countries, to promote democracy and to uphold human rights.

Before passing on to other matters, perhaps we should point out that the worst distortions of American history occur in grade school texts and that as students move up in grade level, textbooks become less goody-goody and quite a bit more accurate. The idea, which certainly is not without merit, seems to be that tiny tots are not ready for unvarnished truth and need to be gently introduced into the "facts of life" over time. What we have stressed here is that even in high school, students are provided a dolled-up version of reality, an account that fails to square with the true history of the United States. (Similar remarks apply to the social studies—civics, government, politics—texts about to be discussed.)

---

[8]From the updated version of *Lies My Teacher Told Me*. New York: Touchstone, a division of Simon and Schuster, 2007.

2. TEXTBOOKS AND INDOCTRINATION

The obvious question to ask is why public school textbooks are written in the way just described. There is no easy answer to this question, but one thing is clear: The ultimate purpose of public schools is to educate the young to fit into adult society. This means, first, giving them the knowledge they will need to be productive citizens and, second, inculcating in them the values, attitudes, and practices that will make them good citizens. Education thus inevitably involves a certain amount of indoctrination.[9]

Applying these thoughts to public school textbooks yields some tentative conclusions as to their likely content, conclusions that are borne out by examining these works. The first is that history and social studies texts are bound to distort their material. The history of every nation has its dark spots as well as bright, and no system works the way it is supposed to. Public school history and civics texts therefore inevitably distort their subject matter so as to make "Our Great Nation" appear better than it really is. No society wants disaffected citizens. Embarrassing matters have to be papered over somehow or other; exactly how depends on social and political factors that change from time to time. Today, these factors are more favorable for providing students with greater accuracy and less indoctrination than ever before. (But not all is sweetness and light by any means, as we shall see shortly.)

The second tentative conclusion is that noncontroversial topics, such as mathematics, will be presented in a much more straightforward way than are history and social studies texts, with indoctrination at a minimum. Society wants just about everybody to be able to do arithmetic.

Finally, a third tentative conclusion is that controversial or touchy topics will be approached gingerly, papered over, or simply not discussed at all. Examples include the effects of campaign contributions on the performance of elected officials; most controversial economic issues; and social justice or its lack. As remarked on before, all of these tentative conclusions turn out to be accurate.

An unexpected new trend in education may modify the indoctrination built into American textbooks and, for that matter, the schoolbooks of other countries as well. Education, like big business, is going global. For example, a Swiss-based secondary school program developed by the International Baccalaureate Organization is being used in hundreds of schools throughout the world, and curricula for elementary and middle schools are in the works. Since publishers will be selling to an international community with potentially far more consumers than any single country could provide, textbooks will be much less likely to favor the bias of any one nation. It's worth keeping an eye on this trend.

---

[9] Although the primary intent of the adults who write and adopt public school textbooks is indeed to educate the young of their society, human nature being what it is, they also have other motives: to defend their own collective contribution to the history of their nation and to deny or play down their collective mistakes and misadventures. It's always difficult to notice how this creeps into the content and tone of the works of one's own group, but it becomes more evident when we examine those of other societies.

3. TEXTBOOKS AND POLITICS

When discussing the mass media in the previous chapter, we pointed out how the various interested parties—media owners, governments, big business, readers, and viewers—exert their power both in the political and the business arenas. The textbook arena also is the scene of power encounters, although, as should become evident, the various strengths and roles of the players are modestly different from what they are in the mass media. The players in the textbook political arena are: voters, in particular parents of schoolchildren and organized groups of interested individuals; teachers, educators, and other scholars; and textbook manufacturers. Governments, of course, particularly on the state and local levels, have a large say in the matter, but they more or less act in response to guidance and pressure from the interested parties and in particular to voter demands.

There is nothing new in the fact that politics plays an important role in determining textbook content. It has always played a big role in the field of education. Even the idea of universal literacy was once fought over in the political arena. Until well into the nineteenth century, education in Europe and America was confined to the upper classes, with very few exceptions. Indeed, the dominant upper-class worldview held that the masses of people were easier to control if they remained ignorant. (It also self-servingly held that the lower classes were too loutish to be able to learn to read and write with any facility.) The push for universal literacy began only with the nineteenth-century growth in the size and political power of the middle classes. Textbooks, in fact, themselves are an invention, more or less, of nineteenth-century educators. In Shakespeare's day, for instance, studying the great classical writings and other treatises constituted a relatively large part of grammar school education.

Nineteenth-century textbooks had just as strong a political orientation as those used in schools today. For half a century after the Civil War, southern states insisted on a sympathetic account of their part in the war, whereas northern states demanded inclusion of the South's treason, so publishers came up with the two different versions of the war for their respective clients. After the First World War, patriotic groups like the American Legion and Veterans of Foreign Wars criticized textbooks that failed to arouse patriotic fervor, and ethnic groups insisted that their heroes be included in history books.[10]

In the 1960s and 1970s, the civil rights movement galvanized minority groups to rebel against Eurocentric curriculums dominated by the work of "dead white males." Colleges and universities devised new courses and revised their reading lists to include the work of black authors and to expand the list of women writers. Classes in women's studies and black studies sprang up around the country, followed by a broader range of courses like gay studies and multicultural literature. When a movement begins in colleges and universities, it usually trickles down to high schools and grade schools. Textbooks began to include more African-Americans, more women, and more prominent people from other cultures, though homosexuals remain off limits. As textbooks became more diverse, so did the controversies surrounding them. The "culture wars" (as they came to be known)

---

[10]For more history on textbook bias see Ravitch, Diane. *The Language Police.* New York: Vintage Books, 2003. Chapters 3 and 4.

sparked by these controversies pitted conservative interpretations of traditional values against liberal ones. (In truth, though, most teachers fell somewhere in between.)

These culture wars have continued to the present day. One perennial textbook battleground is Texas, where conservative and liberal board members recently haggled over whether to eliminate Thomas Jefferson, who coined the phrase "separation of church and state," from the history textbook list of great thinkers. They voted against including coverage of the late Senator Edward Kennedy, Hillary Clinton, and Thurgood Marshall (the first black justice)—and voted for adding Phyllis Schlafly (conservative activist), the National Rifle Association, and the Heritage Foundation (a conservative think tank.)[11] These are among the long list of changes to social studies standards that were considered for Texas schools and textbooks—most of them politically driven and most of them reflecting controversies occurring across the country. Like it or not, textbooks are weathervanes of political activities.

How Textbooks Are Selected

In the United States today, textbooks are selected and purchased on the local level. School boards either select the texts to be used or provide teachers and school principals with lists of approved books from which to select. In practice, of course, local boards follow the advice of teachers, except when under political pressure or higher-level direction of the kinds about to be described. Teachers, quite naturally, are influenced in their selection of texts by what they were taught in schools of education, and thus by dominant members of their disciplines. (Similar remarks apply to the way things work in most democratic countries, including Canada and most of the European democracies.)

School boards, elected by the public or appointed by elected officials, tend to be rather vulnerable not only to the advice of teachers and educational theorists but also to lobbying by politically active groups. These groups thus indirectly influence textbook publishers intent on satisfying the requirements of local and state boards. This is perhaps the most important reason for the textbook revisions in the treatment of class, gender, and race briefly described a while back. Publishers today wouldn't dream of using a title like *Man and His Changing World,* to cite a 1930s example, any more than they would illustrate a textbook exclusively with pictures of white, middle-class males. Minority groups with increasing political power are insisting that textbooks reflect more accurately the historical and cultural experiences and contributions of nonwhites, of women, and of other minority groups. Women's rights organizations have successfully reduced the use of sexist language in textbooks, and the hotly debated traditional canon of Western literature has been broadened to include a wider selection of multicultural writers. As noted in the previous section, all of these changes have been politically driven.[12]

---

[11]For a more complete report see Staly, Terrance. "History Teaching Standards Tilt to the Right for Texas High Schoolers." *Dallas Morning News* 16 January 2010.

[12]Of course, as in most cases of this kind, success usually depends on a readiness to change on the part of many ordinary citizens, the point being that perhaps organized groups can succeed only to the extent that the times are ripe, even though, without organized political pressure, little change might take place. In any case, organized political agitation surely was (and is) an important cause of widespread changes in attitude concerning minorities and women.

Nor should we overlook political fights over ideological issues concerning the quality and standards maintained in textbooks. Over the past two decades, the American school system has been intensively scrutinized and extensively criticized. Textbooks have come under fire, in particular, for being dumbed down in both content and linguistic sophistication. Educators are under pressure to raise textbook standards, to standardize content, and to link material to an increasing number of state and national achievement tests.

In times now long gone, funds spent by local boards in America came exclusively from local taxes—chiefly property taxes—and each district controlled its own choice of textbooks. Nowadays, a great deal of school money comes from state coffers, and even from the federal government, with the inevitable consequence that school boards are restricted from above as to their textbook choices. Political power concerning education thus has been dispersed from being almost exclusively local, to spreading to entire states and even, to a lesser extent, to the nation as a whole. Nearly half of the states in America now have state textbook-adoption committees that screen publisher offerings—in particular, those concerning basic or sensitive topics, and books intended for the first six school grades. Local boards in states with textbook committees must choose books from lists approved for adoption within their state. Inevitably, politicking on the state (and to a much lesser extent) national levels increasingly shapes the content of the textbooks from which local boards must choose.

The Power of Big Business

All of this means, by the way, that big business has less power in determining textbook content than it does in shaping the news offered by the mass media. But textbook publishing companies still exert a good deal of power in the textbook arena. State and local boards, after all, are forced to choose from the books offered to them by textbook publishers (whose number grows smaller every year because of the same market-driven forces that have been shrinking the number of mass media outlets). But publishers, in their turn, are guided by the demands of state and local agencies, especially of textbook committees in two key states: California and Texas. (Pressure groups are particularly strong in Texas. And when you consider that almost $500 million was budgeted for textbooks in 2010, you can understand the clout that state has.)[13] That is why the power that publishers derive from their role as commodity supplier is not as large as one might suppose. A textbook that makes neither the California nor the Texas list is going to have a hard time hanging around long enough to find a sufficiently large constituency in other states, and so the major publishers pretty much have been forced to tailor their offerings accordingly. (The very few low-budget books intended for use in a single state or locality are obvious exceptions.) Furthermore, because local boards also generally specify a pool of potential texts from which individual schools in their districts must select, publishers also have had to take these boards' preferences into account. The requirements of big city school boards (remember the extent to which the United States has become an urban society) thus are an important influence on textbook publishers.

---

[13]A state committee in California approves all books used in kindergarten through the eighth grade; in Texas, through grade 12. But California does lay down requirements that all texts used in every grade must meet.

How Authors Influence Textbook Content

Authors and experts in the various fields also inevitably have a say as to textbook content. Although under the thumb of political and market forces of the kind just discussed, authors do generally have scruples concerning truth telling and do tend to be constrained by professional standards. They aren't inclined to stray from the straight and narrow (as they see it!) any more than they are forced to do so. (There no doubt are rotten apples in this barrel, just as in every other, and let's pass over the charge occasionally heard that some authors of public school history and social studies texts do not have a realistic grasp of their subject matter.) But they rarely, if ever, have a genuinely free hand to "write it as they see it." (We also should mention the disgraceful fact that the authors listed on some public school textbooks sometimes have had little or nothing to do with the actual writing of their books.)

Although content is the most important element of textbooks, the clarity, the style, and the author's ability to engage the reader's interest go a long way in making the material palatable. It's little wonder that students' eyes glaze over when the style is turgid, the presentation dull, and the writing unclear. Too often books written by committees fall into this category.

But Students Have Little Influence on Textbook Content

Oh, yes, students also have an indirect say in textbook content, particularly as to style and level of difficulty. Unliked books, or those that are too difficult, tend to be unread books. Teachers want the textbooks they select to be read—indeed, to be studied. Anyway, that's why, in the case of public school textbooks, the term *indoctrination* isn't far off the mark. In the case of the mass media, the ultimate users of the commodity wield great power (as should be evident from the discussion in the last chapter). In the case of public school textbooks, the ultimate users, students, have relatively little say. (But then, most mass media audiences consist of "responsible" adults, while public school textbook audiences are considered to be "just children" or, extrapolating from other currently popular lingo, just "preadults.")

4. CENSORSHIP

It's very difficult to determine in particular cases whether books have been censored, but the earlier discussion about the ways in which local and state boards influence textbook content should make it clear that censorship does occur. Government agencies, from the federal government down to local school boards, do in fact force changes in the content of public school texts (and also nonprint materials). Authors definitely are not free to write the books that they might prefer to; at least they cannot do so with any serious hope of having their efforts published and adopted. Textbook writers these days try very hard to tailor their works so as to be politically correct (more will be said about this shortly), just as, you will recall, do writers in the mass media.

The Controversy Concerning the Teaching of Evolution: An Instructive Example

All controversial topics are subject to censorship, or at least to serious attempts at censorship. The theory of evolution is an especially interesting case because, perhaps more than any other scientific theory, it goes against the grain of many deeply held religious beliefs.

Starting in 1859 with the publication of Charles Darwin's book, *On the Origin of Species,* the theory of evolution has been challenged and denied countless times and for several different reasons. But the most important of these reasons has always been that evolution theory runs counter to literal interpretations of the Old Testament. In a famous 1925 court case, commonly referred to as the "Scopes Monkey Trial," John Scopes was convicted of violating a Tennessee law against the teaching of the theory of evolution in public school classrooms. In more recent times, however, courts have systematically struck down laws like the old Tennessee statute, notably in 1968 when the U.S. Supreme Court declared unconstitutional an Arkansas law that banned the teaching of evolution.

After the 1968 Supreme Court decision, religious fundamentalists invented the theory they call "creation science" in an attempt to make their biblical view at least be taught alongside that of evolution theory in science classes. Creationists believe in the Genesis explanation of God as the architect of the universe and the creator of each species on Earth. They reject the theory of evolution and try to discredit it in the classroom. But in 1987, after several lower court decisions, the U.S. Supreme Court declared creation science to be religious advocacy, not science, and thus not to be taught as science in public school science classes. Although this has dealt a blow to those advocating creationism as science, it has not stopped attempts at state and local levels to flout the law; in fact, creationism is still espoused in some schools where community sentiment is highly in favor of this being done, and evolution theory is slighted in many others because of that pressure. However, because of the Supreme Court's ruling, fundamentalists now often avoid the terms *creation* and *creation science,* and instead use *intelligent design.* Intelligent design holds that life is too complex to be explained by the theory of evolution and therefore must have been created by a higher power as part of a purposeful design, but that power may or may not be the biblical God.

Fundamentalists continue to attempt to picture evolution as just one theory (as the name "theory of evolution" implies to those who don't understand scientific lingo) and to get the biblical account in Genesis taught alongside it. In fairness, it needs to be said that at least some advocates of creation science or intelligent design believe it to be scientific—so, for that matter did the second President Bush, who endorsed the teaching of intelligent design even though it put him at odds with scientific thinking.

Nevertheless, the relative failure of religious fundamentalists in their attempt to counter the teaching of evolution and to get intelligent design taught in science classes has not reduced their efforts. Indeed, in recent years, pressure on state and local school boards and on individual schools has increased, no doubt due to the increase in enthusiasm for fundamentalist religion in the United States (as in many other countries).[14] Americans remain astonishingly resistant to accepting evolution as a bedrock idea of science.[15]

Evolution is often discounted as "just a theory," and, in fact, the concept was extremely controversial in the past. But with the continued gathering of substantiated evidence for 150 years, it has finally been validated. Here is an explanation of why scientists today would accept evolution not merely as a theory, but as an overarching set of principles or laws. *

[T]he concept of evolution is at the law level, as it summarizes the results of a large number of observations or facts about organisms. The analogous theory is natural selection or other means by which evolution is achieved. Unknown nearly 150 years ago to Darwin, explanations of macroscopic evolution in terms of microscopic genes and molecular sequences of nucleic bases in DNA are known to us. Placing the concept of evolution at the law level clarifies its status; it is not a theory.

*Taken from Martin, Bruce and Frances. "Neither Intelligent nor Designed." *Skeptical Inquirer* November–December 2003.

According to a 2009 Pew Research Center poll, nearly one third of Americans believe that human beings and other living things have existed in their current form since the beginning of time (and thus reject or question the theory of evolution) in contrast to 81 percent of scientists who accept evolution as scientific law. Further, a third of Americans believe that there is still scientific debate about the issue, but in fact there is no credible disagreement. Another interesting finding is that two-thirds of the public hold scientists, physicians, and engineers in high esteem—but the feeling isn't mutual. A whopping 85 percent of the scientific community think that Americans' ignorance of science is a major problem—not to mention media coverage of scientific issues, which a large majority rate fair or poor.

This disconnect between the scientific community and social conservatives fuels court battles over evolution that continue to rage in this country. In 2011 alone, seven states proposed nine different bills aimed at undermining the theory of evolution, according to the National Center for Science Education.[16] Often couched as "academic

---

[14]Note, however, that other sorts of books espousing the creationist viewpoint sometimes are used in public schools, especially in states such as Louisiana and Texas, where fundamentalist interpretations of the Bible are widely accepted. Also of interest is the fact that the influence of fundamentalist Jewish and Muslim groups on public school education has been comparatively slight because these groups constitute only a tiny minority in America today.

[15]The survey was conducted by the Pew Research Center for the People and the Press and the American Association for the Advancement of Science (the world's largest science organization).

[16]The National Center for Science Education, a group that defends the teaching of evolution in public schools, keeps close track of developments. This report was from their April 8, 2011 "Anti-evolution Legislation Scorecard."

freedom" bills, they typically allow teachers "to help students understand, analyze, critique, and review. . .the scientific strengths and. . .weaknesses of existing scientific theories"—including evolution. (Tennessee). Or they require a "thorough presentation and critical analysis of scientific theory of evolution." (Florida). Interestingly, the bills died in committee in six states: Florida, Texas, Missouri, Kentucky, Oklahoma, and New Mexico—but not in Tennessee. The law passed in 2012, despite thousands of scientists, educators, and civil libertarians petitioning the governor to veto it.

As many studies have shown, a significant number of high school science teachers do not have a satisfactory grasp of their subject matter, and many teachers believe in creationism and would like to teach it. What is equally troubling is that some teachers who accept Darwin's theory as a scientific law are afraid to teach it for fear of getting into trouble with school administrators and fundamentalist parents. Or they find ways to present evolution obliquely by discussing it without actually mentioning the word or by assigning a chapter on the subject without discussing it in class.

It is worth noting that Darwin himself did not believe that his theory of evolution was antithetical to belief in the existence of a creator. In fact, the last sentence in his classic book *On the Origins of Species* affirms such a belief:

> There is a grandeur in this view of life, with its several powers, having been originally breathed by the Creator into a few forms or into one; and that, whilst this planet has gone cycling on according to the fixed law of gravity, from so simple a beginning endless forms most beautiful and wonderful have been, and are being evolved.

It is difficult to be sure why the very well-organized fundamentalists are not winning more battles than they do, but one reason has to be the pressure exerted by an aroused scientific community, worried that a generation of scientific illiterates will be raised in the United States. Eminent scientists, for example, testified in the court cases mentioned before that creation science is not a science and convinced courts to hold that this is the case. Nevertheless, fundamentalists have not given up the fight by any means and, indeed, have had success at the local level in many places where large numbers of parents do not want students to be taught that evolution theory is a fact. Ah, well, at least we don't convict scientists on the charge of heresy any longer, as the Inquisition did to Galileo for his "heretical" belief that the Earth went around the sun.

Interestingly, religious fundamentalists are largely responsible for one of the improvements in recent public school textbooks—namely, the very modestly improved treatment of the topic of religion in American life. After World War II, and up to just a few years ago, religion tended to get mentioned only in the colonial period, except for accounts of the Mormons' great trek west in the nineteenth century and the inauguration of the first (and so far only) Catholic president, John F. Kennedy, in 1960. Most of the newer texts today provide much more information than that about the role religion has played in American life, even if their accounts still have a bit of the flavor of a token gesture.

Publisher Self-Censorship

Given what has been said so far, it shouldn't come as a surprise that publishers have become exceedingly cautious in the editing of public school textbooks or that they try very hard not to offend powerful special-interest groups. This is especially true with respect to grade school textbooks, as might be expected, because most parents want their children apprised of the harsher realities of life rather slowly. (Few see anything wrong in telling tiny tots that there is a Santa Claus or a tooth fairy.)

This caution on the part of publishers sometimes has rather ludicrous consequences. For example, a West Coast publisher asked one of its illustrators to remove the stem from a picture of a plum because it cast a shadow that might be construed as phallic. Harcourt Brace, a very large textbook publisher, once had an artist remove a mother's apron from a drawing picturing a typical eighteenth-century family scene because the apron was seen to be "demeaning to women." (Never mind that the portrayal was accurate.) Some publishers no longer allow udders on drawings of cows or zippered flies on drawings of little boys' trousers.

In the old days, when Dick and Jane reigned supreme, the world was portrayed as having a gardenlike quality. Slums did not exist, nasty people were restricted to fairy tales, almost everyone was white, and women were primarily pictured as housewives and mothers. The pressures on publishers were different, so the product was different. Textbook publishers inevitably try to make their products be as politically correct as possible; what changes over time is what counts as politically correct.

Currently the most significant source of self-censorship is the bias guidelines issued by every educational publisher. They all conduct bias and sensitivity reviews that regulate the way textbook authors discuss ethnic and minority groups, including women, the disabled, and the elderly, and they respond to both liberal and conservative pressure groups. In one sense, this is understandable, given the strong impetus to eliminate discrimination since the 1960s, but guidelines have gone way beyond their original intent, as Diane Ravitch points out in *The Language Police* (2003), an excellent analysis of test and textbook bias. Here are a few examples she cites to give you the flavor of constraints placed on authors. (These are drawn from the Scott Foresman-Addison Wesley and McGraw-Hill guidelines.)[17]

Writers must include women in equal numbers with men in both the text and illustrations (despite the fact that men have dominated Western culture up to and including much of the twentieth century—like it or not). But they must avoid such stereotypes as passive, weak, gentle, illogical, short, or emotional women and active, strong, brave, logical, tall, or unemotional men. Sexist terms like *sissy, tomboy, lady, hen-pecked husband,* and *forefathers* are out. Disabled people must never be referred to as "the disabled" but as "people with disabilities." The blind and the deaf should be called "people who are blind" and "people who are deaf," and midgets and dwarfs are "people of small stature." But it's just as bad to call someone "normal" or "able-bodied"; the correct term, instead, is "a person without disabilities" or "a person who is nondisabled"!

The discussion of ethnic and racial groups is closely monitored as well. Writers must present "a fair and balanced representation" of racial, ethnic, and gender groups in text and illustrations. Here is a random sampling. Authors cannot refer to "primitive cultures" because there are no primitive cultures. African tribes have been replaced by ethnic groups, and they don't live in huts but in little houses. Illustrators must not draw African-Americans in loud colors or prints, straw hats, and white suits—or in middle-class

---

[17]Above, note 10. See Chapter 12 of *The Language Police* for a full account of these bias and sensitivity reviews.

In The Mad, Mad World of Textbook Adoption, *Chester Finn, Jr., and Diane Ravitch have this to say about the Alice-In-Wonderland world of textbook guidelines:*

Textbooks are now judged not by their style, content, or effectiveness, but by the way they live up to absurd sensitivity guidelines. Do literary anthologies have more male than female story characters? Do textbooks portray stereotypes such as female nurses or male mechanics? Do history textbooks suggest that religious strife has been a cause of conflict in human history? Do they mention junk food, magic, or prayer; suggest that the old are wise or the young are vigorous; or leave out any ethnic, racial, or religious group, no matter how small? If they do, that is grounds to have a textbook rejected.

clothes. They can't show these people in tenements and bright cars or in "dull, white picket-fence neighborhoods." Given these constraints, one wonders how African-Americans *can* be depicted, or for that matter, why anyone would want to write a text-book to begin with (except, of course, the intrepid authors of this text).

Even science textbooks are skewed by politically correct bias. In *Life Science,* a middle school biology textbook, Navajo physicist Fred Begay rates a half-page discussion on his study of Navajo medicine, but no mention is made of Nobel Laureates James Watson, Maurice H. F. Wilkins, or Francis Crick—the co-discoverers of DNA. In *Discovery Works,* a fifth-grade science textbook, students wade through three pages of Algonquin Indian myths about season changes before they find out that the tilt and rotation of the Earth affect climate change—not the migration of crows. In distortions like these, the scientifically sound sinks under the weight of the politically correct.[18]

Nontextbooks Also Often Are Censored

Books that are not explicitly textbooks often are subjected to censorship. The censor in most of these cases is the local school board, but state boards have been getting into the act in recent years.

Almost any kind of book may be censored, but most that are contain passages alleged to be obscene, racially or ethnically biased, slighting or demeaning of women, or they provide a favorable portrayal of a lifestyle claimed to be immoral. A Tennessee county school board, for example, removed the old standby *Drums Along the Mohawk,* by Walter D. Edmonds, from an assigned list because it contained words judged to be obscene, such as *hell* and *damn.* Shakespeare's *The Merchant of Venice* is sometimes censored because Jewish groups object to its portrayal of Shylock, and a New Hampshire school banned *Twelfth Night* because it violated a school board ruling that prohibited alternative lifestyle instruction. (Viola, the heroine, is disguised as a boy who inadvertently becomes romantically entangled with another woman, Olivia.)

---

[18]Examples taken from Winnick, Pamela R. "A Textbook Case of Junk Science." *Weekly Standard* 9 May 2005.

A bit sillier was the removal from California's annual English exam list for tenth graders of the short story "Am I Blue," by Pulitzer Prize-winning author Alice Walker—removed primarily because it was "anti-meat-eating." But perhaps silliest of all, surely the most ironic, is the fact that one of the most frequently censored books is *The Adventures of Huckleberry Finn.* Sam Clemens would have been amused, but not surprised. The Clemens classic has two groups on its back: fundamentalists and others offended by its portrayal of religion and by the way Huck flouts conventional morality, and African-Americans offended by its portrayal of Negroes and by the racist language it puts into the mouths of bigoted slave owners. A recent effort to sanitize the book was a new edition that got rid of the n-word. In its place the word "slave" was used—219 times! As might be expected, the revision set off a storm of controversy over meddling with a classic, but it had its defenders, who were uncomfortable using the racial slur. Probably no other book in our literature has been so continuously controversial as *Huck Finn.* Irony of ironies: One of the schools that has censored *Huck Finn* turns out to be Mark Twain Intermediate School in Fairfax County, Virginia. Censoring *Huck Finn* is ironic, of course, because Clemens intended his great work to expose the evils of slavery—precisely what civil rights groups today want every American to remember.

It would be provincial, however, to conclude that public school book censoring is a uniquely American phenomenon. On the contrary, this sort of censorship, like most other kinds, is less frequent and less severe in the United States than in most, perhaps all, other countries. Every nation dolls up its past, for the same reasons that we do so in the United States, and many censor on religious grounds or out of a sense of propriety. In Germany, starting after World War II and continuing to a lesser extent until the mid-1990s, history texts have understandably played down the atrocities committed by Germans during that most horrible of all wars—so far!—and teachers still sometimes engage in their own kind of censorship by simply never quite finding sufficient time to cover that period in German history adequately. Similar remarks, incidentally, apply more or less to the teaching of Japanese history in Japan. And Soviet texts didn't bother to mention the millions killed by the Soviets during Stalin's reigns of terror or the smaller but still extremely large number of people worked to death in Siberia even after his death.

Needless to say, authoritarian regimes have absolute control over the education of their young. Before Saddam Hussein was ousted, schoolbooks in Iraq were vehicles for Baathist party propaganda. History books traced the dictator's ancestry back to a cousin of the prophet Muhammad and compared him to great leaders of the past. His quotes were sprinkled throughout math texts, and his name was incorporated into English primers in birthday greetings and songs to Father Saddam. Iraqi teachers are now at work deleting this garbage from their schoolbooks.

Although the censoring of books outside public schools' walls (and also most schools that are church sponsored) always has been, and still is, much less common than it is within these walls, it does occur, and this obviously limits what students as well as adults can read. Favorite targets are books with sexual content and those affecting national security.

In the long history of censorship, however, all sorts of books have been banned. Way back in 1526, the first English translation of the New Testament was banned and

*The number of books and magazines censored out of public school classrooms and libraries runs into the thousands every year. Here are a few striking examples:**

Of Mice and Men (John Steinbeck)
The Sun Also Rises (Ernest Hemingway)
The Catcher in the Rye (J. D. Salinger)
The Grapes of Wrath (John Steinbeck)
Look Homeward Angel (Thomas Wolfe)
The Invisible Man (Ralph Ellison)
Native Son (Richard Wright)
Brave New World (Aldous Huxley)
Slaughterhouse Five (Kurt Vonnegut, Jr.)
To Kill a Mockingbird (Harper Lee)
The Naked Ape (Desmond Morris)
I Know Why the Caged Bird Sings (Maya Angelou)
(The *American Heritage Dictionary* was banned because it includes "gutter words" like *ball, nut,* and *tail* and cites certain uses of the term *bed* as a transitive verb.)

Oh, yes. Perhaps in an attempt to prove that George Orwell is the Nostradamus of the twentieth century, lots of school districts have banned use of . . . 1984.

*See the American Library Association's *Newsletter on Intellectual Freedom.*

[W]hen American scholars talk about . . . Soviet texts which blatantly indoctrinate, they are called brainwashing. When our own texts are biased, prejudiced, one-sided and unfair, it is called "transmitting a favorable view of our democracy."

—S. Samuel Shermis

---

printed copies burned; in Spain, a similar fate awaited the first translation into Spanish. Indeed, the Bible may be the most censored book in history. For decades, *Lysistrata, Canterbury Tales, Decameron, Moll Flanders,* and versions of the *Arabian Nights* were banned from U.S. mails under the Federal Anti-Obscenity Act (the Comstock Law of 1873), and *Fanny Hill,* the story of a prostitute told with explicit sexual descriptions, has been suppressed on and off since its publication in 1749. D. H. Lawrence's *Lady Chatterley's Lover* was in and out of obscenity trials until the 1960s, and James Joyce's *Ulysses,* voted the best novel of the twentieth century by the Modern Library, was banned in this country for 11 years (1922–1933) because of its obscenities.

In the 1980s, censorship focused more on sex and swear words, but as we moved into the new millennium, the emphasis switched to witchcraft and wizardry. For several years, the Harry Potter series headed the American Library Association's list of most challenged (that is, banned) books. Although most readers enjoy as fantasy the tales of sorcerers and magic spells, some take them literally as corrupting forces of evil; others are concerned about the clash between Christianity and witchcraft, still others by the depiction of family dysfunction and violence. For several years, though, Harry Potter has dropped off the list. The big winner from 2006–2010 was *And Tango Makes Three*, a true story about two male penguins in the Central Park zoo who were given a penguin chick to raise. (You can guess why that one was censored.) Authors must love it when their books are banned. *And Tango Makes Three* surged in popularity once it made the banned book hit list. But suddenly that one dropped out of sight when the *ttyl* series topped the 2011 list. A young adult novel written in the style of instant messaging conversation, it ranked first because of sexual content and offensive language. If fairy tales were as popular now as the *ttly* series, they'd probably be banned too. (In fact, they have been cleaned up over the years—for example, in Grimm's version of "Cinderella," her mean stepsisters were brutally punished at the end when pigeons plucked out their eyes in the wedding procession. How many kids hear that version today?)[19]

EXERCISE 12-1

A school superintendent from Burlingame, California stopped eighth-grade classes from reading *Kaffir Boy,* by Mark Mathabane, when a parent complained that her child was disturbed by the subject matter. The award-winning memoir describes the author's experience growing up in South Africa when blacks had no civil rights and were brutally treated. (The word *kaffir* is a highly offensive racial slur.) The controversial section includes two paragraphs describing grown men preparing to rape young boys in exchange for giving them all the food they could eat, a powerful incentive since the boys lived in poverty and were desperate for food. In the memoir, Mathabane ran away, and as a consequence, the other boys shunned him. The point of the story, he explained, was to show that "resisting peer pressure is one of the toughest things for young people to do," and he was concerned that "it's a lesson that seems to be lost on people who want to censor my book." But given the graphic nature of the paragraphs in question, the superintendent considered it inappropriate for eighth graders. (Story reported in Asimov, Nanette. "Burlingame Schools Pull 8th-Grade Book from Class." *San Francisco Chronicle* 12 April 2007.)

What would you do if you were the parent of a 13-year-old eighth grader? Would you want the book censored or not? Or would you take the middle road and allow the book to be taught as long the controversial section was deleted? Write an argument defending your position.

---

[19]For more examples see "Frequently Challenged Books of the 21st Century." *Banned Books.* American Library Association. Web. www.ala.org/advocacy/banned/frequentlychallenged/21stcenturychallenged

5. TEXTBOOKS FAIL TO GIVE STUDENTS GENUINE UNDERSTANDING

From what has been said so far, it should be clear that public school textbooks fail to give students a true understanding of the history and workings of their society. They, and schools in general, fail to orient students in space and time—fail to help them understand how life is different from place to place and, in particular, from one time to another. These failures are due primarily to defects in style and content of the kinds we have been at pains to describe—defects, we have suggested, that result from the various forces at work shaping the finished products, in particular, conflicting pressures from interested social groups.

But it is important to understand that these defects do not result from something peculiar to the American system. The textbooks of any democratic society are bound to reflect the different opinions and interests of its citizens. To have it otherwise would be to surrender control of this important part of our lives to others, as is the case in most authoritarian societies around the world. While fighting to make textbooks better than they are today, we should not forget how much they have improved since, say, the authors of this college text went to school (eons ago, when dinosaurs still roamed the Earth).

One final comment. The praise that has been somewhat begrudgingly given to today's public school textbooks[20] in this chapter should not cloud the fact that the writers of this college text do not care for the large doses of indoctrination they contain. This text was written in a completely different spirit. A student who accepts its contents uncritically, without thinking carefully about the subjects discussed, has missed its main point, which is that in important or controversial matters, free men and women must become their own experts, or at least must be able to judge for themselves the opinions and advice of those who call themselves experts. The success of a free society depends on an informed and thinking electorate, not on an indoctrinated one. To that end, we have stressed the importance of thinking critically by avoiding fallacious reasoning, overcoming impediments to rational thought, and bringing to bear good background knowledge when dealing with important sources of information like textbooks. Eternal vigilance in critical thinking is the price of liberty.

6. POSTSCRIPT ON COLLEGE TEXTS

The question naturally arises about college textbooks: Do they distort American history and practice as do public school texts? Do science texts fudge in their portrayal of evolution theory? If the forces at work are the same with respect to college as public school texts, we should expect the results to be roughly the same (taking into account the

---

[20]The history and social studies books used in private schools are, with rare exceptions, quite similar to those discussed here, except for some of the textbooks used in schools run by organized churches. Of course, in some of the very best private schools, original sources—books intended for adult readers—are more in evidence than are texts designed explicitly for schoolroom use. (Yes, the schools attended by the offspring of the rich are indeed better than the ones the rest of us are subjected to.)

If you're still wondering whether all that much progress has occurred in textbook quality in recent years, this snippet from a really bad textbook still in circulation as late as 1970 should provide a bit of evidence:

As you ride up beside the Negroes in the field they stop working long enough to look up, tip their hats and say, "Good morning, Master John." You like the friendly way they speak and smile; they show bright rows of white teeth. "How's it coming, Sam?" your father asks one of the old Negroes. "Fine, Marse Tom, jes fine. We got more cotton than we can pick." Then Sam chuckles to himself and goes back to picking as fast as he can.

—Mentioned in *The New Republic* 25 July 1970; the book's title is best omitted here.

If that sort of writing doesn't make every current textbook look wonderfully good, nothing will.

greater maturity of college students). If they aren't, we should expect the finished products to be different. What do our worldviews tell us about this question?

Note first that the publishers of college texts have exactly the same motives as those who produce public school textbooks. In fact, most publishers in one field also publish in the other. Second, most college texts are adopted by the teachers who will use them in their own classes (or, in the case of courses having several sections, by group faculty decisions), not by school boards or state agencies. (Students buy them but can't choose which ones to buy.)

The reason for this important difference is the history and the current funding of higher education in the United States as compared to primary and secondary education. Primary and secondary school traditions are largely "homegrown" and intended for a mass audience. Public school teachers have always had their rights to academic freedom infringed upon by local school boards or, more accurately, never had such rights. Teachers who express controversial opinions in the classroom have little legal protection and may be fired if school administrators consider their opinions inappropriate. Although individual cases have been appealed, so far, the federal courts have ruled consistently that teachers do not have free speech rights in grade school or high school classrooms.

American colleges and universities evolved on the model of their European counterparts (chiefly in Germany and England), which were intended for an elite clientele. Professors, at least, were granted a great deal of academic freedom. (They were, of course, more constrained under monarchical systems, and professorial freedoms were nonexistent during the Nazi period in Germany and, to a lesser extent, during the Fascist period in Italy.) The result of transplanting this tradition to the United

States, the freest Western society, has been academic freedom for almost all faculty members; thus, college teachers have always had the privilege of selecting the books they and their students will use.[21] It follows, then, as night follows day, that college textbook publishers will try to produce books that please college teachers—their potential adopters.

College teachers, however, do not operate in a vacuum. They, too, have an audience to consider—their students—and many students, unfortunately, are not as well prepared to do college work as typical students were, say, 40 years ago. (This obviously tends to be less true of students in "elite" colleges and universities.) A recent federal study done by the National Center for Education Statistics found that only 31 percent of college graduates are able to read and understand complex prose passages—almost 10 percent less than college grads in 1992. One reason for this fact is that a larger proportion of young people go to college today than in times past, when only brighter students (and a few who were merely rich) went to college. Other reasons, not fully understood yet, are that students read less now, watch more TV, and learn to read and write on computers, which involve a different kind of literacy. But a contributing factor, often overlooked, is that more and more students have become victims of the dumbing down of grade school and high school texts mentioned a while back and find it difficult to comprehend some of the more high-powered college texts. They are more easily intimidated by thick books or those written in past centuries in a dense or a different style. College teachers, being human, often react (consciously or unconsciously) to the problem this raises by selecting textbooks and works of literature that are relatively brief and more easily understood. Reading lists have been shortened; books perceived as "weighty tomes" tend to get neglected in introductory courses.[22]

Anyway, college texts, wherever they may rest on an absolute scale, are genuinely unlike their public school counterparts. College teachers want widely differing textbook content and levels of difficulty, creating a market in which all sorts of views and qualities find a constituency. College texts even tend to be less dull than their lower-level counterparts, a happy note on which to end this particular—immensely interesting, entertaining, and completely unbiased—college textbook.

---

[21]More precisely, almost all *tenured* faculty members. Nontenured faculty still have to worry about offending those who determine who will be rehired and who "terminated." This benefit of the tenure system often is overlooked but is of great importance. (Nontenured faculty also usually are paid a good deal less than the tenured variety. But that is a topic for another time, another class.)

[22]There also is the fact that what is "in" at one time may well become "out" at another; textbook selection tends to reflect these changes, especially the dramatic changes in course offerings. Forty-five years ago, for example, there were no courses in critical reasoning. Most schools required courses in formal logic, usually taught in philosophy or math departments, and these obviously did deal with the principles of good conclusion drawing. Critical reasoning was taught by English department instructors primarily in the context of the writing of argumentative essays. That is why there was only one true critical reasoning textbook (Monroe Beardsley's *Thinking Straight*, mentioned in Chapter 7) in common use prior to *Logic and Contemporary Rhetoric*'s appearance on the scene in 1971.

SUMMARY OF CHAPTER 12

Public school textbooks in America have improved a great deal in the past 30 years or so.

1. History and social studies texts are more accurate in their portrayal of minorities and women and in the way in which they deal with the dark side of the social system and history of the United States. But textbooks still are written in a dull, one-fact-after-another style that makes true understanding, and also retention of specific facts, quite difficult. They also have reflected the general dumbing down that has occurred in public schools and colleges during the past several years.

2. History texts tend to bombard students with almost endless lists of forgettable facts that tend to bury important information. They also distort reality so as to satisfy the various interested pressure groups and to mold students into good, loyal citizens. They portray American presidents and heroes in a one-sided manner (for instance, not mentioning the vicious, bloodthirsty side of President Theodore Roosevelt). They also exaggerate the American role in world affairs (as in World War II) and play down the nasty side of U.S. history. *Example:* Putting down the Filipino attempt to gain independence.

3. The ultimate purpose of public schools is to educate the young to fit into the adult world. Textbooks are intended to provide students with the knowledge they will need to be productive citizens and to inculcate the values, customs, and attitudes of the society as a whole. (That is why it is accurate to speak of indoctrination.)

   We can expect, then, that noncontroversial topics will be presented in a more or less straightforward manner, while topics that are controversial, or sensitive—in particular, those connected to the history and social practices of society—will tend to pull punches and portray matters in the best light possible.

4. Just as in the case of the mass media, politics enters into the textbook business. Because they are a commodity, textbooks are written so as to satisfy potential buyers, which means primarily local school boards, state agencies, and the professional educators who are empowered to make selections. Political considerations enter in at every level—local, state, and national.

   Although the details change from time to time, there is nothing new in this intrusion of politics into the educational arena. Even the very idea of public school education is political, there being no public schools whatsoever in the United States until some time in the nineteenth century.

   Big business, of course, has some power over textbook content, but less than it does, say, concerning how the news is presented in the mass media. But it does have some power, including power derived from its ability to lobby state legislatures and local school boards.

   The most important of the state agencies concerned with textbook selection are those of California and Texas.

5. Pressure groups have been rather successful—indeed, sometimes oversuccessful—with respect to their demands that textbooks be politically correct by increasing coverage of minorities, women, and religion in American history and life, leading publishers to tailor their products to fit expected pressure-group preferences. Many of these demands have been incorporated into bias guidelines that are the most significant source of self-censorship for educational publishers. But attempts to have discussions of creation science or intelligent design included in biology texts, either alone or alongside evolution theory, on the whole have not been successful.

   It should be noted that nontextbooks also sometimes are censored by public schools, including classic works of literature (by such writers as Ernest Hemingway, Mark Twain, and more recently J. K. Rowling for the Harry Potter series) as well as dictionaries listing four-letter words.

6. The result is that textbooks fail to provide students with genuine understanding or even, because of their dull styles and piling on of facts, knowledge of particular facts that is retained for any length of time. They do, however, reflect what organized groups and professional educators want students to read, which is as it should be in a democratic society.

7. But college texts, having a different sort of clientele, are different. (Vive la difference.)

EXERCISE 12-2

Look through a high school or college textbook for examples of the following types of hidden bias:

1. Pictures in the text that either reflect a bias (like photos dominated by Caucasians) or portray multiracial groups but devote little discussion to them in the text.

2. Gender, ethnic, or racial stereotypes like women described as caregivers or men as strong, successful professionals.

3. Exclusion of groups such as Latinos or people with disabilities or members of non-Christian religions.

4. Sexist or slanted language that subtly conveys a bias.

Describe the examples you found and explain the biases they reveal.

EXERCISE 12-3

1. Here is a famous quote by Northrop Frye: "Censorship is to dissent (and democracy) what lynching is to justice." Evaluate this quote, in particular, discussing the charge that it contains a fallacy.

2. Here is a (fortunately) much less famous quote by Mel Gabler, of Educational Research Analysis (a pressure group that has had success, particularly in Texas):

"When a student reads in a math book that there are no absolutes, suddenly every value he's been taught is destroyed. And the next thing you know, the student turns to crime and drugs."

    a. What is Gabler's (unstated) point? What is he advocating, and why?

    b. Evaluate his argument, again considering the charge that his reasoning is fallacious.

3. The Alabama State Education Department required that the following disclaimer be included in all biology texts used in Alabama public schools that include an account of evolution and evolutionary theory:

> This textbook discusses evolution, a controversial theory some scientists present as a scientific explanation for the origin of living things, such as plants, animals, and humans. No one was present when life first appeared on the earth; therefore any statement about life's origins should be considered as theory, not fact.

Critically evaluate this disclaimer.

EXERCISE 12-4

1. At what point in their educational careers do you think students are ready to be taught the biological facts concerning human sex and reproduction? Or do you think these topics should not be broached in public schools? Defend your answers.

2. It has been forcefully argued that very young children are tender shoots who need to find out the bad features of their society (as of life in general) rather gradually, so that it would be wrong to tell them too quickly that quite a few presidents (including such "heroes" as Franklin Roosevelt and John Kennedy) had mistresses, or that America's history is filled with nasty deeds and steeped in blood and conquest. The point of these arguments is that we don't want to destroy the pride and loyalty of the young, and we don't want to make future citizens into cynics.

    a. Do you agree or disagree with this line of reasoning? Defend your answer.

    b. Does it tend to undercut one of the themes of this chapter—that less indoctrination means better education?

    c. At what age, if ever, should students be given a completely accurate and balanced account of these matters?

    d. It has been argued that, in a society such as exists today in the United States, where several religions flourish and there is no single moral code accepted by all, public schools should not attempt to teach students about alleged values, customs, or traditions of the culture. What is your opinion on this question and, of course, why do you think so?

*3. Does the term *creation science* ring a bell with respect to a topic discussed in Chapter 7? Explain.

4. Recall how the Boston Massacre was described in your history textbooks back in high school. Then look up that event in a first-rate history book and describe the differences. (Hint: If there are no differences, either your high school history text was the best ever published, or your memory is poor or your new source is not a first-rate book.)

5. Evaluate the following argument:

> Because evolution cannot be reproduced in the laboratory, it should not be taught as though it is the only theory believed by sane individuals concerning the origins of life on Earth.

EXERCISE 12-5

Here is Lewis Lapham in a *Harper's* magazine essay (August 2000) explaining why he believes that today's public schools are as poor as he thinks they are:

> Why . . . do the public schools continue to decay . . . [?] Possibly because the condition of the public schools is neither an accident nor a mistake. The schools as presently constituted serve the interests of a society content to define education as a means of indoctrination and a way of teaching people to know their place. We have one set of schools for the children of the elite, another for children less fortunately born, and why disrupt the seating arrangement with a noisy shuffling of chairs? Serious reform of the public schools would beg too many questions about racial prejudice, the class system, the division of the nation's spoils. A too-well-educated public might prove more trouble than it's worth, and so we mask our tacit approval of an intellectually inferior result with the declarations of a morally superior purpose. . . .

What do you think of some of Lapham's claims, for instance, that we have a two-tiered school system, that issues concerning racial prejudice and our class system (is there one?) intrude, and that there is tacit approval of the intellectually inferior result?

*EXERCISE FOR THE ENTIRE TEXT

This text, like all others, is based on certain presuppositions (only some made explicit) and no doubt contains fallacious reasoning, in spite of the authors' best efforts to reason cogently. So, as the final exercise, write a brief critique of this textbook with respect to (1) its major presuppositions (that is, the worldviews of the authors as stated or implied in the text); (2) possible fallacious arguments; (3) biased selections of material; and (4) rhetorical devices used to persuade readers to accept the authors' opinions on this or that. (Be sure to defend your findings, including examples to back up your claims.)

---

*Starred (*) items are answered in a section at the back of the book.

Appendix: More on Cogent Reasoning

The object of reasoning is to find out, from the consideration of what we already know, something else which we do not know.
—Charles Sanders Peirce

A simple person believes every word he hears; a clever one understands the need for proof.
—Proverbs 14:15

1. More on Cause and Effect

In Chapter 1, we said a few words about how inductive reasoning is used to discover causal relationships—to discover how one thing causes another. But just as in the case of most interesting concepts, that of causation is really a cluster of related concepts, mostly with blurred edges. When we call one thing the cause of another, we can mean simply the *sufficient condition* for bringing it about. In this sense, the cause of Marie Antoinette's death was being guillotined—having one's head cut off certainly suffices to bring about death.

On the other hand, we often mean by the cause of a thing or event whatever is a *necessary condition* for bringing it about. Striking a match on a rough surface (thus heating it) can be thought of, for example, as a necessary condition of the lighting of a match, even though it is only part of what must be true for the effect—the lighting of the match—to occur. It is a necessary condition, but not a sufficient condition: Matches also need to be dry and struck in the presence of oxygen if they are to light. Being in the presence of oxygen and being dry and being heated together constitute both the necessary and the sufficient conditions for a match to light.

The point here is that, even though striking a match (heating it) cannot alone cause a match to light, we still in everyday life talk as though striking a match is what makes it light. It usually makes perfectly good sense to say, for instance, that the match lit because it was struck on a rough surface (which heats the match to the required temperature), even though a match struck on a rough surface in a vacuum will not light (because of a lack of oxygen). But we would not say, for example, that it lit because it was in the presence of oxygen. The difference, roughly speaking, is *human agency*—in everyday life, it's easy to make a match light by striking it (heating it), but we can't usually make it light by providing oxygen. (For one thing, the oxygen already is there; for another, the match still won't light because ordinary air temperatures are too low.)

Also of interest is the fact that we sometimes need to distinguish between *proximate causes* and those that are more *remote*. Suppose that a truck jackknifes on an icy highway, blocking three of four lanes, and that an auto, call it auto *A*, has to swerve into the unblocked lane and that another auto, *B*, then crashes into auto *A*. The ice on the road would be said to be the proximate cause of the truck's jackknifing but a much more remote cause of the accident between autos *A* and *B*.

The difference between proximate and remote causes can be important in everyday life, in particular in legal cases. Clearly, auto *A*'s swerving into the last unblocked lane is a proximate cause of the crash between *A* and *B*, yet the driver of *A* may well not be held responsible, since his need to go into that lane was caused by more remote events. The guilty party more likely will be held to be the driver of the truck for driving without sufficient care on an icy highway.

This example brings to mind the fact that, in everyday life, a given effect can be explained in terms of more than one cause. Which one we select usually depends on our particular interest in that effect. In assessing blame, say, in the case of a knife murder, we don't care about the neural and muscular causes of the murderer's arm movement, but we do care very much about his having consciously willed to do the act. A biologist, on the other hand, might be very interested indeed in neural firings in the guilty party's body, and in a court of law might well testify to neural and muscular causes of the knife blow. So it makes sense to say either that the willing caused the event or that the neural firings and muscle contractions did so.[1]

2. SCIENTIFIC METHOD

Scientific method is just common sense writ large, sharpened, fine-tuned, and applied (in the best cases) with creative persistence and patience. There is nothing mysterious or impenetrable about how scientists go about justifying their hypotheses.

Common sense requires that beliefs about the nature of the world be justified, more or less, by cogent arguments, as discussed in earlier chapters. Scientists have no other way, no magic formulas or wands, for coming to justified beliefs about the nature of the world. Science's "secret" lies in the persistent accumulation of knowledge by thousands (now literally millions) of practitioners who have required of each other the elimination so far as is possible of the shoddy, wishful thinking that peppers everyday reasoning. The rules of the scientific game force scientists to reject unjustified theories[2] and to give up their most cherished ideas when experience shows that they are false (or unsupported by good evidence).

---

[1]For more on causation and related matters, see Hausman, Alan, Kahane, Howard, and Tidman, Paul. *Logic and Philosophy*. 12th edition. Boston: Wadsworth, Cengage Learning, 2013.

[2]Scientists use the terms *theory* and *hypothesis* in at least two ways. In one sense, both of these terms refer to untested speculations or to insufficiently confirmed patterns. In another, they refer to well-established, well-confirmed, and accepted patterns. The second sense is synonymous with the expressions "scientific law" and "law of nature."

Typical scientific theories result from a complicated mixture of deductive and inductive arguments, but the key arguments are inductive. Good scientists try to find *patterns* in what they have observed so far, in particular in their scientific experiments,[3] and project these patterns via inductive reasoning to larger slices of reality. In everyday life, common sense reasons by inductions from past experiences that sugar sweetens, vinegar sours, bread nourishes, and drought kills crops. Scientists, using the same commonsense methods, but much more persistently and stringently, conclude that copper conducts electricity, cigarette smoking causes cancer, the Earth's path around the sun is an ellipse, and radioactive substances have half-lives. (They also, of course, use viewing instruments they have learned to construct by means of inductive reasoning—telescopes, microscopes, X-ray machines, and so on—that we ordinarily don't have at our disposal in daily life.)

So science is just the accumulated knowledge gained by huge numbers of individuals observing nature, proposing theories (patterns) that explain what has been observed, and testing by additional observations to confirm their theories (hypotheses). When scientists claim to have discovered a new pattern, others will try to duplicate their findings; when they succeed, a theory tends to be accepted into the scientific canon; when they cannot successfully duplicate the findings, a theory will be discarded, or at least modified so as to take account of what has been learned by the failure to confirm. It is this that distinguishes science from pseudoscience: A scientific theory predicts what will be experienced under certain conditions; if it is not experienced, the theory must be rejected or revised to conform to what has been discovered. Those who believe in pseudosciences—for example, extrasensory perception—cling to theories that are disconfirmed by experience and that do not make successful predictions about what will be experienced in the future.

Speaking of pseudoscience brings to mind the fact that a truly scientific theory must conform not just to evidence directly supporting it but also indirectly to all scientific theories whatsoever. Pseudosciences, on the other hand, never conform to the whole body of scientific knowledge or even, sometimes, to ordinary everyday thoughts. Creation science, for example, asserts that all human beings except for Noah and his family perished about 5,000 or so years ago in the biblical flood. This means that all of the human genetic variety we see today—all racial differences—must have evolved in just a few thousand years from the common Noah family stock, and this contradicts everything we know about how human beings, or any mammals, evolve and propagate. So anyone who accepts creation science on this point must reject virtually everything known about genetics, along with a great deal of the rest of modern biology.

Note, by the way, that failure to confirm a proposed scientific theory does not mean that the attempt to do so was of no value. On the contrary, failure can be very revealing; indeed, it often is more enlightening than success. For example, the failure of experiments conducted in the 1880s to prove the existence of an "ether," believed in those days

---

[3]A scientific experiment is just a kind of deliberately arranged experience. Instead of waiting for an event to happen, scientists arrange for it to happen, perhaps in their laboratories. For instance, they may mix two chemicals in the laboratory that rarely, if ever, are found mixed in nature, to see the result. But whether an event is "found" in the laboratory or found in "nature" is irrelevant to scientific procedure.

by scientists to be the medium through which light (and other electromagnetic waves) traveled through space, led to a crisis in Newtonian physics that was finally resolved by Einstein's special theory of relativity. So, in a sense, one of the most important scientific advances of the twentieth century grew out of the failure to confirm a previously widely accepted scientific theory.

Students often misunderstand this aspect of scientific investigation. They often object, for example, to biological research done on animals because what works with respect to other animals frequently does not do so in the case of human beings; students often see this as proof that animals were made to suffer with no offsetting increase in knowledge about how human diseases can be conquered. They don't understand that failures of this kind may lead investigators away from a wrong path and on to a right one. (They also often overlook the many cases in which, say, drugs that work well on close mammalian relatives also do so when tried on human beings.) Note, by the way, that those who champion pseudosciences generally do not learn from failures to confirm their theories; they tend simply to sweep this sort of counterevidence under the nearest metaphorical rug.

Pseudoscientists also tend to ignore ways in which their theories run counter to simple facts and ideas about how things work that we all hold in everyday life. Creation science, for example, fails to take account of what we all know about the abundance of species in today's world. There are thousands of mammal species, thousands of bird species, thousands of amphibian and reptilian species, and millions of insect species, all of which could not have fit into one ark that even today's technology might with great effort construct. So even forgetting that lions can't be expected to lie down with lambs; forgetting that the ark would have had to be stocked with an incredible amount and variety of food and water so animals would not starve or dehydrate; forgetting that literally millions of plant species would have had to be collected; forgetting the physical impossibility of Noah and his family going around the world to collect all of these animals and plants and food; forgetting about bacteria and viruses; and forgetting fussy details about getting rid of huge amounts of fecal material, it should be clear that the creation science story violates not just dozens of extremely well-confirmed, high-powered scientific theories, but also all kinds of everyday ideas about how the world works, *while predicting nothing about what sorts of (earthly!) experiences the future may hold for us!* The scientific theory of evolution, on the other hand, is consistent with every other well-confirmed scientific theory and has predicted all sorts of things that have been and continue to be discovered to be true, including how and where fossils might be found, and so on.

Finally, let's take a look at a rather simple and truly scientific theory—the "sea-of-air" hypothesis—and at how scientists test and confirm their hypotheses. The theory was proposed by the seventeenth-century mathematician and physicist Evangelista Torricelli, a disciple of Galileo. It was well known then that water can be pumped from a well only from a maximum of about a depth of 34 feet (without the aid of auxiliary power); Torricelli proposed to explain this and other facts by his theory that a sea of air surrounds the surface of the Earth and presses down on it because of the force of gravity, just as water presses down on something at the bottom of the ocean. Pumps thus can raise water from a well (at most) to a height of about 34 feet, Torricelli theorized, because of this *air pressure.*

Torricelli's theory can be, and was, confirmed by performing several different sorts of experiments. For instance, if the limit that water can be pumped from a well is about 34 feet, and if mercury is about 14 times heavier than water (it is), then if the sea-of-air theory is correct, it follows that air pressure will hold up a column of mercury only $\frac{1}{14}$ as high as a column of water. So we can confirm the sea-of-air hypothesis by constructing a mercury device (we call these things *barometers*) and finding that this is the case. Torricelli's followers also confirmed his theory by testing at higher-than-sea-level elevations where, according to the sea-of-air theory, a column of mercury should be held up a lesser amount than at sea level, because there is less air pressing down on the mercury. (We now use this fact in other ways—for instance, in measuring fluctuations in air pressure at a given elevation, part of the knowledge needed to predict changes in the weather.) Notice, by the way, that had the results of experiments not conformed to Torricelli's theory, his hypothesis would not have been accepted by the scientific community.

The point of all this is twofold. First, scientific method is not some mysterious entity; and second, although in practice it leads to extremely complicated experiments and arguments, the basic underlying patterns of scientific inquiry are rather simple. We also should mention that it is the incredibly diverse evidence that supports scientific theories that is the reason why they are so reliable and why we should not reject what science has to say on any subject without having *extremely good reasons* for doing so.

3. CALCULATING PROBABILITIES AND FAIR ODDS

Billions of dollars are legally wagered on games of chance each year in the United States, and billions more are wagered illegally. The popularity of Atlantic City, Reno, and Las Vegas testifies to the fact that many millions of people in America gamble every year. Yet most who gamble have no idea how to calculate fair odds, one reason almost all gamblers lose in the long run. (Another reason, of course, is that the odds on all legal gambling games, including in particular slot machines and state lotteries, are rigged against the player—the odds *always* favor the house.)

Legitimate, fair odds depend on the *likelihood* (*probability* or *chances*) that a given outcome will occur. For example, when you flip a symmetrical coin, the chances are *one out of two,* or ½, that the coin will land heads up because there are two possibilities, and both are equally likely. *Fair odds* on heads thus should be even money—one to one— and someone who bets a dollar and wins should win a dollar. (Note, though, that very few coins are absolutely symmetrical. They tend to be very slightly heavier on one side or the other. Also notice that the dice at places like Las Vegas are specially made to be as close to symmetrical as possible. Just any old pair of dice will not do, because of possible numbers "bias" favoring some numbers over others.)

Most games of chance are designed to present players with a specific number of equally likely alternatives, or combinations of alternatives, on which they must wager. To find the *probability* of combinations of outcomes, simply divide the number of favorable outcomes by the total number of possible outcomes, favorable or unfavorable. (Remember, though, that this works only in cases in which all individual outcomes are equally likely and outcomes are *independent* of each other—a matter to be discussed soon.)

Suppose we want to calculate the chances of getting a 7 on the next toss of an honest (symmetrical) pair of dice. There are exactly 36 possible outcomes on each toss, of which exactly 6 add up to 7 (namely, the combinations 1 and 6, 2 and 5, 3 and 4, 4 and 3, 5 and 2, and 6 and 1). So the probability of getting a 7 on a given toss equals $6/36$, or $1/6$. Out of six tosses, the average wagerer will win once and lose five times. That is why fair odds on 7 in a dice game are 5 to 1 and why someone who wins a dollar bet should win $5.

At a casino, someone who bets a dollar is required to place it on the table, so that, if winners were paid fair odds, they would get back $6—their own dollar plus $5 in winnings. But no casino in history has ever paid fair odds. Gambling establishments are in business to make money, not to run fair games of chance!

At Las Vegas and other places where gambling is legal, perhaps the best odds for average players are at the dice tables. Slot machines provide the worst odds (except for wagers on sporting events or horse races). Yet the slots are without doubt the most popular way to lose money at every legal gambling casino. But state lotteries very likely offer players (one is tempted to say "suckers"!) the worst odds of any legal popular games of chance, since they pay back in winnings only from one-half to at best two-thirds of what they take in.[4]

Anyway, probabilities being what they are, when the odds are less than fair, virtually everyone who gambles must lose in the long run. But people being as so many of us are, all sorts of foolish theories have gained wide currency among those who like to gamble. The most foolish theory, of course, is that there is something called luck and that in certain situations luck is on our side.

But there are also two other, more sophisticated theories that should be mentioned. One is the belief that doubling a bet after a losing play, say, at the dice table, assures victory in the long run even when the odds are stacked against you. After all, you must win sooner or later, thereby recouping all losses plus a nice profit.

Alas, there is no gambling Santa Claus. First, the odds are against you on every play; doubling the bet cannot change that fact. Second, unless you are a Bill Gates or a Warren Buffett, the house always has a very much larger pile of reserve cash than you do and therefore can withstand a greater run of losses. In the battle between house and gambler, the gambler thus almost always gets wiped out first by a streak of bad luck. (There are old stories and even a song about "the man who broke the bank at Monte Carlo," but if it ever happens, it is a rarity.)

According to a variation of the double-the-bet gambit, a bet made after previous losses should cover just what has been lost so far plus just a small amount extra—say, the amount of the first bet—so that if you bet $2 on the first play and lose, the second play is for $4, the third for $8, and so on until you win, at which point you start over with a $2 bet. This method certainly increases the average number of plays until a gambler will get wiped out, but it still can't change the inevitable failure lurking in the distance.

---

[4]That is why playing a state lottery amounts to paying a voluntary state tax. Thomas Jefferson, among other illustrious figures, favored lotteries for that very reason. Ordinary taxes are compulsory; lottery "taxes" are completely voluntary. Good point. Of course, human nature being what it is, plenty of people who regularly toss money away on state lotteries complain bitterly about having to pay state sales and income taxes.

This method also has the disadvantage that, even if you beat the odds and end up a winner, you've just won the tiny amount of your initial wager. (A friend of the authors of this text tried this system at Las Vegas several years ago—at $10 a pop—and actually lasted over two hours before losing her bankroll.)

The other cute fallacy that gamblers fall for is to believe that the less often, say, a 7 has shown up lately at the dice table, the more likely it is that it will show up on the next toss of the dice. The odds, gamblers are fond of saying, have to "even out." Wait until 7 has not shown up for a specified number of tosses, say, ten in a row, and then bet heavily on 7.

The trouble with this system is that each toss of the dice is *independent* of every other toss, which means that what happens on one toss is independent of what happens on any other. The point is that the dice don't know (or care!) what has shown up on previous tosses. The conditions that determine the odds on any given toss determine them to be the same for all tosses, no matter how previous tosses turned out. The dice, after all, are still the same symmetrical devices obeying the same laws of physics on every toss.

True critical reasoners, of course, don't need to know anything about correct odds to be sure that systems like this don't work. The house is in business to win; if they let you play, you can bet your system is no good.[5]

Although the theory about how to calculate fair odds in general is quite complicated, there are a few simple rules that cover most common cases. Using the lowercase letter *a* to stand for a first event or outcome and *b* for a second, and *P* as shorthand for probability, here are four such rules:

Restricted conjunction rule:

If two events are *independent* of each other (the occurrence of one has no effect on the occurrence of the other), then the probability of both occurring is equal to the probability of the first times the probability of the second. In symbols, this reads:

$P(a \ \& \ b) = P(a) \times P(b).$

For example, the probability of getting two 7s in a row with a fair pair of dice is equal to the probability of first getting a 7 ($1/6$) times the probability of 7 on the second toss ($1/6$), and thus is $1/6 \times 1/6 = 1/36$.

General conjunction rule:

$P(a \ \& \ b) = P(a) \times P(b, \text{given that } a \text{ occurs}).$

---

[5]There have been very few exceptions to this rule. One occurred many years ago when card-counting systems were devised for blackjack that changed the odds so that they were in favor of adept card counters. At first, casinos refused to let card counters play—they actually kept lists—but then they simply increased the size of blackjack decks or used mechanical devices spewing out an endless series of cards, thereby ruining the card-counting game. (The card counters proved to be not much of a problem, because extremely few players were sufficiently adept at keeping track of cards played, and anyway, the idea that there is a way to beat the odds is good for business.) Another exception also occurred many years ago when college students discovered the tiny bias of a particular Las Vegas casino roulette wheel by patient observation over several days. They were allowed to win several thousand dollars, because of the great publicity, before the house ruined the game simply by changing the wheel.

For instance, the probability of drawing two spades in a row out of an at-first-complete deck of cards is equal to the probability of drawing the first spade ($^{13}/_{52}$, because 13 of the 52 cards in a deck are spades) times the probability of drawing a second one, given that the first spade is not replaced in the deck ($^{12}/_{51}$), and thus is $^{13}/_{52} \times {}^{12}/_{51} = {}^{1}/_{17}$.

Restricted disjunction rule:

If a and b are mutually exclusive events (an outcome cannot be both a and b), then:

$P(a \text{ or } b) = P(a) + P(b)$.

For example, the probability of drawing a spade or a heart on a given draw is equal to the probability of drawing a spade (¼) plus the probability of drawing a heart (¼), and thus is ¼ + ¼ = ½. (Drawing a spade and drawing a heart are mutually exclusive because no card can be both a spade and a heart.)

General disjunction rule:

$P(a \text{ or } b) = P(a) + P(b) - P(a \& b)$.

For instance, the probability of getting at least one head in two tosses equals the probability of getting a head on the first toss (½) plus the probability of doing so on the second toss (½) minus the probability of getting heads on both tosses (¼), and thus is ½ + ½ − ¼ = ¾. (Note that we can't just say it is equal to ½ + ½.)

It should be obvious, by the way, that the probability of a contradiction equals zero and of a tautology (logical truth), one.

EXERCISE A-1

*1. What is the probability of getting either 2 or 12 on a given toss of an honest pair of dice?

2. How about one or the other in two tosses?

3. What is the probability of getting a red jack, queen, or king with an ordinary deck of cards on one random draw?

*4. If a state lottery paid fair odds, how much should a $2 wager pay a winner who picked the correct five-digit number?

5. Can we use the general disjunction rule in cases in which the events are mutually exclusive, as in the spade/heart example just mentioned? Explain your answer, and give an example.

---

*Starred (*) items are answered in a section at the back of the book.

EXERCISE A-2

Here is a "system" promoted in a book on gambling.[6] (A tiny part of the system has been omitted here.) Explain why it doesn't work (hard question, but well worth figuring out).

> There is only one way to show a profit. Bet light on your losses and heavy on your wins.
>
> *Bet minimums when you're losing.*
>
> You recoup losses by betting house money against the house, not your own. When you win with a minimum bet, let the winnings ride and manage to come up with a few more wins. . . .
>
> *Bet heavy when you're winning.*
>
> Following a win with your minimum bet, bet the original minimum plus the amount you won. On a third win, drag [keep?] the minimum and bet the rest. You now have a one-minimum-bet profit on the round, regardless of what happens. . . . As soon as you lose, go back to the minimum bet. . . .
>
> *Always make your heavy bets with the other fellow's money, not your own.*
>
> The worst thing you can do betting house money against the house on a bet is break even on that particular wager. Actually, you've lost money on the round—but it was money that you got from the other fellow, not part of your original venture money. . . .
>
> *Don't limit your winnings.*
>
> Always ride out a winning streak, pushing your skill to the hilt. . . .
>
> *Quit on a losing streak, not a winning streak.*
>
> While the law of mathematical probability averages out, it doesn't operate in a set pattern. Wins and losses go in streaks more often than they alternate. If you've had a good winning streak and a loss follows it, bet minimums long enough to see whether or not another winning streak is coming up. If it isn't, quit while you're still ahead.

---

[6]*Gambler's Digest: The World's Greatest Gambling Book.* 2nd edition. Ed. Clement McQuaid. Iola, Wisc.: DBI Books, 1981.

Answers to Starred Exercise Items

These answers certainly are not presented as revealed truth. They represent the authors' thoughts on the matter, which it is hoped will prove useful to the reader.

EXERCISE 1-1 (PP. 3–4)

4. *Premise:* We are sinners all.
   Implied premise: All sinners should forbear to judge (others).
   Conclusion: We all should forbear to judge (others).

5. *Premise:* We would get rid of crime syndicates.
   Premise: The government would rake in billions in taxes.
   Conclusion: Drugs should be legalized.

8. *Premise:* Michael Vick has paid the penalty for his criminal behavior and has made amends by volunteering with the Humane Society.
   Premise: He is a great quarterback.
   Conclusion: His criminal record shouldn't prevent him from getting into the Hall of Fame.

EXERCISE 1-2 (PP. 5–6)

1. *Premise:* If we keep burning so much coal and oil, the greenhouse effect will continue to get worse.
   Premise: But it will be a disaster if it happens.
   Conclusion: So we've got to reduce our dependency on those fossil fuels.

4. No argument. Just a narrative of summer activities.

9. *Premise:* We all think ourselves so abundantly provided with good sense that we don't desire any more.
   Implied premise: If everyone is satisfied with the amount of good sense he or she has, then good sense must be equally distributed.
   Conclusion: Good sense is equally distributed.

   (The bit about it being the most equally distributed item is, we can assume, a rhetorical flourish. By the way, do you suppose Descartes was being a bit ironic?)

EXERCISE 2-3 (P. 38)

4. Disjunctive syllogisms have the form

   A or *B*

   Not *A*

   B

   If we replace the *A*s by the *sentence* "Snow is white" and the *B*s by the *sentence* "Snow is pink," we get the following argument:

   Snow is white or snow is pink.

   Snow isn't white. (Not snow is white.)

   Snow is pink.

   The term *or* in this disjunctive syllogism serves as a *sentence connective* (grammarians would say it serves as a coordinating conjunction); it connects whole sentences. In this case, it connects the sentences "Snow is white" and "Snow is pink." "Snow is white or snow is pink" is said to be a *compound sentence* composed of the two *atomic sentences* "Snow is white" and "Snow is pink," joined together by the sentence connective *or*.

   Contrast this with the following syllogistic form and argument:

All *S* are *M*.	All sinners are betrayers.
All *M* are *P*.	All betrayers are untrustworthy.
All *S* are *P*.	All sinners are untrustworthy.

   In this case, we replace the *S*s, *M*s, and *P*s not by the whole sentences but by parts of sentences—namely, sentence *subjects* or sentence *predicates*. The term *are* serves not as a sentence connective but rather as a *verb* (the verb *to be*); it connects the subject of a sentence with its predicate. In the case, say, of the atomic sentence "All sinners are betrayers," the verb *are* connects the subject *sinners* with the predicate *betrayer* to form the atomic sentence "All sinners are betrayers." (The term *all* serves as a *quantifier*, indicating how many sinners, but that is another story, discussed in formal logic texts.)

EXERCISE 2-4 (P. 39–40)

3. Contingent. It certainly is not a contradiction, and it also is not a tautology because there is no law of logic that forbids one from running for both president and vice president in the same election. (Is there a legal law of the land?)

EXERCISE 3-1 (PP. 67–72)

1. Appeal to authority. Doctors are specialists in medicine. They don't necessarily know anything more about moral issues than anyone else. Anyway, don't we all need to make up our own minds about moral matters?

2. Straw man. This was a cheap shot that misrepresented Obama's position by distorting a minor segment of his stimulus plan.

8. Questionable premise: In this infamous statement—much quoted at the time—Obama attempted to explain the attitude of workers in a series of negatives—guns, clinging to religion, antipathy, and zenophobia. Whereas this explanation may apply to some workers, it certainly doesn't apply to all of them. He made the mistake of not qualifying his sweeping generalization—though he tried mightily to justify it after the fact.

14. Appeal to authority, questionable premise, suppressed evidence. A doctor who is setting guidelines shouldn't be profiting from a company who stands to benefit from those guidelines. Under those circumstances, his authority may be suspect. And it is questionable that banning conflicts of interest would limit the number of doctors available for work. After all, 44 percent of the medical evaluators were conflict free. Finally, the fact that some well-regarded doctors conducted company-sponsored research doesn't mean that they remained untainted or that they were essential for setting the guidelines.

17. Suppressed evidence. Most of us are in our own home a lot more than we are in these other places. The rape rate per unit of time is much greater in the other places mentioned by Dr. Brothers than in one's own home.

20. No fallacy if this was a humorous jab at Washington insiders. If serious, appeal to authority. It is certainly doubtful that God was messaging Washington—but one never knows.

25. Inconsistency. Doesn't the phrase "heritable disposition" mean a disposition caused by a genetic inheritance?

33. Questionable premise and possibly either/or. It is certainly questionable to refer to WikiLeaks as a "high-tech terrorist," whether you are for or against its unauthorized publication of classified information. An either/or fallacy is conceivable if the argument is couched in terms of two possible alternatives, one good, the other bad.

EXERCISE 4-1 (PP. 89–93)

4. Irrelevant reasons.

6. Slippery slope.

10. This is one of those juicy quotes that is loaded with fallacies. For starters, there are the ad hominems—calling the student a slut and prostitute. Then there is the straw man in Limbaugh's claim that she is asking Congress to pay her for having sex, a gross distortion of her argument that the schools should provide coverage for contraception. On top of that is the irrelevant reason that because she is asking for coverage, she must be a prostitute. Throw in a couple questionable premises and you've got a veritable minefield of fallacies.

14. Equivocation. You don't have to make the past or future present in thought. What you make present, the "it," is thoughts about the past or present. The term *it* is used equivocally, the first use denoting the past or present and the second the thought of the past or present.

24. Equivocation. To imagine our own death is to visualize what it would be like to experience it. In this sense, we can and do imagine our own death. Freud changes the meaning of *imagine* so that to imagine it we would have to not visualize it, which, of course, is impossible.

33. Irrelevant reason, ad hominem, questionable premise. Even if all our poor people were fat, which they aren't, it doesn't logically follow that food stamps should be cut. This is just a cheap shot at welfare recipients.

EXERCISE 5-1 (PP. 113–115)

6. Students taught this way could be, and very likely are, different from "average" students in having more concerned parents (than average), more affluent parents, homes in which books and the like form a larger part of life, and so on. We already have good reason to

believe that "booked" households produce children who generally score higher than average. The point is bringing background beliefs to bear. You may have specific, relevant background beliefs, as above, or just general ones that should lead you to have some doubts about the implication of the stat—that home teaching is better than public schools.

EXERCISE 5-2 (PP. 115–118)

1. Questionable cause. No study of vaccine side effects has found a link between the vaccine and mental retardation. This is simply an anecdote and anecdotes do not equal evidence. There is also a hasty conclusion in the argument: Since my daughter was vaccinated and she became mentally ill, the vaccine must have caused the mental illness.

13. Hasty conclusion. Being interested in people doesn't necessarily insure that Morgan would be a great interviewer.

20. Questionable premise and hasty conclusion. The first part of the premise, that same-sex marriage is contrary to divine law, may not seem fallacious to someone with a conservative, religious world view, but the second half, that it is contrary to natural law, certainly is questionable and leads to the hasty conclusion that same-sex marriage should be illegal.

EXERCISE 5-3 (PP. 119–123)

1. Questionable analogy. Here's an example for which some background information is essential. (Precise figures aren't necessary.) On a trip to Saturn, the *Titan 4, Cassini,* carried 72.3 pounds of plutonium—the most carcinogenic substance known to man—with far greater radioactivity than was in the Chernobyl reactor at the time of its meltdown. The failure rate of *Titan 4* is 1 in 12.5. If *Cassini* disintegrated at its closest point (500 miles) in encircling the Earth, scientists estimate that millions of people would die—vastly more than the fatalities in a car crash. It's also worth noting that the chances of having an accident when driving a car are very much less than 1 in 12.5.

2. Suppressed evidence. In a nation where most people live in cities, where pigs cannot be kept, forbidding the sale of pork, bacon, and such is tantamount to forbidding the eating of these items. Inconsistency. So Rabbi Shapira came close to being inconsistent when he claimed that the ultrareligious Jews in Israel want the sale but not the eating of these kinds of meat to be forbidden, since the one is tantamount to the other.

8. Questionable statistics. Having extolled scientists for their generally correct handling of statistics, here is a case where they goofed. The problem isn't that a rough statistic did not follow from their evidence, but rather that precise ones such as 968.1 billion tons of carbon stored 18,000 years ago did not. Note, for instance, that they estimated how much carbon dioxide was locked within plants, and so on.

11. Suppressed evidence. (1) Superstition is more accurately defined, in part, as belief without good evidence, or in the face of contrary evidence. (So the article changed the meaning of the term *superstition,* and some readers may have been guilty of falling for the fallacy equivocation.) (2) Some of the greatest scientists may have been superstitious, Isaac Newton being perhaps the best candidate. But the parts of their beliefs that became incorporated in science were not superstitions, Newton again furnishing perhaps the best example. (3) In addition, a great deal of what scientists once accepted, *on good evidence,* they now reject, or have modified or sharpened, because of better evidence (for example,

the rejected ether theory). Rejecting or modifying well-supported theories because of better evidence in favor of more accurate theories is the heart of science and is definitely not superstition.

15. No fallacy. His analogies are apt.

21. Hasty conclusion. The evidence cited certainly is relevant to the question and favorable to Pierce's claim that the ads caused a rise in teen smoking, but it is not conclusive. Many other factors were at work (was there a similar increase in the use of other harmful drugs such as alcohol or marijuana?) and need to be evaluated along with the ads. Questionable statement. Why isn't banning cigarette ads a First Amendment issue? It's true that we don't think a ban on ads for illegal substances would violate the First Amendment prohibition on censorship of speech, but, on the other hand, we wouldn't be inclined to agree that nothing can be advertised that causes serious illnesses (for instance, high-fat foods).

22. Hasty conclusion. There certainly are plenty of good background reasons for concluding that raising the speed limit will increase traffic fatalities. But we can't automatically credit the 55-mph speed limit with reducing fatalities. (For one thing, that limit was generally flouted anyway; for another, cars have been made safer, and perhaps drivers on average are more sober.) Still, it would have been a good guess, based on background beliefs, that increases in speed would result in increases in fatalities. (Experience so far is mixed as to whether in fact the new higher maximum speed limits have resulted in increased highway deaths.)

24. Questionable analogy. The issue is not the similar sizes of California and Iraq, but the populations. There are 35 million Californians but only 140,000 U.S. soldiers in Iraq. California homicides would amount to 125,000 if people in that state were actually killed at the same rate as our soldiers were dying in Iraq.

EXERCISE 5-4 (PP. 123–124)

Questionable cause/hasty conclusion. To begin with, if we subtract the U.S.'s figures, the stats look much different (suggesting the criminal population in the United States is high for other reasons). Also, Ireland, with 88 percent church attendance, has a lower jail rate than four of the six low-church nations and lower than the average. This raises all kinds of questions. Are the Irish secret sinners? Are their police incompetent? How many criminals are behind bars in the United States because they committed victimless crimes (such as smoking dope) or because of race prejudice?

In any case, the statistics cited completely fail to support the implication that churchgoing leads to criminal behavior, nor do any other statistics known to the authors of this text.

EXERCISE 7-2 (PP. 181–182)

3. Translation: Printed on paper that is at least 10 percent recycled, with a minimum of 40 percent new material.

Is there something sneaky about this? Yes, indeed. Starting out with the statement "Printed on recycled paper" leads one to suspect that the item is printed on 100 percent recycled paper, thus playing to those who like to use recycled materials. The bit about post- and preconsumer materials is bound to be confusing to most of these people, who will then rely on the (misleading) first statement—the one they can understand. At the same time, the manufacturer is protected from fraud by the statements about pre- and postconsumer materials.

6. What the good admiral said in militaryese was that navy teams had gone around the country trying to find ways to get naval installations to spend more money. (It was close to the end of the fiscal year, and the navy had not used up its appropriation for that year. Yes, bureaucracies, with very few exceptions, do work this way.)

EXERCISE 7-4 (P. 182–183)

1. Actually, two of the sayings might be challenged. Charles Beardsley's quote may be thought to be doublespeak, and the Chinese proverb clearly does use the pronoun *he* when people in general are meant. But Beardsley deliberately employed "pompous prolixity" in order to rail against that very kind of language. And it makes not a great deal of sense to change ancient sayings (or should we commit to flames the King James version of the Bible with its sexist sayings, such as "He that is without sin among you, let him first cast a stone at her"?).

    Confucius's precept does exaggerate the slipperiness of the slope he describes. But it is slippery!

EXERCISE 8-1 (PP. 190–193)

3. *Thesis:* None of the historical or anecdotal parts of the Bible are the word of God.
    Reason (premise): What I've seen (or know?) needs no revelation.
    Conclusion: Revelation is that which reveals what we don't know (haven't seen) before.
    Reason: Revelation is that which reveals what we don't know (haven't seen) before.
    Conclusion: Revelation can't tell us about earthly things men could witness.
    Reason: Revelation can't tell us about earthly things men could witness.
    Conclusion (thesis): None of the historical or anecdotal parts of the Bible count as revelation. (Paine assumed an equation between revelation and the word of God.)

EXERCISE 8-7 (PP. 203–204)

2. It is very difficult to construct margin notes or a summary for material such as these excerpts from *Mein Kampf,* because confusion and ambiguities abound. Nevertheless, here is a reasonably accurate summary (omitting Hitler's anthropomorphization of laws of nature):

    1. It is a law of nature that animals mate only with members of their own species.

    2. Breeding higher with lower within a species produces a medium that will lose out eventually to the higher.

    3. If a law of nature did not exist forbidding breeding higher to lower, still higher could not develop.

    4. The struggle for food and mates results in a higher development of a species.

    5. Just as mating stronger with weaker *individuals* goes against nature, so does mating higher with lower races.

6. Proof: Aryans in North America remained pure and became masters of the continent; Latins in Central and South America mixed with the natives and produced an inferior culture, of which they are not complete masters. (This isn't exactly what Hitler says, but it is what he means. Remember that a good deal of Latin America was still in a colonial status in the 1920s when Hitler wrote his tome.)

EXERCISE 10-1 (P. 242)

2. Clearly there's a contradiction here. Certificates that cost $1 aren't free.

6. This Nike commercial wins the *Logic and Contemporary Rhetoric* "Most Offensive Commercial of the Decade" Award for telling those who have just proved to be the second best at an activity (perhaps by the tiniest margin) among the several billion people on the planet that they are losers, instead of crediting them with their great accomplishment. (The underlying offensive message is captured by Vince Lombardi's famous remark, "Winning isn't everything; it's the only thing." Compare that to "It isn't whether you win or lose but how you play the game.")

10. Appeal to authority. Agronsky is no authority on the subject. Straw man. No one claims coconut oils are "poisoning" America. Suppressed evidence. (1) Although some fats are healthier than others, coconut oil is low on the healthy list. (2) It is total amount of fat intake that is most important. (3) No single fat source supplies more than a small portion of total intake of fat, so that "only" 1.5 percent coming from coconut oil proves nothing. The point is that it's prudent to reduce one's total amount of fat intake well below the national average and to reduce intake of some kinds of fat—coconut oil being a prime example—more than others. (4) If true that the fatty acids in coconut oil are beneficial, that would be a good reason to prefer this oil to others—say, when cooking. But this claim is generally not accepted by the medical profession. On the contrary, it is fats such as olive oil that seem to be the most beneficial.

EXERCISE 10-2 (PP. 243–244)

3. This commercial points to a profitable use of air travel—to foster face-to-face business relationships. That is why this has been an extremely successful ad—it reminds business executives of the value of catering to customers in person. But the commercial gives no reason to fly United instead of other airlines. (The implied reason that United flies to more than 200 locations is not a good reason for choosing United. For one thing, some other airlines fly to that many cities; and for another, what difference does it make if you intend, say, to fly to Chicago, whether the airline you choose also flies to 199 other cities or just to half that many?) Jargon-type slogan. "United. Come fly the friendly skies." Identification. Casting the right actors for TV commercials is crucial, and this ad does it beautifully. Ben is someone most people in business will identify with.

EXERCISE 12-4 (PP. 342–343)

3. The topic is the one discussed in Chapter 7 entitled "Those Who Control the Definitions"—defining oneself into victory. Those who favor teaching the biblical account of creation in science classes were trying to define themselves into victory by calling the biblical account "creation science," very much like businesses do who call employees "subcontractors."

EXERCISE FOR THE ENTIRE TEXT (P. 343)

You didn't really expect an answer to this one, did you? (If you did, go back to page 1 of Chapter 1 and start reading—carefully this time.)

EXERCISE A-1 (P. 351)

1. Since it isn't possible to get both 2 and 12 on a given toss, we can use the restricted disjunction rule. And given that the probability of getting a 2 $= \frac{1}{36}$ and of a 12 $= \frac{1}{36}$, the probability of getting 2 or 12 $= \frac{1}{36} + \frac{1}{36} = \frac{2}{36} = \frac{1}{18}$.

4. There are 100,000 five-digit numbers, each one equally likely to be picked. Thus, the odds on any given number are 100,000 to 1. So a winning $2 bet should pay $200,000 plus the $2 wagered. (None do. But note that in lottery cases of this kind, how much is paid to winners usually depends on how many people pick the correct number and whether there was a winner of previous plays. When there is no winner for several plays and the pot becomes very large, the number of people who play increases dramatically [people are not always rational!], so that, even though the amount of prize money increases, the probability that there will be several winners increases, thus dividing each winner's share. Of course, when the odds against winning anything are 100,000 to 1, the chances of winning are so miniscule that it is a waste of time to play. It almost never makes sense to wager at such poor odds, even if they are statistically in your favor; doing so loses you the opportunity to profit in some more likely ways. Human irrationality makes most of us see things differently, but that's just one of the tendencies that a good rational thinker fights against.)

Bibliography

Asterisks indicate works mentioned in the text.

Cogent Reasoning

Carroll, Lewis. *Symbolic Logic and the Game of Logic*. New York: Dover, 1958.

Dewey, John. *How We Think*. Lexington, Mass.: Heath, 1910.

*Hausman, Alan, Kahane, Howard, and Tidman, Paul. *Logic and Philosophy*. 12th edition. Boston: Wadsworth, Cengage Learning, 2013.

Kahane, Howard. "The Proper Subject Matter for Critical Thinking Courses." *Argumentation* 3 (1989).

Lemmon, E. J. *Beginning Logic*. Rev'd. G. N. D. Barry. Indianapolis, Ind.: Hackett, 1978. (A strictly formal logic text.)

Fallacious Reasoning

*Bentham, Jeremy. *The Handbook of Political Fallacies*. New York: Harper Torchbooks, 1962. (A reprint of a classic nineteenth-century tract.)

Broad, C. D. "Some Fallacies in Political Thinking." *Philosophy* 29 (April 1950). (Interesting article by an important twentieth-century philosopher.)

*Cerf, Christopher, and Navasky, Victor. *The Experts Speak: The Definitive Compendium of Authoritative Misinformation*. New York: Pantheon, 1984.

*Dixon, Paul. *The Official Rules*. New York: Delacorte, 1978.

Ekman, Paul. *Telling Lies: Clues to Deceit in the Marketplace, Politics, and Marriage*. New York: Norton, 1992. (Fascinating book that will help readers to perceive when they are being lied to.)

Hamblin, C. L. *Fallacies*. Newport News, Va.: Vale, 1986. (A reprint with new preface of the definitive history of fallacy theory.)

Huff, Darrell. *How to Lie with Statistics*. New York: Norton, 1954.

*Jackson, Brooks, and Jameison, Kathleen Hall. *Unspun, Finding Facts in a World of Disinformation*. New York: Random House, 2007.

*Kahane, Howard. "The Nature and Classification of Fallacies." In *Informal Logic: The First International Symposium*. Eds. J. Anthony Blair and Ralph H. Johnson. Inverness, Calif.: Edgepress, 1980.

Miller, James Nathan. "Ronald Reagan and the Techniques of Deception." *Atlantic Monthly* (February 1984). (Nice illustration of how statistics can be misused for political advantage.)

Morgan, Chris, and Langford, David. *Facts and Fallacies: A Book of Definitive Mistakes and Misguided Predictions*. Exeter, England: Webb & Bower, 1981. (One of several excellent books illustrating expert feet of clay.)

Morgenstern, Oscar. "Qui Numerare Incipit Errare Incipit." *Fortune* (October 1963). (Still one of the best explanations of how government statistics on business and such can be and are manipulated for political purposes.)

*Fireside, Daniel, Miller, John, and Snyder, Bryan. *Real World Macro: A Macroeconimics Reader from Dollars and Sense.* 25th ed. Boston: Dollars and Sense, 2008. (How statistics can be manipulated, in particular by the federal government.)

Smith, H. B. *How the Mind Falls into Error.* New York: Darby, 1980. (Reprint of the 1923 edition.)

Thouless, Robert H. *Straight and Crooked Thinking.* New York: Simon & Schuster, 1932.

Wheeler, Michael. *Lies, Damn Lies, and Statistics: The Manipulation of Public Opinion in America.* New York: Dell Laurel, 1977.

Impediments to Cogent Reasoning

Batholomew, Robert E., and Goode, Erich. "Mass Delusions and Hysterias: Highlights from the Past Millennium." *Skeptical Inquirer* (May/June 2000). (Fascinating article on human irrationality during the just-completed thousand years. Great companion to the Charles MacKay book listed later.)

*Bentham, Jeremy. *The Handbook of Political Fallacies.* New York: Harper Torchbooks, 1962. (A reprint of a classic nineteenth-century tract.)

*French, Christopher C., Fowler, Mandy, McCarthy, Katy, and Peers, Debbie. "Belief in Astrology: A Test of the Barnum Effect." *Skeptical Inquirer* (Winter 1991).

Gardner, Martin. *Science: Good, Bad, and Bogus.* Buffalo, N.Y.: Prometheus, 1981. (Debunking of pseudoscience.)

———. *Fads and Fallacies in the Name of Science.* New York: Dover, 1957. (The classic debunking of pseudoscience.)

*Gilovich, Thomas. *How We Know What Isn't So.* New York: Free Press, 1991.

*Goffman, Erving. *The Presentation of Self in Everyday Life.* New York: Anchor, 1959. (A classic.)

*Goleman, Daniel. *Vital Lies, Simple Truths.* New York: Simon & Schuster, 1985. (The best understandable explanation of recent scientific ideas about self-deception, its biological functions, and the unconscious.)

MacKay, Charles. *Memoirs of Extraordinary Popular Delusions and the Madness of Crowds.* New York: Harmony, 1980. (Reprint of 1841 edition, with foreword by Andrew Tobias. An excellent account of several disasters—the Crusades, the seventeenth-century Dutch tulip madness, the South Sea Bubble—driven by mass hysteria.)

Nickell, Joe. *Inquest on the Shroud of Turin.* Buffalo, N.Y.: Prometheus, 1982. (An example of sanity on a foolishness-provoking topic.)

Nisbet, Robert. *Prejudices.* Cambridge, Mass.: Harvard University Press, 1986.

Peirce, Charles Sanders. "The Fixation of Belief." *Popular Science Monthly* (1877). (A classic article by America's premier philosopher.)

Sagan, Carl. *The Demon-Haunted World.* New York: Random House, 1996. (A protest by an eminent astronomer against superstition and the uncritical acceptance of pseudoscientific claims.)

Shermer, Michael. *Why People Believe Weird Things: Pseudoscience, Superstition, and Other Confusions of Our Time.* New York: Freeman, 1997.

Twain, Mark. *Mark Twain on the Damned Human Race.* Ed. Janet Smith. New York: Hill & Wang, 1962. (The great American humorist on all sorts of human foibles. If you think of Sam Clemens as just a writer of stories, you should read this book. For one thing, it will make evident to you how ridiculous it is to censor *Huckleberry Finn* on grounds of racism.)

Vyse, Stuart A. *Believing in Magic: The Psychology of Superstition.* New York: Oxford University Press, 1997.

Language

*American Philosophical Association (APA). *Guidelines for Non-Sexist Use of Language.* (Publication of the APA, available from their national office in Washington, D.C.)

*Carroll, Lewis. *Alice's Adventures in Wonderland.* New York: New American Library, 1960. (Reprint. The Reverend Dodgson, by the way, was a first-rate logician.)

"Guidelines for Equal Treatment of the Sexes in McGraw-Hill Book Company Publications." (Eleven-page, in-house statement of policy that has been generally adopted in the publishing business.)

Hall, Edward T. *The Silent Language.* New York: Doubleday, 1973.

*Jacoby, Susan. *The Age of American Unreason.* New York: Pantheon Press, 2008.

*Lakoff, George. *Don't Think of an Elephant.* White River Junction, VT.: Chelsea Green Publishing Co., 2004.

*———. *Moral Politics: How Liberals and Conservatives Think.* Chicago: University of Chicago Press, 2002.

Lutz, William. "Notes toward a Description of Doublespeak." *Quarterly Review of Doublespeak* (January 1987).

*———. *Doublespeak Defined.* New York: HarperCollins Publishers, Inc., 1999.

*Orwell, George. *Nineteen Eighty-Four.* New York: New American Library, 1949. (Shows how language control helps control thoughts and thus behavior.)

*———. "Politics and the English Language." *A Collection of Works by George Orwell.* New York: Harcourt Brace, 1946.

Postman, Neil. *Amusing Ourselves to Death: Public Discourse in the Age of Show Business.* New York: Penguin, 1986.

Solomon, Norman. *The Power of Babble: The Politician's Dictionary of Buzzwords and Doubletalk for Every Occasion.* New York: Bantam Doubleday Dell, 1992.

Evaluating and Constructing Extended Arguments

Cavender, Nancy, and Weiss, Len. *Thinking/Writing.* Belmont, Calif.: Wadsworth, 1987.

Flew, Antony. *Thinking Straight.* Buffalo, N.Y.: Prometheus, 1977.

Lanham, Richard. *Revising Prose.* New York: Scribner's, 1979. (A good guide to clear writing.)

St. Aubyn, Giles. *The Art of Argument.* Buchanan, N.Y.: Emerson, 1962. (A beautifully written little book on argument.)

Writing Cogent (and Persuasive) Essays

*Hayes, John R., and Flower, Linda S. "Writing as Problem Solving." *Visible Language* 14:396–398.

*Kahane, Howard. *Contract Ethics: Evolutionary Biology and the Moral Sentiments.* Lanham, Md.: Rowman & Littlefield, 1995. (Helpful in bringing value judgments to bear when evaluating arguments.)

Advertising

Baker, Samm Sinclair. *The Permissible Lie.* Cleveland, Ohio: World, 1968.

*Beiler, David. *The Classics of Political Television Advertising: A Viewer's Guide.* Washington, D.C.: Campaigns and Elections, 1986. (Companion guide to a 60-minute videocassette containing some of the great TV campaign spots. Great fun and educational, too.)

Benn, Alec. *The 27 Most Common Mistakes in Advertising.* New York: AMACOM, 1978.

*Clark, Eric. *The Want Makers.* New York: Viking, 1988.

*Collins, Thomas L. *Beyond Maximarketing.* New York: McGraw-Hill, 1994.

Faucheux, Ron. "How to Win in '94." *Campaigns and Elections* (September 1993). (Interesting to compare with how campaigns were run in 1994.)

*Feldstein, Mark. "Mail Fraud on Capitol Hill." *Washington Monthly* (October 1979).

Glatzer, Robert. *The New Advertising: The Great Campaigns from Avis to Volkswagen.* New York: Citadel, 1970.

Hopkins, Claude. *Scientific Advertising.* New York: Crown, 1966. (Reprint of one of the classics on advertising.)

Iyengar, Shanto, and Ansolabehere, Stephen. *Going Negative: How Political Advertisements Shrink and Polarize the Electorate.* New York: Free Press, 1996.

Jamieson, Kathleen Hall. *Dirty Politics: Deception, Distraction, and Democracy.* Oxford University Press, 1992. (How campaigns dominated by 30- and 10-second TV spots fail to provide voters with adequate information.)

———. *Packaging the Presidency: A History and Criticism of Presidential Campaign Advertising.* 2nd ed. New York: Oxford University Press, 1992.

*Kilbourne, Jean. *Deadly Persuasion: Why Women and Girls Must Fight the Addictive Power of Advertising.* New York: Simon & Schuster, 1999.

*Lemann, Nicholas. "Barney Frank's Mother and 500 Postmen." *Harper's* (April 1983).

*Marks, Steven. *Confessions of a Political Hitman.* Naperville, IL: Sourcebooks Inc., 2007.

McGinnis, Joe. *The Selling of the President 1968.* New York: Trident, 1969. (Still the best inside account of a presidential campaign—Nixon's successful run for the presidency.)

*Ogilvy, David. *Confessions of an Advertising Man.* New York: Atheneum, 1963.

Preston, Ivan. *The Great American Blowup: Puffery in Advertising and Selling.* Madison: University of Wisconsin Press, 1975. (Interesting account of what legally qualifies as mere puffery rather than false advertising.)

Rowsome, Frank, Jr. *They Laughed When I Sat Down.* New York: Bonanza, 1959. (Perhaps still the most interesting book on the history of advertising.)

*Sabatim, Karry J., and Simpson, Glenn R. "When Push Comes to Poll." *Washington Monthly* (June 1996).

Savan, Leslie. *The Sponsored Life: Ads, TV and American Culture.* Philadelphia: Temple University Press, 1995.

Stauber, John, and Rampton, Sheldon. *Toxic Sludge Is Good for You: Lies, Damn Lies, and the Public Relations Industry.* Monroe, Me.: Common Courage Press, 1995.

*Washburn, Katharine, and Thornton, John, eds. *Dumbing Down: The Strip-mining of American Culture.* New York: Norton, 1996.

In addition to the books already listed, several excellent videocassettes are available from Campaigns and Elections, Washington, D.C., including the June 1986 *The Classics of Political Advertising* (with an accompanying booklet by David Beiler); *Prime Time Politics,* a 1989 cassette primarily concerned with the 1988 elections; and *The 25 Funniest Political TV Commercials* (actually, not all that funny, but instructive). There also are several other modestly interesting videocassettes available, including *30-Second Seduction,* a 1985 cassette by Consumer Reports.

Managing the News

Bagdikian, Ben. *The Media Monopoly,* 4th ed. Boston: Beacon, 1992.

Bennett, James. "The Flack Pack: How Press Conferences Turn Serious Journalists into Shills." *Washington Monthly* (November 1991).

*Bradlee, Ben. *A Good Life.* New York: Simon & Schuster, 1995.

Cohen, Jeff, and Solomon, Norman. *Adventures in Medialand: Behind the News, Beyond the Pundits.* Monroe, Me.: Common Courage Press, 1993.

Cohen, Richard. "Making Trends Meet." *Washington Post Magazine* 28 September 1986. (How *Time* and *Newsweek* exaggerate and invent trends and fashions.)

Crossen, Cynthia. *Tainted Truth: The Manipulation of Fact in America.* New York: Simon & Schuster, 1994.

Croteau, David, and Hoynes, William. *By Invitation Only: How the Media Limits Political Debate.* Monroe, Me.: Common Courage Press, 1997.

Day, James. *The Vanishing Vision: The Inside Story of Public Television.* Berkeley: University of California Press, 1995. (A good account of how and why public television [PBS] succeeds in some ways and comes short in others.)

*El-Nawawy, Mohammed, and Iskandar Faraq, Adel. *Al-Jazeera: How the Arab Network Scooped the World.* Boulder, CO: Westeview Press, 2002.

Fallows, James. *Breaking the News: How the Media Undermine American Democracy.* New York: Pantheon, 1996. (Important book by the now [1997] editor of *U.S. News & World Report.*)

Faludi, Susan. *Backlash: The Undeclared War Against American Women.* New York: Bantam, 1991.

Fineman, Howard. "The Power of Talk." *Newsweek* 8 February 1993. (How "call-in democracy"—TV and radio talk shows—is influencing elections and the legislative process.)

Hansell, Saul, and Harmon, Amy. "Caveat Emptor on the Web." *New York Times* 26 February 1999.

Hausman, Carl. *Lies We Live By: Defeating Double-Talk and Deception in Advertising, Politics and the Media.* New York: Routledge, 2000. (One of the best books on these related topics.)

Hess, Stephen. "Television's Self-Fulfilling News." *Washington Post,* National Weekly Edition 30 October–5 November 1989. (How TV shops around for expert opinion that conforms to the view they want to air.)

Hitt, Jack. "Warning: CIA Censors at Work." *Columbia Journalism Review* (July/August 1984).

*Jensen, Carl, and Project Censored. *Censored: The News That Didn't Make the News—and Why.* New York: Seven Stories Press, 1996. (A [hopefully] yearly publication about censored news stories.)

*Knightly, Phillip. *The First Casualty.* New York: Harcourt Brace Jovanovich, 1975. (The first casualty in war is, of course, truth.)

Levine, Richard M. "Polish Government versus the Workers: Why TV Is the Prized Weapon." *TV Guide* 7 November 1981. (An illustration of how important TV has become for politics everywhere.)

Lieberman, David. "Fake News." *TV Guide* 2 February 1992. (How video press releases, created by public relations firms, are surreptitiously slipped into TV news programs.)

McChesney, Robert. *Corporate Media and the Threat to Democracy.* New York: Seven Stories Press, 1997. (Interesting critique of corporate media power, plus some suggestions for improving the fairness and accuracy of the mass media.)

Miller, John J. "MLK, Inc." (How the Martin Luther King family is making big bucks by charging high permission fees to reprint from King's "I Have a Dream" speech and other writings, thereby inadvertently acting as censors.)

Perkins, Ray, Jr. *Logic and Mr. Limbaugh.* Chicago: Open Court, 1995. (A nifty account of how Rush Limbaugh mangles truth and logic.)

*Perry, David L. "No Way to Celebrate." *Columbia Journalism Review* (July/August 1990). (On how increasingly large jury awards in libel cases are putting a chill on investigative reporting.)

Smiley, Xan. "Misunderstanding Africa." *Atlantic Monthly* (September 1982). (How government intimidation and interference mangles news from Africa. An old article, but not that much has changed.)

Waters, Frank. *The Earp Brothers of Tombstone.* Lincoln: University of Nebraska Press, 1976. (The most accurate account of the exploits of the famous "Wild West" Earp brothers, Wyatt and Virgil, including a reasonably accurate account of the so-called "gunfight" at the O.K. Corral. A good antidote to the baloney the media dish out on this and other aspects of western U.S. history.)

*Zepezauer, Mark, and Naiman, Arthur. *Take the Rich off Welfare.* Tucson, Ariz.: Odonian, 1996.

In addition to the books just listed, there are several excellent videocassettes on managing the news, perhaps the most revealing being *Fear and Favor in the Newsroom,* distributed by California Newsreels, dramatically illustrating how corporate power influences news coverage.

Textbooks: Managing Worldviews

American Indian Historical Society. *Textbooks and the American Indian.* San Francisco: Indian Historical Press, 1970. (Shows how textbooks in those days—pre-1970—covered up the horrible treatment of Native Americans by European invaders.)

Barzun, Jacques. "The Wasteland of American Education." *New York Review of Books* 5 November 1981. (Still very relevant.)

Black, Hillel. *The American Schoolbook.* New York: Morrow, 1967.

Chubb, John E. *Politics, Markets, and America's Schools.* Brookings Institution, 1990.

Cockborn, Alexander, and St. Clair, Jeffrey. *Al Gore: A User's Manual.* New York: Verso, 2000.

*Darwin, Charles. *The Origin of Species.* London: John Murray, 1859.

DelFattore, Joan. *What Johnny Shouldn't Read.* New Haven, Conn: Yale University Press, 1992.

*Elson, Ruth M. *Guardians of Tradition: American Schoolbooks of the 19th Century.* Lincoln: University of Nebraska Press, 1964.

*Finn, Jr., Chester E., and Ravitch, Diane. *The Mad, Mad World of Textbook Adoption.* Washington: Thomas B. Fordham Institute, 2004.

*Fussell, Paul. *Wartime: Understanding and Behavior in the Second World War.* New York: Oxford University Press, 1989.

Henry, Jules. *On Sham, Vulnerability, and Other Forms of Self-Destruction.* (Unfortunately out of print.)

*Hirsch, Jr., E.D. *The Making of Americans.* New Haven: Yale University Press, 2009.

"History/Social Science Framework for California Public Schools, Kindergarten Through Grade Twelve." *California Department of Education.* 2005. Web. http://www.cde.ca.gov/ci/cr/cf/documents/histsocsciframe.pdf (The basic document governing California schools.)

Kasarda, John D. "The Jobs-Skills Mismatch." *New Perspectives Quarterly* (Fall 1990). (The economy needs highly educated workers; schools produce "low achievers.")

*Loewen, James W. *Lies Across America: What Our Historic Sites Get Wrong.* New York: New Press, 1999.

———. *Lies My Teacher Told Me: Everything Your History Textbook Got Wrong.* New York: New Press, 1995. (Terrific book explaining how and why public school textbooks distort history the way they do. Probably the best book on the topic ever written.)

*Loewen, James W. *Lies My Teacher Told Me.* New York: Simon & Schuster (A Touchstone Book), 2005. (A revision of the previous edition.)

Lynch, Michael W. "Rampaging Toward Choice." *Reason.* (Libertarian slant on the issue of school vouchers and charter schools.)

*Nelson, Jack, and Roberts, Gene. *The Censors and the Schools.* Boston: Little, Brown, 1963. (The best book on the topic up to 1963.)

Paulos, John Allen. *Innumeracy: Mathematical Illiteracy and Its Consequences.* New York: Hill & Wang, 1988.

Raloff, Janet. "Errant Texts." *Science News* 17 March 2001. (Very good article on the poor quality of public school science textbooks.)

*Ravitch, Diane. *The Language Police: How Pressure Groups Restrict What Students Learn.* New York: Knopf, 2003.

Schrank, Jeffrey. *Understanding Mass Media.* 2nd ed. Skokie, Ill.: National Textbook, 1986. (One of the best public school social science texts.)

*Shenkman, Richard. *Legends, Lies and Cherished Myths of American History.* New York: Morrow, 1988.

Stotsky, Sandra. *Losing Our Language: How Multicultural Classroom Instruction Is Undermining Our Children's Ability to Read, Write, and Reason.* New York: Free Press, 1999.

Washburn, Katharine, and Thornton, John. *Dumbing Down: Essays on the Strip-mining of American Culture.* New York: Norton, 1996. (Several fascinating essays on how the dumbing down of American public schools is harming society.)

Zinn, Howard. *A People's History of the United States.* New York: Harper & Row, 1980. (Perhaps the easiest-to-understand antidote to the history learned via public school history texts.)

Selected List of Periodicals

One of the themes of this text is that good reasoning requires reasonably accurate background beliefs, and one of the best ways to acquire a good stock of general information and theory is by reading some of the literally thousands of periodicals—magazines and journals—that are readily available these days. Here is a selected list of (primarily) non–mass media periodicals, the majority concerned mostly with social–political issues, the media, or science, which the authors of this text happen to dip into at least now and then. (The comments represent our opinions and are not to be taken as some sort of revealed truth.) Most of these publications have websites. For a complete list of magazine reviews see *Magazines for Libraries,* ed. Cheryl LaGuardia, available in the reference section of most college libraries.

American Heritage. Perhaps the most interesting history magazine, covering a broad range of topics in American history, some by well-known authors of historical pieces. Most articles are well-illustrated, and the writing style is engaging. *Examples*: "The State of America 72 Years Ago" and "The New Mexico and Arizona Centennials" in the Winter/Spring 2012 issue.

American Spectator. A wild-swinging, right-wing publication that has as its mission "to provide its unique view of American conservative politics, with a keen sense of irreverence." The writing is often humorous, particularly in regular columns like "Current Wisdom," "Political Hay," and "High Spirits."

Amnesty International. Magazine publication of Amnesty International, reporting on government torture around the world. (Reading this publication makes one appreciate living in a democratic society.)

Atlantic Monthly. One of the best general magazines, with some excellent articles and fiction. It always covers foreign affairs and the Washington scene, plus a wide variety of articles on everything from the London Olympics to the continuing saga of JFK's mistresses. *Examples*: "Why Women Still Can't Have it All" and "The Last Days of Foie Gras," in the July/August 2012 issue.

Black Enterprise. A business magazine oriented toward African-Americans in the business world whose mission has always been centered on "closing the black wealth gap and financially empowering African-Americans." It regularly covers such topics as family finances, money management, business opportunities, and home ownership.

Bloomberg BusinessWeek. A good business magazine, written for those in business on a level that the general reader can appreciate and understand. In addition to a wide range of business articles, it covers social issues and lifestyles as well. Editorials are generally moderate in their position.

Columbia Journalism Review. One of the best journalism publications, full of interesting, newsworthy articles as well as articles on the field of journalism and a particularly good book review section. *Example:* The cover story of the July/August 2012 issue: "Women, 40 Years Later." Other articles, "Piecemeal Existence" on the tough job market for young writers, and "Cell Coverage" on the jailhouse reporting of a convicted murderer.

Congressional Digest. A monthly publication providing impartial coverage of the pros and cons on controversial issues before Congress, as well as legislative and judicial background information. *Example:* The June 2012 issue that summarizes and debates the federal response to violence against women.

Consumer Reports. Publication of Consumers Union, an unbiased, nonprofit organization; a very good source of information about consumer products. All products it tests are purchased, no free samples are accepted, and no revenue comes from outside advertising—all of which make for objective dependable reviews.

Discover. Perhaps the best of a bad lot of mass media popular science magazines. Articles cover research from all science disciplines, profiles well-known scientists, reviews books, and reports on other science related issues. *Examples:* July 2012 issue with articles on the environment ("Great Floods" and "Conspiracy of Winds") and biology ("Microbes You Can't Clean Away").

The Economist. A very informative British newsweekly, well-respected internationally for articles on business and economics, world politics, science, technology, and the arts. *Examples:* Articles in the July 14, 2012 issue on election laws ("Voting Right, Voting Wrong"), Prostitution in France ("On the Game") and Cholera in Cuba ("Under Observation").

Editor and Publisher. Important trade magazine and a good source of information about how those in the business see things. Its newsy articles are aimed at industry leaders.

Environment Nutrition. A very good concise newsletter on diet, nutrition, and health that covers a wide range of topics, including food safety, nutrition comparison charts, herbal remedies, and best buys in brand-name foods. It is edited by a team of doctors, nurses, academics, and other health professionals.

Extra! The best magazine on the media, the main publication of FAIR (Fairness and Accuracy in Reporting). *Examples:* A special section on Iran and War in the June 2012 issue, including "U.S. Media Duck Legality of Attacking Iran" and "Lost in Translation."

Free Inquiry. Secular humanist publication that defends the importance of free inquiry in all areas of human endeavor. *Examples:* Articles on controversial topics like the use of religious-based charities in the secular sphere and homosexuality and atheism in the U.S. Armed Forces.

Harper's. Very good general monthly, with some of the best writing on politics and culture in the country. The Harper's Index is famous for its illuminating statistics and facts about a wide variety of subjects. *Examples:* July 2012 articles "Breeds of America," on current attitudes about race, and "Nature's Perfect Package," on euphemistic food labels.

Harvard Health Letter. An eight-page newsletter containing reasonably reliable medical information. The editorial board is staffed with doctors in different specialties, but the writing is geared to the general public.

Index on Censorship. A chronicle of censorship around the world that acts as a political forum with an international outlook. *Example:* Recent articles addressing suppression of freedom of expression in the United Kingdom and Internet privacy issues.

In These Times. Left-wing, socialist publication. Analyzes social, environmental, and economic justice in popular movements and discusses politics that shape our lives, but the magazine is critical of the Left when writers think it is warranted.

Mother Jones. Successor to *Ramparts:* radical Left viewpoint, with occasionally very good exposés. Investigates politicians, corporations, and governments, sometimes irreverently, and champions environmentalism. *Examples:* July–August 2012 articles "Undoing Citizens United" and "Follow the Dark Money."

The Nation. Long-established left-wing magazine, very much improved under the current editor and now very good indeed. It covers politics extensively, as well as economics and the arts, and has a searchable index of items in every issue from 1865 to the present. *Examples:* July 16/23, 2012 articles "Mitt Romney and the Gilded Age," "The Washington Post's Problem," and "Is There Freedom After Torture?"

National Geographic. The long-established special-topic magazine. Tends to make the world look somewhat better than it is, but nevertheless has interesting articles, with very good, sometimes stunning, visuals about interesting places around the world. *Examples:* August 2012 articles "Life After Wounded Knee" and "Tibet's Golden Worm."

National Review. Perhaps the most interesting conservative magazine. It covers mainly current political issues, with a long cover story for each issue as well as columns, book reviews, and political cartoons. *Examples:* Articles in the July 9, 2012 issue, "The Immigration Population," "The Bush-Obama Years," and "Sex and the Social Scientist."

Natural History. A publication of the American Museum of Natural History. An attractive magazine with good nature photography, featuring articles written by scientists or naturalists for a general audience.

Nature Conservancy. Magazine sent to contributors to the Nature Conservancy, an organization that purchases land in the attempt to preserve natural habitats. *Examples:* July 2012 e-newsletter articles "Artists Find Inspiration in Nature" and "Honoring the Military Who Honor Nature."

New Internationalist. Excellent, very left-wing publication intent on reporting issues of world poverty and inequality and the unjust relationship between the powerful and the powerless. *Examples:* The July 2012 issue articles, "Can Co-operatives Crowd Out Capitalism" and "What Would Che Say About Co-ops?"

New Republic. Long-established liberal (sort of) political magazine, but recently more middle-of-the-road. *Examples:* July 12, 2012 articles, "Why I Wish Obama Would Stop Inviting Me to Dinner" and "Mormons on the Potomac."

Newsletter on Intellectual Freedom. American Library Association newsletter containing lists of censored books.

Newsweek. Mass media, general news weekly recently made over with updated graphics and more celebrity profiles. Trendy, good for summarizing a week's happenings, but generally fails to scratch the surface. As of 2013, it will be available online only. *Examples*: July 16, 2012 issue includes "Champagne Flows While Syria Burns," "Hey, Buddy, Can You Spare $20 Million?" and a profile of the late Nora Ephron.

New Yorker. A very good general magazine, with funny cartoons (several reprinted in this textbook), great photos, plus information on goings-on in New York City. *Examples:* Articles in the June 25, 2012 issue include, "Unpopular Mandate: Why do Politicians Reverse Their Positions?" "Adversity Basketball," and a review of the book *Barak Obama, The Story.*

New York Review of Books. Very good left-wing publication with excellent, indeed sometimes superb, lengthy reviews and articles. *Examples:* July 12, 2012 articles, "American Male Novelists: The New Deal," "Burmese Days," a review of books by Burmese authors, and "In Mitt Romney's Schoolroom," a review of Diane Ravitch's book *A Chance for Every Child.*

Nutrition Action Health Letter. Publication of the Center for Science in the Public Interest. An excellent source of information about food and health. Each issue tends to focus on topics in the news.

Politico.com. Online magazine covering national political news (about Congress, elections, lobbying, etc.) Started by two former *Washington Post* staffers, it has brought some big-name journalists on board. *Examples*: On July 19, 2012, "Rupert Murdoch Warms on Romney" and "YouTube Restores Romney's Ad."

Reason. Perhaps the most interesting of the libertarian (pro-free-enterprise, con-big-government) publications. *Examples:* Recent articles cover topics like the fiscal soundness of the Affordable Care Act and perspectives on medical marijuana in Los Angeles.

Salon.com. Online magazine with a liberal slant that focuses on U.S. politics but covers a range of issues from technological advances to book, music, and film reviews. *Examples:* July 20, 2012 articles, "The Tiny GOP Zone of Decency," "America's Grand Tax Lie," and "Journalism v. Propaganda."

Science News. Very good weekly, packed with information about what is new in science. *Examples:* Articles in the July 14, 2012 issue, "Alzheimer's May Be Prion Disease," "Volcanoes Belch Up Ozone—Depleting Bromine," and "Mosquitoes Remade."

Scientific American. Excellent science monthly, often difficult going for lay readers, but worth the effort. *Examples:* July 2012 issue includes "Secrets of the HIV Controllers," "Witness to an Antarctic Meltdown," and "Machines That Think for Themselves."

Skeptical Inquirer. Publication of the Committee for the Scientific Investigation of Claims of the Paranormal—the best periodical on pseudoscience. *Examples:* Articles in the July/August 2012 issue, "The Social and Symbolic Power of AIDS Denialism," "Political Myths That Influence Voters," and "Why the GOP Distrusts Science."

Slate. A liberal online magazine of news, culture, and politics—plus *Doonesbury* cartoons. *Examples:* July 20, 2012 articles, "How Obama Defies Gravity" and "Nice Assassination" on the killing of high-level Syrian officials.

Time. Mass media general news weekly. Trendy, but often doesn't scratch the surface. *Examples*: Articles in the July 23, 2012 issue, "The Insidious Enemy" on military suicides, "The Syrian Arms Race," and "Definite Particle" on the Higgs boson particle.

Utne Reader. Reprints "the best of the alterative press" and is perhaps itself the best of the magazines that reprint material from other magazines. *Examples:* Articles in the July-August 2012 issue, "The PhD Now Comes With Food Stamps," "The Other Arctic," and "Life in the Bike Lane."

U.S. News & World Report. A mass media general newsweekly that is tilted a bit to the right. *Examples:* It has cornered the market on issues that tally national rankings like "America's Best Colleges," "Best Hospitals," and "Best Places to Retire."

Vanity Fair. A style magazine filled with lush celebrity photos and reams of ads that also features some serious, in-depth articles on a wide range of topics from business and politics to literature and film. *Examples*: Articles in the June 2012 issue, "Murdoch's Civil War," "Unearthing Obama," and "A Splash of Marilyn."

Washington Monthly. One of our favorite magazines on how our political system works. It offers a balanced approach to a wide-range of issues. Examples: Articles in the July/August 2012 issue, "How to Save Our Kids from Poverty in Old Age" and "The Slow-Motion Collapse of American Entrepreneurship."

Wired. Nerds' online magazine on computing, the Internet, and other areas of science and technology. *Examples:* July 2012 articles, "How I Accidentally Kickstarted the Domestic Drone Boom" and "New Videogame Lets Amateur Researchers Mess With RNA."

Women's Health Watch. A very good Harvard University health letter for women. *Examples:* July 2012 articles, "8 Secrets to a Good Night's Sleep," "What Clinical Studies Can Do for You," and "I Can't Eat That!"

World. A weekly newsmagazine reporting from a right-wing Christian perspective. *Examples:* July 28, 2012 articles, "Ice Age-4: Continental Drift," "Hope in the Heartland," and "Democracy and Dualism" on the Muslim Brotherhood victory in Egypt.

Glossary

ad hominem An attack on one's opponent rather than one's opponent's **argument**. (An *ad hominem* argument, literally, is an argument "to the person.")

affirming the consequent Arguing in a way that has the following invalid form (also called *asserting the consequent*):

1. If *A* then *B*.
2. *B*.
∴3. *A*.

analogical reasoning Reasoning from the similarity of two things in several relevant respects to their similarity in another.

appeal to authority Accepting the word of an authority, alleged or genuine, when we should not.

appeal to force An alleged fallacy committed when a conclusion is accepted after a threat of force of one kind or another. (Traditionally known as *argumentum ad baculum*—"argument to the cudgel," or "appeal to the stick.") A threat of force usually coerces people into accepting a certain idea or action, usually out of self-interest, but doesn't necessarily convince them of the merits or demerits of the case. Thus they are not guilty of fallacious reasoning in accepting the argument, at least not according to the criteria set up in this text.

appeal to ignorance Believing that something is true because there is no good evidence that it is false. (Traditionally known as *argumentum ad ignorantiam.*)

argument One or more statements (premises) offered in support of another statement (a conclusion).

argumentative essay A passage (usually consisting of at least several paragraphs) that argues for a **conclusion**.

background belief A belief that is brought to bear in evaluating an **argument's** cogency.

begging the question Assuming as a premise some form of the very point that is at issue—the conclusion we intend to prove.

biased statistics Fallaciously **reasoning** from a sample that is insufficiently representative of the population from which it is drawn.

categorical proposition A proposition (statement) that asserts or denies a relationship between a **subject class** and a **predicate class**.

cause (of an event) Something necessary to bring about a particular result, or part of what is sufficient to bring it about.

claim The **argument's** conclusion.

cogent reasoning **Valid reasoning** from justified premises (**warranted premises**) that include all likely relevant information.

cognitive meaning The part of the meaning of a word or expression that refers to things, events, or properties of one kind or another.

common practice The fallacy in which a wrong is justified on the grounds that lots or most others do that sort of thing.

comparison of alternatives Arguing for a course of action by showing that likely alternatives are less desirable.

composition The fallacy in which it is argued that a particular item must have a certain property because all or most of its parts have it.

concatenated reasoning Reasoning that employs several inductions and deductions, concluding to a pattern that fits what has been observed so far.

conclusion What the **premises** of an **argument** are claimed to prove.

contingent statement A statement that is neither necessarily true (a **tautology**, **logical truth**) nor necessarily false (**inconsistent**, a **contradiction**).

contradiction A statement that is necessarily false (**inconsistent**, a contradiction), or a group of statements that taken together are inconsistent.

correct A criterion of **cogent reasoning** requiring that the premises of an **argument** genuinely support its conclusion, either deductively or inductively. (See also **valid**.)

culture lag The tendency of practices and beliefs to persist long after whatever conditions made them useful or sensible have disappeared.

deductively valid An **argument** that guarantees that if all its premises are true, then its conclusion also must be true, because the claim asserted by its conclusion already has been stated in its premises, although usually only implicitly

deductively invalid Any **argument** that does not have a **deductively valid** form.

delusion A strong belief held despite strong evidence invalidating it.

denial Denying the existence of painful situations, thoughts, or feelings or reinterpreting them to make them seem less threatening.

denying the antecedent Arguing in a way that has the following invalid form:
1. If *A* then *B*.
2. Not *A*.
∴3. Not *B*.

dilemma An **argument** that presents two alternatives, both claimed to be bad.

disjunctive syllogism A **deductively valid argument** having the following form:
1. *A* or *B*.
2. Not *A*.
∴3. *B*.

division The fallacy in which it is assumed that all (or some) of the parts of an item have a particular property because the item as a whole has that property.

either–or fallacy Mistakenly **reasoning** from two alternatives, one claimed to be bad (to be avoided), so that we ought to choose the other alternative in particular when there is at least another viable alternative.

emotive meaning The positive or negative overtones of a word or expression.

equivocation Use of a term in a passage to mean one thing in one place and something else in another.

evading the issue A fallacy in which a question at issue is avoided (usually) while appearing not to.

exposition An explanation of an issue, idea, or other specific subject.

fallacious reasoning Reasoning that is not **cogent**, because it suppresses relevant evidence, contains a **questionable premise**, or is invalid.

false charge of fallacy Wrongly accusing others of a fallacy.

false dilemma A dilemma that can be shown to be false because either one of its **premises** is false or there is a third alternative.

faulty comparison A questionable analogy.

form (of an argument) Its logical or grammatical structure.

guilt by association Judging someone guilty solely on the basis of the company that person keeps.

hasty conclusion   The fallacious drawing of a **conclusion** from relevant but insufficient evidence.

herd instinct   The tendency to keep our beliefs, and thus our actions, within the bounds of what society as a whole will accept.

higher-level inductions   Very general inductions that can be used to evaluate those that are less general.

hypothetical syllogism   A deductively valid **argument** having the following form:
1. If A then B.
2. If B then C.
∴3. If A then C.

identification advertisement   An ad aimed to motivate its intended audience to identify either with a particular product or with the product's manufacturer or distributor.

inconsistent   Contradictory.

indirect proof   An **argument** in which the opposite of a desired conclusion is assumed as a **premise**, leading to a **conclusion** that is false, contradictory, or patently absurd, justifying acceptance of the desired conclusion.

induction   **Reasoning** that a pattern of some sort experienced so far will continue into the future.

induction by enumeration   An **inductively valid argument** moving from a premise stating that all so far examined As are Bs to the conclusion that all As whatsoever are Bs.

inductively valid   Correctly **reasoning** that a pattern experienced so far will continue into the future.

irony   Locutions that literally say one thing although their intended meaning is something else, usually opposite to its literal meaning.

irrelevant reason   A broad fallacy category containing several narrower fallacies in which a **premise** of an **argument** is irrelevant to its **conclusion**.

logical truth   A statement that is necessarily (logically) true; a statement that can be proved to be true by logic alone.

loyalty   Unwavering allegiance to one's group.

major term   The predicate of the **conclusion** of a **syllogism**.

margin note and summary method   A method for evaluating an extended passage by constructing a summary of that passage and evaluating the summary.

middle term   The term that occurs once in each **premise** of a **syllogism** but not in its **conclusion**.

minor term   The subject of the **conclusion** of a **syllogism**.

modus ponens   A deductively valid **argument** having the following form:
1. If A then B.
2. A.
∴3. B.

modus tollens   A deductively valid **argument** having the following form:
1. If A then B.
2. Not B.
∴3. Not A.

mood (of a syllogism)   The classification of a **syllogism** depending on the kinds of propositions (A, E, I, or O) it contains.

obfuscate   To be so confused or opaque as to be difficult to understand.

particular affirmative proposition   A proposition having the form "Some As are Bs"; an I proposition.

particular negative proposition   A proposition having the form "Some As are not Bs"; an O proposition.

partisan mind-set   An attitude of strong, often biased, allegiance to a faction, cause, or person that results in viewing everything in terms of "us" versus "them."

plagiarism   Verbatim, or close to it, use of someone else's writings without acknowledging the source, making it appear to be one's own material.

predicate class   The items referred to by the predicate of a **categorical proposition**.

prejudice   Thinking ill of others without sufficient warrant, particularly members of a specific group, race, or religion.

premise   A **reason** offered in support of an **argument's conclusion**.

pro and con argument   An **argument** that considers **reasons** in favor of and against a thesis or conclusion.

procrastination   Putting off for tomorrow what common sense tells us needs to be done today.

promise advertisement   An ad that promises to satisfy desires or allay fears.

provincialism   A limited perspective shaped by the ideas, interests, and kinds of behavior favored by the groups with which we identify.

pseudoscientific theories   Theories that are without scientific foundation.

questionable analogy   **Reasoning** by an analogy that is not apt, not justified.

questionable cause   Labeling *A* as the cause of *B* on evidence that is insufficient, negative, or unrepresentative, or is in serious conflict with well-established high-level theories.

questionable premise   Accepting a less than believable **premise** or other statement.

quibble   To attempt to take advantage of the failure of one's opponent to cross every *t* and dot every *i*, to spell out what should be taken for granted.

rationalization   A psychological ploy we use to justify our actions or beliefs, however wrong, by coming up with self-satisfying but incorrect **reasons** to explain them.

reasoning   Inferring from what we already know or believe to something else; the conclusion reached by reasoning.

reasons   Statements (**premises**) offered in support or acceptance of another statement (**conclusion**).

reductio ad absurdum proof   An **argument** in which the opposite of an untenable **conclusion** is assumed in order to show that the conclusion is false, contradictory, or patently absurd.

refutation to counterargument   An attempt to refute one's opponent's **argument**s against one's own position.

scapegoat   One who is blamed for the ills of the world.

self-deception   Consciously believing at a deeper level what we know to be dubious.

slanting   A form of misrepresentation in which a true statement is made to suggest something else (usually either known to be false or not known to be true). Also, the careful selection of facts so as to imply something else (usually something false).

slippery slope argument   Objecting to a course of action on the grounds that once it is taken, another action, and then perhaps still others, are bound to be taken; or arguing that whatever would justify taking the first step would justify the others, where, given that the last step is not justified, then neither is the first.

slippery slope fallacy   Arguing that a slope is slippery without providing good **reasons** for thinking that it is. (Also see **slippery slope argument**.)

small sample   Drawing **conclusions** about a population on the basis of a sample that is too small to be a reliable measure of that population.

statistical induction   An induction that moves from the **premise** that a certain percentage of a sample has a particular property to the **conclusion** that the whole population from which it is drawn has the same percentage of that property.

stereotype   A conventional oversimplification, often negative, of characteristics that describe a specific group of people.

straw man A fallacious form of **reasoning** in which an opponent's position, or a competitor's product, is misrepresented or a weaker opponent is attacked rather than stronger ones.

subject class The items referred to by the subject of a **categorical proposition**.

superstition An irrational belief, based on biased evidence or on small or unrepresentative samples, that ignores logical evidence to the contrary.

suppressed evidence The fallacy in which evidence contrary to one's position is neglected, overlooked, or slighted.

suppression Avoiding thoughts that are stressful by either not thinking about them or by thinking nonstressful thoughts.

syllogism An **argument** containing exactly three **categorical propositions**, two of them **premises**, one a **conclusion**.

tautology A statement that is logically, or necessarily, true or so devoid of content as to be practically empty.

thesis The conclusion of an extended argumentative passage; its **conclusion**.

tokenism Mistaking a token gesture for the real thing, or accepting a token gesture in lieu of something more substantive.

tone The attitudes or feelings expressed by a passage.

traditional wisdom Accepting an unsuitable practice because doing so follows a traditional or accepted way of doing things.

two wrongs make a right Justifying a wrong by pointing to a similar wrong done by others, usually by one's accuser.

universal affirmative proposition A proposition having the form "All *S* are *P*"; an A proposition.

universal negative proposition A proposition having the form "No *S* are *P*"; an E proposition.

unrepresentative sample Fallaciously **reasoning** from a sample that is insufficiently representative of the population from which it is drawn.

valid A criterion of cogent **reasoning** requiring that the **premises** of an **argument** genuinely support its **conclusion**, either deductively or inductively.

warranted premise A **premise** that is believable given one's background beliefs and other evidence.

weasel word A word that appears to make little or no change in a passage, while in fact sucking out most of its content by being so **equivocal** or qualifying that it negates the substance of what is being said.

wishful thinking Believing what we would like to be true, no matter what the evidence.

worldview The most important of one's background beliefs (including those about morality, God, the "meaning of life," etc.), usually but not always very general; one's philosophy.

Indexes

Name Index

Media Index